ASPECTS OF ROMAN HISTORY,
AD 14–117

Aspects of Roman History, AD 14–117 charts the history of the Roman Imperial period, from the establishment of the Augustan principate to the reign of Trajan, providing a basic chronological framework of the main events and introductory outlines of the major issues of the period. The first half of the book outlines the linear development of the Roman Empire, emperor by emperor, accenting the military and political events. The second half of the book concentrates on important themes which apply to the period as a whole, such as the religious, economic and social functioning of the Roman Empire.

The book includes:

- a discussion of the primary sources for Roman imperial history;
- clearly laid out chapters on different themes in the Roman Empire, such as patronage, religion, the role of the senate, the army and the position of women and slaves, designed for easy cross-referencing with the chronological outline of events;
- maps, charts and illustrations;
- a guide to further reading.

Richard Alston's highly accessible book is designed specifically for students with little previous experience of studying ancient/ Roman history. *Aspects of Roman History* provides an invaluable introduction to Roman Imperial history, which will allow students to gain an overview of the period and will be an indispensable aid to note-taking, essay preparation and examination revision.

Richard Alston is a Lecturer in Roman History at Royal Holloway, University of London. He has also been a senior examiner in ancient history at A-level. He is the author of *Soldier and Society in Roman Egypt: A Social History* (Routledge).

ASPECTS OF ROMAN HISTORY, AD 14–117

Richard Alston

London and New York

First published 1998
by Routledge
11 New Fetter Lane, London EC4P 4EE

Simultaneously published in the USA and Canada
by Routledge
29 West 35th Street, New York, NY 10001

Reprinted 1999, 2002, 2003

Routledge is an imprint of the Taylor & Francis Group

© 1998 Richard Alston

Typeset in Garamond by Routledge
Printed and bound in Great Britain by T J International Ltd

British Library Cataloguing in Publication Data
A catalogue record for this book is available from the British Library

Library of Congress Cataloguing in Publication Data
Alston, Richard, 1965–
Aspects of Roman history, AD 14–117 / Richard Alston.
Includes bibliographical references and index.
1. Rome–History–Empire, 30 B.C.–284 A.D. 2. Rome–Politics and
government–30 B.C.–284 A.D.–Historiography.
3. Emperors–Rome–Biography. 4. Rome–History, Military–30
B.C.–476 A.D.
I. Title.
DG276.A44   1998   97-24205
937'.07–dc21

ISBN 0–415–13236–3 (hbk)
ISBN 0–415–13237–1 (pbk)

CONTENTS

ILLUSTRATIONS

Maps

Figures

Tables

ILLUSTRATIONS

PREFACE

This book has been written very quickly and with very modest aims. It has been a task additional to other research work and has been very largely written in the evenings of the last year. I have accumulated various debts in the writing of this text. I give thanks to *The Society for the Promotion of Roman Studies* and to Dr John Patterson for permission to use his maps of Rome. I thank Kate Gilliver who has read a large proportion of this and commented constructively on it. Most of all, I thank Sara, my wife, whose support and understanding are essential to everything. Sara has also cast her 'lay-person's eye' over this and I am very grateful for her comments. She has also put up with (or perhaps enjoyed) the many evenings I have spent with this text. Sam has suffered his father's eccentricities and provided entertainment and commentary as only a three-year-old can, but I dedicate this book to his brother, Joshua, whose arrival in the middle of the reign of Nero has given immense pleasure, though it delayed the delivery of the manuscript. It almost goes without saying that all mistakes and errors of fact and judgement remain my own.

ABBREVIATIONS

Abbreviations of journals and authors follow the standard abbreviations of *L'Année Philologique* and the *Oxford Classical Dictionary*.

BMC = Mattingly, H. (1932–62), *Coins of the Roman Empire in the British Museum*, London.

EJ = Ehrenberg, V. and Jones, A. H. M. (1976) *Documents Illustrating the Reigns of Augustus and Tiberius*, Oxford.

Campbell 1994 = Campbell, J. B. (1994) *The Roman Army: 31 BC–AD 337: A Sourcebook*, London, New York.

IGRR = Cagnat, R. (ed.) (1901–27) *Inscriptiones Graecae ad res romanas pertinentes*, Paris.

ILS = Dessau, H. (1892–1916) *Inscriptiones Latinae Selectae*, Berlin.

MacCrum, Woodhead 1966 = MacCrum, M. and Woodhead, A. G. (1966) *Select Documents of the Principates of the Flavian Emperors including the Year of Revolution, AD 68–96*, Cambridge.

Smallwood 1966 = Smallwood, E. M. (1966) *Documents Illustrating the Principates of Nerva, Trajan and Hadrian*, Cambridge.

Smallwood 1967 = Smallwood, E. M. (1967) *Documents Illustrating the Principates of Gaius, Claudius and Nero*, Cambridge.

Map 1.1 The Roman Empire in AD 60 (from Talbert 1985)

- - - Approximate provincial boundaries
- provincial capital or main centre
□ Legionary base (1 legion unless a figure follows)
⊡ Legionary base and provincial capital
BELGICA Province
AFRICA Proconsular province
Pontus 'Client kingdom'
PARTHIA Other territory/peoples

Regnum Bospori

VIMINACIUM
NOVAE
Danuvius
MOESIA
OESCUS
THRACIA
BITHYNIA
ET PONTUS
AMASTRIS
MACEDONIA
PERINTHUS
Pontus
Armenia Minor
Armenia
THESSALONICA
NICOMEDIA
GALATIA
ACHAEA
PERGAMUM
ANCYRA
CAPPADOCIA
ASIA
CAESAREA
(MAZACA)
Commagene
CORINTHUS
EPHESUS
CYRRHUS
To
ANTIOCHIA
MYRA
Commagene
SYRIA
PARTHIA
LYCIA ET
(5 legions)
PAMPHYLIA
PAPHUS
CYPRUS
RAPHANEAE
CRETA ET
GORTYN
(2)
CYRENE
CAESAREA
Euphrates
JUDAEA
CYRENE
Nabataea
ALEXANDRIA/
NICOPOLIS (2)
AEGYPTUS
Nilus
E
0   500
km
G   R.J.A.Talbert

1

2

4

5

6

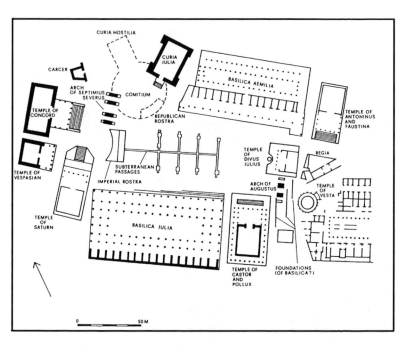

Map 1.2 The Forum Romanum (from Patterson 1992)

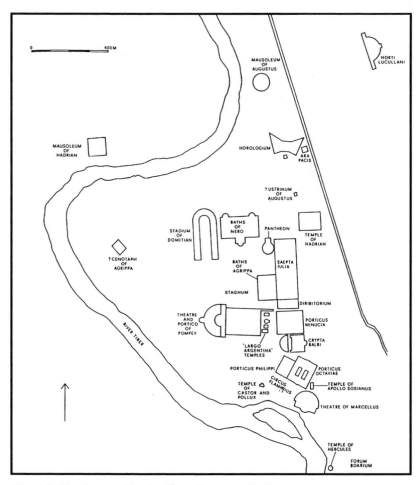

Map 1.3 The Campus Martius (from Patterson 1992)

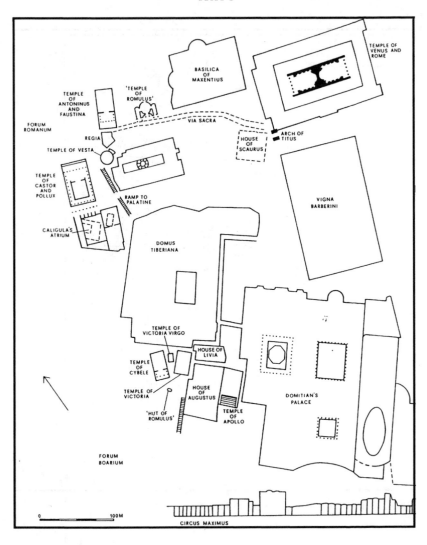

Map 1.4 The Palatine (from Patterson 1992)

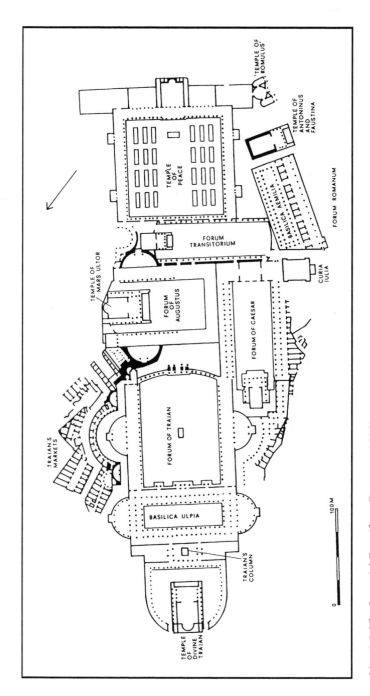

Map 1.5 The Imperial Fora (from Patterson 1992)

1

INTRODUCTION

AIMS

This book is an introduction to the period AD 14–117 aimed at those with little or no previous experience of ancient history. The book's aims are modest. It is intended to provide a basic chronological framework for study of the main events of the period and to give brief introductory outlines of the major issues. In the first section of the book, I consider the major political and military events of the period. The discussion is arranged mainly by emperor. In the second section, I turn to themes which will tend to apply to the whole of the period. There will be times when issues which arise in considering individual reigns are discussed thematically and reference will be made to these discussions. The book need not be treated as a linear account and students are encouraged to switch between chapters as the need arises.

I do not provide lengthy quotations from source material in this book. Most of the major sources are easily available in modern translations and there are also several good collections of documentary material. This work is intended to supplement the study of original sources and expose some of the problems in studying this material. In the sections that follow, I will examine some of these problems and also establish the political and constitutional background of the Principate (as this period is called).

SOURCES: PROBLEMS AND METHODS

Using historians and biographers

The distinctive nature of ancient history lies in our dependence on a relatively small number of mainly literary sources, though we can supplement our knowledge by studying inscriptions, papyri and archaeological material. Historians often express considerable doubts as to the historical value of their sources. There are good reasons to take a sceptical line. Most of the ancient historians and biographers on whom we rely appear to have been interested in historical truth but, of course, there are various levels of historical truth: there is what we know happened and what we think happened. Modern historians are not always careful to make clear such distinctions. Ancient historians are rarely explicit about the nature of their evidence for particular events or whether they are relying on facts or suppositions. Worse, since nearly all our major narrative sources wrote long after the events they describe, our sources are often themselves second-hand. They rely on earlier writers' accounts, the accuracy of which cannot easily be assessed. Even when a story comes to us from several different sources, it may have originated from a single fraudulent source now lost. In addition, material which may have originated in scandalous gossip, especially when dealing with the sex lives of emperors, has reached our sources. The veracity of this material is almost impossible to assess.

Ancient historians judged their work not just by its veracity but also by its literary qualities: they dramatised the past for their audience and in so doing allowed themselves a certain artistic discretion. Many were also politically active and presented their own political agendas through the recounting of events. Ancient historians, like most other historians, reshaped the past to suit their various aims. Although we might be able to take account of the prejudices and methods of our major sources, the methodology of their sources must remain mysterious.

Truth, slander, dramatised accounts and historical speculation are blended in our sources, and there is no obvious way of distinguishing between the various elements. A historian could take the reasonable decision that much of our material is untrustworthy and that no conventional history of the period can be written. Nevertheless, I have not adopted this view here. Although each anecdote must be considered on its merits, I have tended to accept much of the ancient material. There are several grounds for such optimism. It is difficult not to accept the basic honesty of many of our major sources. It was normal for historians from the earliest times to claim to be writing an accurate account of past events, and historians such as Tacitus lay claim to objectivity (Tac., *Hist.* I 1). Although we cannot sensibly reconstruct what sources our sources relied on (except in certain rare cases), it is clear that there was a considerable amount of written material available for them to consult, such as decrees of the senate, memoirs of key figures, the works of other historians, texts of famous speeches, and documents preserved in official archives. Some of our sources may not have bothered to consult this material, but the material was there and provided a basis for the historical compositions of the period. A historian who wrote blatant untruths would have laid himself open to ridicule. When we can check our literary sources against the documentary material, on the whole, our sources do not appear to be misleading.

Of course, the material that cannot be checked – for instance, the material that relates to the inner workings of Nero's government (pp. 109–10) or which is scandalous and scurrilous – is exactly the material over which there is the most doubt and which is so often used by our sources to give an overall impression of the regime. The material that appears in the documentary record is so often uncontroversial and less open to serious doubt. One must take care, often extreme care, and beware the inventiveness of the tradition and Roman political gossip. All historians working on this period are faced with the same fundamental problem. The grounds for dismissing certain accounts and accepting others are normally subjective, based on individual perceptions of the ancient sources. This is why all ancient historians must return time and again to their sources. Others reading the ancient material will undoubtedly reach different decisions to those I have arrived at in this book. The discipline of ancient history involves a continual re-reading and re-interpretation of the ancient sources from which all our research ultimately begins.

Historians and biographers: biographical notes

Tacitus

Cornelius Tacitus is perhaps the major historical source for the period (see also pp. 24–6). His origins are uncertain though his family may have resided in Southern Gaul. He married the daughter of Agricola, a prominent general who conquered much of Northern Britain. He embarked on a political career and was consul in AD 97 and governor of Asia *c*.112–116. He was a prominent orator and spoke at important trials and his first literary work, the *Dialogus*, concerned the history of oratory. Most of his writing dates to after the death of the emperor Domitian. Although Tacitus' political career progressed under Domitian, Tacitus was hostile to the emperor. The *Agricola*, the biography of his father-in-law, was published soon after Domitian's death and expresses this hostility, partly by contrasting the moral qualities of that emperor with the many virtues of Agricola. Tacitus' *Histories* recount the events from the death of Nero to that of Domitian (AD 68–96). Only the first four books and part of the fifth, the books which dealt with the civil wars of 69–70, survived the Middle Ages. Tacitus then turned to the earlier period. The *Annales* covered the period from AD 14–68, but much of this work has also been lost although we have most of his account of the years AD 14–29, 32–37 and 47–66.

Dio Cassius

Sometimes known as Cassius Dio, Dio was a Greek born in the province of Bithynia, part of Asia Minor, in the mid-second century AD. He started a successful political career in the late second century and became consul. He was prominent in Rome at the start of the political traumas which evolved into what some have called the 'third-century crisis'. Imperial rule had long been established in Rome when Dio was writing and, in spite of the fact that the emperors of the period seem to have become increasingly despotic, there was little opposition to the idea of monarchy. Dio's history was a careful work of scholarship and he spent many years gathering material. His history eventually filled eighty books and covered the period from the foundation of Rome by Romulus to his own day. Much of this is, however, only partially preserved. The best preserved sections cover the years from 68 BC to AD 46. In addition to this, we have excerpts and summaries (epitomes) made by Byzantine scholars for most other years. He is a major source for the reign of Augustus and for the early part of our period, and is particularly important for those years for which we do not have Tacitus' account.

Suetonius

Gaius Suetonius Tranquillus was born c. AD 70, the son of a Roman equestrian. He was friendly with the younger Pliny (*Ep.* I 18, I 24, V 10, IX 34), who secured him a military posting (*Ep.* III 8) (which Suetonius eventually transferred to a relative) and a grant of certain privileges from Trajan (*Ep.* X 94). His major patron seems to have been Septicius Clarus who was prefect of the praetorian guard under Hadrian (emperor, AD 117–38). This man may have secured Suetonius his post as *ab epistulis*, one of the major administrative officials in the imperial government (see p. 248). When Clarus and Suetonius became involved in a scandal concerning Hadrian's wife, both were removed from office (HA, *Vita Hadriani* 11.3). Suetonius probably lived in retirement after this date. He wrote many scholarly works, biographies, natural histories, works on grammar, literary studies and on the customs of the Romans. His most famous works are his biographies of the Caesars, starting with Julius Caesar and ending with Domitian. Although the biographies contain brief accounts of the major events in the lives of his subjects, his interest seems to have been mainly in moral character. Suetonius' style is very formulaic and many of the biographies have a very similar structure. He is often accused of merely compiling material without application of critical discretion, and many have dismissed much of Suetonius' more scandalous material as gossip. These accusations, however, are unfair. Suetonius both shapes his material to leave a definite impression and, though he recounts fantastic stories, often makes it clear that he believes gossip to be incorrect. His 'matter-of-fact' presentation of material allows the reader to make independent political and moral judgements, though Suetonius' own views are often implied. Unlike many other ancient biographers and historians, Suetonius quotes from original documents to which he may have gained access during his time in the imperial administration. He makes less use of archive material in the biographies of emperors after Nero, which might suggest that these were less thoroughly researched.

Josephus

Josephus was a Jewish historian and aristocrat. He was given a rebel command during the Jewish war of AD 66–70, but was defeated and captured by Vespasian (see pp. 156–7). He was jailed, but prophesied that Vespasian would become emperor, and was released when Vespasian made his bid for the throne. He then acted as spokesman for the Romans in their attempt to win over Jewish rebels and was present at Jerusalem when the city was sacked. Following the end of the war, Josephus moved to Rome where he composed a history of the war (*Bellum Judaicum*). He was forced to defend his position against those who thought his activities during the war somewhat disreputable and produced an extended autobiography (*Vita*) and a defence of the Jewish people (*Contra Apionem*) against anti-Semitic pamphlets published by an Alexandrian Egyptian named Apion. His previous major work was a history of the Jewish people, originally written in Aramaic and subsequently translated into Greek (*Antiquitates Judaicae*).

Velleius Paterculus

Velleius was a military officer who served under Augustus and Tiberius. He wrote a summary history of Rome, a guide to a proposed much larger work, which concentrated on the reigns of Augustus and the early years of the reign of Tiberius. He presents a picture of Tiberius as a military hero. Some have seen him either as a propagandist for Tiberius or as seeking to win the favour and patronage of that emperor and Sejanus, his praetorian prefect.

Plutarch

Plutarch was born in the 40s AD and was still active in the 120s. Although he visited Rome and was interested in Roman themes, most of his writings were on topics unrelated to contemporary political events in Rome. His main works were a series of essays known as the *Moralia* and a number of 'parallel lives' in which Greek and Roman historical figures were compared. The *Moralia* essays deal with a range of topics, though religion is an important theme. Some are academic discussions of philosophical works while others are more 'morally improving' exhortations. The biographies are more commonly used by historians. For our period, the two most interesting are the lives of Galba and Otho.

Using poetry and fiction for social history

Another oddity of ancient history is that historians often use poetry and sometimes prose fiction as source material, normally more often for social than political history.

Many of the poets of the period wrote in the first person and, in so doing, appear to describe their own attitudes and experiences. The autobiographical appearance of much of the poetry has encouraged historians to use these texts. Unfortunately, these poems are less straightforward than sometimes appears. Several writers of this period make it clear that they adopt a 'voice' for their poetry, and that they may have different 'voices' which might say contradictory things in their various poems. For instance, the poet Ovid, who produced several erotic poems and guides to seduction, later claimed that these were the products of his 'character' and that his 'life' was chaste (Ovid, *Tristia* II 353–4. Compare Catullus, 16. 5–6; Apuleius, *Apol.* 11). The credibility of these claims is impossible to substantiate. Writers used 'voices' in order to create characters much in the same way that modern comedians write sketches in which their characters might say things that the author would never support or say in his own 'voice'. Some ancient writing, like modern comedy, may be funny simply because its vision of society is far from the truth and yet, as modern readers, we have little way of getting the joke.

In addition, one of the major concerns of poets was literature itself. All the poets, and indeed all other writers from this period, were very familiar with a body of Greek and Latin literature. The culture was so refined that poets could quote, or even slightly misquote, a line of another's work and expect it to be recognised by the audience even if the line had been written a century or more previously. Literary works imitated and parodied earlier works and worked in a sequence of imitation and literary creation that went back to the earliest Greek literature. Very often, the works imitated are lost and we can only guess how much was a writer's own invention and how much borrowed. We may then be presented with an unreal literary world with elements of contemporary culture blended with elements from previous centuries and elements from Greek culture, of which some parts might have been almost pure invention.

Nevertheless, the historian should not despair. The fictional and poetic writing of the period was liberally laced with contemporary references and some of the attitudes expressed find parallels in other types of writing. One might also argue that interest in literature would have rapidly waned if all literature referred to a never-never land. The historian must, however, be warned and pick his or her way through this minefield with extreme care, avoiding placing too much trust on individual stories or attitudes as evidence for Roman society.

Major poets and fiction writers: biographical notes

Juvenal

Very little is known about Juvenal's life and it is unclear whether his various ancient biographers had any more information than we have. He may have been related to a Junius Juvenalis, an equestrian (see p. 215) attested in an inscription from Aquinum, south of Rome. His historical references date him to the reigns of Domitian, Nerva, Trajan and Hadrian. He is alleged to have been exiled during the reign of Domitian (possibly to Egypt which he says he visited). His surviving literary output post-dates that emperor and he was still writing after AD 127. His work consists of sixteen vitriolic *Satires*, mostly directed at aspects of life in Rome.

Martial

Born in Spain, Martial came to Rome in the reign of Nero and worked there for over thirty years. He does not appear to have held any official posts but earned his living from poetry. He wrote a very large number of very short poems, many of which are obscene. These *Epigrams* cover most aspects of Roman social life, including notably the relationship between patrons and clients and the games in Rome.

Petronius

Tacitus tells us that C. Petronius was consul and governor of Bithynia, probably in the early part of the reign of Nero. Nero, however, brought him back to Rome where he became a member of the emperor's intimate circle. He was appointed as 'judge of taste' (*arbiter elegentiae*) and showed considerable erudition and skill in adding to the luxury of Nero's court. His influence made him enemies and Tigellinus, fearing that Petronius' greater knowledge of sensual pleasures would lead to him supplanting Tigellinus in Nero's affections, arranged his fall (Tac., *Ann.* XVI 18–19). He was probably the author of a novel, *Satyricon*, the surviving parts of which tell of the disreputable adventures of two characters in the

Greek towns of Italy. The most famous episode is a particularly luxurious and tasteless dinner party held by the freedman Trimalchio.

Other literary sources

The Younger Pliny

Pliny was born in c. AD 61 to a family prominent in the north Italian town of Comum. The most notable member of his family was his maternal uncle, Pliny the Elder, who not only wrote an encyclopaedia, but also commanded the fleet at Misenum on the Bay of Naples. When Vesuvius erupted in AD 79, the elder Pliny sailed to the rescue of the fleeing populations of Pompeii and Herculaneum. He was, however, overcome by fumes and died. In his will, he adopted his nephew who became Gaius Plinius (son of Lucius) Caecilius Secundus. Pliny inherited his uncle's estates and probably also his political connections, both of which aided his subsequent political career. He started as a lawyer (*Ep.* V 8) and then served briefly in the army in Syria, where he seems to have managed the military accounts (*Ep.* VII 31). He held several offices during the reign of Domitian, but his political prospects, and indeed his personal safety, may have become much less secure as Domitian became more tyrannical. After Domitian's assassination, Pliny's political standing improved and his skill as an orator led to him taking part in many of the most prominent trials of the period. In AD 100, Trajan rewarded him with a consulship and in 111 appointed him to deal with something of a political and financial crisis in Bithynia, in which post Pliny died. Pliny was one of the leading literary figures of his day and dabbled in many areas. He wrote poetry which he tells us was recited to some acclaim (*Ep.* VII 4), though the fragments which have survived suggest that a two-day recital of his poetry was more of a tribute to the kindness and perseverance of his friends than the quality of his verse (*Ep.* VIII 21). He and Tacitus were the leading orators of the day and Pliny published or circulated many of his works. His only surviving speech is the *Panegyricus*, a revised version of a speech thanking Trajan for his consulship, in which he contrasted Domitian and Trajan and lavished praise on the latter. His most famous works are his letters. These were published in ten books and offer a remarkable insight into the life of a leading senator of the period. They must, however, be treated with caution. Unlike Cicero's letters, these were mainly selected by Pliny for publication and may have been substantially revised. The image of Pliny and his friends is carefully contrived to emphasise their achievements and their political and moral integrity. Book Ten is a little different since this contains his correspondence with Trajan and, as such, offers valuable insights into the role of a governor and the relationship between emperor and governor in the early second century AD.

Strabo

Strabo was a geographer who wrote during the reigns of Augustus and Tiberius. He described the whole of the known world, using the works of earlier geographers and visiting many places himself. He wrote in Greek.

Philo

Philo was a Jewish theologian living and working in Alexandria in the 30s AD. Little is known of his life. He was a very prominent member of the Jewish community and represented that community on an embassy to Rome to obtain civic rights. Most of his work, written in Greek, interprets biblical texts through a complex method of analogy and literal interpretation, owing much to Greek traditions. Historians chiefly consult two of his works, the *Legatio ad Gaium* (*Embassy to Gaius*) and the *In Flaccum* (*On Flaccus*). In the latter, he describes the activities of a governor of Egypt and, in the former, recounts the story of his visit to Rome to petition the emperor.

Documentary sources

There are two major types of documentary sources: papyri and inscriptions. Papyri, ancient texts written on paper made from the papyrus reed, are preserved in desert regions in Egypt and the Near East. The texts are preserved either as archives, a collection of documents which someone thought worth keeping, or as stray finds, often from rubbish heaps. The texts are very varied in nature. Most deal with official business, though there are some private letters.

Inscriptions on stone or bronze are more central to the topics that we will be covering in this book. Most of the individuals we know of from the ancient world are only attested by their tombstones. These were often displayed prominently by the major roads and

provide more than just a marker for a grave. The words, and sometimes the pictures, send a message to those passing about the status
of the individual and his heirs. Devotional inscriptions (erected
following the completion of a vow) were also 'public' in that they
displayed the religious loyalties of the individuals concerned, as
well as thanking the deity for the normally unspecified help.

Communities also erected inscriptions. The subject matter of
these varied. They might thank an individual for services rendered
and summarise her or his claims to virtue and status. Some of these
inscriptions come from statue bases, the statue for which has often
disappeared. Letters from the emperor, or from provincial governors,
or important decrees of local councils might also be displayed. Some
civic constitutions were engraved on bronze tablets.

All inscriptions were public monuments and although many read
as matter-of-fact statements, they tend to give an 'official view' of
individuals and events. Tombstones, for instance, might give legal
status, possibly profession and age at death, but are not likely to tell
us what an individual was really like. Inscriptions erected by
communities are even less likely to give us anything other than an
official line on events.

Attempts to use inscriptions as sources for social history are
hampered by peculiar patterns in the evidence. The majority of our
inscriptions are in Latin or Greek, yet a majority of the population
of the empire spoke languages other than Latin or Greek. Certain
provinces have produced very few inscriptions, or the inscriptions
that have been published tend to come from specific areas and date
to specific times where and when it was somehow fashionable to put
up inscriptions. Some groups, especially the poor and the provincials, may not have wished or been able to afford to put up
tombstones or devotional inscriptions. Some communities may have
commemorated their gods and their dead on wooden plaques rather
than on stone. Inscriptions are, therefore, a very imperfect reflection
of ancient society.

POLITICAL LIFE: FROM THE REPUBLICAN
TO THE AUGUSTAN CONSTITUTION

The main features of Republican government were the mix of
democratic and aristocratic institutions. Much of this arrangement
was carried over into the Augustan period and is summarised in
Table 1.1. The most potentially powerful Republican assembly was

the *comitia tributa*. This assembly elected the tribunes and passed laws. As the tribunes had the right to veto any governmental action and could imprison even senior magistrates, they could paralyse the Roman state. More positively, they called the assembly and could propose legislation to it. These powers could be used to force through reforms unpopular with the aristocracy or to break a political wrangle when no consensus had emerged among the magistrates or in the senate. Legislation seems to have been used sparingly in the early Republic and it was only after 133 BC that serious attempts were made to realise the potential power of the tribunes, many of these attempts ending in violence.

The most powerful offices were those of the consuls and praetors. These magistrates held *imperium*, power. This enabled the magistrates to control the administrative and legal machinery of the state, to instruct junior magistrates, to command troops, and to employ limited powers of coercion. Initially, the tribunate was founded to restrain the powers of these magistrates and to protect the people from tyrannical consuls. The people were extremely suspicious of any consul who used these powers against Roman citizens without recourse to public trial. Their power was also checked by the collegiality of office. The two consuls held equal powers and it was not unusual for consuls to be political rivals.

All magistracies were normally held for a single year. The brief tenure of office made it difficult for any magistrate to use his post as a basis for lasting power. After that year, the magistrate would be answerable in the courts for his actions and would become an ordinary senator once again, dependent on the political support of the plebs and fellow senators (see below). This knowledge restrained the magistrates.

The Republican senate was the advisory council of the consuls who chaired its meetings. The decisions it reached were published in the form of advice but this advice was not legally binding either on the consuls or on other persons or states. Its power lay in its personnel. All the magistrates and former magistrates of Rome sat in the senate. Collectively, the senators had vast political experience and immense political power. To oppose the stated wishes of the senate was, therefore, to stand against the political class of Rome, and, in normal circumstances, the consuls, other magistrates and, indeed, the rest of the population of the empire abided by decisions of the senate. In effect, the senate became the governing council of the Republic.

The power of the political establishment was enhanced by the nature of Roman political contests. There were no parties as such seeking the support of different groups in Roman society. Some individual politicians were able to build up considerable personal political followings, either due to their success as military leaders or to their support for popular causes. Many relied on their *clientes* (dependants) and the support of their friends and their clients to mobilise popular support at elections (see pp. 219–22 for a discussion of the nature of this relationship). Aspiring politicians needed to attract the patronage of senior figures who would lend the support of their often more extensive network of friends and clients. Thus, most Roman political figures were dependent for their political power on a network of political alliances and friendships. Some were born into this network, but others had to establish themselves from scratch, carefully cultivating powerful friends. The system advantaged a hereditary aristocratic group and men without those inherited connections found it very difficult to break into Roman political life. Any politician who alienated the Roman political elite risked the loss of all political support and of being consigned to a virtual political wilderness. The system encouraged conservatism and created a close-knit political elite, some of whom regarded political power as almost a birthright.

THE AUGUSTAN CONSTITUTION AND POLITICAL SETTLEMENTS

The Roman historical tradition dated the emergence of this powerful aristocratic political elite to 509 BC when Tarquinius Superbus, the last of the kings of Rome, was expelled from the city. The subsequent period saw the transformation of Rome from an insignificant city state in the centre of Italy to the wealthy capital of a huge empire. Much of the credit for that transformation was due to the achievements of this traditional elite and they had shared in many of the benefits. In 28 BC, Augustus faced this elite as conqueror of the Roman world, and in this and subsequent reforms attempted to reconcile his power with the system of government which they had dominated for the previous centuries.

Table 1.1 summarises the major features of the constitutional arrangements after the reforms of Augustus and Table 1.2 summarises Augustus' constitutional powers.

The bundle of powers and titles accumulated by Augustus remained the constitutional basis for imperial power throughout

Table 1.1 The Augustan constitution

1. Social orders	Senators	Owned property worth 1,000,000 sesterces or more. Members of the senate.
	Equites (knights)	Owned property worth 400,000 sesterces or more.
	Plebs	Freeborn Roman citizens.
	Liberti (freedmen)	Former slaves with varying political rights. They owed some residual service to their former masters.
	Slaves	Owned by their masters, slaves had no civil rights.
2. Major magistracies	Quaestors	Financial posts held by men of 25 years or over.
	Aediles	They were in charge of the administration of the city of Rome.
	Tribunes	The tribunes protected the Roman plebs from the more senior magistrates and could veto all state business. They could call assemblies of the people.
	Praetors	These were assistants to the consuls with powers equal to them, but subordinate. They were primarily legal officials, though former praetors served as governors.
	Consuls	Two consuls presided over the Senate and had supreme legal authority. They were in charge of all government business. The former holders of the post had great prestige.
3. Assemblies	Senate	Constitutionally, the senate was the advisory council to the consuls, but was in fact the governing council of Republican Rome. Their advice was published in the form of decrees. Members were former magistrates.
	Comitia tributa	This was a semi-democratic assembly of the people. It elected minor magistracies and passed laws.
	Comitia centuriata	This was a popular assembly of voting centuries controlled largely by the aristocracy. It elected the senior magistrates and could pass laws.

Table 1.2 Main powers and titles of Augustus

Power	Date awarded (BC)	Description
Proconsular power (*Imperium proconsulare*)	27	Governorship of a number of provinces and command of the armies in those provinces. The provinces were ruled by legates of the emperor.
Greater proconsular power (*Imperium proconsulare maius*)	23	This gave the emperor authority over governors in the provinces.
Tribunician power (*Tribunicia potesta*s)	23	Powers of the tribune without the office. This included the right to call assemblies, to veto the actions of magistrates and gave Roman citizens the right to appeal to Caesar.
Consular power (*Imperium consulare*)	19	The powers of the consul without the office. This included legal and administrative powers and the right to call the senate and chair meetings.
Pontifex Maximus	12	This effectively made the emperor chief priest.
Censorial powers	Taken occasionally	This gave the emperor the right to revise the membership of the senate and other social orders, to take a census of the Roman population, and gave authority in moral issues.
Right to make treaties	—	Free rein in foreign policy.
Ius prima relationis	23 (?)	The right to propose the first item of business in the senate.
Freedom from legal compulsion	24	
Imperator	40–38	A title awarded by acclamation after
Augustus	27	This name, 'revered one', was granted following the first constitutional revision.
Princeps	from *c.* 23	Not an official title, but an acknowledgement of Augustus' role as 'first citizen'.
Father of the Native Land (*Pater Patriae*)	2	No powers. A purely honorific title.

our period. The development of the constitution was not, however, smooth. The changes in the imperial position over the first twenty years of his reign seem to attest a debate about and a political struggle over the role of the emperor. From 31–23 BC Augustus had held one of the two available consulships. After 23 BC, he was consul rarely, and then only for part of the year, a model followed by most later emperors. From 23–19 BC, a period of some turmoil in Roman politics, he held no consular authority and the granting of consular power in 19 BC may represent a political victory for those who wished the emperor to have greater constitutional powers. The ultimate result of these revisions was that the emperor received the powers of the most important magistracies of the Republican constitution (those of the consul and the tribune) without actually having to hold the offices. The emperor also had ultimate authority in the empire and either governed provinces directly through his representatives or indirectly through his *maius imperium*. Emperors were also members of all the main colleges of priests in Rome, and the position of Pontifex Maximus seems to have given them authority over all religious matters. The constitutional powers of the emperors were so great that their authority seems unquestionable. These powers form the constitutional basis of a monarchy in the original sense of the word: rule by an individual.

Although, constitutionally, Augustus' powers seem monarchic, Augustus claimed to restore Republican government. This claim refers to the settlement of 28–27 BC when the powers that Augustus had accumulated during the triumviral period and the civil wars were laid down and new powers were granted by the senate. This was a political settlement designed to break with the illegality of the previous years and restore law and order. There appears to have been no intention on the part of Augustus to retire from public life. The settlement was designed to give his preeminence legitimacy and to build a new consensus which would bring stability to his regime. To achieve this consensus, he had to abandon some of his powers and restore authority to the senate. The freedom and power of the senate were the cornerstones of constitutional government, yet that freedom was to exist in a system in which Augustus was pre-eminent. Such a settlement had inherent contradictions, and these led to political tensions in the early years of the Augustan Principate which came to the fore with an embarrassing trial and a political conspiracy in 23 or 22 BC. The discontent of these years led to Augustus seeking a new constitutional settlement and to his withdrawal from Rome. From 23–19

BC, Augustus spent much of his time in the provinces, but the political problems in Rome continued and Augustus was able to return with renewed authority in 19 BC after a diplomatic triumph in the East and enforce a third constitutional settlement which brought him increased powers.

Augustus' political power was reflected in the legal powers he was granted, but was actually dependent on his ability to build a political consensus and to persuade the Roman political elite that they were involved in the running of the state. When Augustus summarised his career at the end of a long inscription placed outside his tomb in Rome, he attributed his supremacy not to any constitutional powers but to his *auctoritas* (authority) (*Res Gestae* 34.3). *Auctoritas* was a personal quality: an attribute of character, not something that could be granted by the senate. It would, of course, be naive to take Augustus at his word. Nevertheless, the association of his political power with his character, rather than his constitutional position, is significant. Anyone could possess his constitutional powers, but his character could not be inherited. At the last, Augustus emphasised the personal nature of his power. Descriptions of Augustus' political behaviour tend to emphasise his affability. He knew the names of the senators and would greet them all in turn. He took part in debates and allowed and even encouraged fierce questioning. Some have described this relationship between Augustus and the senate as a partnership but, if so, it was clearly a partnership of unequals. The emperor had far more power than any individual senator. Yet, he needed the senate. Senators commanded his armies. Senators governed the provinces. Senators made the administration work. The involvement of senators gave an air of legitimacy to government and linked the new regime with the traditions of the previous centuries. Augustus remained politically reliant on the goodwill of the senate. Augustus was not an absolute monarch, but a politician continually striving to assert his power.

The competition of Roman politics did not, therefore, end with the constitutional revisions which established the emperor's legal supremacy. Legal power brought the technical ability to command but this was limited by the political necessity of ensuring the compliance of those over whom he had authority. This compliance was achieved by political influence (*auctoritas*) and not legal power (*imperium*). Later emperors then acceded to constitutional supremacy, but needed to translate that into political influence.

THE WORKINGS OF POLITICS

Roman politics in the Republican and Augustan periods was very much a personal matter. Political alliances were composed of friends and family. To a very great extent, this system seems to have continued throughout the imperial period. There were, however, significant changes. Popular elections were gradually phased out (see p. 61). This meant that the people who mattered and who secured office for a senator were the emperor himself, who was in a position to appoint to office, and the other senators. There does seem to have been competition for posts (especially the senior posts) and success in this competition probably depended on the support that senators could gain from their colleagues. Friends and associates could be called on to give their support and bring with them the support of their own social connections. Favours were begged and were recalled and a network of mutual debts was created and extended.

The workings of this system of patronage will be explored more fully elsewhere (see pp. 219–22). It is sufficient to note here that these social networks extended across the senatorial order and united large numbers of people. We can try to understand Roman politics in the imperial period as a competition between the various factions (groupings of family and friends). The prominence of an individual would lead to the advancement of his friends and family and, it has been suggested, that we could understand and reconstruct the dynamics of Roman senatorial politics if we understood the composition of the various factions. Clearly, this is at least part of the answer. We do see factions advance. The prominence of Sejanus under Tiberius led to his family and friends enjoying political advancement and his fall ruined them (see pp. 40–6). We can replicate the pattern across the period. On such an interpretation, what mattered in Roman politics was who was in charge. This emphasises the scramble for power rather than any ideological conflict and suggests that for the vast majority of ordinary people, it probably mattered little who was currently winning the game.

Politics in the modern era has revolved to a greater or lesser extent around issues. Political groupings coalesce around shared beliefs, even if party coalitions are sometimes very loose. In the Republican period, it is possible to interpret some of the political activities of the period as also being 'issue-politics'. Politicians of the time would talk of *optimates* (the aristocratically oriented) or *populares* (the popularly oriented), by which they did not mean that these men belonged to a political party or even to a particular political faction. It meant that the particular politicians would tend to propose certain types of measures either designed to give influence to and perhaps spread financial benefits among the lower classes or to retain power and wealth in the upper echelons of society. Even within a system of competition between factions, there were real issues that were debated and fought over.

The advent of the Principate brought an end to such labels and seemingly ended the '*popularis* movement', since the emperor (normally) took care to look after the material needs of the urban poor and their support would anyhow have been of only limited use to senatorial politicians. The issues that motivated politicians were not the same as in the Republican period, but they can be detected.

Perhaps the most important issue facing Roman politicians was the role of the emperor and his relationship to the senate. Different views could and were taken of the proper role of each body within the Roman state. It is certainly arguable that the struggle to accommodate monarchy within an essentially republican political system was at the heart of the various political events of the period. Essentially, some politicians took a minimalist line: the emperor was just a senator with special authority and should be treated as any other senator. Others took the view that the emperor was a monarchic figure who should have the trappings of a monarchic position and be treated as if he was an absolute monarch. These are, of course, extreme views and most politicians did not position themselves at these extremes.

Although these were probably issues that convulsed the Roman aristocracy, we cannot detect 'Republican' or 'monarchic' parties operating during the period. As in the Republic, alliances of friends and family remained crucial for everyday political life. We do, however, sometimes see how 'issue-politics' related to 'faction-politics'. The so-called 'philosophical opposition', which was active from the reign of Nero to the reign of Domitian, was a faction (see pp. 129–32; 170–1; 181–3). At the centre of the faction was a single family whose activities spanned this period. Around them was a looser group of friends who were sometimes interrelated, sometimes not. It seems very unlikely that the actions of the members of this family and their associates were motivated simply by a desire to see their group rise to political prominence. They had a particular view of the Roman state and how senators should behave towards the emperor. It was this view that got them into trouble. Yet people joined this faction because they admired the political stance of its leading members. Marrying into the family was to take a position on a political issue, and joining in a patronage network with these people was at least in part an ideological statement. Although this was a faction, it was a faction formed both around a family and an issue. When emperors turned against leading members of the family, those on the edge of the group or remotely related also suffered. The two forms of political motivation were not in fact distinguishable. One must understand political events as a conflict of ideologies and a conflict of political factions.

FAMILY POLITICS: AUGUSTUS, TIBERIUS AND THE SUCCESSION

The emperor's supremacy realigned Roman politics. Political power was no longer dependent on office holding or on influence in the senate but could also be achieved through influence over the emperor. This was court politics. The inner workings of the Augustan court are mysterious, but some of the tensions and political groupings can be seen in the struggles that surrounded the issue of the succession. The struggles divided the imperial family and the Roman aristocracy and those divisions continued into the reign of Tiberius.

On the death of Augustus in AD 14, Tiberius was the leading man in the Roman state. He had been Augustus' political partner since AD 4 and had been adopted by Augustus. He was Augustus' most experienced general and had been at the forefront of his campaigns in Germany and Pannonia. Recently, he had suppressed the extremely dangerous Pannonian revolt and had led Roman attempts to retrieve the situation in Germany after Varus' legions had been wiped out in AD 9. Towards the end of his life, Augustus had come to rely on Tiberius. Tiberius had become his obvious successor.

Twenty years previously, the situation had been very different. Augustus had only one child, Julia (see Figure 1.1). His closest male relative was his nephew Marcellus, and Marcellus' marriage to Julia established him at the centre of Augustus' dynasty. Marcellus died suddenly in 23 BC. Julia, as a woman, could not succeed to Augustus' political position, but she could be expected to produce grandchildren for Augustus who would eventually inherit. The choice of a father for Augustus' grandchildren was crucial. Augustus used family members for important military and political tasks.

Julia's husband would be close to the heart of the imperial household. Augustus turned to Agrippa, his leading general. The alliance bore fruit: Gaius, Lucius, Julia, Agrippina and Agrippa Postumus. Augustus had his heirs. When Agrippa died in 12 BC, Augustus' grandchildren were still young. In the event of Augustus' death, they would need protection. Augustus turned to Tiberius.

Tiberius was the son of Livia, Augustus' third wife, and her first husband, Tiberius Claudius Nero. He was not a blood relation of Augustus, but his closeness to the imperial family had led to a series of important military postings. He and his brother Drusus shouldered the military burden of Augustus' policies in Germany and both were married into the imperial family. Tiberius was married to Vipsania (Agrippa's daughter by an earlier marriage) and Drusus was married to Antonia (Augustus' niece). Augustus overturned Tiberius' marriage to find Julia a new husband and his grandchildren a new protector. Tiberius appears to have opposed this, perhaps because of a reluctance to fulfil his designated role as guardian of the imperial grandchildren or, as our sources have it, devotion to Vipsania, or hostility towards Julia. In 6 BC, although Augustus had just honoured him with the grant of extensive powers, Tiberius withdrew from Rome and went into voluntary exile. This must have been a great blow to Augustus. He had lost his leading general, his son-in-law, and the guardian of his grandchildren. Also, the breach within his family had become obvious, a breach that became wider in subsequent years.

Tiberius' exile is a manifestation of a power struggle around the ageing emperor. The two halves of the imperial family jostled for

Figure 1.1 Simplified family tree of Augustus

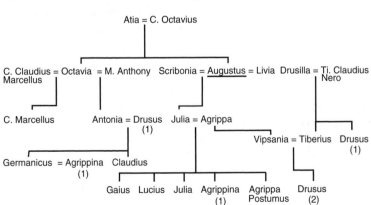

position. Time was against Tiberius. He and Drusus (who died in 9 BC) had effectively replaced Agrippa as Augustus' most trusted associates. Nevertheless, Julia and her children seemed destined to triumph and Tiberius' prospects gradually diminished. After Tiberius' withdrawal, Augustus simply waited for his grandchildren. Gaius was introduced into public life in 5 BC. Lucius followed in 2 BC.

The year 2 BC was intended as an *annus mirabilis* (a wondrous year) for Augustus. He was sixty years old, an old man by the standards of his day, and his active career was coming to an end. It was the year in which he completed his most magnificent building project: the *Forum Augusti*. This remarkable monument to Augustus and his family contained the temple of Mars Ultor, which Augustus had promised at the very outset of his political career. It was associated with Julius Caesar and the divine ancestors of the Julian family, Venus and Mars. The temple contained the standards Augustus had retrieved from the Parthians and was thus a monument to his greatest diplomatic achievement. The forum was lined by statues of the famous men of Rome, paralleled by statues of the famous members of the Julian family into which the emperor had been adopted. The centrepiece, the culmination of Roman history as displayed in the forum, was a statue of Augustus himself. An inscription on the base of the statue proudly proclaimed the title the senate had voted to him that year: *Pater Patriae*, the Father of his Country.

It was also a year in which family disputes resurfaced. His daughter Julia was accused of adultery and sent into exile. Her alleged lovers included many of the most prominent men of the Roman aristocracy. Historians have argued as to whether this was a sexual or a political scandal. Some have wanted to see the charge of adultery as a convenient excuse to rid Augustus of a dangerous political grouping. Others have preferred to delve into the psychology of a royal princess forced into three arranged marriages, widowed twice and deserted by her third husband. The argument is futile since with Julia (whose marital bed had always been a political pawn in the complex dynastic arrangements of the emperor) sex and politics were inextricable. For Julia, adultery had obvious political implications, as she and her alleged lovers must have known. Accusations of adultery, whether or not they were true, were political charges and Augustus' decision to act on those charges was a political act. Julia and her friends or lovers were a political grouping, whatever their sexual habits, and, in 2 BC, they were ruined.

In spite of a conciliatory letter when Julia was disgraced, relations between the two halves of the family remained hostile. Gaius was given a command in the East in AD 1, and there were rumours that Gaius talked openly of having Tiberius killed. Despite the fall of Julia and her group, Tiberius' prospects improved only marginally. Julia's children were still likely to inherit. But Tiberius' star was ascendant. In AD 2, he was recalled to Rome, where he would at least be safe from Gaius, even if he had no official role. In the same year, Lucius died. The blow to imperial hopes was such that Tiberius was moved to compose a poem lamenting Lucius' death (Suet. *Tib.* 70.2). Two years later, Gaius died after a long illness. He may already have been politically isolated. His mother and her friends were in exile. He had apparently requested to be relieved of his duties in the East and to return to Rome. Augustus was once again without an adult male heir and was once more forced to turn to Tiberius, who was now too busy for poetic composition.

Augustus' dynastic settlement involved a series of adoptions. He adopted Tiberius and Agrippa's surviving son Agrippa Postumus. Tiberius adopted Drusus' son Germanicus, husband of Agrippa's younger daughter, Agrippina. Germanicus was the grandchild of Augustus' sister Octavia and was thus a blood relative of both Augustus and Tiberius.

Tiberius' position was far stronger in AD 4 than it had been in 12 BC. His adoption shows that he was the immediate political heir. A huge revolt in Pannonia in AD 6 demonstrated that Tiberius was indispensable. Agrippa Postumus was still too young to take an active political role, but he was not allowed to become a potential replacement for Tiberius. In AD 7, he was exiled. In AD 8, his sister was accused of adultery with a prominent Roman aristocrat. Both were exiled. Her husband, L. Aemilius Paullus, a prominent senator who was distantly related to the imperial family, was executed for conspiracy. Of the children of Agrippa, only Agrippina remained in Rome, safely married to Tiberius' nephew and adopted son. Tiberius had triumphed.

This victory came at a cost. The family had been split. Members of the aristocracy had sought to associate themselves with the various factions and to show their loyalty and support to either Julia and her children or Livia and her children in the hope of eventual reward. Many of those who had supported Julia, Gaius and Lucius must have regarded Tiberius with suspicion. Augustus had killed many of his political opponents in the proscriptions and on the battlefields of the civil wars before 27 BC. Tiberius was to face them in his family and in the senate.

2

TIBERIUS (AD 14–37)

TIBERIUS AND TACITUS

All the major literary sources for the reign of Tiberius, with the exception of Velleius Paterculus, are hostile. Most attention has been given to Tacitus' depiction of the reign and Tacitus' portrayal has dominated modern perceptions. In part, this is due to the literary quality of Tacitus' work, which is generally regarded as being far greater than that of other writers, and is a tribute to his compelling portrait of the political events of the period.

Like many Greek and Roman historians, Tacitus was an annalist. His history was written within a fairly rigid framework in which the events of each year were recounted in order. Thus, an event which continued through more than one calendar year would be described under each year, whereas a modern historian will usually collate the events of two separate years to produce a single narrative account. This structure has certain strengths in that it allowed Tacitus to describe the events as they unfolded and to establish chronological links and coincidences which might escape a more thematically organised work, but it also has certain weaknesses in that it provides few obvious opportunities for summation and conclusions. When a modern historian might spend pages analysing the importance of certain events, Tacitus moves on to the next event. It is a tribute to his literary skill that although Tacitus' opinion of Tiberius is clear from the start, the methodical relating of events gradually lends support and credibility so that the stated 'facts' of Tiberius' reign seem to rule out other interpretations. Any assessment of the reign of Tiberius must start from Tacitus' devastating and brilliant depiction and from an acceptance that the *Annales* are a work of literature, carefully shaped and constructed by its author to represent his opinions and historical viewpoint.

This does not, of course, mean that we ought to reject Tacitus' opinions, but there are reasons to exercise caution. Tacitus was writing more than sixty years after the death of Tiberius. There will have been few who could remember Tiberius' reign and Tacitus must have been dependent on literary sources whose identity, quality, veracity and significance cannot normally be assessed. Since Tacitus rarely discusses his sources, it is virtually impossible to detect or evaluate interpretations borrowed from earlier writers. Biases, lies, misunderstandings and rumours may be integrated with the facts and the modern historian has few resources to reconstruct the processes that led to the formation of Tacitus' historical account (see pp. 2–3 for a general discussion of the difficulty of using this type of source). Nevertheless, we can at least attempt to understand the forces that are likely to have shaped the historical tradition and to have influenced Tacitus' historical thought.

Tacitus was a senator. His history concentrates on the relationship between the senatorial aristocracy and the emperor. Rome, and especially the senate, are presented as the crucial areas of political activity, as they had been during the Republic. His political interests and career must have affected his historical interests. It is likely that he presents a pro-senatorial viewpoint and largely used sources that shared his perspective. We may compare this with the rather different perspective offered by Velleius Paterculus (see p. 6), a writer who had followed an equestrian career (see pp. 255–6 for a discussion of the equestrian career structure) before entering the senate. We may accuse Velleius of flattering a dictatorial regime and must take account of the probability that the expressions of hostility towards Tiberius may have resulted in trial on the charge of treason. Nevertheless, the notably positive presentation of both Tiberius and Sejanus suggests that some, at least, may have had a rather different perspective on political events from that of the senators. Neither Velleius nor Suetonius show the same obsessive interest as Tacitus in the relationship between the senate and Tiberius.

Tacitus lived through the reign of Domitian, which was marked by a deterioration in the relationship between emperor and senate culminating in what is now known as 'the reign of terror', a period vividly described by Tacitus in the *Agricola* (1–2, 45) (see pp. 183–4). There were superficial similarities between the reigns of Domitian and Tiberius which were probably generally recognised at the time: Suetonius (*Dom.* 20) tells us that Domitian 'read nothing except the journals (*commentarii*) and register of deeds (*acta*) of Tiberius'. Nevertheless, there were differences in the way in which the emperors presented themselves and behaved towards the senate. Tiberius seems to have wished to present himself as the servant of the senate while Domitian may have seen himself as the senate's master. The reign of Tiberius was not a blueprint for that of Domitian. The influence of the Domitianic period on Tacitus was probably more subtle. Tacitus' experiences probably led to him adopting a more pessimistic view of the relationship between the emperor and the senate, rather than leading to a fundamental remodelling of the history of Tiberius to reflect the reign of Domitian.

Like all historians, Tacitus writes with the benefit of hindsight. If we date the formation of the monarchy to 31 BC, then Tacitus was writing after more than 130 years of monarchic government, when the imperial throne had had thirteen incumbents and there was no realistic alternative to imperial monarchy. Tiberius became emperor less than fifty years after the formation of the monarchy and when there had only been one previous incumbent. Tacitus knew that the principate would develop and that the senate would suffer the tyrannous rules of Caligula, Nero and Domitian without ever making a serious bid for a return to Republican government. Furthermore, Tacitus was writing for a knowledgeable audience. His contemporaries, even if not historians, will have known something of the reign of Tiberius. This shared knowledge lends the account a certain irony and a sense of inevitability. Everyone knows the eventual outcome of the story, though, of course, the participants at the time cannot have known. Let us take a modern parallel: any modern account of the international developments of 1910–14 must be overshadowed in the minds of readers and the historian by the eventual outbreak of the First World War. Thus, for Tacitus and his contemporaries, the events of the reign of Tiberius are a prelude to the history of the rest of the century, and the respect paid by Tiberius to the senate in the first years of the reign especially becomes bitterly ironic when writer and audience know what is to happen. Yet to understand why people behaved as they did in AD 14, we must free ourselves from this knowledge of the future.

THE ACCESSION

Velleius tells us that Tiberius was at Augustus' bedside when the old emperor made his farewells and 'returned his heavenly spirit to heaven' (Velleius Paterculus, II 123.2). Tacitus is not so certain.

Tiberius was summoned by his mother and arrived at Nola to find the emperor either dead or almost so. Livia had taken control of the situation and managed the flow of information from the emperor's bed-chamber so that news of the emperor's death was issued only when Livia and Tiberius were ready (Tac., *Ann.* I 5). Immediately after the announcement was made, Tiberius issued the watchword to the praetorian guard thereby establishing control over the only significant armed force in Italy. He then set out to Rome to arrange the formalities of the funeral and to secure his accession.

Tiberius' most serious dynastic rival was the surviving son of Agrippa and Julia, Agrippa Postumus. Tacitus (*Ann.* I 5) relates rumours that Augustus had visited Postumus in his island exile on Planasia, raising the possibility that Postumus would be summoned back to Rome. Fear of Agrippa Postumus' political resurrection allegedly led to Livia hastening Augustus' final illness. The story of an aged emperor making a secret journey to see his grandson and the allegation that Livia poisoned her husband seem far-fetched. In any event, action was taken to remove the potential threat to Tiberius' position. Tiberius later asserted that Augustus had left orders for Agrippa's death, but this was regarded with suspicion: Tacitus (*Ann.* I 6) wonders why Augustus, who had never murdered any of his relatives, would remove his own grandson to ease the way for his stepson. Tiberius' motive was straightforward.

On arrival in Rome, Tiberius convoked the senate to decide arrangements for Augustus' funeral. This was the only business which he allowed to be discussed. There was a pause in the business of state. The funeral was conducted with due solemnities. Augustus was deified. Only after this, did the senate turn to the accession of Tiberius.

The debate seems to have been long. Tiberius refused to receive the powers that Augustus had held. The senate demanded that he should assume Augustus' role and powers. Tiberius ordered a document to be read which summarised the military and financial status of the Empire: obviously providing the senate with crucial information if it was to take over the administration of the Empire. The senate again appealed to Tiberius to take on the burden. Tiberius weakened. He stated that he would not take on all aspects of the state but would accept any cares the senate chose to entrust to him. The senate pressed him and asked him to make his wishes clear. Tiberius claimed he desired none of the responsibility. There were signs of frustration and the senators pressed him again. Eventually, Tiberius was broken down and accepted Augustus' powers (Tac.,

Ann. I 11–12). Velleius (II 124.2) writes that Tiberius 'almost struggled longer to refuse the principate than others had fought to obtain it'. Whereas Velleius sees in this Tiberius' modesty, Tacitus portrays it as an example of Tiberius' hypocrisy.

The senatorial debate itself parallels events in 27 BC when Augustus established his constitutional position. There may have been a certain ritualistic quality to the debate: the prospective emperor had to be seen to be reluctant to accept the burdens thrust upon him. Yet, clearly, the staunch resistance of Tiberius was something of a surprise and led to a certain amount of frustration. Even Velleius seems somewhat bemused. Is Tacitus right, therefore, to dismiss the debate as an elaborate charade?

Tiberius was certainly the senior figure in the state. He had been Augustus' partner in power and was the leading and most experienced general. The political conflicts within the imperial family over the previous twenty years reflect the intention that the Augustan system would survive the first emperor's death. Most must have assumed that Tiberius would succeed in some way to Augustus' position. On Augustus' death, Tiberius had acted to secure his position. Agrippa Postumus was killed. Tiberius had assumed control of the imperial guard. Arriving in a Rome publicly grieving the loss of their Princeps, Tiberius was accompanied into the Forum by the guard, a potent symbol that imperial power had already passed into his hands. Tacitus (*Ann.* I 7) also places before his account of the senatorial debate a ceremonial occasion at which the consuls, commander of the guard, prefect of the corn supply, the senate, the army and the people all swore allegiance to the new emperor. This oath of loyalty reinforced the supremacy of the emperor and gave a religious authority to his position. Yet, if we are to believe Tacitus, the same senate that had sworn loyalty to the *princeps* then engaged in this very long debate over whether he was to become *princeps*. If Tiberius had received oaths of loyalty from the consuls and senate, what was the point of seeming reluctant to take a position he had already in large part assumed? If the debate was really about whether Tiberius would retire into private life, then the charade must have been so obvious that one wonders at its purpose.

The politicians of Rome were dealing with a new problem: there was no established procedure to deal with the succession to the imperial position. We have epigraphic evidence for the accession of Vespasian which seems to show that the assumption of the imperial position would be ratified by the passing of a *lex de imperio* which granted the emperor all the powers and privileges that went with the position. These powers and privileges had been gathered by Augustus in a series of constitutional settlements (see pp. 13–17). There was no precedent to which Tiberius or the senate could turn and no single enabling bill which the senate could pass. There was also the issue of which powers and titles were peculiar to Augustus and whether Tiberius would fulfil exactly the same role as the old emperor. Indeed, although it was recognised that Tiberius was in some sense the political successor of Augustus, as Augustus had succeeded Caesar, we need not assume that it was clear to all or any of the participants to what exactly Tiberius had succeeded. For Tacitus, and most of the later writers, the constitutional and political role of the emperor was established and known, but in AD 14 the matter was probably not so clear cut. When Asinius Gallus asserted that by asking Tiberius which part of the state he wished to control he had not intended to suggest that one should divide what could not be separated, but to argue that the body of the state was one and needed to be ruled by the mind of a single man, he was discussing the issue central to the debate: the nature of the imperial position (Tac., *Ann.* I 12).

Even given these constitutional difficulties, we might have expected the senate to have recognised Tiberius as the political heir of Augustan supremacy and that Tiberius would have allowed them rapidly to establish his constitutional position, following the Augustan model. This was, after all, the decision the senate reached eventually. By forcing the senate to discuss the issue at length, the senators were driven to give Tiberius their public support. Tacitus (*Ann.* I 7) explains this convoluted process (typically) by reference to Tiberius' twisted character, but he also provides us with another, more interesting explanation: fear of Germanicus.

Tiberius was in a strong, even dominant, position on the death of Augustus and was the most obvious and credible candidate as Augustus' successor. This does not, however, mean that his position was secure. Augustus had secured the principate on the battlefield. Tiberius had secured his position through dynastic politics. The dynastic squabbles had created tensions in the imperial family which were probably still reflected in divided loyalties among the senators. The rumour of Augustus' visit to Agrippa Postumus, unlikely though it may have been, illustrates these continued tensions. We are hampered by the lack of good chronological data, but as he sat in the senate in AD 14, Tiberius probably had little solid information about the attitudes of the armies on the Rhine and Danube. He may already have had reason to fear that he would not secure the German and Danubian legions as easily as he had secured the praetorian guard. Until the loyalty of the troops and their commanders was assured, Tiberius was threatened by over-whelming military force. The political realities of the first months of his principate meant that Tiberius could not afford to alienate the senate. He needed all the political support he could muster. This uncertainty more than anything else explains Tiberius' cautious approach to the senate. He needed his accession to appear constitu-tional to minimise potential disaffection among the generals and governors and their friends in the senate.

Although we can see the political pressures that may have lain behind Tiberius' behaviour in this debate, there is a further possible explanation. Not only was Tiberius' political position rather different from that of Augustus, but he also differed in character. We view Tiberius and Augustus with the knowledge of the centuries of monarchic government that followed. Tiberius had a different perspective on history. There had been more than four centuries of Republican government, then about fifty years of Augustan rule. Augustus provided a model for Tiberius to follow, but Tiberius could look to other ways of maintaining his power, ways which would suit him and his political situation. In his early years, Tiberius consistently looked to the senate to give him advice and guidance. He avoided taking initiatives. In many ways, this first debate sets the tone for the first years of the principate (certainly in Tacitus). Tiberius may have been trying to establish closer ties to the senate than Augustus had maintained, perhaps even some genuine sharing of power. If this is the case, then the opening debate was at least in part about establishing a style. The policy ultimately failed and Tacitus cynically suggests that it was a charade never intended to succeed. As we shall see, however, the reasons for its failure are more complex.

GERMANICUS

Germanicus is very much the hero of the early years of Tiberius' reign. His early death in suspicious circumstances may have enhanced his reputation. As Tiberius' standing declined in the later years of his reign, the loss of Germanicus may have been felt more deeply by the Roman people and the rifts that opened in the im-perial dynasty subsequent to, and in part resulting from,

Germanicus' death made his reputation and family a focus for the disaffected. Even though he died in AD 19, he was a central figure in Tiberius' principate.

Germanicus, not Tiberius, stood at the centre of the Augustan family (see Figure 2.1). Tiberius was the son of Tiberius Claudius Nero and Livia. He was the adopted son of Augustus and had been married to Vipsania, daughter of Agrippa, and then to Julia, daughter of Augustus. Germanicus was the son of Nero Drusus and Antonia, grandson of Mark Antony and Octavia (sister of Augustus), Livia and Tiberius Claudius Nero. He was Tiberius' nephew and adopted son. He was married to Agrippina, daughter of Julia, granddaughter of Augustus. Germanicus, unlike Tiberius, could claim a blood relationship with Augustus, through his maternal grandmother, and his children were direct descendants of Augustus. By arranging for Tiberius to adopt Germanicus, even though Tiberius had a son, Drusus, and by marrying Germanicus to Agrippina, Augustus restructured the dynasty to place Germanicus and Agrippina at the heart of the family. In so doing, he made it possible for some to see Germanicus as the rightful or intended heir of Augustus and those who were in some sense disaffected with Tiberius could look to Germanicus to provide a focus of opposition. After the feuding in the family in the last years of Augustus' reign, the final dynastic settlement retained the possibility of continued conflict between the party of Tiberius and Drusus and that of Germanicus and Agrippina.

The first crisis of Tiberius' reign (described below) illuminated that potential. Its successful outcome, with a clear demonstration of the loyalty of Germanicus to his uncle, probably reassured a nervous emperor and brought much needed stability to the initial years of Tiberius' rule. Germanicus' early death, however, meant that this stability was short-lived.

Soon after the news of Augustus death and Tiberius' accession to the throne, the legions in Germany and on the Danube sought to take advantage of the weakness of the new regime to obtain better conditions, including provision for retirement at the correct age and an increase in pay. The revolt broke out in Pannonia (Tac., *Ann.* I 16–30), but was paralleled by a mutiny in Germany (Tac., *Ann.* I 31–49). The Pannonian outbreak was dealt with fairly quickly. Tiberius sent his son Drusus, Aelius Sejanus (joint prefect of the praetorians) and a detachment of praetorians to Pannonia. A sudden and mysterious diminishing in the brightness of the moon at a critical moment helped convince the soldiers their mutiny was doomed.

Figure 2.1 The family of Tiberius in AD 14

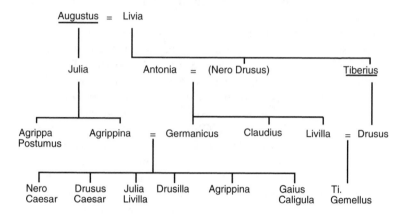

Drusus took advantage of the decline in the morale of the mutineers to execute their leaders. The elements continued to conspire against the mutiny. Storms and floods convinced the soldiers that the gods disapproved of them. Drusus was able to leave the camp before a delegation that had been sent to negotiate with Tiberius could return. He had quickly and efficiently ended the mutiny.

The German mutiny was more serious. When Germanicus returned to the legions following the news of Augustus' death he found all four legions mutinous. Germanicus attempted to restore their loyalty but they proffered their complaints and offered to support Germanicus in an attempt on the throne. If Tacitus' story is true, the offer may have been tempting. Most of Tiberius' military career had been spent commanding the legions in Germany or on the Danube. He had had little contact with the legions in the East. Clearly, these German forces did not have sufficiently fond memories of the new Emperor to bind them in loyalty to him. The mutinous legions in Pannonia, though Drusus was with them, may well have come over. Tiberius would not have had time to summon legions from the East, and it is far from certain that they would have been loyal. Nevertheless, Germanicus stood with his uncle and adoptive father. Family loyalty determined his attitude.

It was his family which, according to Tacitus, ultimately saved the day. The troops had returned in disorder to their winter quarters, two legions heading to Vetera, two to Ubii. After rioting at Ubii where Germanicus and his family were also staying, Germanicus sent Agrippina (who was pregnant) and his son Gaius

Caligula to safety. The sight of the granddaughter of Augustus and her son, who seems to have been adopted as something of a mascot by the troops, ignominiously retreating from the mutinous legions who should have been their protectors, was too much for the troops and two legions were brought round. The ringleaders were executed. Germanicus was confident enough to threaten the legions at Vetera. Before he arrived at the camp, the leading mutineers were overpowered and killed and the legions' loyalty was secured.

Germanicus' reaction to the mutinies was to launch campaigns into Germany. The first raid was destructive and punitive. Although his troops were attacked returning to base, the mission was accomplished successfully. The attack was a preliminary to an extended series of victorious and destructive raids in AD 15 and 16, somewhat marred by a naval disaster in 15 (Tac. *Ann.* II 24). No substantial territory was won in these battles and Roman losses were heavy. Tiberius recalled Germanicus. Tacitus (*Ann.* II 26), who may have had access to at least some of the correspondence between Tiberius and Germanicus, claims that Germanicus was reluctant to leave since he believed that the Romans were on the verge of significant gains. Tiberius, however, thought that the frontier had been stabilised and that diplomacy offered more immediate gains. Germanicus returned to Rome and in AD 17 celebrated a triumph.

In the next year, Germanicus was consul with Tiberius and was sent east. He was given *maius imperium*, a power greater than that of the provincial governors. Germanicus clearly went as an imperial deputy. In the same year, a new governor was sent to Syria, the most powerful province in the region. Gnaeus Calpurnius Piso was a trusted and experienced politician. He had been consul with Tiberius in 7 BC. His wife Plancina was a friend of Livia, Tiberius' mother. Tacitus depicts him as something of a monster, arrogant and violent. His relationship with Germanicus was disastrous. Even by the time he arrived, Piso's behaviour on the journey to Syria had suggested that he was hostile to Germanicus. After Germanicus provided a diplomatic resolution to the brewing Armenian crisis, relations between Piso and Germanicus worsened, but open confrontation was avoided. In AD 19, Germanicus visited Egypt. On his return to Syria, there was another disagreement with Piso. Germanicus fell ill and Piso, who had been leaving the province, delayed. Signs that magic was being employed against Germanicus were found in the dying man's room (Tac., *Ann.* II 69; Dio, LVII 18.6–10). Germanicus, apparently convinced that Piso was behind the magic and his illness, formally renounced his friendship with

Piso and ordered him from the province. The former was a serious act: it was a public declaration of hostility. Germanicus died.

At this stage, Piso behaved in an extraordinarily odd manner. He had been expelled from Syria, but had not rushed back to defend his cause in Rome. He heard of Germanicus' death when on the island of Kos. He allegedly celebrated publicly the death of his enemy, the emperor's son, a death for which, as he must have known, some would blame him. He then returned to Syria to challenge the new governor. He bribed some troops and raised an army. He was not, however, able to dislodge Germanicus' friends. After being besieged and defeated, he was sent back to Rome under escort (Tac., *Ann.* II 74–81).

The death of Germanicus was a great shock. The transportation of his ashes from Syria to Rome gave rise to an outpouring of national grief. Agrippina was at the centre of the ceremony. She disembarked at the South Italian port of Brundisium carrying the ashes. The praetorians met her at the port. They carried the ashes in procession across Italy. As the ashes reached each town, the populace and the leaders of the community would show their respect by public sacrifice and mourning. Drusus, Claudius and the consuls journeyed to meet the ashes and accompany the mourning procession into Rome. The ashes were laid to rest in the mausoleum of Augustus. Tiberius and Livia did not appear (Tac. *Ann.* III 1–5).

Piso slowly returned to Rome. His suspected aide in the death, a woman named Martina who was a friend of Plancina and who had been arrested in Syria, died in mysterious circumstances at Brundisium on her way to Rome (Tac., *Ann.* III 7). A public interview between Piso's son and Drusus led to Drusus expressing a certain hostility (Tac., *Ann.* III 8). The trial followed and is reported in detail by Tacitus. Piso was accused of inciting rebellion, corrupting the troops, black magic and poisoning. Only the poisoning charge was defended stoutly. The case was lost, and Piso committed suicide. His son survived and, more surprisingly, so did Plancina, after a plea from Livia (Tac., *Ann.* III 12–19).

Tacitus adds an allegation concerning Piso's death which provides us with an excellent example of Tacitean innuendo (Tac., *Ann.* III 16). Some said (Tacitus deliberately distances himself from this rumour) that Piso had an incriminating document: a letter from Tiberius. Piso held on to the letter, hoping to secure his acquittal, but the document disappeared after his death. Both this disappearance and the 'suicide' were said to be the work of Sejanus. Tacitus does not even suggest that he believes it was true, but simply by repeating the story, backed by certain unnamed contemporary witnesses, he suggests to the reader that Piso was murdered and that Tiberius was behind the death of Germanicus. He also foreshadows a main theme for the reign: the rise and fall of the sinister Sejanus. Dio, whose narrative is incomplete for this period, does not mention the story.

The outlines of the Germanicus story may be comparatively clear but the motivations of the main participants are shrouded. We must ask several basic questions. Was Tiberius afraid of or hostile towards Germanicus? Was Piso instructed to obstruct Germanicus? Was Germanicus the victim of a conspiracy? What were the results of his death?

The evidence is, of course, mixed. Curse tablets, human remains left in Germanicus' room and the other evidence of a magical conspiracy to kill Germanicus are mysterious and it must be allowed that many in the ancient world believed that magic worked. It is possible that Piso commissioned this and that he, or Plancina, arranged for Germanicus to be poisoned, but there was no convincing evidence to connect Piso to the magic or the alleged poisoning. In an era of limited medical knowledge, people, even young, fit people, could die suddenly of no obvious cause. It seems, however, unquestionable that Piso was reluctant to accept Germanicus' authority in the East and his behaviour was calculated to annoy Germanicus and undermine his position.

The sentiments of the family were well known. Piso's father had followed the Republicans Pompey, Cassius and Brutus and had held a consulship in that crucial year in Augustus' early reign, 23 BC. Piso's brother was to continue to offend the imperial family: he publicly announced that he was fleeing the moral corruption of Rome and was only persuaded to return by Tiberius' personal intervention. He prosecuted Urgulania, a woman closely connected to the imperial family, seriously embarrassing Tiberius and Livia (Tac., *Ann.* II 34), and was to be prosecuted for treason in AD 24 (Tac. *Ann.* IV 21). Piso himself had served in Spain (*CIL* II 2703) and possibly Africa before his appointment to Syria and had gained a reputation for brutality (Seneca, *De Ira*, I 18). He had opposed a motion of Tiberius and Drusus in the senate in AD 16 (Dio, LVII 15.9) and in a debate that year argued that senatorial business should continue to be transacted in the absence of the emperor (Tac. *Ann.* II 35). He made deliberate show of his independence. He and Tiberius had been consuls together in AD 7 and the evidence points to at least some friendship between the Pisones and Tiberius.

Tiberius must have been aware of his character and that he would have clashed with Germanicus. It is difficult to believe that his elevation to the governorship of Syria was a coincidence, or that Piso acted without some feeling that Tiberius would support him.

The sending of Piso to such a crucial posting could be interpreted as a sign of hostility towards Germanicus, and was later interpreted as such. If we examine the relationship between Germanicus and Tiberius, there is little other evidence to support this thesis. Germanicus had inflicted major defeats on the Germans but suffered significant losses. Tiberius may have been unwilling to absorb such losses for comparatively little gain. Roman power had been reasserted after the Varian disaster of AD 9 after almost ten years of campaigning. Whatever Germanicus' instincts, Tiberius' judgement that Rome would be better served by a period of consolidation on the German frontier cannot be dismissed as merely a convenient excuse to withdraw Germanicus. Germanicus returned to a triumph: the greatest military honour available. He progressed through the streets of Rome honoured by the population. This was also a political triumph: Germanicus was portrayed before the Roman people as a great hope whose victories enhanced the whole imperial house. In his absence on the frontier, he had been associated with Drusus in public games, at which Drusus had obviously presided (Tac., *Ann.* I 76). On his return to Rome, Germanicus held the consulship with the emperor. Augustus had held the consulship only irregularly between 23 BC and his death. Tiberius was to hold the consulship with Drusus in 21 and with Sejanus in 31. Germanicus was sent to the East with *maius imperium*. To all appearances, Germanicus was held in the greatest honour. Relations between Drusus and Germanicus seemed notably good and Tiberius seemed happy with the successes of both his 'sons'. There was no division in the imperial house.

Germanicus was granted great honours following his death. The *Tabula Hebana* (EJ 94a) notes that a statue was to be set up to Germanicus and his father on the Palatine Hill near the temple of Apollo in which meetings of the senate were often held; his name was inserted into the hymn of the Salii (see p. 319); five of the voting centuries were to be named after him; a curule chair (see p. 319) was to be placed for Germanicus at the games of the Divus Augustus and the chair was to be kept in the temple of the new god, the temples were to be closed on the day that Germanicus' ashes were interred and sacrifices were to be made on that day each year at his tomb. On the same day the equestrians were to parade in

Germanicus' honour. In public, all due honours were granted to Germanicus. The only oddity was that Tiberius and his mother did not attend the internment. Some bad feeling may have been read into this by Germanicus' supporters, but this would seem to be an over-reaction. Although the ashes were interred with great public ceremonial in the mausoleum (the Augustan family tomb), this was not a public funeral. The funeral had been conducted in Syria. The role of Tiberius at such an event would be unclear and Tiberius anyhow tended to avoid ceremonials. Tiberius' absence allowed Agrippina centre stage. She dominated the event. At worst, we see here only a political misjudgement on the part of Tiberius and Livia, though in such a comparatively small community such misjudgements could have dire consequences. Nothing was done which would suggest that Tiberius was satisfied at the loss of Germanicus.

Tacitus argues that the imperial court was divided between Germanicus and his supporters and those of Tiberius and Drusus. It is, however, difficult to find evidence of this. Drusus acted with Germanicus to have Haterius Agrippa appointed praetor. Agrippa was a relative of Germanicus and had caused controversy in AD 15 by vetoing a proposal to beat pantomime actors who were held responsible for inciting a crowd that attacked some soldiers. Since one presumes that these were praetorians, a source of loyal support for Tiberius, it may be seen as a veto directed against an important element of Tiberius' power and we would therefore have expected Tiberius and Drusus to have opposed Agrippa. That they did not shows the unity of the imperial family (Tac., *Ann.* I 77, II 51). After Germanicus' death, Piso's son approached Drusus in order to secure his support in the forthcoming trial, Drusus being potentially the greatest beneficiary of Germanicus' death. He was refused a private audience and publicly rebuked. Drusus then left for Illyricum. There is no evidence of any division between Drusus and Germanicus, though Germanicus' relationship with Tiberius appears to have been a little more complex.

We might view Piso as a maverick, a throwback to the days of the fiercely independent Republican nobility and consider his actions in the East as those of an autonomous Republican. He was irritated by the regal honours granted to the young man by the Easterners. Germanicus appears to have been comfortable in the East and to have adapted his behaviour to the cultural values of the cities that he visited, notably the great cultural centres of Athens and Alexandria. There is some sign that Tiberius may also have been unhappy at the ease with which Germanicus adapted to the role of Eastern (deputy) monarch. Yet, this is probably too simple a reading of Piso's character. The Piso brothers were well connected, but it is difficult to see how they could have risen so far if they had been openly subversive. Piso's closeness to Tiberius may have been a more important factor in the hostility between him and Germanicus than any alleged 'Republicanism'. It seems very likely that Piso was appointed as a check on the young man and that his appointment represents a lack of trust in Germanicus on the part of the emperor. The behaviour of Piso, and his subsequent trial, was probably a significant political embarrassment for Tiberius. It threatened to expose his relationship with Germanicus. Such an exposé of Tiberius' lack of faith in the national hero in a time of such grief may have been distinctly discomforting for the emperor.

The death of Germanicus, and subsequent events, gave focus to increasing discontent with Tiberius. Tiberius was unwilling, or temperamentally unable, to curry popular favour. He was to sponsor very few sets of games during his reign. The result was a fairly rapid loss of political support among the plebs of the city which quickly manifested itself in public opposition. Dio has a story dated to AD 15, before Tiberius had paid the legacies given by Augustus to the Roman plebs. A corpse was being carried through the Forum when a man stopped the bearers, bent over and whispered a message in the corpse's ear. When he was asked what he said, he replied that he had sent word to Augustus concerning Tiberius' failure to pay the legacies. Tiberius had the man killed, so that the message would be delivered directly (Dio, LVII 14.1). Another sign of the weakness of Tiberius' position came in AD 17 with the emergence of a pretender. Clemens, a slave of Agrippa Postumus, who had made a futile attempt to save his master, stole Postumus' ashes and retreated to Cosa. After some time he re-emerged declaring himself to be Postumus, miraculously saved. Word spread and Clemens eventually made his way to Ostia. Tiberius did not move openly against him, but supposedly had him kidnapped and executed. Tacitus clearly has the story from a number of sources and believed that Clemens had powerful supporters (Tac., *Ann.* II 39; cf. Dio, LVII 16.3–4).

Discontent was clear even before the death of Germanicus. Although his death removed a potential rival to Tiberius, it was to focus attention on Agrippina. Agrippina had returned with her children to a nation in mourning. The passing of the cortège through Italy was an opportunity to unite the people in grief. The torch-lit procession in Rome, a procession with military honours, to the mausoleum in which Augustus had been laid to rest just a few years before and the silent placing of the ashes in the family tomb brought together the community of Italy and Rome, a community which had so recently united to celebrate Germanicus' triumph over the Germans. Ceremonials are important and here was a great ceremonial, orchestrated around and centring on Agrippina, not on the emperor. Consciously or otherwise, Agrippina's role in these ceremonies and her position as grandchild of Augustus and the mother of Augustus' great-grandchildren, had made her a central political figure.

The marriage of Germanicus and Agrippina had united the imperial family. After the death of Germanicus, Agrippina had no family tie to Tiberius. It seems very likely that Tiberius or Livia had been behind the exile of Agrippina's sister and the death of her brother. Her mother, Julia, starved herself to death in AD 14, presumably seeing no hope of a return from exile now that her former husband had seized power. Agrippina may have suspected that Tiberius was in some way involved in the death of her husband. The tensions that had divided the imperial family for almost thirty years were once more obvious and Agrippina was a natural, if vulnerable, focus for the growing opposition to Tiberius. Her popularity and that of her sons could only increase as Tiberius' standing declined. In an increasingly tense political atmosphere, Tiberius came to rely more on a close friend and less on his family. His failure to manage his family and his gradual loss of popularity and authority led him to look for a new approach. The death of Germanicus created the conditions for the rise of Sejanus.

SEJANUS

Tiberius' first prefect of the guard was L. Seius Strabo. This man offered Tiberius crucial support at his accession and his loyalty was rewarded with a posting as Prefect of Egypt, the senior equestrian magistracy (see p. 256). Although an equestrian, Seius Strabo was connected to several prominent senatorial families through his mother and wife or wives and his career brought him considerable wealth (*CIL* IX 7285 = *ILS* 8996 = EJ 220). His son was adopted, probably into a prominent senatorial family, and his name was changed to L. Aelius Sejanus. Instead of pursuing a senatorial career, Sejanus followed his natural father and became first joint commander of the praetorian guard with his father and then sole commander of the guard.

Sejanus first appears in our historical record in AD 14 when he was sent with the young Drusus to quell the mutinous legions on the Danube (Tac., *Ann.* I 24). He had been among the friends of Gaius Caesar (Augustus' grandson) (Tac., *Ann.* IV 1), but after Gaius' death, had become an associate of Tiberius. Although Tacitus mentions him briefly in the story of the trial of Piso, we next sight him in AD 20 when he betrothed his daughter to Claudius' son (Tac., *Ann.* III 29). By AD 21, he was an emerging power and Tacitus (*Ann.* III 35) alleges that Marcus Aemelius Lepidus, a member of one of the most aristocratic families of Rome, stepped aside to allow Sejanus' uncle to assume a command in Africa for fear of making an enemy of Sejanus. The following year, after Sejanus was praised for prompt action to prevent a fire that burnt down the theatre of Pompey spreading to other areas, a bronze statue was erected to him in the theatre, a notable honour (Tac., *Ann.* III 72). Tiberius had allowed him to concentrate the praetorian guard in a single camp in the city, so that the entire guard would be under his direct authority.

Sejanus was becoming increasingly prominent in the imperial government and Drusus is said to have become increasingly hostile and to have complained at the trust that his father placed in this interloper (Tac., *Ann.* IV 7). Sejanus was, however, only remotely connected to the imperial family. Drusus was his father's natural political ally and successor. Drusus' hostility seriously weakened Sejanus' position. Tiberius may have called him *socius laborum* (ally in my work) in early 23 (Tac., *Ann.* IV 2), but his position was clearly subordinate.

In 23, however, his prospects were transformed. Drusus died, allegedly poisoned by Sejanus and Drusus' wife Livilla (Germanicus' sister). Tiberius was left without an adult male member of his family on whom he could rely. The closest male surviving members of the imperial family were Claudius, who was regarded as unsuitable for high office, and the sons of Germanicus and Agrippina. Drusus appears to have acted as a guardian for these children and his loss left them and their mother vulnerable. Sejanus was now in a similar position to that of Tiberius following the death of Agrippa. He was the closest collaborator of the emperor and the second most powerful man in the state, but he was not ultimately expected to succeed.

The truth of the poisoning allegation is difficult to substantiate.

The allegation of poisoning resurfaced when Sejanus fell. His former wife, having seen her and Sejanus' children killed, returned home and alleged in a suicide note that Sejanus and Livilla had murdered Drusus (Dio, LVIII 11.6–7). Tiberius had the slaves of the household tortured until confessions were extracted. It is clear that Sejanus was the obvious beneficiary of Drusus' death. There may have been rumours of foul play at the time, some of which connected Tiberius himself to the death of his son, though Tacitus regards them as ridiculous, and we must remember that virtually any and every death in the imperial family was thought by at least someone to be the result of foul play. There may, however, have been other motives behind Sejanus' wife's allegation, which was made at a time of the most intense personal distress, and other reasons why Tiberius might have found the allegation credible or convenient in AD 31 (Tac., *Ann.* IV 10–11).

There was no immediate threat to Sejanus' position after Drusus' death. Ultimately, however, the young sons of Germanicus and Agrippina would usurp his position. The next years appear to have been marked by increasing hostility between Sejanus and Agrippina and her sons and, as in earlier imperial power struggles, various groups among the aristocracy allied themselves with either Sejanus or Agrippina. The extent of Sejanus' power in these years cannot be assessed. His power over the emperor was not complete, as was apparently demonstrated in AD 25 when his request to marry Livilla and thus become a member of the imperial family was refused. (Tac. *Ann.* IV 39–40).

The episode disclosed Sejanus' ambition and may have been a significant blow to him, but the continuing dissensions in the imperial family were working to his advantage. Relations between Agrippina and Tiberius became so bad that Agrippina apparently refused to eat food at Tiberius' dinner parties for fear that it had been poisoned. She also petitioned Tiberius to be allowed to remarry, a request Tiberius refused (Tac., *Ann.* IV 53).

These two blocked marriages illustrate the growing political crisis in Rome. Sejanus' bid to marry Livilla offered a means for Sejanus to be brought within the family and therefore provided Tiberius with an alternative route to an heir. The implications of such an alliance were clear. In AD 25, Tiberius was unwilling to turn aside from his own grandchild or the children of Germanicus and contemplate Sejanus as imperial heir or guardian of any such heir. Agrippina's remarriage could not be allowed either and it is difficult to believe that her alleged appeal was more than rhetorical.

She requested male protection for herself and her children, but this would be to place a man, of necessity from outside the imperial family, in the position of protector and step-father of possible imperial heirs. He would be in a powerful political position. It was also an implied rebuke. Tiberius himself should have been the protector of the imperial family. One ought, however, to be a little cautious. These stories were obviously of dramatic importance, but dealt with matters internal to the imperial family and one must wonder how they reached the historical tradition. They do not reflect well on Tiberius or Sejanus and their publication may be part of a hostile tradition. Certainly, the circle around Agrippina might have leaked the stories, or they could have emerged at the time of the fall of Sejanus. The stories are plausible, though not certain to be true.

Tiberius was in a difficult position, faced with a conflict between his friend and his family and perhaps an increasingly restive political class in Rome. His solution was startling. He left Rome and retired to Capri, an island in the bay of Naples. It is difficult to see anything other than a personal motive for the retreat. Tiberius cut himself off from the day-to-day politics of Rome, isolating himself from the factions and the fighting. The senate was thereby somewhat marginalised since, with the emperor taking decisions on Capri, there could be little consultation. Also, his retreat meant that Tiberius needed someone to manage Rome while he was away, to represent his political interests, and to ensure that the business of government that had to be conducted in Rome was correctly managed. For this, he had to turn to Sejanus. It was therefore a decision of sorts, and the retreat to Capri led to a significant increase in Sejanus' power. Sejanus became Tiberius' first minister, an extremely powerful position, though, as we shall see, Sejanus always depended on the support of the emperor.

In 28, the senate voted altars to *Clementia* (mercy) and *Amicitia* (friendship). The former was an 'imperial virtue', for only the powerful may show clemency. The latter was flanked by statues of Sejanus and Tiberius (Tac., *Ann.* IV 74). Sejanus' birthday was to be honoured, a privilege normally reserved for members of the imperial family. According to Dio, various groups in Roman society erected statues to Sejanus and he was included in the usual prayers and sacrifices for the fortunes of the emperor (Dio, LVIII 2.7). Sejanus was associated with Tiberius in the symbols and rituals of imperial power, an association which must have at least suggested to the people that Sejanus was to be further elevated.

It is no coincidence that the very next year saw a direct attack on

Agrippina and her son Nero Caesar. Nero was accused of shameful sexual activity and Agrippina's attitude was criticised. The senate, however, refused to act. It would not launch highly unpopular prosecutions of members of the imperial house without clearer direction (Tac., *Ann.* V 3–4). We do not have a complete narrative for the following years and do not know what Tiberius' reaction was to this rebuff, but Nero and Agrippina were eventually exiled, presumably after a clear statement of the emperor's wishes. Nero was killed or encouraged to kill himself in 31 (Dio, LVIII 8.3–4; Suet., *Tib.* 54). Drusus Caesar was to follow into exile and eventually to death, also accused of sexual misdemeanours (Dio, LVIII 3.8).

Sejanus' rise now looked inevitable. His principal enemies were exiled and it seemed that the emperor, who already relied on him so much, would eventually raise him to the imperial position. He was, however, still an equestrian – not a suitable candidate for imperial office. Tiberius changed this. Sejanus was appointed to the consulship of AD 31. He was to have the very rare honour of sharing his consulship with Tiberius himself, a clear mark of favour. Dio dates Tiberius' use of the phrase *socius laborum* (ally in my work) to 30, a phrase that might suggest that he would become ally in his title as well.[1] The senate voted that Sejanus and Tiberius would hold joint consulships every five years and similar ceremonies were to be conducted whenever either of them entered the city. Dio tells us that sacrifices were made to images of Sejanus, suggesting his integration into the imperial cult (Dio, LVIII 4.1–4). He was betrothed to a daughter of the imperial house, and Sejanus could hope that he would be marked as Tiberius' heir or co-emperor by the grant of tribunician power or by adoption. Most must have expected both these developments. Neither happened. Tiberius decided to destroy him.

Sejanus' status in 31 was such that Tiberius had remaining few choices. The next logical step was to raise Sejanus still further, but that would have been to make him virtually co-emperor. Gaius Caligula, the third son of Germanicus and Agrippina, had remained with Tiberius on Capri. Tiberius may have found this young man congenial company. It was becoming clear that to promote Sejanus would mean the death of Gaius. Removing Gaius may also have raised the issue of the security of Tiberius' young grandson: could he be protected? If Tiberius was to promote Gaius, then he had to deal with Sejanus. He was too mighty to be just a subject. Whatever the rationale, Tiberius decided to rid himself of his praetorian prefect.

This was no easy task. Sejanus had control of the praetorians, the major military force in Rome. He did not, however, control the *vigiles*, the night-watch, a kind of military police force stationed within the city. It was this force that took control of the streets of Rome while Sejanus was in the senate-house (*curia*) awaiting the reading of a letter which Macro, who was to be Sejanus' replacement as prefect of the praetorians, had assured him would bring further honours. Instead of honours, the letter condemned Sejanus. He was taken from the senate-house and imprisoned. The senate met again on the same day and had him executed. The speed of his fall was notable. Tiberius had successfully disposed of his ally (Dio, LVIII 8–11; Suet., *Tib.* 65).

Sejanus was more than prefect of the praetorian guard and Tiberius' *socius laborum*. He was a politician of some importance. This aspect of his career does not emerge clearly from the ancient accounts, but can be detected in the story of his death and its aftermath. In Dio, we see a popular reaction against Sejanus which appears to pre-date his fall, if only slightly, and which was savagely expressed following his death. Dio claims that Sejanus saw himself as a popular leader and this may be confirmed by a mysterious fragmentary inscription which suggests that Sejanus held some sort of gathering on the Aventine Hill in Rome in the year of his consulship. The Aventine was traditionally associated with plebeian political activity and a gathering there would suggest some kind of anti-senatorial activity (EJ 53). In courting popular opinion, Sejanus may have attempted to weaken the position of the family of Germanicus, which seems to have had consistent popular support in this period (Tac., *Ann.* V 4–5). Dio (LVIII 9.1) suggests that Sejanus was surprised by the strength of feeling in favour of Gaius in 31, though we may question the reliability of Dio's information, and that Tiberius only acted decisively once he had evidence for Sejanus' popular support failing.

Sejanus second source of power and influence was his support in the senate. This should not be overestimated: it seems likely that the majority of the senate were hostile towards Sejanus. When the fateful letter was read, however, the consul Memmius Regulus, who was in on the plot, did not immediately propose the death penalty or put a proposal before the senate that Sejanus be arrested for fear that Sejanus' supporters, including the other consul, would cause a disturbance. He took advice from a single senator (Dio, LVIII 10.8). In the aftermath of the fall of Sejanus, his most prominent supporters were tried in the senate for various charges. His uncle, Quintus Julius Blaesus who had campaigned successfully in Africa and had been awarded great honours as a result, was probably executed. Publius Vitellius killed himself. Livilla was executed. Publius Pomponius was arrested, but was able to drag out proceedings until the death of the emperor. Sextius Paconianus was accused of complicity with Sejanus and brought down Lucianus Latiaris (Tac., *Ann.* V 8–9; VI 4). Others, whose names we do not have, also perished.

Sejanus' fall reverberated through Italy, and the town of Interamna in Umbria erected an inscription in AD 32 to commemorate Tiberius' saving of the state from the threat posed by Sejanus (EJ 51). Even among the legions there must have been shock. All the legionary armies, with the exception of those in Syria, had consecrated images to Sejanus in their camps (Suet., *Tib.* 48.2). This was not just the death of a courtier, but the removal of a powerful political group and seemed to be a shift in the political balance in Rome.

The savagery of the assault on Sejanus and his followers (Sejanus' children were brutally murdered) suggests that they were held responsible for the actions against senators, members of the imperial family and others in the preceding years. In AD 32, Haterius Agrippa (see p. 37) attacked the consuls of the previous year for not prosecuting the adherents of Sejanus sufficiently vigorously (Tac., *Ann.* VI 4). The supporters of Agrippina celebrated their triumph by exacting revenge.

If we examine the ultimate result of these dramatic events, however, the fall of Sejanus appears in a rather different light. Tiberius remained on his island retreat. The loyalty of the praetorians was secured by the payment of a generous bonus. More significantly, Agrippina remained in exile and in 33 killed herself, having been savagely beaten and tortured. Drusus died in the same year. He was starved to death. Tiberius apparently felt able to make the details of the manner of their deaths known (Dio, LVIII 22.4–5; Tac., *Ann.* VI 23–5; Suet., *Tib.* 53–4.). The essentials of the policy towards the imperial family, for which Sejanus had been blamed, remained unchanged. Tiberius simply dropped the man who had been carrying out the policy and deflecting some of the odium from the emperor himself. In this, Sejanus had proved useful, but not indispensable. The continuation of prosecutions of prominent senators and of the persecution of Agrippina and her two sons suggests that Sejanus had been a tool of the emperor and ultimately his power had depended on the emperor's support. What seemed such a dramatic change in 31 may, in reality, have been just a demonstra-

tion of the realities of imperial power: it was Tiberius who had ultimate control and no matter how impressive the political factions of
Sejanus or others, this remained the case.

THE SENATE

Tacitus depicts the relationship of the senate and the Emperor as
starting badly and getting progressively worse. To a large extent
this picture can be accepted. It is not contradicted by our other
sources and is confirmed by the failure of the senate to vote Tiberius
the posthumous honours his adopted father and many subsequent
emperors received. Tacitus may have exaggerated the hostility; it is
unlikely that he fabricated it.

Modern historians have tended to emphasise the exaggeration
and to point out that Tiberius himself initiated few prosecutions of
senators, that many senators were undoubtedly guilty of the crimes
of which they were accused, and that the number of senators killed
during Tiberius' reign was quite small. This is to miss the point.
Tacitus especially presents a depressing catalogue of prosecutions
and trials from almost the first days of Tiberius' rule. There is no
guarantee that Tacitus included all those tried during the period,
and indeed it is more than likely that some of the less spectacular
cases were omitted from this litany. Numbers, however, are less
important than the political atmosphere that such trials created.
The senate was a relatively small body. The senators were also a
close-knit group. Political marriages, remarriage, the frequent use
of adoption (even of adults), and such sociological features of Roman
society as patronage (see pp. 219–22) meant that senators usually
had an extensive network of family connections and friendships.
The fall of a politician would not just affect that man but also his
friends and family, several of whom might also be in prominent
political positions. The exile or death of a friend or family member
could lead to a desire for revenge. Further prosecutions could follow.
Such feuding could easily escalate.

Under Tiberius, we seem to see just such an escalation. Sejanus
and his supporters seem to have initiated prosecutions against the
friends of Agrippina, probably tacitly supported by the emperor.
The friends of Agrippina initiated prosecutions following the fall of
Sejanus. With the growth in political trials, there came to be an
increasing use of *delatores*. These were people who received substantial rewards for providing information leading to prosecution. It

was not just treason that produced these trials but corruption and sexual misdemeanours, the very stuff of gossip and rumour in small communities.

The trials dominate our accounts. We must see them from the viewpoint of the senator who would know, if only slightly, most or all of the victims, whose friends and relatives might fall foul of malicious prosecutions and who himself might fear that someone would launch a potentially life-threatening prosecution against him based on the flimsiest of evidence. It does not take many trials and deaths to produce an atmosphere of paranoia in which people might look for radical and possibly treasonable solutions to their problems. Tiberius' political standing fell as a result and his relationship with the senate worsened.

It is easy to understand the process by which support could be alienated, but less easy to see how Tiberius could have allowed this to happen. He seems to have started his reign with good intentions and to have made every effort to honour the senate. He was Augustus' choice: the most obvious man for the job. What went wrong?

Our ancient sources tend to emphasise character. Tiberius is depicted as a secretive man, hiding his true nature and desires behind a mask. He did not assert his policy and when others produced decisions different to Tiberius' preferred but unstated option, he stored up the memory of his defeat. Those who caused offence did not know, perhaps could not know, until Tiberius' hostility manifested itself on a different, unrelated and perhaps more dangerous occasion. He appears to have been a very difficult man to understand. The senate could not establish a view of him and or gain a sense of what he required. They, therefore, became uncertain and unsure of the implications of any political position they took up. They believed the worst about the character behind the mask, assuming him to be cruel and perverse. Evidence of his cruelty abounds in the ancient sources. His perversions were rumoured, rumours reported to us mainly by Suetonius. Rapacious sexual appetites were the preserve of the tyrant (the man who abused his power for his personal pleasure).

This is not an interpretation that can be lightly dismissed as mere court gossip. The emperor's character mattered since this was an age when politics was largely a matter of the personal interaction of the emperor and the small aristocracy. Sexual perversion was a failing of character and could be taken as a sign of other failings, such as irrational cruelty. If the emperor used his power to seduce or to sexually abuse aristocratic women in Rome, it would reflect on his relationship with other members of the political class. He would be judged as a tyrant: a man who might use his power unpredictably to harm others. Such failings of character demonstrated unsuitability to hold that power. Such gossip was treason.

We can, however, look beyond day-to-day politics to the complexities and tensions of the relationship between senate and emperor. Augustus claimed in his *Res Gestae* to have based his control largely on personal authority rather than legal powers (see p. 17). Tiberius seems to have attempted to continue with this system of government and even enhance the traditional Republican elements. He allowed the senate to debate and decide many issues and was reluctant to give his opinion. He depicted himself as the servant of the senate and not its master. Yet Tiberius and other members of the imperial family retained immense power. Political success could be guaranteed by the support of the emperor. The political realities led ambitious men to cultivate those who could wield imperial power and only the brave or the foolish would knowingly oppose that power. The senate then could not offer impartial political guidance to the emperor since its members were not impartial but were seeking the political backing of the *princeps* or other members of his family. Few could exploit the independence Tiberius offered the senate since they themselves were not independent. The situation was so frustrating that Tiberius famously remarked that these were 'men ready to be slaves' (Tac., *Ann.* III 65).

The situation was made worse by the divisions in the senate. The last years of Augustus had been marred by the problems in the imperial family and we must suppose that groups within the aristocracy offered their support to one or other of the family groups. The imperial family may have been united briefly following the accession of Tiberius but, as we have seen, there were probably residual tensions between Tiberius and certain members of the Roman elite. Some of these may have surfaced in factional disputes between groups who offered support to Germanicus or to Drusus, but until Germanicus' death the unity of the imperial family probably reduced senatorial conflict. Divisions within the imperial family were manifested following the death of Germanicus and were probably worsened after the death of Drusus. Nevertheless, our accounts suggest that many of the prosecutions of this period were unrelated to divisions within the imperial family. Some were part of more minor disputes between individual senators, the background to which cannot be reconstructed. In many ways the senators were behaving no differently to those of the Republican period who had pursued their political enemies through the courts. Tiberius did not intervene decisively to prevent these prosecutions. The legal system had penalties for malicious prosecution. As it became clear that Tiberius might allow prosecutions, senators brought test cases on the charge of *maiestas* (treason). This was an ill-defined offence which came to include offences, verbal or other, against the person of the *princeps*, his predecessor or family. This placed Tiberius in a difficult position. The prosecution in itself was a demonstration of loyalty to him and the alleged offence may have been personally insulting. He could always show *clementia* by blocking these prosecutions. He was in a more difficult position with offences against the *Divus Augustus*. Augustus was responsible for Tiberius' accession and his acts had been given a religious authority by the deification of the emperor. Criticism or insulting behaviour was irreligious and struck at the heart of the principate. Tiberius may have been reluctant to block prosecutions that the senate had initiated and seemed eager to bring to appropriate conclusions but, by not blocking all prosecutions, Tiberius gave senators the means of pursuing their competition. Since the charges often related to the emperor's person, the emperor himself would carry some of the blame. Tiberius was in an invidious position. The very freedoms he allowed the senate were reducing his political standing and making him seem a more autocratic figure.

There can be little doubt, however, that Tiberius was not an innocent figure in this process and that he exploited the situation by using exactly these mechanisms to rid himself of his political enemies. After all, there is no reason to believe that Tiberius was immune to the increasingly vitriolic political atmosphere in Rome, and a man who killed so many of his relatives and former friends would hardly be squeamish about the removal of his political opponents. Eventually, there could be no pretence that Tiberius would preserve Republican freedom and more than a hundred people were charged with *maiestas* during the reign.

We need not see in Tiberius' dealings with the senate the actions of a malicious or perverted character. The tensions of the relationship between a Republican institution, handled in a comparatively republican manner by the early Tiberius, and a monarchic system of power could not easily be resolved and even Augustus, who had created this delicate balance, had problems. Tiberius failed to resolve this defect in the principate, but then so did most of the emperors who followed him. Yet, it was not just Tiberius who was at fault. Tacitus' Tiberius is cruel and vindictive, but he is aided, even encouraged, in this by a pliant senate ever eager to ruin one of their colleagues. For Tacitus, the most depressing element in the catalogue of prosecutions, executions and suicides that eroded the freedoms of the senate was that it was the senators themselves who were at the forefront of these prosecutions. The tensions in the political system were played on by all those involved.

ADMINISTRATION

Our major ancient literary sources tended to view the world from the perspective of Rome and from the perspective of the senatorial elite. Their judgements are not, therefore, primarily motivated by the administrative efficiency of emperors, though this does play a part in assessments. Modern historians have been far more concerned with the issue and have here, as elsewhere, sought a fresh perspective on the emperor. Assessment of administrative efficiency of any emperor is hampered by the very nature of our sources. Extreme results of administrative failure, such as bankruptcy or revolts get reported, but the absence of such is hardly adequate grounds for categorising an administration as efficient. Tiberius remained solvent during his reign, but the quality of his administration of Rome and of the provinces is questionable.

While in Rome, Tiberius appears to have been assiduous in the performance of his administrative and legal duties. He passed as much business as possible to the senate for consideration and the evidence of these senatorial debates suggests that Tiberius and the senate were careful administrators. The situation does not seem to have altered significantly after his departure for Capri. Technically, since the imperial position was a creation in addition to and an amalgam of pre-existing administrative positions, the emperor's presence was not necessary for the proper functioning of Rome's administration. Indeed, since Augustus had also spent many years away from the city, there is no suggestion that the imperial presence was intended to be integral to the administration's daily functioning. Tiberius still retained influence over Roman affairs through the employment of ministers and could have cases he wished to hear transferred to Capri for his personal attention. Indeed, the retreat to Capri must have freed Tiberius from the daily ceremonials, the formalities of regular attendance at the senate, and allowed him to delegate much legal business which, in theory, might have allowed him to concentrate on the most important issues. Nevertheless, Suetonius (*Tib.* 41) claims that Tiberius ceased to pay any attention to administrative issues following his retreat. Tiberius did not neglect Roman business entirely. In 27, Tiberius provided compensation for those who had lost property in a fire on the Caelian Hill (Tac., *Ann.* IV 64) and he did the same in 37 when fire destroyed part of the Aventine and the Circus Maximus (Tac., *Ann.* VI 45). In 32, he wrote to the senate asking them to issue a stern proclamation against the people who had been rioting because of a threatened failure of the corn supply (Tac., *Ann.* VI 13). The following year Tiberius enforced a pre-existing law on interest rates and inadvertently caused a financial crisis which he stabilised by prompt and generous action (Tac., *Ann.* VI 16–17; Dio, LVIII 21.4–5). This is admittedly quite sparse evidence for administrative intervention in the affairs of the city, but it is probably sufficient to suggest that Tiberius remained concerned with administrative matters and managed the affairs of the city quite competently.

There is more information concerning policy in the provinces, but even here it is difficult to reach evaluative judgements. One of Tiberius' most famous phrases was 'I want my sheep to be shorn not shaven' (Dio, LVII 10.5) referring to the Prefect of Egypt's unexpectedly large transfer of revenues from the province. This shows some concern for the state of the province but, as Seager points out, it is firmly from the point of view of the sheep farmer and not the sheep.[2]

Another notable feature of Tiberius' reign is the between eight and eleven trials for *repetundae* (corruption). This evidence may be read in two ways: either as showing Tiberius' determination to prevent governors of provinces unduly oppressing the provincials, or as demonstrating the level of corruption during Tiberius' reign. Tacitus and Dio, interestingly, treat them as political trials, though Tacitus is quite willing to admit that several of the accusations were well founded (Tac., *Ann.* VI 29). They see the trials as symbolising the divisions of the elite and the state of politics, not abnormal corruption, but perhaps we should take a more charitable line towards Tiberius and see in these trials at least some attempt to control the activities of the governors.

There were two cases in which corruption led to revolts. The major revolt in Gaul led by Florus and Sacrovir in AD 21 seems to have been caused by oppressive Roman taxation and the burden of debts (Tac., *Ann.* III 40–6). The Frisii revolted in AD 29 due to Roman extortion: the Romans had taxed the Frisii in hides, but the size of the beasts had not been specified in the treaty. A senior centurion (*primuspilus*), who was in charge of the region, specified that very large hides were required and, in so doing, bankrupted the Frisians, causing a major revolt. The Romans suffered a military setback but Tiberius refused to commit to a major campaign (Tac., *Ann.* IV 72–4).

The other major characteristic of Tiberius' provincial administration is the length of time he left the governors in office. Dio tells us that praetorian governors served for three years while consular governors served for six (Dio, LVIII 23.5). Suetonius (*Tib.* 41) produces a litany of military disasters due to Tiberius' administrative mismanagement of Armenia, Moesia and Gaul. It is unclear to what events in Gaul and Moesia Suetonius' précis was referring. Tacitus' account of the problems in Armenia and Parthia suggests rather that Tiberius, through the effective diplomacy and military tactics of Lucius Vitellius, was initially successful in supporting the Roman's preferred candidate for the Parthian throne (Tac., *Ann.* VI 31–7) until the puppet's support dissolved (Tac., *Ann.* VI 41–4). In any case, Rome secured a peace treaty and brought stability to the borders, though this had to wait until the reign of Gaius (Dio, LIX 27.3–4; Suet., *Gaius.* 14.3). Tiberius did detain governors appointed to Spain (Dio, LVIII 8.3) and Syria in Rome, for reasons which are again unclear. Aelius Lama had remained in Rome after his appointment to Syria but was sufficiently trusted to be given the urban prefecture (see p. 252) by Tiberius (Tac., *Ann.* VI 27; Dio, LVIII 19.5).

Tiberius followed a very conservative policy in the provinces. He seems to have dealt with those military problems that arose with reasonable efficiency but to have avoided any major expansion, especially in the latter years of his reign. There is no evidence to suggest that his government was any more or less efficient than that of other emperors. His policy of leaving governors in place for extended periods and his rather strange decision to detain the governors of Syria and Spain in Rome were probably not conducive to administrative efficiency in the long term. His largely pacific policy left the empire undamaged and avoided the military disasters that had marred the final years of Augustus' reign.

CONCLUSION

If we were to accept the ancient judgement on Tiberius, we would see his reign as a failure and judge Tiberius himself a tyrant. We must, however, recognise that Tiberius' position in AD 14 was far from easy. He was the first to inherit the imperial position. He had many enemies and his position within the dynasty was questionable, though he was clearly the most powerful man in Rome. He inherited the role of a monarch within an oligarchic political system. Augustus seems to have been able to manipulate his formal and informal power to control the empire with reasonable success, though Augustus himself suffered considerable political setbacks. Tiberius seems to have attempted to perform the same trick during his early years, but for various reasons, some unfortunate (like the loss of Germanicus and Drusus), some related to his character (like his failure to curry popular support), he was unable to control the senate and Roman political life.

In the end, he turned to other methods of control. He used Sejanus as a first minister and removed himself from the heart of Republican government. He allowed Sejanus to build a powerful political faction through which he could rule. The tyranny of a faction proved efficient, if brutal. Once he removed the faction, he still ruled from his retreat. The role of the *princeps* was clearer and odium was not diverted onto a chief minister but control was maintained. The effect of this rather brutal governmental method was to upset the Augustan balance. Imperial power was not wrapped in the clothing of Republican traditionalism but stood clear and independent of the supervision of the senate. If Augustus had been able to claim that his power was Republican, Tiberius could make no such claim. He was a monarch and passed on his power to a young and inexperienced relative who had no claim on power other than the accident of birth. This was true monarchy. In a monarchic system, successful monarchs die in bed, the succession secure and their empires intact. Tiberius achieved this.

The empire itself seems to have been comparatively well managed. We should not see in Tiberius a brilliant administrator, though certainly in the early part of his reign he took considerable pains over his administrative duties. In his old age, government may have become more lethargic. We do not see the expansion that had marked the early years of Augustus' reign or major civil projects. In administrative terms, Tiberius passed on to Gaius an empire which was largely unchanged.

Politically, Gaius' inheritance was very different from that of Tiberius. The Augustan political system had largely collapsed. In some ways, the imperial position was much stronger. There were none of the doubts that marked the debates in AD 14. Tiberius had firmly established a hereditary monarchy.

Main events in the reign of Tiberius

Date (AD)	Event
14	Deaths of Augustus, Julia, Agrippa Postumus, Sempronius Gracchus. Mutinies in Pannonia and Germany. Germanicus campaigns in Germany.
15	War in Germany. Treason law revived.
16	War in Germany. King of Parthia deposed. Trial of Libo for treason. Revolt of Clemens.
17	Triumph of Germanicus. Deaths of kings of Cappodocia (executed), Commagene and Amanus. Unrest in Syria, Judaea and Armenia. Germanicus receives *imperium maius* and sent to the East. Revolt of Tacfarinas in Africa.
18	Germanicus settles Armenia, Cappodocia and Commagene, but quarrels with Piso.
19	Germanicus visits Egypt, but returns to Syria to depose Piso. Germanicus dies.
20	Agrippina returns to Rome with Germanicus' ashes. Trial of Piso. Tacfarinas resumes revolt in Africa. Emergence of Sejanus (Dio).
21	Revolts in Africa, Thrace and Gaul. Successful prosecution of the poet Priscus for treason.
22	Drusus given *tribunicia potestas*. Tacfarinas defeated. Sejanus given a statue in the theatre (Dio).
23	Emergence of Sejanus (Tacitus). Death of Drusus.
24	Prosecutions of Calpurnius Piso, C. Silius, Cassius Severus, Plautius Silvanus and Vibius Serenus. Death of Tacfarinas.
25	Prosecution of Cremutius Cordus, Fonteius Capito and
26	Rebellion in Thrace. Prosecution of Claudia Pulchra. Tiberius leaves Rome for Campania.
27	Collapse of the amphitheatre at Fidenae.

(Continued)

Date (AD)	Event
28	Entrapment of Titius Sabinus.
29	Trial and death of Sabinus. Death of Julia. Revolt in Germany. Statues dedicated to Tiberius and Sejanus. Altars to Clementia and Amicitia associated with Tiberius and Sejanus.
30	Death of Livia. Charges brought against Drusus (son of Germanicus) and Agrippina. Images of Sejanus receive sacrifices. Death of Fufius Geminus. Death of Mucia.
31	Fall of Sejanus. Rise of Macro. Gaius Caligula made heir.
32	Trials and deaths of the supporters of Sejanus.
33	Deaths of Agrippina and Drusus. More treason trials. Credit crisis in Rome.
34	Political trials. Rumours that the governor of Germany threatened revolt if summoned back to Rome.
35	War in Parthia and Armenia. Treason trials.
36	War in Cappodocia. Treason trials. Tiridates crowned in Parthia. Fire in Rome.
37	Political trials. Death of Tiberius. Accession of Gaius Caligula.

3

GAIUS CALIGULA
(AD 37–41)

ACCESSION AND PROBLEMS

The death of Tiberius must have come as a great relief to many in the senate and elsewhere. He appears to have been unpopular with virtually everyone in Rome. Gaius was welcome. He was the son of Agrippina and the beloved Germanicus, and great-grandson of both Augustus and Antony. In him, the imperial house, so long divided, was united. The friends of Agrippina would have been pleased at the accession of her son. The friends of Tiberius could console themselves that he had been chosen by the old emperor. He was a young man, 24, and great things could be expected of him. The senate accepted him enthusiastically and voted him all imperial powers. They also set aside the will of Tiberius which had made him co-ruler with his cousin, Tiberius Gemellus (Tiberius' grandson), who was still a minor. The people had hated Tiberius and had supported Gaius' family in the face of imperial persecution. The troops probably also welcomed him as the son of Germanicus. It is to the troops that we owe Gaius' nickname (by which he is perhaps now more familiar), since as a child he had wandered the camps of his father's armies dressed in a miniature version of military uniform and the troops named him Caligula (little boots). Supported by the senate, people and army, Gaius assumed power smoothly. Within six months his support was ebbing away and Gaius was acting like a tyrant. Within four years, he was dead.

The standard modern explanation for the rapidity with which Gaius' fortunes declined is that he was insane. Gaius suffered an illness which can be associated with a change in the nature of the reign. He suffered from insomnia, from vivid nightmares, from fainting fits and from headaches (Suet., *Gaius* 50); his moods changed rapidly; friends suddenly became enemies; he loved bloodshed and killed without compunction; he was astonishingly brutal; he apparently talked to gods and made attempts to seduce the moon; he represented himself as divine. Nevertheless, at this distance, we cannot ascertain whether he was suffering from a serious mental disorder. No reasonable psychiatrist could collect the correct medical information from the surviving accounts to be able to pronounce on his mental health. There are two reasons for re-evaluating Gaius. First, his contemporaries may have had difficulty coping with his behaviour, but he was sufficiently sane that many followed him for nearly four years. By the standards of the time, his outward appearance and behaviour cannot have suggested to all that he was unfit for office. Philo's *Legatio ad Gaium*, an eyewitness account of Gaius' behaviour, suggests a man who refused to give a fair hearing, who cruelly set out to humiliate, but not someone who was completely insane. Second, our two main sources, Suetonius and Dio, were working with a profoundly hostile senatorial tradition, a tradition which made no attempt to understand Gaius' actions. Our Jewish sources, Josephus and Philo, saw him as a persecutor of their people. All were content to display Gaius as a model tyrant, irrationally cruel, driven by insatiable desire for pleasures, be they food, wine, sex or money. One who was so much a slave to the sensual and was so obviously not in control of his desires could not, in their view, continue a coherent policy. It would also be difficult to credit that policies represented as wholesale slaughter of the aristocracy or as an assault on the Jewish people could have an intelligent rationale, however morally disreputable. We, on the other hand, while making no excuse for Gaius' behaviour, can look for that intelligence and try to understand what, if anything, Gaius was trying to achieve.

We are, of course, hampered by the mythology that surrounds Gaius. Almost more than in any other reign, fact and fiction are blended in our accounts. As stated in the introduction (pp. 2–3), there is no convincing method for reversing the process and separating the factual information from the mythical. However, some of the better attested stories concerning Gaius suggest that the emperor himself was concerned to surround himself with a mythology, representing himself as something more than human, and this argues against simply dismissing the more colourful stories of the reign. One must, of course, be cautious and try to identify later inventions or additions to the tradition but, with Gaius, the myth is a fundamental part of the history of the reign.

THE FAMILY

Gaius' position on accession was strong but his claim to power was rather different from that of the two previous emperors. Whereas Augustus had fought to obtain his position and Tiberius had been without doubt the leading man in the state, Gaius' claim for the imperial position rested solely on his birth. He had held no office, he had had no experience of military or magisterial responsibilities, and although most senators would have been well disposed towards him, few if any were bound in loyalty to him through previous favours and all were older and more experienced. Gaius' political education had been to watch the last years of Tiberius, when Tiberius had dominated a frightened aristocracy. He had not seen an emperor advise, bully and cajole to build a political consensus. Augustus' claim that his rule rested on personal authority rather than on constitutional or legal powers emphasises the difference between his position and that of Gaius (see p. 17). Gaius had no *auctoritas* on which to rely. He had his family (see Figure 3.1 for his family and ancestry). He also had legal and military power.

His first steps were cautious. He relied on the advice of Macro, Tiberius' praetorian prefect (see p. 44), and probably Silanus (his former father-in-law), and attempted to build a consensus with the senate, deferring to their authority and experience in the first days of his reign. The nervous were reassured when Gaius burnt the letters relating to the persecution of his mother and brothers (Dio, LIX 6.1–4). Exiles were recalled. At the same time, Gaius set about

Figure 3.1 The family of Gaius

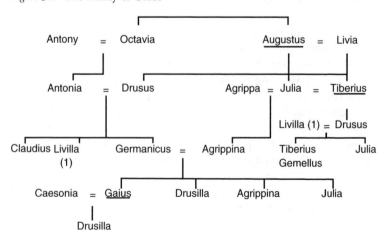

establishing his credentials and securing the support of key elements of the Roman state. The praetorian guard had been secured through the good offices of Macro. Their loyalty was assured by the payment of 2,000 sesterces (Dio, LIX 2.1–3). The loyalty of the plebs was similarly cemented by the payment of generous legacies on behalf of Livia and Tiberius and by payments made by Gaius himself. The rapid resumption of public games and festivals sponsored by the emperor was also popular. Most notable, though, was the treatment of his family. Antonia, Gaius' grandmother, was granted extensive honours, equal to those that had been enjoyed by Livia. His mother's and brothers' ashes were returned to Rome and interred in the mausoleum of Augustus. His sisters were honoured by association with Gaius. They were included in the public oaths taken to the emperor and appeared with Gaius at the games (Dio, LIX 3.4–5). Most surprisingly, Claudius was plucked from obscurity and was awarded the consulship with Gaius (Dio, LIX 6.5).

The implications of these actions ran deeper than just demonstrating Gaius' family loyalty: it was a claim to power. Power did not come from the constitution, from the legal grant of the senate, still less from the will of Tiberius (which was overturned on the grounds, ironically enough, of insanity), but from birth. This is, of course, a monarchic ideal. From the first, Gaius was committed to the idea that he ruled because of his inherent qualities, not because of achievements or law. Indeed, his position depended on this assumption. This emphasis on family and monarchy was the cornerstone of his legitimacy as a ruler.

In AD 38, his sister Drusilla died. Her death provided Gaius with another opportunity to emphasise the status of his family. She was granted a public funeral. Gaius associated her with the goddess Venus. Statues were placed in the Forum. A senator claimed he had seen her rising to heaven, a sure sign of divine status. He was well rewarded (Dio, LIX 11.1–4). The deification of his sister pre-figured Gaius' own growing association with the gods (see pp. 62–4) and was a further representation of the peculiar status of his family.

Like so much else in Gaius' brief reign, relations with his family soured. We can only guess at the reasons for this. The emperor's family associated with other members of the aristocracy who must have made up their social circle. They were in a position to be aware, probably more aware than the emperor himself, of the intolerable strains under which the aristocracy was placed. We need not assume that Gaius' family was insensitive to the pressure of their aristocratic friends or even approved of Gaius' policies. The pressures of living with an absolute monarch who revelled in his ability to inflict sudden death may also have begun to tell. Antonia, his grandmother, killed herself (Suet., *Gaius* 23.2). In 39, while on campaign in Gaul, Gaius claimed to have discovered a conspiracy which involved the governor of Germany, Lentulus Gaetulicus, who had served in the post for ten years, M. Lepidus, and his sisters Agrippina and Julia (Dio, LIX 22.5–7). Lepidus was killed; the women were exiled. Gaius claimed it as a great victory and the senate were made to congratulate him. The senate, hundreds of miles away and probably deeply concerned and mystified at the fall of Gaius' beloved sisters and Lepidus, with all of whom he was rumoured to have had sexual relations, chose Claudius to forward congratulations (Dio, LIX 23). This was a mistake. The fall of his sisters marked a dramatic change of policy: Gaius had turned against his family. He marked Claudius' arrival by having him thrown into a river and the emperor's uncle was perhaps fortunate to escape with his life.

This change of policy may be related to his marriage plans. His mistress, Caesonia, was pregnant. Gaius married her and she bore him a daughter. Gaius had a child and the prospect of more. His claim for legitimacy changed. He placed increasing emphasis on his own personal qualities, rather than those family qualities he shared with his sisters. Perhaps to compensate for this change, he chose to lay further emphasis on his divinity and to make what may have been an implicit part of his representation explicit. The imperial house was effectively reduced to the nuclear family of Gaius, Caesonia and the baby Drusilla, with the addition of uncle Claudius. The unfortunate Caesonia and her daughter were to share Gaius' fate (Dio, LIX 29).

POPULAR SUPPORT

The people had demonstrated against Tiberius when Agrippina and her children were threatened. They had celebrated when Sejanus fell from office and when Tiberius died. Gaius inherited the popularity of his mother and brothers and, in marked contrast to his prede-cessor, made efforts to maintain his popularity with the masses and his political control over them. He did this through lavish displays of generosity and through expensive and extended games. According to the tradition, he made no effort to conceal his pleasure in the games and theatrical displays. He surrounded himself with actors, notably Apelles and Mnester (Dio, LIX 5.3; Suet., *Gaius* 33, 36, 54), whom he was seen to kiss as friends (a normal Roman form of greeting) while senators were obliged to kiss his hand or foot (Dio, LIX 27.1–2). Gaius himself is said to have performed in both theatrical productions and as a gladiator at the games (Dio, LIX 5; Suet., *Gaius* 54, 32.2). He further associated himself with popular opinion by becoming an active supporter of one of the circus teams, the greens (Dio, LIX 14.6). This interest in dramatic performance and in the theatre as an arena in which the emperor displayed himself before his people foreshadowed the much more extensive use of theatrical display by Nero (indeed one might suspect that the stories were created later in order to attack Nero), and one presumes that many of the same factors that influenced Nero would have affected Gaius (see pp. 112–17). Such behaviour was seen as beneath the dignity of the emperor by more conservative members of the Roman elite. Gaius' supposed wish to act in a tragedy and his prolongation of a festival by three days to make time for this theatrical extravaganza may, in fact, have been the immediate spur for the conspirators to take action (Dio, LIX 29.6–7).

Gaius sought to increase the political authority of the people by restoring popular elections (Suet., *Gaius* 16.2; Dio, LIX 20.3–5), which appear to have been effectively brought to an end in the late Augustan period when Augustus ceased to attend the elections. Tiberius had allowed the senate to co-opt its own members. Throughout this period, the electoral assembly continued to meet, though it had merely ratified the election of the candidates placed before it.[1] One supposes that Gaius removed the right of the senate to nominate and officially allowed competition, though Suetonius tells us that normally there was the same number of candidates as posts.

The relationship between Gaius and the people also soured. In 39, there were demonstrations against Gaius' treatment of the senate. The people were becoming concerned at the number of killings. Gaius is supposed to have responded by wishing that the people had but one neck to be cut (Dio, LIX 13.3–7). Gaius' frustration was showing and he responded to demonstrations by use of force. His power was shown in other ways. He closed the public granaries that provided the people with the free grain supplies and thus threatened the people of Rome with starvation. On summer days, he withdrew the awnings from the theatre and closed the exits so that the crowd roasted in the hot sun (Suet., *Gaius* 26.5). These were conspicuous displays of his power which demonstrated to the people that he could inflict great hardship upon them.

Gaius also lost support through his attempts to raise taxes to fund his extravagances. The problem was caused not so much by the increase in taxes but by his failure to publicise adequately the tax regulations so that many found themselves subjected to heavy fines. There was a popular campaign to force publication of the regulations, but when Gaius eventually succumbed to pressure the material was inscribed in lettering so small and on a notice placed so high that no one could read it. The outcry may have resulted in the killing of many of the protesters (Suet., *Gaius* 40–1; Dio, LIX 28.10–11).

THE DIVINE EMPEROR

More attention has been focused on Gaius' pretence of divinity than almost any other aspect of his reign. This is, of course, understandable since his divinity poses a problem for both ancient and modern religious traditions. For us, it is very difficult to concede that a man could become a god. It seems self-evident that a man does not possess the necessary attribute of the divine. For the ancients, the position was more complex. Worship of the emperor was established under Augustus and continued throughout the period (see pp. 309–12). It was, however, only the 'bad emperors' who went so far as to declare themselves to be gods. There was still a distinction between the mortal human and the immortal divine and to claim to cross that divide as a human was to risk divine retribution.

Gaius' own religious beliefs cannot be assessed. Suetonius (*Gaius* 51.1–2) tells us that although he mocked the gods and stories of their miracles by day, he was afraid of thunder (a sign of divine displeasure) and Mount Etna, though these are hardly sufficient grounds to describe him as religious. The many stories (some of which may have been invented) of Gaius showing disrespect for the statues of gods suggest that he had no profound religious belief. Some of the elite would have shared this view. Why then did Gaius consistently present himself as a semi-divine figure, and, towards the end of his reign, apparently demand the public acknowledgement of his divinity?

Although both Augustus and Tiberius had been superior in authority to members of other senatorial families, they had taken care to behave as if they were among equals. They were *principes*, the leading men, but the senate contained many *principes*, men of authority and political stature to whom respect needed to be shown. Gaius was not, however, a *princeps*. He was inferior in political stature and experience. He was notably sensitive about his comparative youth (Dio, LIX 19.1–6). He needed, therefore, some way to assert his superior status over the nobles in the senate.

Suetonius provides an anecdote explaining Gaius' development of divine aspirations (*Gaius* 22.1–2). At a dinner party, Gaius listened to several client kings disputing among themselves as to who had the most glorious ancestry. Gaius had been experimenting with titles. He had tried *'pius'*, *'castrorum filius'* (son of the camp), *'pater exercituum'* (father of the army) and *'optimus maximus Caesar'* (best and greatest Caesar), but none were satisfactory. To display greater authority, to rise above the level of the client kings and the rest of the Roman aristocracy, he decided to assume divine status, a status which would reflect his pre-eminence.

The great advantage of divine status was that it allowed the development of new ways of representing imperial power and of forcing others to displays of loyalty, ways normally reserved for the gods. Gaius remodelled the entrance to the imperial palace so that visitors would pass through the temple of Castor and Pollux, two divine gatekeepers for the house of the living god. He built temples to his *numen* (his divine spirit) on the Capitoline and Palatine hills (Suet., *Gaius* 22.2; Dio, LIX 28.5). He instituted his own priesthood into which Caesonia and Claudius were enrolled (Dio, LIX 28.5–6). He appeared in the guise of Apollo, Neptune, Hercules, Bacchus, Juno, Diana and Venus (Dio, LIX 26.5–10). The senate and court were forced to acknowledge his divinity and statues were altered so that the gods would have Gaius' features. His more than human power was acknowledged through his association with the divine.

By rising above the level of the human, Gaius could also rise above the normal constraints of social behaviour. Indeed, as the ways of the gods were beyond human comprehension, so Gaius' capricious cruelty became an attribute of his great power. Like the gods, Gaius could strike at any moment and, like the gods, Gaius must be feared and obeyed.

He rose above normal social *mores* in his sexual life. While Tiberius' alleged perversions had been dark secrets hidden by his island retreat and were only matters of gossip in Rome, Gaius' sexual misconduct was a matter of public display. His sexual promiscuity rivalled that of Jupiter and, like the father of the gods, he had relationships with both men and women. Women were seized at banquets or at their own marriages, dragged from the feasts and, one presumes, raped (Dio, LIX 8.7). This sexual terrorism was somewhat more controlled after his marriage to Caesonia (Suet., *Gaius* 25). M. Lepidus (see above) was supposed to have been his lover. He was also said to have had sexual relations with his sisters (Suet. *Gaius* 24; Dio, LIX 3.6, 11.1, 22.6). The Olympian deities were promiscuous and incestuous. The Ptolemies, the Hellenistic rulers of Egypt from 323–30 BC, had similarly formed incestuous relationships. Incest in royal families could symbolise status in two ways: either their behaviour was to be governed by the practice among the gods, or, as divine figures, they were expected to form relationships with people of similar status, which left them with little choice. Gaius, therefore, had two possible models on which to base his behaviour. We cannot know whether Gaius did have sex with his sisters, but the manner with which he associated with them in public and the deification of Drusilla as Venus was deliberately suggestive of a sexual relationship. Myth and historical reality blend in stories of Gaius' sexual behaviour and it is probable that the myth originated with Gaius himself, whatever the reality.

Gaius' assumption of divinity was an extreme reaction to his problems, but it was not, in itself, the act of a madman and may be seen as a rational way of displaying authority when interpreted in the context of contemporary religious practice and attitudes towards the imperial position. We must remember that Gaius numbered among his ancestors Venus, Mars, Romulus, Hercules, Divus Julius, and Divus Augustus. His sister had been seen rising to heaven. Gaius' policy may ultimately have been misconceived, but it was not revolutionary.

THE SENATE

Gaius was remembered deservedly for the hostility he showed towards the senate, but it is important to reconstruct events carefully for, by paying attention to Dio's account especially, we can see that Gaius' policy changed during his brief reign and we can attempt to understand the factors that motivated such a change.

On accession, Gaius acted to secure his political position. As a young emperor, he needed to develop a way of dealing with the senior men of the state, most of whom were in the senate. He seems at first to have attempted to build a consensus. The burning of the papers relating to the deaths of his mother and brothers was a declaration of amnesty after the political disputes of the previous years. He also temporarily abolished the charge of *maiestas* (see p. 49; Dio, LIX 6.1–4). In other ways, his behaviour was also exemplary. It was expected that Gaius would assume the senior constitutional office, the consulship, immediately after his accession. The consulship was not just an important political and ceremonial office, but it conferred status on all holders and former holders of the office. As Gaius had not held the office, he needed a consulship in order to join the elite within the senate. Instead of deposing the two consuls who already held the office, Gaius delayed his assumption of the consulship until the end of their normal period of office (six months). He then took the consulship with his uncle Claudius (Dio, LIX 6.5).

Following the lead of Tiberius in AD 14 (p. 27),[2] Gaius also published the public accounts (Dio, LIX 9.4–6). Publication of the information necessary to formulate policy and govern the empire was a declaration of his willingness to bring government out from behind the closed doors of the palace and share power with the senate. The world could see how Rome was to be financed. Secret papers were burnt. Gaius could really claim to be *demokratikotatos* (most democratic) (Dio, LIX 3.1–2).

The consensus-building of this early policy may be related to insecurity. The young man probably looked to more experienced heads for advice, perhaps to Claudius, probably to Marcus Silanus and Macro. In some ways, this again follows his predecessor in the use of chief ministers and foreshadows Nero. The policy was not to last. The inevitable fate of Tiberius Gemellus had only been postponed at the start of the reign. The youth, as Tiberius' grandson, was a latent threat to the emperor since he had as good a claim to the throne. Gaius had him killed in late 37. Marcus Silanus killed himself following expressions of outright hostility from Gaius (Dio, LIX 8.4). In the following year (38), Macro and his wife Ennia were forced down the same path (Dio, LIX 10.6–8). More worryingly, already in 38 the senate was witness to Gaius' macabre sense of humour, a feature of his treatment of the senate in later years. After his illness, Gaius was informed that Publius Afranius Potitius had promised to give up his life if Gaius would be spared; Atanius Secundus had promised to fight as a gladiator on Gaius' recovery. Such grandiose gestures of loyalty may have been foolish, but, like that of the senator who claimed to have seen Drusilla on her way to heaven, were sometimes rewarded. Gaius, however, applied logic and forced the two senators to keep their words (Dio, LIX 8.3). Atanius Secundus won his fight (Suet., *Gaius* 27.2).

Gaius was deeply concerned with his own comparative lack of experience and *auctoritas* in comparison with many in the senate. He compensated for this by emphasising the status of his family and, eventually, assuming divine characteristics. A natural corollary of this was to attack those other families in the senate that had claims to special status, thereby further differentiating the Julians. Some of the most noble families of Rome had peculiar traits of dress or names that recalled their places in the legends and history of Rome: the Torquati had a collar; the Cincinnati a lock of hair; and the Pompeii the name 'Magnus' (great). All these features were removed by Gaius (Suet., *Gaius* 35.1).

This was comparatively mild treatment. If the stories are to be believed, Gaius emphasised his authority by humiliating individual senators. Senators were forced to attend him by running alongside his chariot for miles. Others had to wait at table, the occupation of a slave (Suet., *Gaius* 26.2). His posturing towards the senate became even more violent during his Gallic campaigns. He declared that he wished no triumph but berated the senate for not granting him one. He met an embassy from the senate and threatened them with his sword. He proclaimed that he returned as a friend to the people and the equestrians (Suet., *Gaius* 48–9). On his return from Gaul, he called a meeting of the senate and announced that there were only a few senators against whom he harboured animosity (Dio, LIX 25.9). The effect of such an announcement must have been electrifying since it portended death to a number of the senators and, as Gaius seems to have struck with a certain randomness, all must have been terrified. It is difficult to believe that this was not the intended result.

It is in this context that we should place the story of Gaius' horse, Incitatus. The horse was apparently a champion at the games and so pleased Gaius that he decided that it would make a good dinner companion. Impressing Gaius with its political insight and intelligence, he promised to elevate Incitatus to the highest office in the senate, but, in the end (and perhaps rather sadly), Gaius was killed before Incitatus became the first horse to hold high political office in Rome (Dio, LIX 14.7). If taken seriously, here is a sign of madness, but surely we see here an insult, calculated and witty, aimed at the senate and their pretensions. Gaius could have a horse as social companion. He could have a horse as political advisor. The senate was without influence. The story of him suddenly laughing while at dinner with the consuls shows the same sense of humour and power. When the consuls inquired why their emperor was laughing, he said that it had occurred to him that he could, at a moment's notice, have them both killed (Suet., *Gaius* 32.3).

Gaius' humour was a serious problem, as is illustrated by Philo's account of the interview of the Jewish embassy. Gaius set out to humiliate the ambassadors. They followed him through a palace as he gave orders for its redecoration, interrupting their most cogent arguments with arrangements for the hanging of pictures. He changed the subject, asking them spurious questions about their attitude towards the imperial cult and dietary laws. When the ambassadors responded that they did not eat pork as it was forbidden to them and that many peoples had similar laws, some being unable to eat lamb, Gaius responded, 'Quite right! It's not nice' (Philo, *Legatio ad Gaium* 361–3). The ambassadors, arguing for the rights of their people to live unmolested after anti-Semitic riots in which many were killed, were reduced to discussions of the relative merits of pork and lamb. Gaius ended the interview by announcing that the Jews were unlucky rather than wicked in not acknowledging Gaius' divinity (Philo, *Legatio ad Gaium* 367). Gaius was accompanied by both the opponents of the Jews and a crowd of servants, friends and hangers-on who encouraged Gaius' performance. It was theatre: a public humiliation of the Jews and a demonstration of the power of the emperor. It was just these tactics that Caligula employed against the senate.

Gaius knew that he made enemies and avoided giving those enemies power. The province of Africa, the last senatorial command which had brought control over significant numbers of troops, remained a senatorial province though the troops were transferred from the control of the governor (Dio, LIX 20.7).

We do not have a complete list of those senators prosecuted. Calvisius Rufus and his wife were tried for their behaviour during Rufus' long governorship (Dio, LIX 18.4). Titius Rufus was rumoured to have noted a difference between the votes and thoughts of senators. Junius Priscus was wealthy (Dio, LIX 18.5). L. Annaeus Seneca caused offence, but was spared because it was reported that he was terminally ill (Dio, LIX 19.7–8). Domitius Afer was attacked because of a statue he erected to the emperor that carried an inscription which Gaius regarded as critical, noting Gaius' youth. Afer saved himself by refusing to make a speech in his defence: he simply claimed to be in awe of the rhetorical skill of his emperor and, in the face of such genius, could only beg for mercy.

His friends ensured his survival (see below) and it is likely that Gaius never intended to kill him (Dio, LIX 19.1–6). Here again is surely the same warped sense of humour that sent Afranius Potitius and Atanius Secundus to fulfil their vows, since even a brazen act of servility became dangerous. Fathers were killed together with their sons: Anicius Cerealis and Sextus Papinus and Betilini Bassus and Capito (Dio, LIX 25.6–26.2). Capito sought to revenge himself by admitting conspiracy and listing his enemies as fellow-conspirators. He over-reached himself when he named Kallistos (see below) and other of Gaius' closest associates. Cassius Longinus, governor of Asia, was slain because rumours had reached him that he should fear Cassius (Suet., *Gaius* 57.2). Either news of the conspiracy was leaking or men were looking for a Cassius like the man who had removed Julius Caesar. Most dramatic of all, and a symbol of the paranoia gripping the senate, is the story of the death of Scribonius Proculus. Soon after Gaius had announced that few remained against whom he retained animosity, a leading prosecutor who was supposed to be close to the imperial court entered the senate and was greeted by all the senators, fearful of such a powerful man. When Proculus greeted him, this man replied, 'And do you who hate the emperor so, welcome me?'. The senators responded by killing Proculus in the senate-house (Dio, LIX 26.1–2).

Our sources emphasise the indiscriminate nature of the slaughter, though again we must beware of invention and distortion. It forms part of their depiction of a madman, a tyrant out of all control. Such a depiction of Gaius is certainly possible. We have all the available materials to paint such a portrait. But we must set Gaius' actions in context. In Gaius' theory of government, in which power was inherited by the emperor who ruled on the basis of his personal authority, there was little room for a representative body such as the senate, and Gaius may have been one of the few Roman emperors who seriously considered abolishing this revered political institution. On return to Rome from his victories in Gaul, Germany and on the beaches facing Britain, Gaius threatened the senate with destruction (Dio, LIX 25.5, 25.9–26.3; Suet., *Gaius* 49). The fear and paranoia created among the senators was such that Gaius probably felt no need to continue with his plan. He had seen, as he reminded the senate (Suet., *Gaius* 30.2), the senators acquiesce in the persecution of his brothers and mother and the dramatic rise and fall of Sejanus. Although all united in praise of the young emperor at his accession, Gaius can have had few illusions about the senate. He must have been aware that there were many who viewed his elevation with fear and distrust and all would try to manipulate the young *princeps* to achieve their personal political ends. Many of the senior senators must have owed their political status and power to Tiberius (and Sejanus). Gaius may have been right to fear and harbour grudges against these men. Our sources do not illuminate the previous political affiliations of the killed and exiled. The attack on Seneca, for instance, seems to have no political justification, yet Seneca's son was clearly closely connected to the imperial family, especially Gaius' sisters, and was to enjoy considerable power as the tutor of Agrippina's son (see pp. 102–12). We do not know what political roles these men played or whether these men on the fringes of our account were major political players or minor victims of Gaius' malice. How many were Sejanus' men, men who had helped destroy the emperor's family?

Gaius eventually fell in what was essentially a palace conspiracy. Unlike Nero, he did not see his generals turn against him and his political position disintegrate. The posthumous tradition is (deservedly) universally hostile, but we need not assume that at the time of his death there were none in the senate who mourned his passing. If we see the reign of Gaius as a continuation of the bloody factional politics of the last thirty or forty years, then our perspectives must change.

Nevertheless, there was something new about Gaius' treatment of the senate. The manner in which he humiliated the senate and elevated his own person above that of the mortal is evidence of Gaius striving for a new representation of imperial power. As Tiberius had been unable to continue the Augustan system and had resorted to a distant manipulation, Gaius also faced difficulties. He had not the rank or the experience, or the confidence in his generals, that had allowed Tiberius to take so distant an interest in the doings of the senate. Gaius needed a more direct role. He needed to exert immediate and decisive authority. He could not afford to allow the senators to question his authority since he was, when compared with Tiberius, so politically weak and inexperienced.

The history to which he looked for inspiration and role models was not the Republican history of Rome, but that of Hellenistic Greece, and especially to Alexander the Great. His absolutism sprang from character and birth. It may have been a possible method of government. The Roman elite had shown themselves willing to acquiesce under tyrannical rule. Gaius' cruelty, his blood-lust, and his psychopathic sense of humour distance him from normal humanity, as they were probably in part intended to do: 'Let them hate me as long as they fear me' is reported as a favourite phrase (Suet., *Gaius* 30.1). We cannot assume, however misguided the policy proved eventually to be, that this policy was not a rational choice of a thinking and troubled politician.

ADMINISTRATION

The practical side of imperial government is said to have dissolved into chaos during Gaius' brief rule. The most obvious symbol of this chaos is the financial prodigality of the emperor which took the treasury from an extremely healthy surplus to bankruptcy. Dio (LIX 2.6) suggests that there were 2,300,000,000 or 3,300,000,000 sesterces in the treasury, while Suetonius (*Gaius* 37.3) opts for 2,700,000,000 sesterces. Even after raising new taxes and reducing the pension paid to the troops on discharge (Suet., *Gaius* 44), Gaius was apparently in such financial straits by the end of his reign that he was selling heirlooms to the Gauls and prosecuting the richest in the empire in order to obtain their wealth. The ancient sources, however, produce no figures for the state of the treasury at this stage and it became a standard criticism of 'bad emperors' to note their financial mismanagement. The financial position of his successor does not appear to have been particularly bad, suggesting either that Gaius' emergency measures were successful or that tradition has distorted the situation (see p. 82).

Another feature of Gaius' government was his treatment of the provinces. Gaius seems to have had a policy of favouring the use of client kings to govern Roman territory in the East. This was a standard technique of Roman imperial policy (see pp. 278–9), but emperors varied in the emphasis they placed on this method of government. For Gaius, this offered several advantages. The greatest threat to his position sprang from the Roman aristocracy, and relying on client kings meant that he had fewer governors who could threaten his position. The kings were dependent on Gaius, who could remove them at a whim. They could not hope to challenge him militarily or for the position of emperor, and they continued to pay taxes to Rome and send the emperor extravagant gifts to retain his favour. The use of kings reflected and emphasised the monarchic principle at the heart of Gaius' government. More importantly, client kings increased the status of the emperor. He could show the Roman people that he appointed kings, and kings were also his servants. If this was the case, what title and position would be suitable for Gaius? Augustus and Tiberius had sought to impose 'Republican' clothing on the position, emphasising the magisterial qualities of the position. Gaius emphasised the regal, but his control over mere kings meant that the title 'King' was unsatisfactory as not representing his real authority. In Medieval and early Modern Europe, the title 'Emperor' came to mean someone who controlled princes and kings. 'Imperator' was formally a military title and did not yet carry this connotation. Gaius had, therefore, to look elsewhere for inspiration and, unsurprisingly, turned to the realm of the divine and to history. Gaius came, as we shall see, to associate himself with that other great ruler of kings, Alexander the Great. Thus, in his use of client kings, two main themes of Gaius' principate come together: absolute power and divine status. As an administrative and political policy, it has a certain logic.

More attention has been focused on Gaius' treatment of the Jews. There were two main areas of conflict: Alexandria and Judaea. In the first, the prefect Flaccus presided over a period of increasing tension which resulted in a violent anti-Semitic outbreak when the Greeks in the city, tacitly or openly supported by Flaccus, attacked the Jews and drove them from most of the city, encouraged by Flaccus' revocation of the Jews' citizenship rights. Our sources suggest that when news of the violence and Flaccus' behaviour reached Rome, through the agency of the newly appointed Herod Agrippa, Gaius acted. He sent a centurion to Alexandria who walked into a dinner party, arrested the prefect, put him on a boat and sailed off to Rome. Flaccus was tried, exiled and eventually executed (Philo, *In Flaccum*). One may believe that Gaius acted to save the Jews, but Flaccus' position had already been fatally undermined. Flaccus had been somehow involved in the prosecution of Gaius' mother and brothers. The reward for this had been his posting to Alexandria. Although at first insulated from Gaius' revenge by the support of Macro, his fall was inevitable once Macro had gone.

Gaius had supported the Herodian dynasty (the Jewish royal family) by appointing his friend Agrippa to the Tetrarchy of Trachonitis and Gaulanitis. As a result of feuding within the Herodian dynasty, the history of which makes the Julio–Claudians seem a model of harmony, Agrippa received yet more territory (Jos., *Ant.* XVIII 237–56), though the Jewish territories of Judaea and Samaria remained under direct Roman rule. Agrippa is depicted as a close friend of Gaius and a man who could exercise some influence over the emperor. He also had some claim to represent all the Jewish people of the region.

As monotheists, the Jews could not worship Gaius, yet worship of Gaius was an essential mark of loyalty to the emperor. Gaius, therefore, instructed the governor of Syria, Petronius, to build a statue of the emperor and install it in the Jewish temple in Jerusalem. This was the most holy of places in the holy city. The population had rioted when non-religious images of eagles had been brought within the temple complex. The conflagration that would have been caused by the installation of a cult statue of the emperor within the temple can hardly be imagined. Petronius delayed. He sent for clarification. He made every attempt to obstruct the project but also to avoid seeming to refuse an imperial instruction. In this latter aim, he was unsuccessful. Gaius wrote an angry missive and further conflict between the governor of one of the most powerful provinces of the empire and the emperor was only avoided by Gaius' timely death. In the former aim, however, he enjoyed some success. Agrippa, who was in Rome, petitioned and, frustrated by delays, Gaius rescinded his order, though he still regarded the Jewish refusal to worship him as a peculiarity (Philo, *Legatio ad Gaium*, 207–333; Jos. *Ant.* XVIII 261–309.).

By rescinding the order, Gaius managed to avoid a catastrophic war in the East though his own anti-Semitism encouraged outbreaks of violence in the cities of the Eastern Mediterranean, many of which had large Jewish minorities. Gaius made an intelligent decision, however misconceived the original policy, and however immoral his policy towards the Jews of the Eastern cities. He had departed from his general policy of imposing his divinity on his subjects.

One further aspect of Gaius' administration deserves recognition, partly because it looks forward to the government of Claudius. One of the shadowy characters of the reign was Kallistos, Gaius' freedman minister. It is difficult to know what duties Kallistos performed, but he was certainly influential. He was allegedly at least partly responsible for saving Domitius Afer (see pp. 67–8) and supposedly chided Gaius for allowing the prosecution to be brought. A man who could save others from the wrath of such an emperor and even criticise the emperor to his face must have been powerful. Kallistos was also closely involved in the plot to kill Gaius (Dio, LIX 25.7–8; 29.1; Jos., *Ant.* XIX 64–9). We glimpse in Kallistos an influential bureaucrat who made sure that the wheels of government turned and provided Gaius with the information necessary to manage the empire.

WAR AND ALEXANDER

Many Roman aristocrats appear to have had an Alexander fixation and a typical portrait style of the Late Republic imitated depictions of Alexander. Roman military policy was frequently shaped by a desire to emulate the achievements of Alexander in conquering the East. Gaius' most splendid display of this Alexander fetish was the bridging of the Bay of Naples, an amalgamation of the Alexander myth with the story of Xerxes' bridging of the Hellespont, but the Romans were unconcerned about historical accuracy in their reconstructions of such remote and mythologised events. The display in 39 was at least in part for the benefit of Darius, a visiting member of the Parthian ruling dynasty. The Parthians had concluded a peace with Gaius on the death of Tiberius. Their reasons for such a generous act towards the new emperor are unclear but the treaty may have been connected with Parthian respect for Germanicus and perhaps even some doubt as to whether the generally restrained policy of Tiberius would be transformed by a young, vigorous ruler out to make a name for himself. If so, such a display of Roman power before the eyes of a Parthian prince had a diplomatic purpose. The bridge was, of course, recklessly extravagant and Gaius' charge across the bridge wearing what he claimed to be Alexander's breastplate seems almost farcical (Dio, LIX 17.1–11; Suet. *Gaius* 19.1–3). Yet, we should not underestimate the impact of the display. Such a mobilisation of resources by the new Alexander could one day be for real and it was no doubt a message that was transmitted back to the Parthian capital. Gaius might enact his historic destiny as the second Alexander on Parthian soil. He never did so.

Gaius' sole military adventure was on the Western frontier. This is again probably significant. It was on this frontier and with these troops that Gaius won his nickname and these troops could be expected to be loyal to the boy whose retreat had once quelled their mutiny (see pp. 32–3). The Gallic expedition can be seen in part as a return to Gaius' political constituency, the men on whose support he relied for his political and personal survival. It came at a particularly difficult point in his reign. He was possibly running out of money and friends and it must be significant that, while in Gaul, he put aside his sisters and Lepidus and took an increasingly hard line with the senate. He returned a man with an army, reassured of their support and prepared to demonstrate his control over the military through elaborate ceremonials, such as a triumphal entry into Rome. It is almost irrelevant that his major triumphs in Gaul had been a quick trip to the seaside, the killing of a governor and chasing a few Germans through the forest.

Much attention has been focused on the 'trip to Britain'. Gaius appears to have completed preparations for a major expedition in the West, either against Germany or Britain. Suetonius (*Gaius* 43.1) tells us that the decision to visit Gaul was sudden, but Gaius levied large numbers of troops (Dio, LIX 21–2) and it is possible that new legions were raised for the invasion. It is difficult to know whether Gaius was ever serious about invading Britain. There were numerous reasons not to go. He had just executed an experienced commander. The troops may have been extremely reluctant. Gaius himself may not have realised the problems that invading Britain posed, and it is possible that the logistical infra-structure, the boats especially, was not ready or that Gaius himself did not feel he had time to engage in such a campaign. Some have suggested that he was distracted by problems in Northern Gaul, or that the whole episode was merely an elaborate training exercise. In any case, he did not go and we are told that the soldiers picked shells from the beach.

Gaius' military policy may have been underestimated. Claudius' accession was marked by a spate of military activity in Germany and Africa (Dio, LX 8.6–7.) and it seems very likely that Gaius commenced these campaigns. Claudius also launched the invasion of Britain very early in the reign, leaving open the possibility that he benefited from Gaius' preparations. Faced with other possible conflicts in the West, a show of force on the beaches of Gaul without committing his forces to a lengthy and costly campaign may have been a sensible policy.

ASSASSINATION

The assassination of Gaius may hardly be described as a surprise. He had bullied and offended, threatened and killed. Dio (LIX 25.7–8) has a story which perhaps provides some of the background to the conspiracy, though its neatness raises suspicions. In his paranoia, Gaius summoned the prefects of the guard and Kallistos and, standing unarmed before them, offered the three an opportunity to kill him: there was an implicit or even explicit suggestion that Gaius had heard of a conspiracy involving these men and here demonstrated that if he had lost their loyalty, his friends were to kill him. They did not, but once Gaius' suspicions had been aroused, these men may have felt that their life-expectancy had been considerably reduced.

The conspiracy (Jos., *Ant.* 19.37–113; Dio, LIX 29) was led by Cassius Chaerea, Cornelius Sabinus and Sextus Papinius, tribunes of the praetorian guard, Kallistos, the influential freedman, M. Arrecinus Clemens, the prefect of the guard, and Minucianus, a friend of the recently killed Lepidus. Many others were involved. In addition, large numbers must have known about the conspiracy and the prompt actions of the consuls on the death of Gaius may suggest their fore-knowledge. The conspiracy appears to have leaked badly, but this was a risk that Chaerea and the others were prepared to take. Modern conspiracies tend to be small affairs, but Chaerea wished to ensure his own survival. To achieve this, he needed to be sure that his actions would receive the support of the political class of Rome. As with the assassination of Julius Caesar, the conspirators were a political group. They needed to act as such and not as a criminal or terrorist band. They discussed the implications of their conspiracy with significant numbers of people. Gaius, however, walked down a private corridor oblivious to the threat. He met first Chaerea who stabbed him and as Gaius fled, he ran into the other conspirators. Dio is at his best reporting this: 'Gaius, having done these deeds as related, over three years, nine months and twenty-eight days, himself discovered that he was not a god.'

Main events in the reign of Gaius Caligula

Date	Event
37	Death of Tiberius.
	Accession of Gaius.
	Payments made from wills of Tiberius and Livia and on behalf of Gaius.
	Honours for Antonia, Drusilla, Agrippina, Julia.
	Repatriation of the ashes of Agrippina (the elder) and Gaius' brothers.
	Abolition of *maiestas*.
	Consulship of Gaius and Claudius.
	Illness of Gaius.
	Deaths of Tiberius Gemellus, Marcus Silanus, Afranius Potitius.
	Gaius marries Cornelia Orestilla and divorces and exiles her.

(Continued)

Date	Event
38	Publication of public accounts.
	Games given.
	Deaths of Macro and Ennia.
	Death of Drusilla.
	Gaius marries Lollia Paulina.
39	Gaius consul.
	Loss of some popular support.
	Building of the bridge from Puteoli to Baiae.
	Trial of Calvisius Rufus and Cornelia.
	Deaths of Titius Rufus and Junius Priscus.
	Attacks on Domitius Afer and L. Annaeus Seneca.
	Gaius goes to Gaul.
	Deaths of Lentulus Gaetulicus and M. Lepidus.
	Exile of Agrippina and Julia.
	Divorce of Paulina and marriage to Milonia Caesonia.
	Banishing of Ofonius Tigellinus.
40	Gaius consul without colleague.
	The British 'campaign'.
	Deaths of Anicius Cerealis, Sextus Papinus, Betilinus Bassus and Capito. Scribonius Proculus killed in the senate.
	Raising of taxes.
41	Assassination of Gaius by Cassius Chaerea and Cornelius Sabinus. Murder of Caesonia and the baby Drusilla.

4

CLAUDIUS (AD 41–54)

ACCESSION

Claudius was born in 10 BC, the son of Antonia and Drusus (see family tree, Figure 4.1, p. 91). He suffered from certain physical disabilities, the exact nature of which is unclear. His mother had a low opinion of him and he was something of an embarrassment to the imperial family. In a culture that valued bodily perfection, infirmities were taken as a sign of physical, mental and perhaps moral weakness. There was obviously some debate as to whether he should have a public role or even whether he should be allowed to become legally independent (Suet., *Claud.* 2–4). He lived in the shadow of his brother Germanicus and engaged in scholarly pursuits, research which he was happy to share with the senate and others during his reign. Under Tiberius, he was given consular regalia, but no office, perhaps in part because of the hostility between Tiberius and Claudius' sister-in-law. He developed a public role as patron of the *equites*, and he seems to have had some support in the senate (Suet., *Claud.* 6). His fortunes improved suddenly with the accession of his nephew Gaius. Claudius was made consul and achieved a certain prominence in the presentation of the imperial house. Nevertheless, although not plucked from obscurity by the praetorians in AD 41, as has sometimes been suggested, he was an improbable candidate for imperial office.

The death of Gaius led to an outbreak of confusion and anarchy. The conspirators do not appear to have had a coherent plan for the aftermath. The killings of Caesonia and baby Drusilla suggest that some wished to remove all the Julio–Claudians and perhaps restore the Republic. Crucially, they missed Claudius. The soldiers rioted and, with several thousand angry armed men roaming the streets, those favouring a clean sweep were unable to complete their plans.

A soldier found Claudius hiding either behind some curtains or in a dark corner. He was recognised and hauled off to the praetorians' camp (Dio, LX 1–3; Jos., *Ant.* 19.212–21; Suet., *Claud.* 10). The soldiers had found the brother of Germanicus, the uncle of Gaius, the last surviving male member of the imperial family and their emperor.

Claudius was initially reluctant to accept his elevation. He knew many in the senate would be opposed to him. He had only limited political experience and no experience of military matters and he had just seen the emperor, his wife and child killed. It looked like a job with rather gloomy prospects. The senate was also reluctant to accept him. The killing of Gaius, like the killing of Caesar, was in some ways a demonstration of the power of the Roman aristocracy. They had suffered at the hands of Gaius and probably had very limited respect for Claudius, his uncle, a man who had been ridiculed by his own family. Claudius had none of the personal characteristics, the political or military experience, or the political support that would have made him attractive to the senate.

The army decided the issue. Claudius, faced with several thousand armed men, acceded to their requests. He had little alternative. It would seem unlikely that the troops would allow him to refuse. Even if he could have resigned his office, it was likely that any subsequent ruler or a restored Republican government would have found him too much of a threat. The senate also had no realistic alternative candidate and the man who had the power to take Rome by force suddenly seemed a reasonable choice (Jos., *Ant.* 19.221–71). Also, all were ignorant of the position on the frontiers. The reaction of the troops could not be gauged, but the senate could probably reckon that a member of the imperial family would be more acceptable to the troops and their generals than any other man they might choose.

For thirty days Claudius stayed away from the senate. When he entered, he was taking no chances: he brought his troops with him (Dio, LX 3.2–3). Claudius' ultimate authority was displayed. He had either no, or limited, political backing in the senate. He therefore needed to look elsewhere for political support while trying to ensure that the senate would acquiesce in his rule.

GOVERNMENT AND ADMINISTRATION

Much has been written about Claudius' government and his supposed reliance on his wives and freedmen. All the ancient sources comment on this reliance. Yet, there were others in Claudius' inner circle who wielded considerable influence. L. Vitellius, for instance, seems to have been very close to the emperor. He supposedly accompanied him in the carriage on what must have been a terrible journey from Ostia to Rome once Claudius had been informed of Messalina's marriage (see p. 93). In his early years, Claudius associated himself closely with his sons-in-law (Dio, LX 25.7–8), Cn Pompeius Magnus and L. Silanus. Nevertheless, the household is particularly prominent in ancient accounts of Claudius' reign (Dio, LX 2; 19.2–3, 30.6; Suet., *Claud.* 28–9; Tac., *Ann.* XII 53; Pliny, *Ep.* VII 29, VIII 6). Claudius made little attempt to cloak the influence of his wives and freedmen. Narcissus, Pallas and Polybius took public roles. Pallas' brother was given command in Judaea. Kallistos, who had survived the fall of Gaius, continued to play an important part in the household administration. Both Messalina's and Agrippina's activities have been somewhat obscured by the tradition, but we may accept that they were allowed considerable independence and Agrippina especially was portrayed almost as a partner in empire.

This use of freedmen and wives insulated Claudius, to a certain extent, from the politics of the senate. The senate was the natural forum for policy discussion for the emperors, but Claudius faced a hostile senate. He had little chance of managing the opinion of this body. By giving the freedmen so much obvious influence, he immediately reduced the authority of the senators who, in their own opinion, should have been influencing the emperor. The public acknowledgement of the power of those in Claudius' household may even have been useful. They deflected political attention. They were at once central to Claudius' political manipulations and dispensable. By moving political debate from the senate to the court, and even by moving certain judicial cases to his household rather than having them heard in the senate, Claudius, to a certain extent, marginalised those who were hostile to him and took a far firmer control over political life.

This may or may not have been a conscious policy. The prospect of leaving sensitive political issues in the hands of a hostile senate may not have filled Claudius with joy, and therefore a policy of dealing with as much business as possible within the household may have evolved. Claudius was always courteous to the senate. He made every attempt to comply with the forms of good and respectful behaviour. The senate was, however, continually made aware that real power lay elsewhere. For a man of limited military experience, Claudius made much of his personal involvement in the British campaign and his military victories. The British campaign was celebrated in coins and arches, triumphs and processions, an extension of the *pomerium* (the sacred boundary of the city of Rome),[1] and in the naming of Britannicus, Claudius' son by Messalina (see p. 85). His link with the praetorians was made obvious in the regular donatives to the soldiers, and was displayed on the coinage and in the guard that accompanied him even into the senate-house.

Claudius also asserted his authority in practical ways. He reformed the senatorial roll. Those who failed to reach the census requirement were encouraged to leave of their own free will. Others were forced to go (Dio, LX 29). He was firm with provincial governors, prosecuting the corrupt and ensuring that those retiring from office would have a period before their next posting when they would be open to prosecution (Dio, LX 24.4, 25.4). He returned the *aerarium* (treasury) to the control of the quaestors, but in order to ensure proper financial management extended their office to three years. He also prevented soldiers taking part in the morning *salutatio* at the houses of senators (see p. 249 for this ceremony), a measure clearly designed to prevent senators taking soldiers into their patronage and possibly inciting them to revolt (Suet., *Claud.* 25.1).

His most notable reform was an extension of senatorial membership to include prominent men from Gallia Comata, the Gallic territory north of the Mediterranean strip which had largely been conquered by Julius Caesar. The Gauls had been within the empire for approximately one hundred years, but had been far from peaceful and the last major revolt had been as recent as AD 21. Many of the Roman aristocracy must have regarded these Gauls as barbarians, and all had been brought up on the myth of bloodthirsty Gauls threatening the very existence of the Roman state. Claudius' speech is preserved both in Tacitus and on an inscription (*Ann.* XI 23–5; Smallwood 1967, no. 369). He 'persuaded' the Senate through use of historical analogy, pointing out that Rome had progressively incorporated new peoples during its expansion and that few of the senators could trace their ancestry back to Romulus' foundation. It was only proper then that as the privileges of citizenship were extended so should the membership of the Senate.

It is arguable whether this shows a notably more liberal attitude on the part of Claudius than his predecessors or contemporaries. Claudius himself was notably fierce with citizens who showed no knowledge of Latin (Dio, LX 17.4; Suet., *Claud.* 16.2, cf. 25.3). Men of provincial origin had infiltrated the senate since the Late Republic, but these tended to be few in number. The vast majority of senators in this period were Italian. Claudius opened the door a little further, but the trickle of provincial senators did not become a flood. Nearly all these senators were from the West. The senate still had a long way to go before it became even vaguely representative of the aristocracy of the Empire and there is no evidence to suggest that this was Claudius' ultimate aim. It seems more likely that he wished to curry favour with, and demonstrate his patronage of, the Gauls. The Gallic chiefs may have been useful allies for Claudius in Gaul, but they were not enrolled in sufficient numbers nor did they have sufficient influence to become a powerful senatorial faction. Their enrolment was a sign of a very gradual change, not a radical policy departure on the part of Claudius.

Claudius also increased the authority of his equestrian procurators. Two new major equestrian governorships were created in Mauretania (Dio, LX 9.6) and, on the death of Claudius' friend Agrippa, Judaea was given an equestrian prefect, as was Ituraea when its king passed away (Tac,. *Ann.* XII 23). Claudius' praetorian prefects were given the ornaments of consular status (Dio, LX 23.1–5) assimilating the honours of the highest equestrian office with those of those of the highest senatorial post. Claudius and his legates were also given powers to make treaties with the power of the Senate and People of Rome (Dio, LX 23.6). The judicial acts of his procurators were ratified, probably increasing their authority in the collection of taxes in senatorial and imperial provinces (Suet., *Claud.* 12.1).[2] Claudius also reformed the equestrian career structure (Suet., *Claud.* 25.1; see also pp. 255–6).

Claudius' reign saw a thorough reform of the Roman aristocracy, a reform carried through by a man who did not have the support of the senior element of that group. The reign does not see a radical shift in power or fundamentally new developments. The senate officially remained at the centre of Claudius' administration. Most of the major governorships continued to be filled by senators. The equestrian role in government was enhanced, but the developments were a natural furthering of Augustus' development of the equestrian career structure. Even the role of the freedmen did not mark a truly radical departure from previous practice. The measures taken did further concentrate authority in the hands of the emperor. Claudius, like Gaius and Tiberius before him, found co-operation with the senate difficult and he too sought a new method of government, but Claudius' solution appears much more conservative than those adopted by his predecessors.

Other aspects of Claudius' administration will be considered in the relevant sections below, but it seems appropriate to comment on Claudius' financial administration at this stage. The sources on Gaius (p. 70) suggest that Gaius was almost bankrupt by the end of his reign and had to resort to desperate measures to raise money. There is no sign of any financial problems during the reign of Claudius. He promised the praetorians lavish donatives (gifts of money) and gave much smaller donatives each year to remind them and the senate of the crucial role they had played in elevating the emperor (Dio, LX 12.4). He also made a substantial distribution to the plebs following his British victory (Dio, LX 25.7–8). He commenced two new huge building projects early in his reign – the harbour at Ostia and the draining of the Fucine lake (Dio, LX 11.1–5) – and he also built a new aqueduct, having completed one started by Gaius (Suet., *Claud.* 20). He was fond of games and put on spectaculars for special occasions (Dio, LX 33.3; Suet., *Claud.* 21, 24.2; Tac., *Ann.* XI 11–12, XII 41). He also funded military campaigns in Britain and Germany and the lavish celebrations that followed his British victory. All this was achieved while gradually withdrawing the taxes that had been imposed by Gaius (Dio, LX 4.1). Claudius did not have to pay for the extravagances of Gaius, but his levels of expenditure must have been high and he is not one of those emperors accused of meanness or (often) of killing aristocrats for their wealth, though the latter charge is levelled at Messalina. Those who were killed during Claudius' reign may have made substantial contributions to the imperial coffers, but this would hardly have transformed the finances of the empire. Notably increased efficiency in tax collection seems improbable. Two conclusions emerge. First, the financial situation in AD 41 may not have been as bad as the sources would have us believe. Second, Claudius' financial administration was probably extremely efficient.

MILITARY AND FOREIGN POLICY

Claudius came to power with no military experience. As the son of Drusus and brother of Germanicus he had inherited a little of their military prestige. Great Roman leaders needed to show their military prowess as well as their political skills, and Claudius needed to demonstrate to the senate, people and soldiers that he was an effective commander-in-chief to bring legitimacy to his position as head of state. He would follow in the tradition of Caesar, Augustus and Tiberius in effectively leading Roman armies and conquering new territory.

He had no shortage of possibilities for new conquests. The Germans were restive and campaigns were probably already underway (Dio, LX 8.7) and although the Roman armies were victorious in 41, there were further campaigns in 47 (Dio, LX 30.3; Tac., *Ann.* XI 16–20) and 50 (Tac., *Ann.* XII 27–30). Political divisions within various German tribes and disputes between tribes provided Rome with an opportunity which Corbulo, for one, was anxious to exploit, and concentrating resources on a German war may have produced significant Roman gains. In Africa, Suetonius Paulinus conducted campaigns against the Moors, campaigns which brought a significant but not conclusive victory in 41 allowing the senate to offer Claudius a triumph. Claudius courteously declined the offer though accepted triumphal *ornamenta* in honour of the victories (Dio, LX 8.6, 9.1–6).[3] The Eastern frontier was also restive throughout Claudius' reign with problems in Armenia and Iberia, and the Parthians suffered a period of internal discord and civil war, but Claudius preferred diplomacy to major conflict.

Claudius chose to invade Britain. In some ways this was an odd choice. There were internal disputes in Britain. Dio mentions a certain Berikos who had been expelled from the island and who appealed to Claudius for help. Numismatic evidence from Britain suggests that the period saw an expansion of the generally anti-Roman Catavellauni at the expense of tribes such as the Atrebates in Sussex. The Dobunni in Gloucestershire may also have been fearful of Catavellaunian imperialism. It seems unlikely that Roman interests were greatly affected by these developments. The Catavellauni would hardly pose any significant threat to Roman power or prestige and, although trade may have been a little more difficult for a time, there is no evidence to suggest that Claudius was remotely interested in protecting the livelihoods of the presumably mainly Gallic traders who transported Roman goods across the Channel. Nor does it seem likely that Claudius felt the slight to Roman prestige from Gaius' failed invasion attempt. Two factors probably motivated Claudius' decision to invade an island that the Romans had left untouched for almost a century. Britain was effectively new territory and its conquest could be guaranteed to impress. In spite of Caesar's expeditions and Roman trading relations, Britain was still something of a mystery and would have the benefit of exoticism. Second, Claudius' invasion could be seen to be in imitation of Caesar.

The relationship between Claudius and Caesar's legacy was complex. As a historian who had studied the period (apparently), it is likely that Claudius was well informed about Caesar's activities and could see some analogies between Caesar's position and his own. Claudius, like Caesar, was faced with a hostile senate and was dependent on the power of the military for his primary political support. Claudius, like Caesar, endeavoured to secure popular support. Claudius also engaged in large-scale administrative reforms, as did both Caesar and Augustus. Also, Claudius was born in Lugdunum, Gaul, and seems to have had a marked partiality for Gauls. Most notable though, is Claudius' echoing of Caesar's building projects in Ostia (Suet., *Claud.* 20.1) and the invasion of Britain itself.

To modern eyes, emulation of Caesar may seem rather a weak reason for choosing Britain as the place to win military prestige, but we must remember that although we conventionally date the beginning of the imperial period to the reign of Augustus, there are good reasons to place this (artificial) chronological division of Republic and Empire in the period of Caesar's dominance and to see Caesar as the founder of the first dynasty. For Claudius, all too aware that the real source of imperial power was the army, it made some sense to emulate Caesar rather than Augustus.

The campaign itself was a success and, with hindsight, it seems obvious that the petty kingdoms of Southern Britain where the terrain presented few notable obstacles to Roman expansion, would have subsided before the sizeable military force collected by Claudius. Yet, the operation was not without its risks. Caesar had failed twice to make significant gains in the province. Tactically, Rome's forces would be dependent on the fleet for reinforcements, some supplies, and as a means of retreat should things go wrong and uncertainties of tide and weather were potentially disruptive. The victory at Medway was clearly hard fought and we need not be too cynical about Aulus Plautius' 'pause' at the Thames to await Claudius, reinforcements, and a decision as to whether to advance. The Romans had used important rivers as frontiers before. But Claudius pushed on and the conquest of Southern and Central Britain seems to have been quite rapid and was a notable military achievement.

Claudius celebrated in style. The news of Claudius' victory was transmitted to the senate by his sons-in-law. His prominent generals were rewarded with political and military decorations. He celebrated a triumph. Arches were erected in Rome and Lugdunum. The victory was celebrated on coins, in sculpture (either depicting Claudius as a conquering divinity or showing a personification of defeated Britannia), and in the name of Claudius' son. Claudius revived an archaic ceremony (previously and typically 'rediscovered' by Augustus), in which the sacred boundary of the city of Rome was extended after new territory had been incorporated into the empire (Tac., *Ann.* XII 24). The final capture of Caratacus, the leading opponent of the invasion, was turned into another ceremonial when Caratacus and his family were presented to the Roman people and Claudius was able to show his magnanimity by sparing the life of his great enemy, who aided Claudian propaganda by behaving as a proud barbarian warrior rather than a man begging for his life (Dio, LX 33.3). In terms of Claudius' political image, as well as in military terms, the invasion of Britain was a success (Dio LX, 19.1–22.2, 23.1–2; Suet., *Claud.* 17, 24.3; *Vesp.* 4.1–2; Tac. *Ann.* XII 31–40).

Claudius inherited a rather disturbed German frontier, and the first years of his reign were marked by extensive campaigning against the Chatti and Chauci especially. These campaigns met with considerable success, but Claudius later changed his policy. The leading general on the frontier was told to cease any further expansion and the manpower of the legions seems to have diverted to construction projects (Dio, LX 30.4–6). Claudius pursued his political and military objectives in Germany through diplomatic means, and the latter part of his reign saw notable tribal conflict in Germany but only limited Roman intervention. This policy is easily explicable. Expansion into Germany in the Augustan and later periods had proved extremely difficult and had required long and bloody campaigns often for very limited territorial gains. There had also been spectacular disasters. Any consistent policy of expansion would have needed considerable resources of manpower and time. The British expedition was a major drain on manpower. In such circumstances, Claudius could not risk losing a substantial force through an expansionist policy in Germany. He had also achieved his military victory so was not as keen to win prestige in Germany. When Augustus had engaged in his major campaigns in Germany and elsewhere in the West, he had either led the armies himself or, more often, relied on his closest associates, Agrippa, Tiberius, Drusus and Varus. Claudius had fewer men he could trust to lead his armies. It would seem unlikely that Claudius would have wished to spend long and hard years on campaign himself. A major campaign in Germany would have meant entrusting many legions to his commanders and providing them with the opportunity to win glory that would have eclipsed Claudius' own triumph in Britain. Claudius did not have the political security to engage in such activities.

In the East, Claudius again seems initially to have followed the lead of his predecessor, but developed his own policy as the reign progressed. He relied on client kings in much of the East and even enhanced the authority of some, most notably Agrippa I who had proved very useful in the negotiations with the senate in the first days after Gaius' death (Dio, LX 8.1–3). These kingdoms caused problems. Rebellions were threatened and kings had to be removed (Dio, LX 28.7). Some even revolted (Dio, LX 32.4; Tac., *Ann.* XII 15–21) but, although suppressing the revolts, Claudius was reluctant to alter fundamentally the political settlement of the East.

Judaea had been given to his close friend Agrippa in 41 (Dio, LX 8.2–3), following very much the policy of his predecessor, but Agrippa's death in 44 without an adult male heir left Claudius little alternative but to annex the province (Tac., *Ann.* XII 23; Jos., *Ant.* XIX 343–63; *BJ* II). The equestrian procurators introduced by Claudius initiated a long period of ineffective government in Judaea which was to culminate in a great rebellion in AD 66.

The period saw problems in Parthia and Armenia. The Parthians engaged in civil war with Vardanes and Gotarzes contesting the throne. Vardanes was victorious but was later murdered, leaving Gotarzes to contend with another claimant, Phraates IV, who had been a hostage in Rome (Tac. *Ann.* XI 8–10). In 49, there was a new outbreak of hostilities and the Romans sent one Meherdates to seize the Parthian throne. The expedition, sponsored by Rome but without Roman troops, foundered (Tac., *Ann.* XII 10–14.) The situation remained disturbed. In 51, a war broke out between Armenia and Iberia which threatened to disturb the region. The governor of Syria was reluctant to commit his forces, but the intervention (unsuccessful) of the equestrian governor of Cappodocia forced his hand. The Parthians under yet another king, Vologeses, would not allow the Romans a free hand and invaded Armenia, though disease and famine meant that the Parthian intervention was no more conclusive than that of the Romans (Tac., *Ann.* XII 44–51). The defeat of the Parthians seems to have discouraged further intervention, though the possibility that there were other problems in the final years of Claudius' reign is reinforced by the next attestation of Armenia and Parthian in the historical account. In the first year of Nero's reign, the young and militarily inexperienced emperor organised a major campaign in Armenia to be conducted by his leading general, Corbulo (see pp. 125–6).

The East was disrupted in the Claudian period and there were clear opportunities for Claudius to intervene militarily, either to take advantage of internal strife in Parthia and Armenia or to reorder the settlement of the Eastern client kingdoms. Claudius seems to have been unwilling to take such action. Again, the dangers and implications of a major campaign in the East may have been at the forefront of Claudius' calculations.

Claudius also inherited a disturbed situation in North Africa and had to fight a long war which culminated in the annexation of Mauretania. Mauretania had previously been controlled by client kings, but the last king clashed with Gaius, with predictable results. The kingdom was not, however, quickly annexed and it seems likely that the Mauretanian kings had either kept the local tribes in check or had formed a series of alliances with the various tribes which now fell apart. Difficulties in Mauretania dragged on until 47, though the peace was probably fragile and Rome had difficulties in the area throughout the following centuries.

With the sole exception of his British invasion, Claudius was notably reluctant to commit forces to major campaigns. In Germany and the East, in spite of the obvious opportunities to take advantage of the discord amongst Rome's enemies, Claudius preferred to proceed through diplomacy, encouraging rival claimants to thrones and only intervening when absolutely necessary.

THE PLEBS

Faced with a hostile Senate, one of the major groups in Roman society to whom Claudius could look for support was the plebs. Claudius invested considerable time and money in securing the support of the plebs. He was a notable giver of games and gave every sign of enjoying them (Suet., *Claud.* 21). Presiding over the games in person, he used the opportunity to communicate with the crowds via notice-boards. Such communication allowed him to test public opinion. The cheers that greeted Domitius Ahenobarbus, son of Agrippina, were in contrast to a polite reception for Britannicus, and, since they could have been interpreted as a measure of the unpopularity of Messalina, may have significantly undermined Messalina's position. The secular games provided a great opportunity for Claudius to demonstrate his links with the past (Tac., *Ann.* XI 11–12; Suet., *Claud.* 21.2). After the adoption of Nero, Claudius associated the young man with his rule by giving games jointly (Dio, LX 33.3; Tac., *Ann.* XII 41). Appearing together before the people at the games was the symbolic parallel to Nero's first political speeches (see pp. 97–8).

Claudius also gave money to the plebs after his British victory, and in this he was aided by his sons-in-law, men with whom he was associating his rule at the time (Dio, LX 25.7–8).

Claudius' attempts to secure the material well-being of the Roman people (Suet., *Claud.* 18–20) were also spectacular. These involved the construction or completion of two aqueducts, one of which had been started by Gaius. Also, Claudius attempted to secure the food supply. This was to be achieved by two measures. The first was an unsuccessful project to bring more land into cultivation by draining the Fucine lake (Dio, LX 11.5; Tac., *Ann.* XII. 56–7; Suet., *Claud.* 21.6). The project involved the construction of a massive drainage ditch and was celebrated by a reconstruction of a naval battle staged on the lake. This descended into farce when the re-enactors refused to fight and had to be cajoled by the emperor, and then the imperial family were nearly themselves swept away when part of the canal wall collapsed.

The construction of a harbour at Ostia was more successful (Dio, LX 11.1–5). The artificial harbour at Ostia provided sufficient space and security to allow the grain to be unloaded there rather than in Campania, where it had been landed previously. The grain was then transported up the Tiber to Rome by barge rather than overland, simplifying the whole operation. This project had first been planned by Caesar, another who needed popular support, but was dropped because of practical difficulties. Claudius was personally involved in the construction project, and indeed was probably supervising the building work at Ostia when news of Messalina's 'infidelities' broke. Claudius' efforts to secure the corn supply were featured on his coinage. The harbour did not solve all the problems. Claudius' reign was marked by several food riots in Rome (Suet., *Claud.* 18.2; Tac. *Ann.* XII 43), possibly before the harbour was fully operational, and Trajan found it necessary to modify the harbour installation at Ostia to provide a yet more secure harbour since the fleet could still be wrecked if a storm blew in.

Nevertheless, Claudius' efforts to secure popular support were probably largely successful. Suetonius tells us of popular dismay following a rumour of the emperor's death (Suet., *Claud.* 12.3), though the story is undated, and, apart from bread riots, which Claudius worked hard to alleviate, there is little sign of unpopularity among the plebs.

FAMILY AND POLITICS

Claudius' reliance on his household for policy advice and his distrust of the senate increased the political importance of the imperial family. Power rested in the imperial court and political debate and activity was largely restricted to that arena. With Claudius, we see politics of the court not the senate. This is, of course, a development largely resultant upon the creation of monarchic rule and can already be seen under Augustus when members of the imperial family, such as Livia and Julia, had ill-defined political influence. Although Claudius showed respect for the senate and took more interest in the senate than some of his predecessors, our sources portray a situation in which the real decisions were taken in private and political power was the ability to manipulate the emperor. Unlike Tiberius, who seems genuinely to have brought problems to the senate and been open to persuasion, Claudius seems to have brought solutions to be discussed and ratified.

Claudius owed his political power to the loyalty of the army to his family and he laid emphasis on his family in the first year of his reign. Claudius' first major problem was how to deal with Gaius' assassins since, although few among the aristocracy would disapprove and the assassins were almost certainly extremely popular in the senate, Claudius could hardly allow such men to survive, lauded by the senate, as visible reminders of the rewards for tyrannicide. He found a compromise and punished some of those responsible for the assassination of his nephew, but only those who had conspired to kill other members of the Julio–Claudian family (Dio, LX 3.4–5). Julia and Agrippina, Claudius' nieces, returned from exile, though Julia was to be exiled again in the same year (Dio, LX 4.1, 8.5). Claudius gave games for Antonia and Drusus, his mother and father and for Livia (Claudius' grandmother), who was given a statue in the temple of Augustus. This may have been a preliminary to full divine honours. Mark Antony (Claudius' grandfather) and Germanicus were also honoured. Although all Gaius' acts were annulled, he did not suffer *damnatio memoriae* whereby all record of his life would be excised from public documents and monuments, and Claudius did not allow the senate to pull down all Gaius' statues, though he arranged for them to disappear (Suet., *Claud.* 11; Dio, LX 4.5–5.2).

The years preceding Claudius' accession had not been kind to the Julio–Claudian family. Claudius found himself surrounded by adult female relatives, but had few close male relatives and was without an adult male heir. The women of the imperial family assumed a greater prominence and, since marriage to a princess of the imperial house brought political influence, the husbands of imperial princesses would be powerful political figures. Should anything happen to Claudius, these men would be in a good position to challenge for the imperial position.

The imperial women also had an invaluable political asset. They could gain access to the emperor and could thereby influence his decisions. These women were not merely decorative or 'heir-producers'; they were serious players of the political game and, given the fatality rate in the imperial family, were playing for extremely high stakes. Livia, Julia and the elder Agrippina had accustomed the Roman elite to powerful imperial women. Claudius was married to Messalina, who had her own interests and those of her children to protect, and the tradition suggests that she was deeply involved in the politics of the period.

In outline, the history of family politics under Claudius is quite simple (see Figure 4.1). Messalina wielded considerable influence, but was caught in adultery and executed. She was replaced by Agrippina who removed any rivals and exerted significant influence over Claudius. She was able to persuade Claudius to adopt her son who, slightly older than Britannicus, became the most likely heir. When Claudius seemed to be about to reject Nero in favour of his natural son, Agrippina removed Claudius and ensured Nero's smooth succession. Behind this relatively simple if sordid tale, lurk complexities which can only be fully understood by looking at the careers of the women in some detail.

Messalina

Messalina was of noble birth, though reconstructing her lineage is complex. She was the daughter of Messala Barbatus, who was the grandson of Claudius Marcellus and Octavia, sister of Augustus. Her mother was Domitia Lepida, who was the granddaughter of the same Octavia and Mark Antony. She was, in fact, more closely

Figure 4.1 The families of Claudius, Messalina and Agrippina

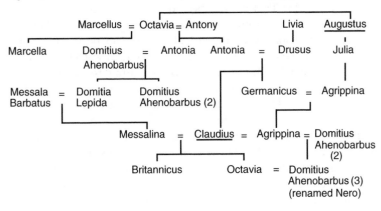

related to Augustus (twice through Octavia) than Claudius (once through Octavia). She provided Claudius with two children, Octavia and Britannicus. In some ways, therefore, she was the ideal consort. The tradition, however, depicts her as the whore-empress whose infidelities and promiscuity strain credulity.

Messalina was clearly a power in the early years of Claudius' reign. It seems that she held a court separate to that of Claudius, and Claudius seems to have approved of this separation. Messalina's influence was seen behind many of Claudius' actions in the early years of his reign. The (re-)exile of Julia, who was accused of adultery with Seneca, was laid at the door of Messalina. Appius Silanus also fell victim to Messalina in an elaborate conspiracy with Narcissus (Dio, LX 14.3–4; Suet., *Claud.* 37). Silanus had been married to Domitia Lepida, Messalina's mother, and was an experienced governor. He was obviously a powerful political figure on the fringes of the imperial family. But the motive ascribed to Messalina by our sources was purely sexual and not political.

Dio links the death of Silanus to the first and probably the most serious conspiracy against Claudius. Annius Vinicianus was the prime mover of the conspiracy. He had been suggested as a possible successor to Gaius and thus may have felt that he was viewed with some suspicion. He gained the support of the governor of Dalmatia, Furius Camillus Scribonianus. But, as the legions were about to depart, a series of omens weakened their resolve and the conspiracy dissolved (Dio, LX 15). The conspiracy involved others in the Roman aristocracy and its dissolution led to a spate of arrests and deaths (Pliny, *Ep.* III 16).

Dio (LX 18) places an extended account of Messalina's growing power in AD 43. This is probably not a coincidence. Claudius was preparing to leave Rome for his invasion of Britain. He had suppressed a major revolt and wished to secure his position in Rome before he left. His trusted friend Lucius Vitellius was left in charge at Rome, but Claudius may have been willing to delegate more authority to Messalina, who was of course deeply committed to Claudius' cause. Dio presents her as building a political group, a group bound together by adultery.

Her authority was seen in the death of Julia, granddaughter of Tiberius, and of a prefect of the guard Catonius Iustus (Dio, LX 18). An alliance of Julia and a praetorian prefect would indeed have been powerful and anything that threatened the loyalty of the praetorians was to be feared. Feminine rivalry, which our sources give as the cause for the removal of Julia, may mask suspected political conspiracy and the removal of a potentially powerful group, possibly in opposition to Messalina.

Other possibly powerful leaders in Roman politics can be divined. Pompeius Magnus, who carried an extremely prestigious name, was married to Claudius' elder daughter by a previous marriage. His connection with the imperial family was paralleled by the betrothal of L. Silanus, already connected to the imperial family down the female line, to the infant Octavia, a prospective marriage that never took place. Both men were advanced to offices at an early age. They brought the news of Claudius' victory in Britain to the senate. They also took part in donations to the plebs in 44 (Dio, LX 5.7, 21.5, 25.7–8). These men were clearly being associated with Claudius' power and presumably groomed for office. Messalina probably had little to fear from Silanus – after all he was committed to one of her children – but Pompeius was a different matter.

The position of others attacked (supposedly) by Messalina is less easy to estimate. M. Vinicius was supposedly killed for refusing to sleep with the empress, i.e. not join her 'group'. He was also the brother of the Vinicianus at the centre of the conspiracy of 42. Presumably, Claudius (or Messalina) could have removed him then. The mode of his death, poisoning, raises further suspicions about the whole story (Dio, LX 27.4).

Decimus Valerius Asiaticus was another victim, killed in 47. The political implications of this are unclear. Asiaticus was a respected senator of provincial origin and cannot easily be seen as a threat to Messalina or Claudius. The killing is explained as a convoluted sexual conspiracy and a plot to seize Asiaticus' gardens in the centre of Rome, gardens in which Messalina was herself to be killed (Dio,

LX 29.1–6; Tac. *Ann.* XI 1–3). Asiaticus went to his death calmly, making arrangements for the funeral, a martyr. In the same year, in a case which cannot be convincingly related to the death of Asiaticus, Pompeius was killed.

The death of Pompeius would seem to have enhanced Messalina's control, yet there are signs of her position slipping. The instrument of her attack on Asiaticus, a certain Suillius Rufus, was himself attacked in the senate, though the debate failed to bring him down (Tac., *Ann.* XI 4–7) and L. Domitius Ahenobarbus received more applause than Britannicus at the secular games of 47, which Tacitus interprets enigmatically as a gesture of sympathy for Agrippina.

Messalina's fall was sudden and the story strange (Tac., *Ann.* XI 26–38; Dio, LX 31.1–5). She became involved with a certain C. Silius. This man was consul designate and the very man who had attacked Suillius Rufus in the senate. For some reason, she apparently underwent a semi-public ceremony with this man, an act of madness according to Tacitus, and then engaged in a post-nuptial revel. Narcissus, Claudius' trusted freedman, organised a concubine to break the news to Claudius while he was staying in Ostia. Claudius hurried back in a carriage with Vitellius and Narcissus, Vitellius refusing to condemn Messalina explicitly. News of Claudius' approach reached the revellers who dispersed in a panic, but no effort was made to raise the army or to oppose Claudius. Messalina was deserted. Her only hope was to reach Claudius. She set out for Ostia to meet him on the road, but could find no carriage and travelled on the city waste cart. The meeting was brief, but she was not arrested. Claudius retreated to the praetorian camp and then the revellers were rounded up and killed, the prefect of the *vigiles* (night watch) among them.

It is difficult to make sense of this and even Tacitus seems to have found the event incomprehensible. Modern historians have seen in it conspiracy on the part of Messalina or Silius against Claudius or the freedmen or even against Agrippina, a rising force. It is difficult to see how a 'marriage' could have been kept secret and how the effective divorce of the emperor by the mother of his presumed heir could be anything less than treason. Yet, there was no organised resistance to Claudius' retribution, a retribution that affected many prominent men. The story is so implausible that it throws into question the whole tradition on Messalina. Can we simply interpret the tradition as a later invention designed to explain and excuse another Claudian purge of the aristocracy or does the novelistic quality of the entire tradition bury historical events behind such a thick layer of invention that the truth cannot be surmised?

Although these solutions are tempting, especially given the trivial motives attributed to Messalina for allegedly removing so many rivals, the tradition surrounding Messalina is so widespread and contemporaneous that we must take it seriously. The imperial women were used as pawns in political and dynastic arrangements. They were married off as suited the emperor. It is likely that heads of other prominent families behaved in a similar way. An aristocratic woman's sexual partners were always a matter of political interest. The tradition, and the tradition is fairly uniform, suggests that the women of the early imperial period were not passive partners in relationships. They expected to be able to influence their husbands and to take an active part in public life. An imperial princess could be expected to have a circle of male friends. Since legitimate political links were formed by sexual relations, it is possible that close illegitimate political ties could be developed through adultery. It is significant that close political co-operation could be interpreted as signifying a sexual tie and that Romans could think it remotely credible that leading Roman women could conduct multiple affairs. Such cementing of a political connection (when extra-marital) was inevitably illegitimate and when it involved an empress, was potentially fatal. This may have added a certain *frisson* to the activity and would have bound the adulterers more closely to each other. Systematic promiscuity was a feasible, if rather odd method of creating a close-knit political alliance. It is possible, therefore, even if we dismiss the wilder stories, that Messalina was less than faithful to her husband. It is also possible that as long as this remained behind closed doors and did not pose a significant threat to the emperor, the creation of such a group was not a substantial problem. With the 'marriage' to Silius, the consul designate, Messalina went one step further.

If we accept Tacitus' view that Messalina and Silius had taken leave of their senses, there is no need for further speculation, but this seems an inadequate explanation for the fall of a woman who had played the political game reasonably astutely. Dio links the fall of Messalina to her disposal of Polybius, a freedman of the emperor, suggesting that she had fallen out with the freedmen so that even in Claudius' assertion of independence from his wife, he was still under the control of his household. Levick picks up this suggestion and, noting that it was Silius who had attacked Suillius after the death of Asiaticus, proposes that Messalina was engaged in a reorientation of her group, an attempt to build bridges with powerful senators.[4] In so doing, she alienated the powerful freedmen who then engineered her downfall. In a struggle between the emperor's wife and freedmen, it is understandable that many would not have wanted to commit themselves. Yet, Claudius' flight to the praetorian camp, his summary execution of so many, and the rapid dispersal of Messalina's supporters in the certainty that they faced death suggest, even if Claudius was influenced by paranoia, that this was more than factional fighting: this was a serious conspiracy, probably intended to remove Claudius.

As with the conspiracy against Gaius, this was a political movement intended to take control and therefore could not be limited to a few people. The politically prominent needed to be included and arrangements put in place for the government. The involvement of the consul-designate would be crucial in the manipulation of the senate in the aftermath of an assassination. Silius' 'marriage' would make him guardian of Claudius' children and place him in position to assume most of the powers of the emperor. He was a logical choice and such an offer may have been seductive. This conspiracy, discovered in advance, could not rally sufficient military support once Claudius reached the praetorian camp. The inclusion of a prefect of the *vigiles* in the conspiracy brought some military force, but even if the *vigiles* could be brought over, and the preparations for this may not have been complete, the military power of the praetorians would overwhelm them. Once Claudius knew, they were lost and all the evidence suggests that they knew it.

The real problem is to explain Messalina's decision to take such desperate measures. Did she fear a rival (Agrippina being the obvious threat), or that Claudius' power was disintegrating in the face of senatorial opposition, or was she becoming increasingly marginalised in the household government? Historical attention has focused on Messalina, and Claudius has been seen as essentially the passive victim of the manipulations of others, but Claudius too was in a position to sense the growing opposition to his regime. He presumably saw the display of public feeling in favour of Domitius Ahenobarbus and the story of Asiaticus, phlegmatically going to his death, a symbol of imperial tyranny, was probably disturbing. Claudius appears to have been sensitive to popular opinion. To see Claudius as a Machiavellian politician manipulating those closest to him runs against the grain of ancient depictions of the emperor, but our sources are committed to a depiction of Claudius as a servant of his wives and freedmen, even though they provide us with sufficient evidence to suggest a wily politician carefully manipulating a rather weak position. An adjustment of Claudius' policy may have left Messalina uncertain of her position. Instead of riding out these difficulties, awaiting a change in the political environment, she may have looked for a radical alternative.

If Claudius had been killed, it would seem likely that the tradition would blame him for the problems of the previous years. By disposing of Messalina, Claudius and the freedmen had a scapegoat who could be blamed for the deaths and the political failures. The death of Messalina in some ways allowed Claudius a fresh start, but much of his meagre political credit had been used up and at least some of his previous supporters were now dead. In an attempt to win popularity and restore the situation, remarkably he chose another woman of the imperial house with whom to associate his power.

Agrippina

After the massacre of Messalina's supporters, Claudius needed to strengthen his political position. One way of doing this was to remarry, which would associate a new group of supporters with his regime. The historians depict a somewhat farcical debate led by the freedmen over whom should be selected. Here, again, the tradition seems dubious. Not only is it difficult to believe that the freedmen might have run such campaigns for their favoured candidates, but also one must wonder how such stories reached the tradition. As with the stories of Messalina, the tradition seems more like historical fiction than real history. We should not, however, assume that the choice was straightforward. There were several available noble women. Claudius' eventual choice was Agrippina, who then nervously encouraged the disposal of her main rivals (Tac., *Ann.* XII 22; Dio, LX 32.4).

Agrippina was perhaps not the ideal candidate. She was Claudius' niece and the marriage would be incestuous. In a family in which close-kin marriage was the norm, such considerations were almost certainly more legal than moral, but the law needed 'rearranging'. These formalities were completed in early 49 and the way was then open for Agrippina to take her place at the side of the emperor (Tac., *Ann.* XII 1–7; Dio LX 31.6–32). More importantly, her son Domitius Ahenobarbus' claim to the throne, already respectable, was improved by the marriage and it was to be further enhanced. The prospective husband of Octavia, Silanus, had his long betrothal cancelled and killed himself. From being a probable heir of the emperor, he had been progressively marginalised and there can have been little doubt that he would have been disposed of at the earliest convenient opportunity (Dio, LX 31.6–8; Tac., *Ann.* XII 8). This left Octavia free for the young Ahenobarbus. In AD 50, he was adopted and given the name Nero (Dio, LX 33.2; Tac. *Ann.* XII 25–6). In 53, he was married to Octavia, a process which, ironically enough, required the adoption of Octavia since Nero was legally her sister. Nero emerged as the heir to the empire. Britannicus remained a problem and a threat to Nero and Agrippina (Dio, LX 33.12; Tac. *Ann.* XII 58). He was, however, still a minor and Agrippina ensured that Claudius was dead before he reached an age when he could realistically assume the imperial position.

In terms of the dynasty, bringing Agrippina into the imperial household tied a lot of loose ends. She was the only surviving child of Germanicus and the elder Agrippina, and the only surviving direct descendant of Augustus (apart from her son). In marrying Agrippina, Claudius consolidated the family and further associated his rule with the popularity of his brother and sister-in-law. The connection seemed to bring stability and unity to the imperial family.

Agrippina immediately assumed a position of remarkable prominence. She was granted the title Augusta as early as AD 50 and seems to have taken her place at Claudius' side at most public occasions (Dio, LX 33.1–2). A colony in Germany was named after her (Tac., *Ann.* XII 27). She is said to have had a hand in the appointment of Burrus as praetorian prefect, a man who proved his loyalty to Nero. Seneca also returned and became prominent within the imperial household as tutor to Nero. Already Agrippina seems to have been playing at least part of the role she was to play in the early years of Nero's reign. She was more than just the wife of the emperor, but acted as a political power in her own right.

Nero's advance was also rapid. After adoption in 50, he received the *toga virilis* in 51, the mark of his adulthood. He celebrated lavish games in association with his new father and was declared *Princeps Iuventutis* (Leader of Youth) (Tac., *Ann.* XII 41). In 53, the year of his marriage to Octavia, he spoke in public to secure grants of privileges for Ilium and Bononia (Tac., *Ann.* XII 58). Both were significant places. Ilium was the original home of the Roman people from where the mythical ancestor of the Julian family led the Trojans to Italy to found the new city. Nero was thereby associated with the family myth of the Julians, surely a symbolic claim for legitimacy. Bononia was a military colony established by his great-great-grandfather Augustus. By representing the colony, Nero laid claim to have inherited Augustus' clients and, to some extent, his political position.

It is reasonable to assume that Claudius planned some role for Britannicus in the succession. The fate of dynastic rivals to previous emperors was not encouraging. Yet, the advancing of Nero would seem to leave Claudius little room in which to manoeuvre. He may have gambled on surviving long enough for Britannicus to reach his majority and then being able to dispose of Agrippina and Nero as he had disposed of Messalina. Perhaps he felt that his position was so weak that he depended on Agrippina's political support to stabilise his regime. Her public presence suggests that he needed to associate himself with her. We cannot know how much political influence she had over the Roman aristocracy. Agrippina could not allow an alternative to her son. She presumably pressed for his elevation. Her timetable was quite tight. Britannicus could not be kept in the background for ever. As the date for his assumption of the *toga virilis* neared, her position and that of her son came under some threat. In AD 54, Claudius died.

It has been alleged that he was poisoned by Agrippina's own hand, avoiding the many elaborate security measures. Most such accusations rest on fairly flimsy evidence. In this case, the evidence is persuasive. His death was remarkably convenient. The sources are remarkably precise. Nero is said to have quipped that mushrooms were surely the food of the gods since his father became a god through a mushroom (Dio, LX 34; Suet., *Claud.* 44–5; Tac., *Ann.* XII 65–9).

Main events in the reign of Claudius

Date	Event
41	Accession.
	Return of Julia and Agrippina from exile.
	Victories in Mauretania and Germany.
	Resettlement of client kingdoms in the East.
	Exile of Julia.

(Continued)

Date	Event
42	Victory of Suetonius Paulinus over the Moors and the founding of two new provinces.
	Work starts at Ostia and the Fucine Lake.
	Death of Appius Junius Silanus.
	Conspiracy of Vinicianus and Camillus Scribonianus
43	Reduction of Lycia.
	Reform of the citizen rolls.
	Deaths of Catonius Iustus and Julia (daughter of Drusus).
	Invasion of Britain.
44	Claudius' triumph.
	Reform of the treasury.
	Distributions to the masses.
46	Asinius Gallus banished.
	Mithridates of Iberia deprived of his kingdom.
	M. Vinicius prosecuted.
47	Reform of the senatorial lists.
	Death of Valerius Asiaticus.
	Campaigns in Armenia.
	Campaigns of Corbulo against the Chauci.
	Secular games.
48	Fall of Messalina and her circle.
	Enrolment of men from Gallia Comata into the senate.
49	Marriage to Agrippina.
	Failure of Claudius' policy in Parthia.
	M. Silanus killed.
	Lollia Paulina killed and Calpurnia exiled.
	C. Cadius Rufus condemned for corruption.
	Ituraea and Judaea incorporated into Syria.
50	Adoption of L. Domitius Ahenobarbus (Nero).
	Honours granted to Agrippina.
	Campaigns and disorder in Germany and Britain.

(Continued)

Date	Event
51	Nero assumes *toga virilis* and presides over lavish games.
	Burrus appointed praetorian prefect.
	War in Armenia.
52	Grant of praetorian rank to Pallas.
	Revolt in Judaea.
	Problems in Cilicia.
53	Nero marries Octavia and takes more active public role.
54	Death of Claudius.

5

NERO (AD 54–68)

INTRODUCTION

With Nero, the Julio–Claudian dynasty came to an end. His reign is often seen as a culmination of tyranny, the final degeneration of the Julio–Claudians, and a period in which bad taste and immorality were in the ascendancy. Nero is portrayed as the undisciplined perpetrator and victim: a spoilt child given absolute power with predictable results, and thus a symbol of the weakness of absolute monarchy. Nero has been attacked across the ages: his responsibility (either directly or indirectly) for the deaths of his father, mother, two wives, his brother and sister (by adoption), his aunt, and numerous other more distant relatives has not endeared him to upholders of family values. His sexual promiscuity, his bisexuality, his reckless financial extravagance, and his showmanship have horrified those who admire Roman restraint and self-discipline. To add to this weight of censure, both the Jewish and Christian traditions remember Nero as a persecutor. His murders and the violence with which he treated his subjects add to his notoriety. While Gaius has been seen to be mad, Nero was just bad. In recent years, however, there have been attempts to re-evaluate Nero's reign. We can make some attempt to understand why Nero went so completely wrong that, in the end, aided by only a few of his closest and lowest status associates, with the guards closing in, he completed a clumsy and rushed suicide. As with Gaius, there are times when our sources have a certain novelistic quality (see p. 57) and Nero the myth seems to overwhelm any historical veracity. Yet, when we gain some insight into the available source material, as with the Pisonian conspiracy (see pp. 133–5), it seems plentiful and trustworthy and it is highly likely that there was a considerable body of evidence available to our main sources. In the end, there seems little reason to dismiss the various and manifest immoralities of the reign or believe that Nero's reputation has merely fallen victim to the hostility of his successors. His was an extraordinary reign in which extraordinary things happened. We need not accept all that is in the literary tradition, but much appears to rest on reasonable evidence.

ACCESSION AND EARLY YEARS

Agrippina had planned Nero's accession with care, and it seems likely that it was the mere possibility that Nero might have a rival that brought a sudden end to Claudius' life. Nero and Agrippina had brought new lustre to Claudius' regime. Their presence re-emphasised the relationship of the family to Augustus (since Agrippina, unlike Claudius, was a direct descendant) and also further associated the regime with the ever-popular Germanicus (see pp. 96–8). Britannicus was confined to the background, yet it was to be expected that he would be joint heir with his adopted brother, who was also his brother-in-law. With Agrippina wielding power within the imperial household, Britannicus' position would always be tenuous. With Claudius dead, it must have been expected that Britannicus would soon follow. Although there can have been little doubt that Nero would become emperor, his position does not seem to have been as clearly superior to that of Britannicus as in these other cases of possible contested claims to the throne (see pp. 27, 65): the differences of age, experience and popularity were not so marked. Nero's rival was a more realistic threat and when Nero left the imperial palace to the acclaim of the praetorian prefect, there was (according to the hostile and possibly inventive Tacitus (*Ann.* XII 69)) a moment of hesitation, an implicit or even explicit request for Britannicus, before Nero was acclaimed alone.

Burrus, the sole praetorian prefect and the appointee of Agrippina, had secured the support of the praetorians. The support of the senate was obtained and maintained at least in part through speeches prepared by Seneca (apparently) but delivered by Nero (Dio, LXI 3; Tac., *Ann.* XIII 3). Much of the success of Nero's early years is attributed to Seneca and Burrus and their loss of influence is seen as leading directly to the degeneration of Nero's regime. This is consistent with ancient standards of historiography and biog-raphy which tended to perceive character as fixed and perceptible changes due to a loss or acceptance of discipline which restrained immoral tendencies. Thus, Nero's early success could not be a feature of Nero's own character, but rather was a feature of the competent management of Nero by those around him (Tac., *Ann* XIII 2). Also, although Dio is clearly hostile towards Seneca (Dio, LXI 10) and Tacitus seems quietly to enjoy elements of the philosopher's corruption, there may have been a largely lost historical tradition that lauded Seneca and saw him as a philosophical martyr to Nero's tyranny, glorifying the years of his influence as if they represented rule by a philosopher-king. Thus, Nero is written out of the political history of the early years of his reign: a few acts of notable brutality excepted.

Yet, the emergence of Seneca and Burrus as leading figures is in itself something of a surprise and suggests that Nero may have taken a keen interest in political developments right from the beginning of his reign. Agrippina had prepared the way for Nero and had been largely responsible for his elevation, and there is little doubt that both Burrus and Seneca owed their prominence to her, but, in spite of initial votes of honours, her appearance on coins alongside her son, and the prominence of the slogan 'best of mothers' (Tac., *Ann.* XIII 2; Suet., *Nero* 9; Dio, LXI 3), Agrippina quickly lost influence. As early as AD 54, when an Armenian delegation was being presented before the emperor, Agrippina was prevented from joining the emperor on the tribunal (would she have done so in the reign of Claudius?) by Nero's sudden descent (Dio, LXI 3.3; Tac., *Ann.* XIII 5). In 55, her favourite at court and alleged lover, Pallas, was forced into retirement and her bodyguard was withdrawn (Tac., *Ann.* XIII 14; Dio, LXI 8.6; Suet., *Nero* 34.1–4). In terms of propaganda, Nero was happy to associate his reign with his mother and give her a remarkable prominence, but in our historical accounts she is firmly prevented from assuming the position of co-ruler.

Nero played a sophisticated political game in his first years. He owed his position to his mother and Claudius and he officially honoured both. Claudius was deified, much to the amusement of all concerned. Seneca, so closely connected to the court, produced a satirical version, the *Apocolocyntosis* (Pumkinification), in which Claudius is not only refused divinity on the motion of Augustus, significantly enough, but also chastised for his crimes and his elevation of freedmen. Nero's speech at Claudius' funeral, allegedly written by the same Seneca, caused laughter in the senate according to Tacitus (*Ann.* XIII 2–3), hardly a suitably reverent attitude on the occasion of the elevation of one so recently departed to the status of divinity. The cultural sophistication of Nero's court was already evident. Nero and his court were capable of playing to two audiences: the traditional audience and another more sophisticated audience ready to see and appreciate the subversive elements of Neronian culture. Even when raising Claudius to the skies, Nero and his court demonstrated their contempt. This may have had a certain appeal to an audience of senators who had become so skilled in dissimulation under various tyrannical rulers that it had welcomed each new horror with praise of the emperor. Such obvious hypocrisy allowed Nero to distance himself from the previous regime while honouring its actions, especially, of course, his own elevation.

In spite of this act of deification, Nero invoked the example of Augustus rather than Claudius as his ideal: it was Augustus' memory he recalled in his first speech in the senate, as it is Augustus who deprives Claudius of his divinity, and Nero's triumphal entry into Rome after his victories in Greece was in Augustus' chariot (Suet., *Nero* 10, 25). His building was on a scale unmatched by any of his predecessors except Augustus. His 'victory' over Parthia was somewhat reminiscent of Augustus' similar victory and the closing of the temple of Janus following the celebration of that victory may have been intended to recall Augustus' similar actions (Suet., *Nero* 13). Nero was the great-great-grandson of Augustus through Agrippina and the great-grandson of Augustus' sister Octavia through his father Cn. Domitius Ahenobarbus. This association with Augustus gave him a claim on the throne separate to his adoption by Claudius, somewhat distancing Nero from his Claudian inheritance and also increasing his status in relation to Britannicus. The association with Augustus may have suited Nero in other ways in that his seizure of the throne at just seventeen could be paralleled by Augustus' acceptance of Caesar's legacy aged nineteen. If the divine Augustus could do it, why should Nero be excluded from power on the basis of his age?

Agrippina was, therefore, central to his dynastic claim. He needed Agrippina to give his regime an air of legitimacy. Yet, he also had an audience in the senate, an audience which may not have taken kindly to the predominance of a woman, even one as exalted as Agrippina. Nero's distancing of himself from Agrippina and the obvious signs that she would be subordinate to him were probably popular with the senate, and we may perhaps presume that Nero himself was interested in exercising his power unrestricted by his mother's control.

With Seneca to advise him, Nero appears to have tried to win over the senate in his first years. He allowed them considerable freedom and they responded with a bout of legislation, mainly concerning administrative matters (Tac., *Ann.* XIII 5). He rejected a proposal from the senate to amend the calendar so that the year would start on 1 December, Nero's birthday (Tac., *Ann.* XIII 10). He also prevented the outbreak of the factional disturbances that had so marred earlier reigns. Those who had been enemies of Agrippina were probably pleased at her apparent loss of influence and delighted at the withdrawal of Pallas, her freedman-supporter. Nero's accession saw only one notable victim, Narcissus, a freedman whose fall would have caused few senators to weep (Dio, LX 34.4; Tac., *Ann.* XIII 1). M. Junius Silanus was allegedly poisoned by Agrippina, always a charge that raises suspicions (Dio, LXI 6.4–5; Tac., *Ann.* XIII 1). Silanus was a great-great-grandson of Augustus, through the maternal line and his brother had been betrothed to Octavia until he was forced to make way for Nero. Others of his family survived until the later, bloodier years of Nero's reign and his death is somewhat out of keeping with the first days of Nero's regime. More significantly perhaps, Plautius Lateranus, a supposed lover of Messalina, returned from exile and a prosecution aimed at two friends of Britannicus was stopped (Tac., *Ann.* XIII 10–11). Nero did not allow tensions past or present within the imperial family to spill over into feuding in the senate. He even showed deference to his fellow consul who was not to be obliged to swear an oath by Nero's *acta* (deeds). It was a quiet and cautious start, designed to secure his position.

In 55, Nero poisoned Britannicus. His killing was unsubtle, poisoned at the emperor's own dinner table. The immediate motive for this action is rather implausibly given as threats from Agrippina to elevate Britannicus in Nero's place (how long would she herself have survived such a coup?). An account of Britannicus winning sympathy after being bullied into a recitation by Nero, and managing to recite creditably a piece which recalled the loss of his patrimony seems to provide a more likely cause for his removal, since it showed that Britannicus was capable of securing sympathy and was sufficiently mature to make a public impression (Suet., *Nero* 33.2; Tac., *Ann.* XIII 14–17; Dio, LXI 7.4). The killing did not bring about any change in policy. Nero maintained reasonable relations with the senate. Although signifying Nero's brutality, few will have been shocked by Britannicus' death.

Nero continued to suppress factional disputes and there may

have been attempts to strike at the heart of the imperial court. Tacitus records accusations against Agrippina, a Rubellius Plautus, Faustus Cornelius Sulla Felix and Burrus (Tac., *Ann.* XIII 19–23) and Dio records an accusation against Seneca (Dio, LXI 10.1). None of these cases came to anything. Nero maintained his court and together they avoided conflict with each other and the senate. It was not until 61 or perhaps 62 that Nero came into conflict with elements of the senatorial aristocracy, but by then Nero's policy had changed and the court of his first years had disintegrated.

THE END OF THE BEGINNING

Although Nero continued to allow the senate notable freedom, which led to some political activity reminiscent of the Republican period (a dispute between a tribune and a praetor which resulted in the senate – not the emperor – intervening and rebuking the tribune and a quarrel between various members of the senate and Helvidius Priscus – of whom we shall hear more – over Priscus' zealous administration of the treasury (Tac., *Ann.* XIII 28)), there were signs that Nero was bored with his role and was looking for new outlets for his energy. The story of Julius Montanus illustrates Nero's own behaviour. Nero had taken to wandering the streets in disguise accompanied by a band of his friends. This gang visited taverns and brothels and got involved in fights – an investigation of the seamier side of Rome that many young Roman aristocratic males had indulged in since the Late Republic. On one of these outings, the gang met Julius Montanus, his wife, and (one presumes) a group of his slaves or friends. Montanus' wife was insulted and Montanus reacted by attacking the gang. Nero himself was beaten up and apparently had to stay out of sight for several days because of his bruises. Nero would have let the incident pass (indeed, what else could he have done, for to let everyone know that he had been roaming the streets and had assaulted a senator's wife would not bring him credit, and to admit that his gang had been beaten up by the said senator and his followers would also bring dishonour), but Montanus wrote a note apologising. Nero could not then pretend that he had not been involved nor maintain the illusion that his disguise had fooled Montanus. By admitting knowledge of what he had done, Montanus changed his offence from having embarrassed his emperor, to having committed treason by knowingly assaulting him. Nero replied, 'So he knew he was hitting Nero'. Montanus' second mistake was made clear and he killed himself (Dio, LXI 9.4; Tac., *Ann.* XIII 25).

Nero's interest in games was also becoming clearer with a new amphitheatre on the Campus Martius in 57 (Tac. *Ann.* XIII 31), though it was not until 59 that Nero seems to have become more interested in exploiting the opportunities that games and theatrical performances gave for self-publicity in more innovative ways.

Nevertheless, the senate continued to gain confidence. C. Cassius Longinus amended a proposal concerning the celebrations for Nero's early successes in Armenia by noting that there was a danger that no work would be done in Rome if the number of holidays continued to increase (Tac., *Ann.* XIII 41). This same Cassius was sent as a senatorial representative to sort out feuding in the Campanian town of Puteoli, though his mission was unsuccessful and, on his request, two brothers, P. Sulpicius Scribonianus Proculus and P. Sulpicius Scribonianus Rufus (see p. 136 for the later career of these brothers) were sent out to replace him (Tac., *Ann.* XIII 48). Thrasea Paetus attacked the over-indulgence of Syracuse in applying to stage more sets of games than were currently allowed, a speech which many must have seen as reflecting on Nero's taste for such events and his love of all things Greek (Tac., *Ann.* XIII 49). The senate appears to have conducted trials free from overt political interference from the emperor, who even allowed some trials to be taken out of his jurisdiction. Pomponia Graecina, wife of Aulus Plautius, the conqueror of Britain, was accused of foreign superstitions. Since Plautius was very prominent and Graecina had made much of her connections to the imperial family, this could be seen as a political trial, but Nero allowed the trial to take place in a family court, according to ancient custom (Tac., *Ann.* XIII 32). Corruption trials took place with varying results and among these trials a certain Cossutianus Capito (who became prominent later) was condemned for corruption and exiled (Tac., *Ann.* XIII 33).

Storm clouds were, however, already gathering. P. Suillius Rufus, who had been a close associate of Messalina's, was tried in 58 on an old charge of accepting payments for his advocacy (see p. 93), which was regarded as a form of corruption (Tac., *Ann.* XIII 42). He responded with an attack on Seneca's corruption, delivered in Tacitus' account in stinging terms. Since Suillius was regarded as one of the best orators of the period, it is likely that the impact and the sentiments are probably authentic reflections of the speech, though the invective and style are Tacitean in our version. Suillius and Cossutianus Capito had come under attack during the reign of Claudius and were probably both associates of Messalina (Tac., *Ann.* XI 6). Old enmities were re-emerging.

Tacitus also dates the first appearance of Poppaea Sabina to this year (Tac., *Ann.* XIII 44–5; Dio, LXI 11.2). Poppaea was well connected within the imperial aristocracy. Her father had been a friend of Sejanus and her grandfather one of Tiberius' prominent generals (Tac., *Ann* I 80, IV, 46–50, V 10, VI 39). Having married an equestrian, she rose through an illicit relationship with Otho, the future emperor and one of Nero's close early associates. Otho married Poppaea and this brought her into the imperial court where she met and became involved with Nero. Otho suddenly became inconvenient and was packed off to Lusitania which he governed with some skill. Nero, however, was faced with a problem. He was married to Octavia and, since he had murdered her brother, the relationship between the two was probably not close. Yet, there would be a political price to pay for her removal. It seems possible, as our sources suggest, that this was opposed by Agrippina and Burrus, but this is one of the places in the tradition that invention must be suspected since our sources' knowledge of this politically sensitive and intimate family business seems too good to be true. For the moment, the relationship with Poppaea remained illicit, though almost certainly public.

Agrippina may have seen the new lover as a further threat to her position and she seems to have made an increased effort to exert influence over her son. It is in this period that accusations of incest are levelled against the pair. Tacitus doubts whether their relationship was incestuous, quoting two sources on the issue, though he notes that Agrippina's previous behaviour would not encourage one to believe anything but the worst about her sexual habits. Dio also questions the tradition, but tells us that Nero kept a mistress who looked like Agrippina (Dio, LXI 11.3; Suet., *Nero* 28.2; Tac. *Ann.* XIV 2).

In 59, Nero decided to murder his mother. We know too little about Nero's psychological state to explain adequately the motivation for such a momentous act (which surely demands a psychological rather than a political explanation). It was a crisis, perhaps a turning point for the regime. One can only speculate that Nero was finding his mother an embarrassment: he could not restrain her political activities, nor fend off her interference and perhaps he feared her disapproval of his relationships. Her exile would require a trial, create a powerful enemy and would look like the actions of an ungrateful son. Nero probably decided that he had to remove her covertly. She was well protected against poison, so traditional means were ruled out. The method chosen was extraordinarily and typically theatrical. Nero had seen a boat built to collapse in the theatre. His admiral, Anicetus, volunteered to build one in order to facilitate Agrippina's accident: a method which one would have thought guaranteed that news of the crime would leak. After dinner with Nero, Agrippina was escorted in this ship towards her villa across the bay of Naples from where Nero was staying. The boat duly collapsed. Agrippina survived and returned to her villa after being picked up by a fishing boat. Now aware of the conspiracy, she had little choice but to ignore it and wrote to her son saying that she had survived an unfortunate accident and although not seriously injured, would prefer to rest without a visit from the emperor. On hearing that the conspiracy had failed, Nero panicked and summoned Burrus and Seneca. They were informed of the failed assassination plot. There was silence. Seneca asked Burrus whether the praetorians would act against Agrippina. He informed Nero that they would not. Anicetus volunteered his disgraced sailors: his life was now in danger. Nero accepted. A dagger was planted on Agrippina's messenger. A party was sent to kill Agrippina. So runs the extraordinary account of our sources (Dio, LXI 13; Suet., *Nero*, 34; Tac. *Ann.* XIV 3–10).

These were dramatic moments, vividly portrayed by Tacitus. Yet, we must wonder at his sources. The meeting with Seneca and Burrus must have been one of the most secret meetings of the Principate, yet Tacitus seems to know exactly what went on and claims that confusion only arose in his sources when Nero came to view his mother's body, a moment which must have offered ample scope to historians with a taste for dramatic embellishment. Tacitus had good sources for the reign of Nero: accounts of earlier historians and probably some memoirs (as well as the official accounts), and much of the life of the emperor was conducted in semi-public, surrounded by a retinue of slaves, freedmen and hangers-on, but who would know what went on in this meeting and would live to tell of it? Many historians, however, might have been prepared to guess at discussions behind the closed doors of Nero's residence and it is possible that this was carried over into Tacitus' account. Although we may accept the broad outlines of the story (the collapsible boat is so ridiculous that it must be true), our interpretation of these events must be cautious, suspicious of the detail contained in the narrative sources.

On the discovery of Nero's plot, the court contemplated stark alternatives. They must connive in the crime of matricide, a crime which naturally horrified, or turn against Nero. Reconciliation seemed unlikely (though was probably Agrippina's only hope). Agrippina was the daughter of Germanicus and was popular with the soldiers. Even if Burrus is not reported correctly, his summary of the likely attitude of the praetorians may have been accurate. They could not be ordered to kill Agrippina. Nevertheless, she had to be killed since she could be a direct threat to Nero, and an experienced political manipulator such as Agrippina could gain both military and political backing. Even if Agrippina could be controlled, the obvious divisions at the heart of the imperial family might seriously weaken its political position and expose Nero to other threats from the Roman aristocracy. With Agrippina dead, there would be more chance of gaining acquiescence in a crime that could not be altered.

Having killed her, Nero wrote to the senate to inform them of the conspiracy against him and met the officers of the praetorians. Both the praetorians and senate acclaimed Nero's 'victory'. Thrasea Paetus walked out of the senate in disgust. Tacitus says that he was 'thus endangering himself without bringing freedom any nearer' (Tac. *Ann.* XIV 10–12) but his judgement is harsh. This was a crucial moment: if a leader emerged in the senate, there would have been a possibility that the praetorians would not defend Nero. Thrasea may have felt that the senate should have taken this extremely dangerous path since the crime itself left no doubt as to the character of Nero. As Thrasea is claimed to have intimated later, with such a brutal leader, death was inevitable anyhow (Dio, LXI 15.3).

Nero entered Rome triumphantly. He had emerged from the crisis with his political position transformed. He made many enemies but, oddly, his power must have looked greater. He had shown that he could commit the greatest of crimes and remain in power, though he can have had little doubt about the senate's real attitude. Nero made some attempt to regain senatorial support by recalling enemies of his mother who had been in exile, but his relationship with the senate was changing. In 60, he invited Rubellius Plautus to retire because of gossip about him as a possible rival to the emperor (Tac., *Ann.* XIV 22). In 61, a scandal involving a forged will led to the exile of three senators; political motivations may be suspected (Tac., *Ann.* XIV 40). Neither were momentous events, though the exile of Plautus suggests an undercurrent of uncertainty and dissatisfaction among the Roman aristocracy.

The crisis may have seriously weakened the existing powers at court (both Seneca and Burrus were originally Agrippina's men), but the end of the old court was delayed until 62. Burrus died of throat cancer, though inevitably there were accusations that his death was assisted (Dio, LXII 13.3; Tac., *Ann.* XIV 51–2). Seneca requested permission to retire and give up his fortune, which was refused, but if this was a bid to restore his power by demonstrating his loyalty to the regime, it failed. Seneca effectively retired with a convenient illness (Tac., *Ann.* XIV 53–6). Most significantly, Nero decided finally to rid himself of Octavia. Octavia was divorced, convicted of infertility, but Nero found he could not put her aside so easily. Crowds demonstrated on her behalf and attacked images of her successor Poppaea. So Nero looked for a more serious charge. Her slaves were tortured in order to extract a confession of adultery. This failed. Nero then turned to Anicetus who had been kept at arm's length from the court since Agrippina's death, either because of the unpleasant associations or the bungled boat trip. He was persuaded to confess and then exiled to Sardinia, probably a comfortable retirement considering the alternatives. Octavia was sent to Pandateria, the prison island, and then executed (Tac., *Ann.* XIV 59–64).

There were other deaths in this year. Antistius Sosianus was charged with reciting slanderous verses about Nero at a dinner party by Cossutianus Capito, now returned from exile. Thrasea Paetus managed to persuade the senate to spare his life, much to Nero's displeasure (Tac., *Ann.* XIV 48–9). Faustus Cornelius Sulla Felix (who had been exiled for conspiracy in 58) and Rubellius Plautus were both killed (Tac., *Ann.* XIV 57–9). Domitia Lepida, Nero's aunt, also died and our sources attribute her passing to the orders of Nero (Dio, LXI 17.1). The freedmen Pallas and Doryphoros were killed (Tac., *Ann.* XIV 65). There may have been a mysterious allegation against Seneca and L. Calpurnius Piso (Tac., *Ann.* XIV 65). Aulus Didius Gallus Fabricius Veiento suffered condemnation for a literary attack on Nero and his works were destroyed (Tac., *Ann.* XIV 50).

This blood-letting demonstrates a change in atmosphere. The old alliance of Burrus and Seneca may have failed to deliver the support of the senate or Nero may have changed policy. Burrus was replaced as praetorian prefect by Faenius Rufus (a popular appointment according to our sources since he had supervised the grain supply with some skill) and Ofonius Tigellinus (Tac., *Ann.* XIV 51). Tigellinus' son-in-law was Cossutianus Capito. Together, these two would conduct Nero's political trials. Both had been exiled by the senate previously and had many enemies. Their prominence gave many just cause to fear. Octavia was replaced by Poppaea Sabina. Nero surrounded himself with a host of others, many (though not all) of relatively low status: freedmen and actors. The court no longer tried to reconcile itself with the senate, but instead searched for new ways of displaying its power and representing the greatness of its central figure. Nero began to make more direct use of his power, a power which had been made clear by the death of Agrippina. Increasingly, they broke with established precedents and transgressed moral and political laws. In so doing, they established the notorious atmosphere of artistic endeavour and moral laxity that characterised Nero's reign.

BREAKING RULES: THE EMPEROR AS ARTIST

By 59, Nero was looking to take a more active part in the artistic life of the empire. He had already built an amphitheatre on the Campus Martius (Tac., *Ann.* XIII 31), but this represented only an indirect involvement. He had an enclosed arena constructed in which he could drive chariots hidden from public view (Tac., *Ann.* XIV 14). This 'private' desire to drive chariots was mirrored by a first 'private' stage appearance at the Juvenalia. This festival of youth encouraged the participation of many among the nobility, including (apparently) a woman of eighty. Some who hid their identities behind masks were forcibly exposed to the crowd, though the festival, held in Nero's gardens, was technically private. Nero also became more interested in philosophy and began to take an interest in poetry (Tac., *Ann.* XIV 14–16, XV 33; Dio, LXI 19).

In 60, Nero introduced the Neronia, which was a festival that imitated the major Greek events in both regularity and in types of competition (Dio, LXI 21; Tac. *Ann.* XIV 20–21, 47; Suet., *Nero* 12.3–4.). Nero himself probably gave no public dramatic performances until 64 when he took to the stage in Naples (Suet., *Nero* 20; Tac., *Ann.* XV 33). Naples was a significant choice since it prided itself on its Greek origins and thriving Greek culture. Nero tested the ground for his appearance on the public stage in Rome, which took place in the following year (Tac., *Ann.* XVI 4–5; Suet., *Nero* 21). We cannot detail Nero's subsequent appearances on stage, though he probably entertained Tigranes in 66 to a display of his singing and chariot-driving (Dio, LXIII 3–6) before he crossed to

Greece. In Greece, he progressed in triumph, winning every prize, even though he fell from his chariot in one race. He completed his trip by freeing Greece from Roman sovereignty and granting Roman citizenship to the judges who had so generously awarded him first place. His return was in triumph. He entered Naples first, the scene of his debut and then marched to Rome, the conquering artistic hero (Dio, LXIII 8.2–10.2, 14, 20; Suet., *Nero* 22–5).

Generally, our sources suggest that stage appearances were demeaning, but even Thrasea Paetus, in some ways a paragon of conservative morality, had himself made a stage appearance in his hometown of Patavium, though perhaps in a semi-private event (Dio, LXII 26.3; Tac., *Ann.* XVI 21). Clearly, this brief stage career was not sufficient to reduce his status in the eyes of Roman traditionalists. It seems unlikely that there was any objection to acting in itself, but it was probably thought contrary to the dignity of a true Roman (many actors were of low social status) to appear on the public stage and to pander to the pleasures of the masses, and that it was unsuitable for the ruler of the world one moment to decide on peace or war and the next to 'give birth' on stage.

Many observers appear to have been confused by the exhibition. Tiridates, for instance, appears not to have understood why the Romans would follow such a man (Dio, LXIII 6.4). One soldier, observing his emperor in chains on stage, rushed to release him (Dio, LXIII 10.2). Such stories demonstrate a failure of normal dramatic convention. Even when acting, Nero remained Nero. In case any failed to notice, Nero was at least sometimes accompanied on stage by the praetorian prefects and in particular roles was bound by golden chains rather than by the normal iron (Suet., *Nero* 21; Dio, LXIII 9.4). The crowds observed their emperor, not the play.

Actors were often very popular and wielded considerable influence. Their position allowed them to turn the lines of a play into political commentary and crowds would cheer a line appropriate to the political circumstances of the day irrespective of the context of the play. For Nero, to perform was to appear before his people. He had his own claque: an organised group of supporters who would clap in a certain rhythmical way in support of the emperor. The praetorians insisted on a rapturous response to Nero's performances. We can also understand his need to involve others of the Roman elite in such shows. By performing alongside Nero, there was no question that they could stand aloof from the display and pretend that it was beneath their dignity to take part. By enforcing participation, Nero could show his artistic superiority, his dominance over the aristocracy politically, artistically and culturally. He displayed this dominance before the largest gatherings of the people of Rome that took place in this period (there were effectively no elections) and their cheers (enforced or voluntary) reinforced this display of power.

His performance of poetry can be considered in the same political light. Tacitus suggests that his verse was weak, not in its metrical correctness, but in direction and thought, since the verse was composed by committee and revised by the prominent poets at Nero's court, and so lost all originality (Tac., *Ann.* XIV 16). Suetonius (*Nero* 52), who refers to Nero's notebooks, suggests that Nero composed and amended the verse himself, though Suetonius' description of the notebooks does not rule out the possibility that the court was responsible for substantial improvements. Nero worked hard at his verse and, although Tacitus pours scorn on the finished product, the criticisms suggest that it was at least of a respectable standard. Dio (LXII 29.1–2) tells us that Nero was composing a historical epic which would cover the whole history of Rome. In some ways, however, what mattered was not content, but the way in which the emperor presented himself. Nero asserted status through verse and there can be little doubt that the 'reviews' will have suggested his superiority over all his poetic rivals. Nero's success at the centre of a court circle of poets asserted his status as a patron and leader of the arts, a cultured man, and one who demanded respect because of his cultural excellence.

Nero's other great contribution was in the field of architecture. In 64, a fire swept through much of Rome. Only four of the fourteen districts survived more or less intact, while seven were badly damaged and three destroyed. Nero made the most of this opportunity and, indeed, was so enthusiastic about the task of rebuilding Rome that it was rumoured (almost certainly falsely) that he had been responsible for the firing of the city.[1] Nero introduced a series of building regulations. The height of buildings was restricted and the partitions between buildings were regulated to stop fire passing so easily and quickly from building to building. The street plan may have been reorganised to produce wider streets and fewer alleys, which would also discourage the spread of fire and aid fire-fighting (Suet., *Nero* 16.1; Tac., *Ann.* XV 38–43).

The most notable monument was, however, the Domus Aurea, the Golden House of Nero. This was a huge construction that bridged the Palatine and Esquiline Hills. The vestibule was of sufficient size to accommodate a 120-foot-high statue of Nero. The palace was fronted by a triple colonnade stretching for a mile. Extensive gardens were attached to the house, including vineyards, woods and pastures, all stocked with appropriate animals and, around a pool, there were models of buildings. There were rooms of immense luxury: a dining room with an ivory ceiling, another that revolved. His baths were filled with sea water and sulphur water. It was a dominating monument: the conspicuous luxury demonstrated his wealth, the building itself monumentalised his domination of the city of Rome, the gardens brought nature, Italy or the country-side within his palace. Here was a representation of the world within a city, and it was all overseen by the towering presence of Nero (Suet., *Nero* 31; Tac., *Ann.* XV 42–3). It is clear from ancient accounts that the palace was filled with crowds of people visiting the emperor or his advisors, and these would have experienced Nero's glorious representation of the world. Nero's house was a public expression of his power.

Nero's final area of artistic genius was rather less conventional. He and his court threw huge parties. The most notorious was a party given by Tigellinus. The gathering took place in the centre of a theatre, turned into an artificial lake. It is the kind of incident that Dio loves to relate. The waters of the lake became a giant wine-cooler and around the edges of the lake were created taverns and booths at which wine flowed freely. In the centre, the lords of misrule Tigellinus and Nero sat watching the unfolding anarchy. The taverns and booths were occupied by women of all statuses, chosen for their beauty. The result was a drunken orgy of rape. Prostitutes and respectable women were involved. Fathers were forced to watch the rape of their daughters. Slaves raped their mistresses. Some of both sexes were killed in the rioting (Dio, LXII 15). Dio's account is sensationalist, while Tacitus (*Ann.* XV 37) provides a more restrained version. Celebrations at the Juvenalia, described by Tacitus (*Ann.* XIV 15) and Suetonius (*Nero* 27), were also orgiastic.

Nero's sexual habits broke rules of conventional behaviour. The details of his relationship with his mother must remain obscure (see p. 108). Nero's acquisition of Poppaea was morally questionable, yet there is no reason to believe that Sabina was displeased by the turn of events. A more serious breach of traditional morals were his two homosexual 'marriages' (both post-dating the death of Sabina), with Pythagoras and Sporus, the latter castrated for this purpose. The open and semi-official nature of these relationships causes more interest than the fact of the relationships themselves. Some Roman men no doubt found male sexual partners, in spite of traditional reservations about homosexuality, but to 'take the female part', as Nero did with Pythagoras, and to do so openly was to break with traditional Roman and Greek conceptions of manhood. Other stories of Nero's sexual activities are wilder. Stories of sadistic attacks on victims while he was wearing animal skins are difficult to verify. All these stories suggested to traditional Roman writers that Nero was out of control. He was enslaved by his passions and incapable of ruling himself or the empire. Such stories justified eventual rebellion (Suet., *Nero* 28–9; 35.4; Dio, LXII 28.2–3; LXIII 13.)

The tradition is so hostile that it is difficult to ascertain any coherent logic or policy behind Nero's artistic adventures. Yet, Nero's court was a place of sophistication and wit as well as debauchery. It sponsored a resurgence in the arts. The writer Petronius (Tac., *Ann.* XVI 17–21) was, for a short time, near the centre of the court until he became another victim of the Pisonian conspiracy (see pp. 133–5). The sophistication of his *Satyricon*, in which a luxurious dinner party is satirised and the artistic and sexual endeavours of his anti-heroes subverted, suggests that Nero's reign was not just about conspicuous consumption, but concerned a demonstration of taste. It is arguable that Nero sought to break away from the achievements of his predecessors to establish his power on a new and revolutionary basis. He would not rule as army commander or as one of the senate or as a god among men, but as a cultural giant.

Nero's urge to experiment with new ways of presenting his power and to subvert traditional morals inevitably led him to the theatre. By looking to popular acclaim, he broke away from the traditional sources of political power in Roman society, the aristocracy and the army, and his subversion of the morals of the aristocracy by forcing them to participate in his cultural events, parties or games, implicated them in a 'cultural revolution'. Nero's artistic revolution created a new form of tyranny and Nero sought to establish the equivalence of that tyranny with past achievements. His triumph in Greece must be understood in this light. There are notable similarities between Nero's triumphal progression and those of the second-century BC Romans who had conquered the region. Nero's cultural dominance was to be seen as an equivalent success which justified his triumphal entry into Rome.

Nero's domination of culture was, however, a dangerous policy. Some responded in kind with ironic attacks on the regime. Thus, Petronius, informed of his death-sentence, responded with a letter detailing and satirising Nero's sexual acts, a letter which apparently drove Nero into a fury. More popular acts of rebellion came at the theatre. Nero's audience was coerced into reaction through the troops, but audiences could subvert by inappropriate laughter or tears. Others simply escaped, leaping from the walls of the theatre or feigning death. More seriously, he might enforce the participation of some of the aristocracy, but others would remain unconverted. Standing in the theatre, receiving the applause of the crowd and backed by the praetorian guard, the opposition of Thrasea Paetus and other killjoys among the aristocracy might not seem serious, but it was this offended aristocracy that was to bring him down. After Nero, coincidentally or otherwise, tastes became much more conservative. Nero failed as a politician and the refined and disciplined behaviour of senators, as reflected in the post-Domitianic literature of Pliny and Tacitus, suggests that he failed as an artistic revolutionary.

ADMINISTRATION, GOVERNMENT AND FOREIGN AFFAIRS

Nero's reign eventually collapsed into an anarchy that resulted in part from his administrative failings. It is appropriate to consider his policy at home and abroad separately, though, as we shall see, the two areas were interrelated.

Home affairs

As with several other regimes, Nero started by promising to break with the past, to behave as a good emperor should and refer matters to open debate in the senate. The particular targets of senatorial ire from the Claudian regime were Claudius' freedmen. To a certain extent, Nero did break with 'freedmen government' and with the administrative policies of his predecessors. Kallistos, Gaius' influential freedman, had died during the reign of Claudius. Narcissus and Pallas, two of the more prominent of Claudius' freedmen, were both removed from power very quickly (see pp. 103–5). Yet, administrative structures were unaltered. The same offices continued to be filled by freedmen and, although these men were initially less prominent, they were probably influential behind the scenes. Nero was generous towards certain of his freedmen: Doryphoros received extravagant gifts (Dio, LXI 5.4–5) and Pythagoras also became prominent, though it is unclear whether his talents were purely sexual. When Nero went on his grand tour of Greece, he left his freedman Helios in effective control (Dio, LXIII 12.1). By this time, however, he had lost confidence in the senate and there were few outside his immediate circle that he could trust. As with Claudius, it is impossible to reconstruct the inner workings of government to ascertain who was making the decisions, yet, although these freedmen were clearly important, it is only with Helios that they seem as prominent as in the reign of Claudius and our sources do not suggest that Nero was dominated by his freedmen. The change in personnel between reigns may have seen a reduction in the independent power of freedmen, though their purely administrative functions remained unchanged.

Nero was, in fact, rather concerned with social status and adopted a conservative policy in this regard. He chose to restrict social mobility by attacking the privileges and wealth of freedmen and their descendants. Sons of freedmen were prevented from joining the senate and those already in the senate saw their careers blocked by a ban on them holding office, a measure which can be interpreted as increasing the dignity of the senate and magistrates (Suet., *Nero* 15.2). Nero also picked on the freedmen when he grew short of money, claiming five-sixths of their estates on death (Suet., *Nero* 32). They were probably a soft target, since the Roman elite would not be affected by the measures and many might even have approved of such severity. Social status was also reinforced in privileges granted to equestrians. The *equites* were to enjoy reserved seating at the circus as well as the theatre (Tac., *Ann.* XV 32). Thus, in both arenas, the Romans would sit in their status groups, reinforcing the boundaries between the different orders.

The most violent example of this concern with social order came with the case of L. Pedanius Secundus. In 57, the senate had passed a law which decreed that if a master was killed by his slaves, those freed by his will who were within the household were to be killed (Tac., *Ann.* XIII 32). This reinforced the law which laid down that all the slaves within the household of a master murdered by a slave were to be considered guilty and executed. This measure seems to reflect a general concern about the disciplining of the servile in this period that can also be seen in a proposal to limit the independence of freedmen, which had been rejected (after detailed consideration) the previous year (Tac., *Ann.* XIII 26–7). In 61, the former prefect of the city (a senior member of the senate), L. Pedanius Secundus, was murdered by his slaves. Secundus was notably brutal and maintained a very large household. There was considerable public and senatorial sympathy for those slaves not directly involved in the killing, but the senate resolved to apply the law and in this were supported by Nero's resolve. The plebs, however, had more sympathy for the slaves and rioted. Nero remained firm. Such a breach of the natural order as a slave killing a master must be punished and the praetorians were called out to enforce public order as the slaves were killed (Tac., *Ann.* XIV 42–5).

Such conservatism contrasts with Nero's seeming willingness to defy social conventions in other areas, but may also partly explain another notorious aspect of Nero's reign: his persecution of the Christians. The reasons for the persecution of the Christians are a matter of some scholarly controversy (see pp. 315–17), but it seems clear that Nero was encouraged to persecute them by the fire of Rome. Some see his actions as distracting attention from his own possible guilt, but perhaps suggestions that the Christians were political or religious subversives encouraged Nero to see them as being in some way responsible for the fire. His attacks on the community were savage and aroused sympathy even in those who were hostile to the Christians (Tac., *Ann.* XV 44).

Nero's administration of justice seems to have been quite careful. He frequently sat in court himself and Suetonius tells us that he took care not to come to an impetuous decision. He took advice (as was the custom among all judges) but, in order to avoid political influence and to encourage considered opinions, he insisted on advice being given secretly and in writing so that he could contemplate the case overnight before giving judgement in the morning. When dealing with a capital case, Nero seems to have signed the death warrants with a show of reluctance, a reluctance which at least suggests careful judgement (Suet., *Nero* 10, 15). Such care is shown in a case of senatorial corruption when Acilius Strabo was prosecuted in 59. Strabo had been presented with a complex legal problem concerning tenure of estates that had belonged to the king of Cyrene before the kingdom had passed to Rome. Strabo's investigation had found that the current holders of the land had no legal right to the land. Though illegally acquired, this land may have been in private hands for 150 years and the landowners took Strabo to court. Nero, to whom the senate passed the case, found in favour of Strabo but offered compensation to the landowners, a careful compromise (Tac., *Ann.* XIV 18).

Nero appears to have curbed the activities of informers. The system whereby informers were rewarded with a portion of the estate of their victim was justly unpopular since it encouraged malicious prosecutions. Nero did not remove the incentive altogether; he merely significantly reduced the portion of the estates that could be claimed by the informer (Suet., *Nero* 10).

Care was also taken in the collection of taxes. Helvidius Priscus first rose to prominence over his assiduous collection of taxes at the treasury, possibly a matter of some controversy since it was often the politically powerful who avoided taxes. Nero published regulations concerning the farming of taxes since the activities of tax farmers had been causing some complaint and he toyed with the idea of abolishing certain taxes altogether in order to end corrupt and unpopular exactions (Tac., *Ann.* XIII 31, 50–1).

Similar care was not exercised over expenditure. Nero was a prodigious spendthrift and appears to have run into substantial financial problems. In some cases, this is the result of ill-luck, in others of overly extravagant spending.

Nero resumed the policy of founding military colonies in Italy that had been discontinued after the early years of Augustus' reign. Military colonies were established at Capua and Nuceria (in 57) (Tac., *Ann.* XIII 31), Antium and Tarentum (in 60) (Tac. *Ann.* XIV 27). Puteoli (also in 60), Pompeii and Tegeanum also received the title of colony, though it is unclear whether any veterans were sent to these towns.[2] Antium was Nero's birthplace and thus marked out for particular honours. It was a favourite haunt of the imperial family. Pompeii was connected with Poppaea Sabina and its elevation marked an end to the disgrace it had suffered after rioting between its population and that of Nuceria in 59 (Tac., *Ann.* XIV 17). Such arrangements were probably expensive as land had to be found for those veterans, if any, who were settled in the colonies and probably civic facilities would have to be built or renovated. It seems unlikely that these colonies were created for economic reasons – to revitalise depopulated areas – and, in any case, Tacitus tells that the veteran colonisation failed since most of the veterans wandered back to the provinces in which they had served.[3]

Nero's personal generosity probably led to the depletion of the treasury. Suetonius (*Nero* 30) has fantastic stories of his gifts. A more serious blow to state finances was probably the extravagance and number of his games and shows. To encourage the actors, when staging a play in which a house burnt down, Nero allowed them to keep all the costly furnishings they rescued from the house. He also used such occasions to distribute largesse to the people by throwing precious objects into the audience (Suet., *Nero* 11–13). One guesses that the Neronia and the entertainments offered for the state visit of Tigranes were expensive, though the scale of the extravagance does not seem to match that of Gaius. The trip to Greece and the huge entourage which seems to have accompanied him must also have weakened the finances of the imperial household. Donatives (gifts of money) to the people and to the praetorians to ease the political crises in his reign also drained the treasury.

Nero's building plans were huge. The Domus Aurea was the highlight of an extensive programme that included amphitheatres and baths, a macellum (a food market), the Domus Transitoria (a precursor of the Domus Aurea burnt down in the fire), and a gymnasium.[4] The fire may have destroyed more than half of the city and Nero used the opportunity to widen streets and build porticoes. It is likely that many public buildings were damaged and, in addition to these longer-term costs, disaster relief must have drained the treasury (Dio, LXII 16–18; Tac., *Ann.* XV 38–41). Public response to Nero's rebuilding of the city was generally favourable, though the Domus Aurea seems to have been something of an exception. Nero's reconstruction of the city may also have been hampered by a plague that broke out in 65.

As ever, the exact state of imperial finances is rather difficult to establish, and the hostility towards Nero is such that any explicit statement by our sources has to be regarded suspiciously, but we have evidence which strongly suggests that Nero was in financial difficulties: the coins themselves. In AD 64–5, a time of financial strain due to expenditure following the fire of Rome, the coinage was reformed. Nero's artistically successful moneyers started getting 5–12 per cent more coins from a pound of gold bullion and 14 per cent more coins from a pound of silver. It seems that the income derived from imperial estates and taxation was insufficient to meet the demands of expenditure and the only way to meet the shortfall was to get more coins from those that came in. Nero also started to issue some low-value token coinage, again probably because he could not collect sufficient bullion to meet his needs. In the short term, such a reduction in metal content probably had only limited economic effects, but it would ease a shortfall in taxation. This fiscal crisis may have encouraged imperial agents to squeeze provincials for new revenue. Taxation was an issue in Judaea where the financial demands of the governor provided the spark that led to the revolt of AD 66–70, and may have substantially contributed to the destabilisation of Nero's regime in other provinces.

Foreign affairs

Provincial governors

The early years of the reign of Nero are marked by a number of corruption trials involving governors (see Table 5.1) and other officials about which, unfortunately, we know very little. Most are briefly recorded in Tacitus (*Ann.* XIII 30, 33, 52; XIV 18, 46).

Unlike the corruption cases under Tiberius, these cases are not seen as examples of factional strife within the senate by our sources. The seeming end to the sequence in Tacitus need not suggest that trials for corruption ceased. Tacitus' pages become filled with more dramatic matters as Nero's relationship with the senate worsened after 60. Such trials may suggest either widespread corruption or a willingness of the authorities to stamp out corruption.

Josephus' history of the administration of Nero's procurators (governors) of Judaea before the great revolt is not encouraging. Felix (brother of Pallas), Festus (who is praised for suppressing political bandits), Albinus (a personally corrupt governor who undid all Festus' work), and Gessius Florus (who made the people long for the return of Albinus) were either corrupt or incompetent. The governors made attempts to raise taxes and illegal charges increased the burden on the Jewish population. Social unrest seems to have been a prominent feature of the period, and in Judaea this

Table 5.1 Trials of governors in Tacitus

Date	Governor	Verdict
56	Sardinia	Condemned
	Achaea	Acquitted
57	Asia	Dies before case comes to trial
	Cilicia	Condemned
	Lycia	Acquitted
58	Africa ·	Acquitted
	Africa	Acquitted
59	Cyrene	Condemned
	Cyrene	Acquitted
60	Mauretania	Condemned

Note: We should probably add to this list Pollio and Laelianus, who served in Armenia (Dio, LXI 6.6).

was tied to religious divisions which led to a very violent situation. The governors proved not only unable to remedy the ultimate source of the rising tension, Roman maladministration, but also failed to take effective measures to secure the province (Jos. *BJ* II 249–408).

The weaknesses of provincial administration are also demonstrated by the Boudiccan revolt. The story of the revolt is detailed in *Annales* XIV 29–39 and by Dio, LXII 1–12. Dio and Tacitus differ in their accounts of the causes of the revolt, but both attribute the problems to financial and political maladministration culminating in a bungled attempt to reorganise the territory of the Iceni in East Anglia. The Iceni joined with another major tribe in the area, the Trinovantes, and, under the leadership of Boudicca, burnt Colchester, London and St Albans to the ground and defeated the Ninth Legion, before succumbing to an army headed by the Fourteenth and Twentieth Legions led by the governor Suetonius Paulinus. Problems faced by the commander of the Second Legion in the south-west suggest that the revolt was supported by tribes other than those mentioned in the literary account. The financial pressure placed on the British, either due to the rapacity of the procurator Catus Decianus or of Seneca (whose greed was a major factor in the revolt according to Dio), was probably the major cause of the revolt and it is likely that such pressures would be felt by all provincials and not just those in the east of Britain. Paulinus conducted a winter campaign against the rebels who had failed to harvest the summer crops, which resulted in great hardship and conflict between Paulinus and the new procurator Classicianus. Eventually, a pretext was found for the recall of Paulinus, who was granted the great honour of a second consulship in 66, and the war was brought to an end.

In spite of this evidence of corruption, Tacitus' account of the trial of Claudius Timarchus of Crete in 63 suggests that the relationship between governors and provincials may have been changing slightly (Tac., *Ann.* XV 20). Timarchus was tried because he was said to have claimed that he arranged the votes of thanks on the governor's term of office. Timarchus seems to have been claiming that he had such authority in the provincial assembly that governors who wished to be recognised and thanked for their administration of the province were dependent on his favour. Such votes would be communicated to the senate and emperor, and it is to be assumed that a governor who failed to win the endorsement of his subjects would find it difficult to secure another appointment.

Although the governor still wielded considerable power and had plenty of scope for corruption while in his province, the state of affairs is rather different from that of the Republic when a governor's power was only limited by the faint possibility that the provincials would be able to bring a successful corruption case against him once he had left office. The result of the Timarchus trial was that such votes of thanks were banned on the proposal of Thrasea Paetus, which was accepted by Nero: a boost, though possibly only temporary, for the powers of governors.

Towards the end of Nero's reign, there is evidence of some disruption in Egypt. Nero may have encouraged Greek groups within Egypt by granting additional privileges early in his reign, further encouraging the changes in Egyptian society brought about by the Roman conquest. Nero planned a visit to Egypt, perhaps to lead an expedition up the Nile against the Aithiopians. He had already sent two military officers to reconnoitre the area. The Prefect Caecina Tuscus was exiled for the crime of swimming in the baths that had been built for Nero's prospective visit (Dio, LXIII 18.1), but there must be a possibility that a more serious charge lay behind this. The tax records of an Egyptian village suggest that the last years of Nero's reign saw a sudden increase in tax avoidance, perhaps a sign of economic difficulties, though such evidence must be treated with caution since it might reflect administrative rather than economic problems. An edict of Tiberius Julius Alexander is equally difficult to interpret (Smallwood 1967: No. 391). This edict was issued in 68 on the accession of the new emperor, Galba. Alexander made allusions to a whole series of petitions and complaints with which he had been presented and the decree was meant to reassure Egyptians of their privileges and stamp out abuses of power. This could be read as a response to real problems and part of a dialogue between prefect and people, but the circumstances of its promulgation, at the start of a new reign, also suggest that it had a propagandist value: the old bad times are over and new, just rule can be expected from Galba.

There is evidence of Nero's concern for the provincials from early in Nero's reign and attempts to ensure good government. There were, however, notable examples of provincial corruption which suggest that even if this was the initial intention, Nero failed to secure good provincial government for his empire.

Armenia and Parthia

The problems of Rome dominate Tacitus' account of Nero's reign, but, as a contrast to these inglorious events and to the depressing listing of deaths, Tacitus also presents an extended account of the campaigns in Armenia. In so doing, Nero is contrasted with a more heroic and praiseworthy figure, Corbulo. This is a familiar technique which Tacitus also used to contrast Tiberius with Germanicus and Domitian with Agricola. Unfortunately, Tacitus' account breaks off before his account of the death of Corbulo and we can only guess what Tacitus made of the destruction of this heroic figure.

Corbulo had been one of Claudius' leading generals and had been recalled by Claudius after a series of campaigns in Germany (pp. 83–5). In 54, the Parthians adopted a more interventionist policy in Armenia, though they were prevented from making significant gains by internal difficulties. Corbulo was sent to Armenia as a precaution against resumed hostilities (Tac., *Ann.* XIII 6). Armenia was something of a 'buffer state' between Parthia and Rome and the scene of much conflict. Both states claimed authority over the region and some compromise normally prevailed. In times of conflict between Parthia and Rome, Armenia was a convenient battleground for the major powers to test their relative strengths.

Corbulo gathered his forces and worked closely with the governor of Syria. Open war may have been delayed until 58 when Armenia was invaded and secured by the Parthians (Tac., *Ann.* XIII 34–41). Corbulo invaded and conducted a long campaign without bringing about a decisive battle. He was, however, finally able to capture and destroy the Armenian capital, Artaxata, and drive the Parthians from Armenia. Campaigns continued into 60 with significant Roman victories in Armenia and neighbouring territories. The Romans were in a position to impose their own candidate on the throne and secure the area under Roman control (Tac., *Ann.* XIV 23–6). The governor of Syria died and Corbulo concentrated all troops in the region under his command. In 61–2, however, war broke out with renewed intensity. By this time Corbulo had relinquished control of Armenia to a new governor, Caesennius Paetus, though he remained governor of Syria. The main action had been on the frontier between Syria and Parthia and although Corbulo did not bring the Parthians to a decisive battle, almost impossible given the far greater mobility of the Parthian cavalry forces, he managed to prevent an invasion of Syria. A Parthian strike into Armenia brought notable success and the defeat and surrender of a Roman army under Paetus. Corbulo's relieving army had come too late (Tac., *Ann.* XV 1–18). Corbulo once more took charge of matters in Armenia and in 63 launched an invasion with a fresh army. The Parthians faced the prospect of another bitter struggle with Corbulo, who had the means to drive them once more from Armenia, and were willing to settle. A temporary settlement of the conflict may have appealed to Nero and Corbulo after a major Roman defeat and almost a decade of conflict. Corbulo negotiated. The Parthians accepted Nero's authority over the province and bowed down to his image. In return, the Romans agreed to appoint the Parthian nominee to the throne provided he journeyed to Rome to receive the honour from Nero personally (Tac., *Ann.* XV 24–31).

Nero made the most of this visit. It was a great ceremonial occasion and an opportunity to display his military glory. The war had in fact achieved very little. Both sides could claim victories. The compromise that emerged, a Parthian ruler of Armenia who needed the blessing of the emperor, was to preserve the peace. Nero is said to have had plans for a further campaign in the East (Suet., *Nero* 19), but the strains of the Jewish revolt and the eventual collapse of his regime meant that these came to nothing. The plans themselves, however, suggest that Nero did not feel that his Armenian settlement had brought him sufficient glory and he needed to reassert military authority.

The West

Germany appears to have been comparatively quiet in this period. Indeed, commanders felt the situation was sufficiently secure that they could devote their attention to major civil engineering projects in order to keep the troops employed. There were problems with the Frisii in 58, who had seized some unoccupied Roman land on which to settle, and with an alliance between the Ampsivarii, Bructeri and Tencteri, but Roman military and diplomatic pressure led to the break-up of this dangerous alliance. The Ampsivarii suffered severe economic difficulties and the tribe dissolved. The same year also saw a battle between the Chatti and the Hermanduri which exhausted both tribes (Tac., *Ann.* XIII 53–7). Effective use of Rome's economic resources, limited military pressure and diplomacy ensured that the borders remained peaceful for much of the reign.

Nero inherited a half-conquered province in Britain. There had been significant unrest in the province and the governors had pursued an active military policy, pushing the boundaries of Roman political and military control further north and into Wales. Nero is supposed to have openly considered withdrawal from Britain, but rejected the idea on the grounds that it would seem to be a move critical of Claudius (Suet., *Nero* 18). However, Nero was critical of Claudius in other ways, and to criticise his major military success can perhaps be seen as another way of disassociating himself from his Claudian inheritance: we must remember that his major dynastic rival was Britannicus. Yet, such a withdrawal was probably politically impossible and it is unlikely that it was ever seriously envisaged.

Nero continued the Claudian policy of expansion until the Boudiccan revolt (see p. 123), after which a more cautious policy was adopted.

The Jewish revolt

The complete mishandling of the province of Judaea in this period is a notable indictment of Roman government. Our source for the revolt is in some ways excellent. Flavius Josephus was a leading figure in the revolt and commanded Jewish forces in Galilee, as well as being a member of the Jewish elite. He was well aware of the diplomatic and political background of the revolt. However, his close involvement clearly prejudices his account. The Jews were themselves divided and the fissures in Jewish society had been manifest long before the outbreak of the revolt. Armed gangs had roamed the countryside, though their political and religious motivations remain a matter of some dispute. Josephus was opposed to these groups, but the quality of the Roman government was such that men such as Josephus found common cause with the more extreme elements and united against the Romans. Political disputes continued between the various elements of the Jewish population and Josephus seems to have spent much of his time as general in Galilee attempting to secure his position against those who wished to revoke his command, or worse. After his defeat in Galilee, he was captured in mysterious and probably dishonourable circumstances by the Romans and then became a vocal supporter of the Roman cause. Josephus, therefore, needed to justify to his Roman audience his actions in revolting and explain his reasons for abandoning that revolt. The result probably seriously distorts the position of Josephus' Jewish opponents, who continued the war and who must have regarded him as a traitor, and confuses our understanding of the origins of the war.

Judaea had been troublesome for many decades and it was common for military forces to be sent from Syria to support the governor of the province. The Romans enjoyed significant support from the Jewish aristocracy in most periods and the aristocrats were probably able to hamper the mobilisation of a large army against the Romans. The problems of the preceding years, however, may have reduced the influence of these aristocrats. In 66, the procurator attempted to increase taxes and extract money from the sacred funds of the Temple. He then violently suppressed a petitioning crowd, but was unable to secure Jerusalem and a stand-off resulted that moved rapidly towards open rebellion. Cestius Gallus, the governor of Syria, marched on Jerusalem but found himself hopelessly outnumbered, though the Jews were probably insufficiently well armed to overwhelm the Roman forces in open battle. Gallus withdrew, but was forced to fight a running battle with the Jews in order to extract even a remnant of his forces from Judaea. Such success encouraged a mass mobilisation of the Jewish population and the Romans were faced with a major military problem.

Nero was in Greece at the time and appointed Vespasian to the command. Vespasian had served with distinction in Britain, but was of relatively humble origin and probably not to be feared. He set about gathering troops from across the East for his expedition. The gathering of forces put an end to any other putative expeditions in the East, but Nero's political position was already so weak that his presence was demanded in Rome. Although there was limited campaigning in 67 and 68, the civil wars that followed Nero's suicide delayed the suppression of the revolt and it was not until 70 that Vespasian's son Titus took Jerusalem (see pp. 156–7).

General policy

With the exception of the Parthian frontier, Nero seems to have been blessed with generally quiet borders. The two major revolts of the period demanded immediate attention and considerable resources. Nero had inherited a fairly pacific policy from Claudius (apart from in Britain) and there is little evidence that he sought to change that policy in the West. Germany had not been an attractive arena for military adventures since the reign of Augustus. Force of circumstances, partly determined by Nero's military policy and the fact that he never himself led a military expedition, reinforces the impression of a non-military emperor. Nevertheless, there are some grounds to doubt the traditional picture. Nero honoured military men such as Suetonius Paulinus and Corbulo (though the latter was eventually forced to kill himself), and at times seems to have taken some care over provincial matters. He may also have had more expansionist plans. He annexed the client kingdoms of Pontus and the Cottian Alps. His policy in Britain prior to 61 seems to have been expansionist. In the East, Nero conducted an aggressive campaign through Corbulo to secure Armenia, though the peace that resulted was essentially a compromise. We also have evidence of mysterious plans for expansion in the East, either to the south of Egypt or towards the Caspian Gates. These could be dismissed as wild romantic projects, but the invasion of Britain could have been placed in that category thirty years earlier. With the frontiers settled in other areas, such expeditions may have seemed a suitable outlet for Rome's military energies, and the building of baths in Egypt for Nero's visit suggests that Nero intended to lead these expeditions himself. Nero may have been aware of a political need to assert his authority as a general but, as in so many other areas, his plans eventually came to nothing.

NERO AND THE OPPOSITION: THE EMPEROR AS TYRANT

Thrasea Paetus

When Thrasea Paetus walked out of the senate on its acceptance of Agrippina's murder, he effectively turned himself into a focus of opposition. Thrasea became a symbol of old-fashioned conservative morality, a representation of the conscience of Rome and the most prominent member of what has been called the 'philosophical opposition'. Several of the figures who came out in opposition to Nero, and who suffered as a consequence, were interested in philosophical ideas and these ideas strengthened their resolution in the face of tyranny. A strong current in contemporary philosophy taught the intelligent man to free himself from emotions and not to fear death. The good man did what was right irrespective of the personal consequences since, although a tyrant could take his life, he could not take his honour. The austere personal lives of many philosophers contrasted with the lifestyle of the emperor and court.

The view that there was a coherent 'intellectual opposition' to

Nero has, however, been discredited. Although it seems to have been the case that Thrasea and those around him were interested in philosophy, and it is likely that their philosophy gave them courage in facing Nero, we cannot identify these men with a particular philosophical school. Men from all parts of the political spectrum might patronise philosophers, and philosophers were active in Nero's court. An interest in intellectual matters did not lead to the adoption of a particular political position. Some took a more liberal view than others and Seneca, to give the most famous instance, was able to co-operate on exactly those issues that proved too much for Paetus.

Not only was there no consistent philosophy, but the group did not form a political party that would be recognisable to modern eyes. There were prominent men and women surrounding Thrasea, such as Helvidius Priscus, L. Junius Arulenus Rusticus, Curtius Montanus, possibly Rufus Musonius and Barea Soranus, though the links between these men are sometimes a little obscure. Thrasea Paetus was married to Arria (see Figure 5.1), whose mother, also Arria, had been married to Caecina Paetus who was involved in the Scribonianus conspiracy against Claudius (see p. 91). Thrasea's daughter Fannia was married to Helvidius Priscus, who was executed by Vespasian (see pp. 170–1). The next generation was persecuted by Domitian (pp. 181–4).

The ideology of opposition to imperial rule passed from generation to generation within the family, and it seems likely that those who formed marital alliances with this family did so because of their approval of their style of politics, so that a dynasty of opposition was formed. Other disaffected individuals associated

Figure 5.1 The families of Arria and Fannia

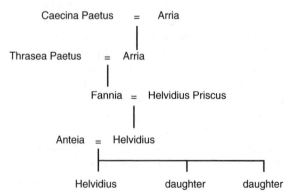

themselves with the group. We do not see a political party, therefore, but a more traditional Roman faction resting on ties of family and friendship as well as ideology.

The group was not really an opposition either. Thrasea was something of an irritation to Nero after his very prominent withdrawal in 59. In 62, he led the senate in proposing exile rather than death for Antistius Sosianus, which provoked Nero into writing a note that confirmed the senate's right to do as it pleased and noted that the senate could even have freed Antistius if it had so chosen (Tac., *Ann.* XIV 48–9). Nero's displeasure was evident. Thrasea managed to secure Nero's support in the debate surrounding the trial of Claudius Timarchus (pp. 123–4), but Thrasea was excluded from the celebrations that surrounded the birth of Nero's daughter in 63 (Tac., *Ann.* XV 23). Thrasea's continued prominence in the senate after 59 suggests that there was no formal break between the two men until 63. Even after 63, friends of Thrasea continued in their political careers and held office. Nero might not have given them important military commands, but he allowed their careers to progress.

Thrasea was marked out as not being a friend of the emperor in 63. Such exclusion from imperial favour was a sign of a greater threat to come. However, he survived until 66. Thrasea was tried in the senate, though his general attitude towards the emperor seems to have been the issue rather than any specific conspiracy. The prosecution was launched by Cossutianus Capito, a man Thrasea had himself successfully prosecuted for corruption. Thrasea apparently debated with his friends whether he should oppose the trial, but they decided that such opposition would be useless and only dignify the proceedings. L. Junius Arulenus Rusticus, who was tribune at the time, offered to veto the trial. Technically, this would have caused something of a constitutional crisis, but there can have been little doubt that Nero would have swept aside such opposition very quickly. Thrasea killed himself when the verdict was announced, instructing his wife to carry on living for the sake of their daughter. Thus, he died a martyr (Tac., *Ann.* XVI 21–35).

Even in what one supposes is the extremely abbreviated form in which Tacitus gives the last acts in Thrasea's martyrdom, it is clear that his career had been mythologised. Tacitus gives us another story about him, included in the account for 63. Nero visited Seneca and boasted to him that he had been reconciled to Thrasea (presumably after Thrasea had been excluded from the birth celebrations). Seneca congratulated Nero (Tac., *Ann.* XV 23). In so doing, he suggested that Nero was the lesser man begging the friendship of the greater, a reversal of political status. It also demonstrates Nero's difficulty. Thrasea's opposition was a symbol of Nero's break with the senate and, by standing against Nero, Thrasea's status was raised far above what it would normally have been. If Nero was to reconcile himself with the senate and return to the co-operative government of the early years, he had to bring Thrasea into line. Killing Thrasea, or acting against his friends, would only further increase Thrasea's status. Thus, Nero had to allow, and was probably even pleased to see, Thrasea's friends following senatorial careers since it showed the break was not absolute and he could continue the pretence of some co-operation. Even in 66, there was a tribune at Thrasea's side when the verdict was announced. Thrasea's death, however, was far from the end of Nero's problems. He could not now hide his break with the senate and it may well have contributed to the last round of paranoid killings in AD 66–7 that marked the collapse of Nero's political position.

Rivals and plots

In 62, Nero broke with the relative restraint of his early years and killed several of those in exile. Three casualties, Octavia, Sulla Felix and Rubellius Plautus (see pp. 110–11) were possibly dynastic threats. Two years later, another possible dynastic rival, Decimus Junius Silanus Torquatus, was killed. He was also a great-grandson of Augustus, and his family's relationship to the imperial house led to their rapid elimination in the period from the marriage of Agrippina to Claudius (a Junius Silanus was betrothed to Octavia) until 65, the year in which Decimus' brother, L. Junius Silanus Torquatus, was killed. There is no evidence to suggest that any of these posed a real threat to Nero. Tacitus tells us an extraordinary tale concerning Plautus. L. Antistius Vetus, who was himself to be killed in 65, wrote to Plautus to tell him of his fate and encourage him to resist, flee to Corbulo and start a revolution. After some discussion with his philosopher friends, Plautus decided not to resist (Tac., *Ann.* XIV 58–9). A possible source for this story is Musonius Rufus, who was himself later exiled. The convenience of such a story both for the philosopher, who could use it as a historical setting for moral discussion, and the historian, for whom it could be used to hint at the fates reserved for Vetus, Corbulo, and perhaps for Thrasea Paetus, raises questions as to its veracity. Decimus Junius Silanus was apparently accused of treason on the basis of his generosity in giving presents to his friends (perhaps he feared for his life and was seeking to dispose of his property before it was seized by the emperor), and because he organised his household by giving his freedmen the same titles as were used in the imperial household (*ab epistulis*, etc., see pp. 248–9) (Tac. *Ann.* XV 35). Dio (LXII 27.2) tells us he was killed because his poverty was such that Nero believed his only method of restoring his fortune would be rebellion. The Junii Silani had survived up to this point through their passivity. They avoided action that could be construed as posing a threat. This studied mediocrity was not enough to prevent their deaths at the hand of an increasingly nervous Nero.

In 65, some of Nero's fears were realised when he uncovered a conspiracy. At the head of the conspiracy was L. Calpurnius Piso, an aristocratic orator who had won fame and popularity in the law courts. He was not a Julio–Claudian and had no claim for imperial office other than his political standing. This was probably a significant weakness in the conspiracy since its two aims, ridding the state of Nero and putting Piso on the throne, were often in conflict. Piso wanted the killing of Nero to be accomplished in such a way that power would pass smoothly into his hands. When obvious opportunities presented themselves to the conspirators (such as Nero staying at Piso's house), they hesitated since they feared they would not be able to control subsequent events. Also, because of its political nature, the conspiracy had to involve a significant proportion of the political class in Rome. Leaks of information became inevitable. Tacitus (*Ann.* XV 48–74) provides us with the full dramatic, tragic story. The story leaked and a freedwoman, Epicharis, was implicated. She refused to give names even under torture. Then a Flavius Scaevinus obtained a dagger from a temple of Fortune or Salus (Safety) from his hometown and, after a long meeting with a certain Antonius Natalis, started behaving so oddly, organising a luxurious (final) dinner party, rewriting his will, sharpening his knife, arranging for bandages to be made ready, that his slaves and freedmen became suspicious. He was betrayed, but conclusive evidence could not be obtained. Then Natalis was brought in and the two failed to agree on what their conference had been about. Torture was applied and gradually the conspiracy was laid before Tigellinus, the praetorian prefect, and Nero. Even then, the conspirators, one of whom was Faenius Rufus, who, as the other prefect of the praetorians was present at the inquisitions, did not act. Gradually, those involved were rounded up to be executed or exiled. Tacitus tells us of suspicions that the conspiracy was a fabrication to enable Nero to rid himself of his enemies, but Nero himself published the confessions, and the details of the conspiracy were confirmed by those involved who returned from exile after Nero's death.

Many of those involved are little more than names to us. There were senators and equestrians; most of the senior officers of the guard, including Faenius Rufus, were implicated. The poet Lucan was also involved, and this brought the conspiracy close to the circle of Seneca. As the numbers of those directly involved grew, and it became clear that even those close to the emperor were involved, more and more of the Roman aristocracy became 'guilty through association' because of their friendships and family ties with the active conspirators. Nero also struck at men who had probably little or no involvement with the conspiracy. One of these was Rufrius Crispinus, killed because he had been married to Poppaea. The philosopher Musonius Rufus was exiled. Another victim was Seneca.

Seneca's death is related at length by Tacitus (*Ann.* XV 60–5) and Dio (LXII 25). Seneca must have expected his death, especially after the conspiracy implicated Lucan. His suicide was ordered and theatrical. He played out the last hours of the philosopher in imitation of Socrates, but his body proved resilient to poisons and bleeding and finally he died after being carried into a steam bath.

Nero cut a swathe through the Roman aristocracy. His confidence may have been partly restored by public demonstrations in his favour at the Neronia (Tac., *Ann.* XVI 4), but he was now fearful of the senate. More deaths followed. The aged, respected and blind senator C. Cassius Longinus was exiled. His crime was keeping and venerating a portrait of his ancestor, as was the custom of the Roman aristocracy, but this ancestor was the Cassius who had led the conspiracy against Julius Caesar (Dio, LXII 27; Tac., *Ann.* XVI 7–9). Even such ancestral treason had become a cause of fear. Cassius had another weakness since his wife, Junia Lepida, was related to the Junii Silani. Lepida was accused of magic and incest with her nephew Silanus, son of Decimus Silanus who had been killed a couple of years earlier (see pp. 132–3). Antistius Vetus (p. 132), another distinguished senator, and his immediate family were also encouraged to commit suicide (Tac., *Ann.* XVI 10–11). A certain Publius Gallus was exiled for having been the friend of both Vetus and Faenius Rufus (Tac., *Ann.* XVI 12). Each exile or death made the friends and family of the deceased fear for their own security and placed them under suspicion. The scale of the conspiracy and extent of the killings are testimony to the rapidity with which Nero's political position was disintegrating.

Nero found a new way of demonstrating his magnificence: April, May and June were renamed Neroneus, Claudius and Germanicus (Tac., *Ann.* XVI 12; Suet., *Nero* 55). The permanence of the imperial dynasty was now even built into the calendar, symbolising the natural order of things, since from March (named after Mars, the divine ancestor of the Julians) the next five months reflected the nomenclature of the imperial family.

Personal tragedy struck in the same year. His beloved Poppaea died. The stories suggest that Nero flew into a fit of rage after a minor domestic disagreement and kicked her in the stomach. She was pregnant again. The blows killed her. Nero had her deified, associating her with Venus (Tac., *Ann.* XVI 6; Dio, LXII 28.1; Suet., *Nero* 35.3). He was now without wife or heir (his daughter had died within three months of her birth). The aristocracy had turned against him decisively. Even reshaping the calendar could not disguise Nero's decline.

The generals

The threat posed by the Roman aristocracy was twofold. They could assassinate the emperor. They also commanded the armies and could use that military force to start a civil war. Since the generals were recruited from the ranks of the senate, and their friends and family remained in Rome, Nero's loss of support among the aristocracy in Rome inevitably led to doubts about the loyalty of the generals. By the winter of 66–7, Nero felt his security sufficiently threatened that he had to remove his leading generals.

Our understanding of events in these years is hampered by the loss of Tacitus' account which ends sometime in the middle of 66, after the death of Thrasea Paetus, and we are forced to rely on items in Suetonius and Dio's imperfect narrative for these years. Much remains obscure, especially a *coniuratio Viniciana* (Vinician conspiracy) dated later than Piso's conspiracy by Suetonius (*Nero* 36) and located at Brundisium. Suetonius is our only source. The location, however, provides a clue in that Brundisium was the port from which Nero set out on his tour of Greece and so places the conspiracy towards the end of 66. The Vinicius, or Vinicianus, is probably Annius Vinicianus who had arrived in Rome as escort to Tiridates (prospective King of Armenia) earlier in the same year (Dio, LXII 23.6). This man was Corbulo's son-in-law and had been serving with Corbulo in 63. His involvement in a conspiracy would implicate Corbulo.

The threat to Corbulo illustrates the interconnection of the politics of the generals and the senate. Cassius Longinus, who had been removed in 65, was Corbulo's father-in-law. L. Antistius Vetus, also removed in 65, was the man who was rumoured to have written to Rubellius Plautus advising him to flee to Corbulo, suggesting some link between Vetus and Corbulo, even if the story was largely fiction (see p. 132). There were other victims in 66 who had some vague connection with the East (Tac. *Ann.* XVI 14-15, XIII 22). Barea Soranus fell victim to the same purge that removed Thrasea Paetus. The attack on Soranus also involved Soranus' daughter Servilia who was married to one Annius Pollio, brother of Annius Vinicianus. The links suggest the elimination of another political group, one member of which was Corbulo.

At some time in late 66 or early 67, Nero summoned Corbulo to join him in Greece. The governors of the two Germanies, Sulpicius Scribonius Rufus and Sulpicius Scribonius Proculus, were also summoned. All three were told of Nero's verdict when they arrived and killed themselves (Dio, LXIII 17). In one blow, the three most powerful generals of the empire were removed. Nero could replace them with men he trusted, but Nero's actions in killing these generals increased the fears of the aristocracy and further reduced Nero's status. If the loyal Corbulo could fall victim, all were at risk. Few were now committed to Nero's cause. The stage was set for the final acts of Nero's principate.

THE DEATH OF AN ARTIST

When the end came, it was from an unlikely source. Helios, the freedman who had been left in charge of Rome, journeyed to Greece in 68 to persuade Nero to return home. He had news of trouble (Dio, LXIII 19.1). Nero returned in triumph: a bold demonstration of his authority. Helios' worries are not clearly stated in our sources, but they may have been the first rumblings of rebellion in Gaul. C. Julius Vindex, a Gallic nobleman and probably a governor of Gallia Lugdunensis had been writing to his fellow-governors to secure support for a revolt. Most forwarded their letters to Nero. There were extensive disturbances in Gaul over the next two years, and some have seen in Vindex's revolt an uprising similar to that in Judaea. Vindex's own propaganda was notably Roman and anti-

Nero. He wished the liberty of Rome to be restored. Yet, although the rhetoric was imperial, the scale of local support he generated may reflect general provincial discontent. It is difficult to imagine that his Gallic followers would have been motivated by the ill-treatment of the Roman senate or by Nero's caperings in Greece and, since Vindex himself may have been governor, taxation rather than local corruption may have been at issue.

Nero acted slowly. He had, after all, just appointed two new governors to control the Rhine legions, Verginius Rufus and Fonteius Capito. He might expect them to be loyal. Faced with the might of the Rhine legions, the revolt of even a major Gallic aristocrat was not a serious threat and emergency measures were unnecessary. From the first, however (and Nero may have been aware of this), Vindex was in close contact with the governor of Hispania Tarraconensis, Servius Sulpicius Galba (Plut., *Life of Galba* 4).

Galba was an experienced general who had made something of a name for himself by the severity with which he treated the troops in Germany following his appointment by Gaius. He had only a single legion, however, and he needed to gather more support than that offered by Vindex before he could march on Rome. Galba delayed a formal declaration of intent, but Vindex forced his hand. He came out openly in support of Galba's undeclared candidature. Vindex's own position was probably becoming increasingly desperate. No other governor had declared with him. Plutarch describes a meeting held by Galba and his counsellors which was attended by the commander of the legion in Spain, Titus Vinius. Vinius declared the meeting a farce. The very fact that they were discussing the issue showed that they were already disloyal to Nero (Plut., *Life of Galba* 4). Galba declared his hand and was quickly supported by the governors of the other Spanish provinces, including Otho, the divorced husband of Poppaea; thus Nero's misdeeds returned to haunt him.

Nero's position now disintegrated for reasons that are not altogether obvious. Galba was a major political figure, much more important than Vindex and would probably be able to rely on a significant senatorial following, as well as being sufficiently respected to be able to secure the support of at least some of the provincial governors. In military terms, however, Galba was no match for Nero. He had only one legion to compare with the combined forces of the empire, and Nero not only had the praetorians close at hand, but could also quickly raise more troops and organise a substantial force. Politically, Nero was disturbed by Galba's rebellion (Suet., *Nero* 42), but he should not have been seriously threatened. At some point, however, the governor of Africa, Claudius Macer, had made an independent bid for the throne (Plut., *Galba* 6).

Nero was threatened on two fronts but took sensible measures, and a supposed loyalist, Petronius Turpillianus, was placed in charge of forces in Italy. The exact chronology of what happened next is uncertain, but, paradoxically, the fatal blow may have come from negotiations before a victory which should have destroyed Galba. Vindex had entered into negotiations with Verginius Rufus. At the conclusion of these negotiations, Verginius' troops attacked and massacred Vindex's forces. Vindex killed himself. When Galba heard the news, he retired, fully expecting death (Plut., *Galba* 6). A few days later, news came of Nero's death and that the senate had called upon him to be emperor.

Verginius Rufus had been acclaimed by his troops as emperor, but had refused the honour. The later tradition, which may have been heavily influenced by Verginius Rufus himself, emphasised that he had not given the order for his forces to attack and made much of his subsequent refusal to take imperial power, yet the motivations of Rufus and his troops at this crucial moment are difficult to reconstruct. By negotiating, Rufus demonstrated disloyalty to Nero, but crushing Vindex seems a demonstration of loyalty to the existing regime on the part of the troops. To declare for Rufus and against Nero seems to contradict their actions against Vindex. We can rule out the possibility that the troops had a collective change of mind and so we must look for another motivation. It seems likely that Rufus was exploring the possibility of an attempt on the throne and by destroying Vindex had established the possibility of an independent claim. For some reason (perhaps because he could not rely on the support of the other German legions), he decided not to continue his attempt and, by refusing the imperial acclamation, he demonstrated that he was not a threat to Galba. He was to use the same technique in 69, when Vitellius' troops pressed Rome and Otho's forces supposedly looked to Rufus to lead them against the Vitellians (Dio, LXIII 24-5; Tac., *Hist.* II. 51).

In Rome, Nero's position was collapsing. Grain prices rose, perhaps from fear that the supply of grain from Africa would fail (Suet., *Nero* 45). Rumours of the disloyalty of Rufus may have been circulating in Rome immediately before Nero's fall. If Rufus turned against him and his own hurriedly raised forces defected, Nero's days were numbered. Turpillianus proved disloyal. The Roman political classes made their calculations and Nero found his support disappearing. Nymphidius Sabinus, who had been appointed prefect of the praetorians after the execution of Faenius Rufus, decided that Nero would lose. The imperial palace emptied of courtiers and Nero himself fled the city, accompanied by only his closest associates. The account of his last days is clearly heavily fictionalised. Vague plans of fleeing to the East or retiring to earn a living on the stage are mentioned, but the disintegration of his position had been so complete and rapid that no confidence could have been placed in the attitudes of the governors of the East. Sabinus chose to act. By fleeing the city, Nero had deserted the praetorians and Sabinus persuaded them to move against him. Cavalry was sent after Nero and in a suburb outside Rome Nero killed himself. His last words were reportedly '*Qualis artifex pereo*' (I, such an artist, perish) (Suet., *Nero* 49; Dio, LXIII 29.2). His final words are so appropriately inappropriate for an emperor, stressing his role on the stage rather than his exercise of political power, that one suspects later invention.

CONCLUSIONS: ART, POLITICS AND POWER

Nero is possibly the most difficult of the Julio–Claudian emperors to understand. The account transmitted through our sources on Nero is almost universally hostile and certainly distorts our understanding of the emperor. Nero was not universally hated during his reign, nor in the aftermath. Otho was to make use of his association with Nero and this brought him a certain popularity (see pp. 150–1). Nero cannot be dismissed as a silly man who strutted about the stage for forced applause and had not a serious political idea in his head.

Although the tradition vilifies his stage appearances, the decline in Nero's political position cannot be directly related to his artistic endeavours, and they seem to have brought him popularity in certain quarters. Nero faced many of the same problems as Gaius and Claudius in coming to the throne with limited experience and, like his two predecessors, his style of government was inventive. He looked for new ways to display his authority and new avenues for his imperial energies. Gaius had turned to a kind of divine despotism by which to control the classes of Rome. Claudius had removed power from the senate by concentrating authority in his inner circle of close friends and household members. Nero looked to culture. In some ways, this device was remarkably successful and Nero presided over a revival for architecture and literature. His subversion of the traditional aristocratic way of life and elevation of an 'artistic ideal' as a governing principle were revolutionary. This could be described as a sensible response to the changed political conditions of the Principate. The emperor now appealed to a wide audience of Romans (of all social classes), troops and provincials, an audience that he could not hope to meet personally or tie to him through personal links of patronage and friendship. The old political habit of going down to the Forum to meet the people or earning political points through associating with the troops in warfare could have only limited effect when the political audience was so diverse. New media had to be found to communicate to such an audience, and mass communication, such as it was in the ancient world, meant the theatre, architecture, art and literature. Portraits of the emperors are found in all provinces and, of course, coinage could be used as a vehicle for imperial propaganda. It is unlikely to be a coincidence that the art on Nero's coinage was of a very high standard. Nero met his people through art and made more use of art to display his status than any emperor since Augustus.

Yet, such excellence did not reconcile the more traditional elements of Roman society to his power. Indeed, by the very act of associating himself with subversive culture, Nero turned traditional values into the values of opposition. Co-operation with traditionalists became progressively more difficult following the death of Agrippina and the worsening of relations with conservatives such as Thrasea Paetus. As a result, Nero moved from co-operation to despotism. The Pisonian conspiracy may not mark a turning point in the reign, since relations with the conservative aristocracy may already have been strained, but led to Nero fearing a considerable section of the political elite. He still had 'conservatives' at his side. Vespasian later made a virtue out of his relatively humble origins, associating himself with traditional values in contrast to the extravagances of the high-born Julio–Claudians. Tacitus also claims that he was a friend of Soranus and Thrasea Paetus (*Hist.* IV 7) and with Tiberius Julius Alexander (who had served with Corbulo) prefect of Egypt, a possible powerful conservative alliance was established in the East by Nero. Similarly, Verginius Rufus in Germany and Galba in Spain were representatives of the traditional Italian aristocracy. Nero's cultural revolution failed in that the very men he relied on to govern his empire were not affected. These men were the powerful, and their obedience would not be won by a particularly fine performance in the theatre. Nero lost the support of the aristocracy and eventually they brought him down as they had brought down Gaius. Nero's fall was a demonstration of their power and suggests strongly that Nero's attempts to win the loyalty of other groups in the Roman empire was fundamentally misconceived. Real power lay not in the crowds that flocked to the theatres of Italy and Greece, but with the generals and aristocrats of the empire.

Given this eventual demonstration of aristocratic power, one must wonder how he managed to survive so long. The lethargy of those attacked by Nero seems notable. Rudich has compared Nero's enemies to the dissidents in the former Soviet Union: a group so overwhelmed by the authority of a powerful state that they saw no hope of salvation through political action and their only hope was to hide their opposition to the regime.[5] There was no formal political organisation opposed to Nero. Opposition consisted of individuals who faced separate and individual persecution. Some may have thought that simply by doing nothing they would demonstrate that they were no threat. Corbulo, for instance, may have calculated that, by going to Greece when summoned, he would demonstrate his loyalty and that this was the safer or more honourable course than plunging the empire into civil war, especially if he had not established the views of other governors. When Vindex finally came out into the open, the hesitation of even one so heavily implicated as Galba suggests the dominant influence of a mentality that taught the Roman elite that the best ways of surviving were to avoid open conflict with the emperor, to keep their mouths shut and to do nothing. As the Pisonian conspiracy unravelled, the passivity of the conspirators, including Piso himself, was notable. With the support of key praetorian officers and a reasonable number of the Roman aristocracy, one might have thought that open rebellion would have had a reasonable chance of success, yet the inaction that had dogged the conspiracy continued and the remaining conspirators seem to have simply hoped that they would not be implicated.

Apart from the psychological explanation, another possibility may be suggested. The Roman aristocracy had seen only temporarily broken Julio–Claudian domination since Caesar defeated Pompey over a century before the death of Nero. There appears to have been no active republicanism at this time. There was no realistic alternative to imperial rule and if Nero was to be removed, who would replace him? As we have seen, Nero killed most of his own family and possible dynastic rivals such as the Junii Silani were also removed. Was there a realistic alternative? The Pisonian conspiracy needed to be so large so that events after the assassination of the emperor (not a substantial problem given the access to the emperor that the conspirators enjoyed) could be controlled. Any subsequent conspirator would face the same problem. A conspiracy needed to secure the future, and to do this they needed an imperial candidate who stood a realistic chance of securing the support of the senate and troops. Nero lasted so long because there was no alternative candidate. This is why Nero was not worried by Vindex. A Gallic nobleman would not be able to secure sufficient support from the Roman elite; he was not a realistic alternative. The declaration of Galba transformed the situation. He was a realistic opponent and, once Galba had declared and the aristocracy accepted the prospect of a non-Julio–Claudian emperor, other possibilities emerged. Verginius Rufus and Claudius Macer were realistic candidates, and so were many others. All a candidate needed was the support of a sufficient number of legions; the scene was set for the civil wars of 68–70.

The crucial change that led to Galba's declaration was probably Nero's purge of his generals in 66–7. Nero had shown that even seemingly loyal supporters such as Corbulo, Nero's greatest general, could be struck down. Corbulo had brought a difficult war in Armenia to an end and presented Nero with his greatest diplomatic triumph. Killing Corbulo showed that none were safe and ultimately there was little alternative but to find an alternative. Although maladministration of the provinces may have been a contributing factor in Vindex's initial outbreak, and may have led to a greater willingness of the provincials to provide immediate support for Galba and others, Nero's fate was decided by the Roman political elite.

Main events in the reign of Nero

Date	Events
AD 54	Accession.
	Deaths of Narcissus and M. Junius Silanus.
	Agrippina 'best of mothers'.
	Corbulo sent to Armenia.
55	Prosecutions of Britannicus' friends stopped.
	Fall of Pallas.
	Death of Britannicus.
	Withdrawal of Agrippina's bodyguard.
	Supposed conspiracy of Agrippina and Rubellius Plautus.
	Cohort on guard in the theatre withdrawn.

(Continued)

Date	Events
56	Nero's gang wanders streets. Death of Julius Montanus.
	Helvidius Priscus becomes involved in dispute over debts.
57	Construction of the gymnasium.
	Cossutianus Capito condemned for corruption.
58	War with Parthia in Armenia.
	Condemnation of P. Suillius Rufus.
	Emergence of Poppaea Sabina.
	Cornelius Sulla Felix exiled.
	War in Germany.
59	Killing of Agrippina.
	Thrasea Paetus walks out of the senate.
	Private stadium constructed for Nero.
	Iuvenalia instituted.
60	Neronia founded.
	Corbulo campaigns in Armenia and takes governorship of Syria.
61	Boudiccan revolt.
	Killing of L. Pedanius Secundus.
	Dedication of Nero's gymnasium.
62	Trial of Antistius Sosianus. Death sentence opposed by Thrasea Paetus.
	Trial of Aulus Didius Gallus Fabricius.
	Death of Burrus. Appointment of Tigellinus and Faenius Rufus.
	Seneca loses influence.
	Assassination of Sulla.
	Assassination of Plautus.
	Divorce, exile and death of Octavia.
	Deaths of Pallas and Doryphoros.
	Seneca and Piso linked in conspiracy charge; charge rejected.
	Caesennius Paetus appointed to Armenia, but defeated.
	Thrasea Paetus speaks against provincial acclamations of governors.

(Continued)

Date	Events
63	Birth and death of Nero's daughter.
	Poppaea becomes Augusta.
	Corbulo brings the war in Armenia to an end.
	Nero's gymnasium burnt down.
64	Nero appears on stage in Naples.
	Decimus Junius Silanus Torquatus killed.
	Nero marries Pythagoras.
	Banquet of Tigellinus.
	Fire of Rome.
65	Conspiracy of Piso. Death of all conspirators and of others.
	Nero appears on stage at the Neronia.
	Death of Poppaea.
	Deaths of Lucius Junius Silanus Torquatus, C. Cassius Longinus, L. Antistius Vetus and family.
	Renaming of months.
	Plague in Rome.
66	Many deaths, including Petronius, Thrasea Paetus and Barea Soranus.
	Tiridates presented in Rome.
	Conspiracy of Vinicianus.
	Nero sets out to Greece.
	Revolt in Judaea.
67	Nero in Greece.
	Deaths of Corbulo and the governors of the Germanies.
68	Revolt of Vindex.
	Galba declares against Nero.
	Death of Vindex.
	Collapse of Nero's position.
	Death of Nero.

6

CIVIL WARS: AD 69–70

INTRODUCTION

The accession of Galba had seen the uncovering of one of the secrets of the Empire: that emperors could be made in places other than Rome (Tac., *Hist.* I 4). The end of the Julio–Claudians led to a period of unprecedented turmoil. In a single year, AD 69, there were four emperors. The armies competed to place these candidates on the throne and, to add to internal turmoil, there was major conflict in Judaea, on the Danube, in Germany and Gaul, and in Britain. Two major cities were sacked, Cremona and Jerusalem, and Rome itself was stormed by the forces of Vespasian.

The result of this internal strife can be explained simply. The man with the biggest army, Vespasian, won. It can be seen as a military struggle in which only those holding armies could take part, which marginalised the senate. Yet, when we examine the detail of these events, the picture becomes more complex and the reasons for the rise and fall of the various emperors less obvious. We are guided through these events by Tacitus. We have only the first four books and the first part of the fifth book of his *Histories*. The complete work probably covered the Flavian dynasty (Vespasian, Titus and Domitian), Nerva and Trajan, but the surviving work concerns only the period AD 69–70. Tacitus claims that he wrote about the period objectively, a bold claim for any historian, yet his political career began under Vespasian and continued under Titus and Domitian. By the later books of the *Histories*, Tacitus was discussing the careers of his friends and enemies. History was blending into politics. Tacitus believed that the Flavian victory was the best result for Rome and that Vespasian, who had certain faults, was the best of the possible candidates. It is, however, notable that the other candidates – Galba, Otho and Vitellius – are not portrayed stereotypically and although Tacitus criticises them all, especially Vitellius, his account allows us to discern some of their better qualities.

GALBA

The death of Nero left Galba in a seemingly strong position. He had replaced Nero who was deeply unpopular with the senate. He was the only declared candidate for the throne. He had a reputation as a conservative, untainted by the excesses of Nero's reign. He had won a military reputation under Gaius and Claudius. He was also a member of an old aristocratic family. He owed his own prominence to a friendship with Livia, wife of Augustus, but his ancestors numbered Republican consuls, and his family had a mythical ancestry to rival the Julians since they claimed descent from Jupiter and the Minoan royal family (Suet., *Galba* 2). He might, therefore, be expected to draw support from the military and from the old senatorial families. He was recognised by the senate, by the armies of the East and, after some delay, by the armies of Germany and the West. This position of seeming strength disintegrated in a remarkably short period.

Part of the reason for this collapse lay in Galba's inability to consolidate his support and his seeming overestimation of his own security. Galba had made a name for himself as a fierce disciplinarian. He did not change his character when he became emperor. The damage was done almost before he reached Rome. Taxes were raised to pay for the excesses of Nero's reign (Suet., *Galba* 12), and some of this money was extracted from Gaul. Galba wished to reward the communities that had supported Vindex and, in so doing, reorganised Gaul so that the communities closest to the legionary bases lost out. The legionaries tended to identify with those local communities. These were also the legionaries who had defeated Vindex, and it must have increased discontent to see communities which they regarded as rebellious rewarded while others suffered (Tac., *Hist.* I 53–4).

Galba also killed several prominent men. The consul designate Cingonius Varro was killed (though his crime is uncertain), Petronius Turpillianus (who had led Nero's army against Galba), Claudius Macer (governor of Africa), Nymphidius Sabinus (Nero's praetorian prefect who also had designs on the throne) and Fonteius Capito (governor of Germania Superior who was also suspected of aiming at the throne). Capito was assassinated by his legionary commanders and Galba may have been only indirectly responsible for his death (Tac., *Hist.* I 7). There were other deaths when Galba reached Rome, such as Helios (Nero's prominent freedman) and Locusta (a renowned poisoner), though some notable Neronians, such as Tigellinus (Nero's other praetorian prefect), survived (Dio, LXIV 3.3–4; Suet., *Galba* 14–15).

Galba embarked on a limited reordering of the provincial commanders. Not only were governors needed in those provinces in which the previous incumbents had been executed or had accompanied Galba to Rome, but also Verginius Rufus had been removed from his post. Galba could hardly reward him since he had been responsible for the death of Vindex, and the negotiations he entered into with Vindex raised suspicions concerning his ambition. New governors were appointed to the Spanish provinces and Africa, and also to the Germanies. Vitellius was sent to Germania Inferior and Hordeonius Flaccus was sent to Germania Superior. Neither were perceived as a threat (Tac., *Hist.* I 9; Suet.,*Vit.* 7). The East was left. Some of the officers of the praetorians, the *vigiles* (watch) and the urban cohorts were also removed (Tac. *Hist.* I 20).

In itself, this policy of removing the potentially dangerous probably increased Galba's sense of security. However, Galba's policy made him enemies and few friends. The killing of so many so quickly, giving evidence of Galba's brutality, may have unnerved members of the senate. There was no reconciliation to bring to an end the brutalities of Nero's reign. Yet, not all Nero's supporters were treated in the same way and so their political enemies remained dissatisfied. Justice had been denied (or so they thought). More seriously, Galba made no attempt to remove or win over former Neronians at lower levels of the military and political structure. Troops raised by Nero remained in Rome and the praetorians (for whom Galba must have been rather a distant figure when he became emperor) were not reorganised. Indeed, Galba offended these powerful groups. A legion raised by Nero from the sailors of the fleet petitioned Galba to be allowed to remain legionaries. Galba refused and they became disorderly. Galba charged them with cavalry, brought them to order and decimated them (every tenth man killed) (Suet., *Galba* 12.2; Dio LXIV 3.1–3). The praetorians had been promised a donative (a gift of money) by Nymphidius Sabinus on their desertion from Nero. Although Sabinus was later killed and Galba cannot have supported the offer at the time, payment would have rewarded the praetorians for their timely defection and tied them to Galba's cause. Galba refused payment: he did not buy his soldiers (Tac., *Hist.* I 5). Tacitus regarded such sentiments as admirable, but extremely foolish. Further, Galba sought the return of gifts made by Nero. Since many of these had been consumed, he threatened to bankrupt members of the Neronian court (Tac., *Hist.* I 20).

Galba also managed to lose some of the friends he already had. Otho had been the first to support Galba and might have expected some reward when he returned with him to Rome. None was forthcoming. Alienus Caecina had represented Galba at crucial moments in Germany and was responsible for the death of Fonteius Capito. He received nothing. Instead, authority was concentrated in the hands of three members of the court: Titus Vinius (who had led Galba's army), Cornelius Laco (a praetorian prefect) and Icelus (a freedman) (Tac., *Hist.* I 6; Suet., *Galba* 14.2). Our sources allege their corruption, but we have no way of assessing their guilt.

In January 69, Galba's rule fell apart. It was customary for an oath of loyalty to be administered to the troops on the first day of the year. The German legions refused, mutinied and turned to the popular Vitellius (Tac., *Hist.* I 12). In Rome, the praetorians grew restless. Otho had ingratiated himself with certain officers and men by generous tips. Galba responded to his political weakness by adopting a young nobleman, Piso Licinianus, as his heir (Tac. *Hist.* I 14–18). All authorities seem to recognise Piso as an honourable young man from one of the best families in Rome, but he had no military experience and was too young to have much political weight. He would be particularly ineffective as a political ally and, as a response to a military revolt, his adoption seems peculiarly inappropriate. Worse still, the troops expected a donative to celebrate such a major family event. These hopes were unfulfilled, Galba's reputation for meanness was confirmed, and the praetorians became more discontented.

Galba was an old man without an heir. His reign was not expected to be long and the question of the succession would have been one of the major issues of the reign. Galba may have calculated that the political problems he was facing in Germany (and possibly he was aware of discontent in Rome) were manoeuvres concerning the succession and he wished to end speculation. Adoption was the only available method. The adoption of a young and inexperienced relative was the action of someone who thought he was enjoying a politically secure position, but Piso brought no new support to prop up the crumbling regime. Galba could have looked elsewhere. Otho would have brought popularity and an ability to reconcile the old Neronians. Vespasian's son Titus would have been another possibility since this would have brought the support of his father, an influential general, and also his uncle, Flavius Sabinus, a prominent senator.

On 15 January, Otho staged his coup. It seems to have been rather disorganised. The situation remained unclear for most of the day. Galba's supporters tried to gather as many troops as possible, but failed to collect a plausible force. Nevertheless, news spread that Otho had been killed but, as Galba and his supporters celebrated in the Forum, the praetorians arrived. Galba's supporters fled and the old general was decapitated (Tac., *Hist.* I 27–41; Suet., *Otho* 6–7; Dio, LXIV 5–6).

Galba's mishandling of the situation seems notable. He faced substantial political difficulties in Germany and the inevitable nervous opposition of those who had supported Nero. Nevertheless, these problems were considerably worsened by Galba's failure to reconcile disaffected and powerful elements. Galba's reputation sprang from his disciplining of the troops, not from the political subtlety of his mind. He seems to have believed that the troops owed loyalty to their commander naturally and to have seen no need to win that loyalty. This may have been the case under the Julio–Claudians when loyalty to the family assured military support on accession, but the troops were no more loyal to Galba than to any other member of the Roman aristocracy. His failure to realise this was a failure to perceive the fundamentals of the imperial position. Imperial power sprang not from legal authority, but from political influence. His successors seem to have understood this and all were notably better at winning the loyalty, sometimes the devotion, of at least elements of the Roman military and civilian population.

OTHO

Otho's accession did not alter the attitude of the legions of Germany. He needed to prepare for the conflict; he needed to secure the loyalty of the troops in Rome and Italy. In this, he was remarkably successful. The praetorians were allowed to choose their own prefects and other troops seem to have been kindly treated (Tac., *Hist.* I 46). Politically, Otho treated the former supports of Galba well and was able to secure the support of prominent generals. Marius Celsus (who had served in the East with Corbulo and was consul designate), Annius Gallus (an able general who later commanded troops for Vespasian in Germany (Tac., *Hist.* V 19), Licinius Proculus (the praetorian prefect) and Suetonius Paulinus (the man who defeated Boudicca) were the main commanders of Otho's troops (Tac., *Hist.* I 87). Otho also managed to gain the support of the legions stationed along the Danube and the legions of the East.

Otho's undoubted early success may have owed much to his policy of associating himself with Nero. Although Otho's support of Galba may have been instrumental in creating the alliance that destroyed Nero, and one of his first acts as emperor was to kill Nero's praetorian prefect Tigellinus (Tac., *Hist.* I 72; Plut., *Otho* 2), Otho seems to have toyed with the idea of renaming himself 'Nero-Otho'. He restored the statues of Poppaea and encouraged the exhibition of portraits of Nero (Tac., *Hist.* I 78; Plut., *Otho* 3). Nero's freedmen and procurators were restored to office and he continued work on the unfinished Domus Aurea. Suetonius tells us that he had intended to marry Nero's widow (Suet., *Otho* 7, 10). A further sexual connection was established by the return to prominence of Nero's lover Sporus, who again appeared in public with an emperor (Dio, LXIV 8). The continued popularity of Nero is shown by the career of a 'false Nero' who caused disruption in Asia and Greece before being killed by the governor of Galatia and Pamphylia (Tac., *Hist.* II 8).

This sudden popularity of Nero questions the dominant literary tradition on the emperor which portrays him as a loathed tyrant. Yet, Nero's political failings and unpopularity in 68 were certain enough. The restoration of his popularity is best seen as a response to events in 68–9. The killing of Nero had not ended the difficulties of the Roman elite or of those who supported them. The subsequent civil conflicts had increased the burdens placed on provincials by the Roman state and the looming civil war increased political uncertainty. The candidates strove for legitimacy in their conflicts and, although none could claim to be Julio–Claudians, association with Nero, claiming to be his spiritual successor, was one way of asserting that legitimacy. Although many had suffered under Nero, many had also benefited and Nero will still have had limited support, especially among the urban plebs who cared little for the sufferings of the aristocracy and had enjoyed Nero's stage performances. Many had made their careers under Nero and would have regarded Galba's revolution with a certain suspicion. Otho's honouring of Nero and limited restoration of Nero's officials could be seen as reconciling the old Neronians to his rule, as well as providing him with a body of experienced administrators to help his war effort.

Otho also attempted to reconcile his potential enemies, the supporters of Galba or other possible contenders, to his accession. With a number of notable exceptions (Piso, Titus Vinius, Laco and Icelus) (Tac., *Hist.* I 42–6), Otho pardoned Galba's supporters (Tac., *Hist* II 71). Even an extremely prominent supporter of Galba, Marius Celsus (who had attempted to organise the military resistance to Otho) was reconciled to the regime and entrusted with a command (Plut., *Otho* 1).

Potential enemies were accommodated by the appointment of Flavius Sabinus, brother of Vespasian, to the important post of Praefectus Urbi (Plut. *Otho* 5; Tac., *Hist.* I 46). Verginius Rufus also achieved renewed prominence in being nominated for a consulship and he may have been a member of the party that accompanied Otho on campaign, since the troops turned to him once they received news of Otho's death (Plut., *Otho* 1, 18; Tac., *Hist.* II 51). Those who had suffered under Nero had those portions of their confiscated property that the treasury still held restored to them, a generous act given the state of the treasury.

Such manoeuvres seem to have been successful in building a powerful consensus behind Otho. We cannot know whether this would have held for any length of time but, although there may have been rumblings of discontent from the East, the fact that there was no rebellious movement until July suggests that Vespasian's bid was not yet planned.

The military position was also encouraging. Otho gathered sufficient troops in Italy to be able to resist Vitellius, and the approaching Danubian legions would have tipped the military balance in favour of Otho. However, the legions did not arrive in time. Both the Vitellian leaders and Otho followed an aggressive policy. Otho sent troops to Gallia Narbonensis where they enjoyed notable success, but the issue was to be decided in Italy (Tac., *Hist.* II 14–15). Otho's camp was apparently divided about whether they should risk a battle against the Vitellian forces before support arrived from the Danubian legions, but early success encouraged the Othonians and they met the Vitellians at Bedriacum. Otho was defeated.

This defeat proved to be decisive, though the strategic situation did not appear to be lost. Otho took counsel from his friends and decided to bring the civil wars to an end. Rather than prolong the war by retreating towards the East, Otho killed himself (Tac., *Hist* II 46–50; Suet., *Otho* 9–11; Dio, LXIV 11–15; Plut., *Otho* 15–17). The historians seem confident that the war could have been continued and that, although the defeat was significant, Otho still had resources on which he could call. His decision is widely praised since Otho's suicide is thought to have been a humanitarian decision taken to avoid further shedding of Roman blood. It may have been encouraged by an assessment of the political situation. Such a defeat often led to defections and Otho may have felt that his political support would waver as the Roman elite and the soldiers sought to back the winning side. In any case, his death brought Vitellius to the throne, but did not end the civil wars.

VITELLIUS

Vitellius' reign poses certain difficulties for historians, since his reputation may have been substantially damaged by later historians influenced by the Flavian view of events. Certainly, the historians appear to be more hostile to Vitellius than the other emperors of 69 but, in spite of Vitellius' personal weaknesses, he still seems to have built a loyal and powerful following in Italy and among the German troops.

Vitellius' family became prominent under Augustus and Tiberius. Under Claudius, Vitellius' father achieved a position of extraordinary importance holding three consulships (see p. 79). The future emperor enjoyed friendships with Tiberius, Gaius, Claudius and Nero, presiding at the second Neronia (p. 112) (Suet., *Vit.* 4). He had governed Africa with exceptional integrity and was appointed to Germania Inferior by Galba (Suet., *Vit.* 7). This was Vitellius' opportunity and he used his talent for winning friends. The soldiers were dissatisfied and disloyal and Vitellius won the loyalty of the troops. On 1 January, when the oath of loyalty was to be administered to the troops in Germania Inferior, they mutinied, refusing to accept Galba as their emperor. There was no declaration in favour of Vitellius, but they swore loyalty to the senate and people of Rome. On 2 January, Fabius Valens greeted Vitellius as emperor and, by 3 January, the legions of Germania Superior had also mutinied. Vitellius began to organise his rebellion (Tac., *Hist.* I 52–8).

The military side seems to have been led by Alienus Caecina and

Fabius Valens. They marched into Italy in two columns with varying success but, once they met outside Bedriacum in North Italy, they inflicted the decisive defeat on Otho and Vitellius became emperor.

The march from Germany to Rome was slow and the Vitellians took every opportunity to extract money from the communities that they passed. Our sources criticise Vitellius' personal morality, especially his eating habits (Dio, LXV 2 gives an implausibly large figure for the costs of Vitellius' dinners during his reign), and the disorder of the march through Gaul and Italy continued when Vitellius' troops reached Rome where there were clashes between the troops and the civilian population (Suet., *Vit.* 13; Tac., *Hist.* II 88).

Many of the Roman aristocracy may have regarded the approach of the Vitellians with some fear. Otho had been effective in reconciling differences, but Caecina and Valens acted sufficiently violently that there must have been doubts as to Vitellius' attitude. The death of Otho and the failure of another candidate, such as Verginius Rufus, to take up the standard left them with little choice. Flavius Sabinus administered an oath of loyalty to the troops remaining in Rome and the armies of the rest of the empire quickly followed (Tac., *Hist.* II 55). Vitellius himself delayed accepting the titles of Caesar and Augustus, though took the constitutional powers that went with the imperial position (Tac., *Hist.* II 62). This reluctance to accept titles may reflect an honouring of the senate and a desire to demonstrate that he would not be an autocratic ruler. Such honouring of the principles of aristocratic government may be behind Vitellius' decision to appoint equestrians to the household offices, breaking with the tradition of employing freedmen (see pp. 248–9). Vitellius seems to have learnt the lessons of Galba's reign and tried to reconcile the aristocracy to his rule. Flavius Sabinus retained his position as Praefectus Urbi. Vitellius also clashed in the senate with Helvidius Priscus, who had returned from exile, but, instead of taking action against Priscus, he merely asked the senate to excuse the quarrels of two senators (Dio, LXV 7.2; Tac., *Hist.* II 91). Although Suetonius (*Vit.* 14) accuses him of cruelty and killing his enemies, Dio (LXV 6) contradicts this. The survival of Flavius Sabinus and Domitian unharmed until the very end of the reign also suggests that Vitellius made every effort to keep the aristocracy on his side.

Vitellius also tried to win the support of the Neronians. He made funerary offerings for Nero on the Campus Martius in Rome (Suet., *Nero* 11; Dio, LXV 7.2–3). He tried to bring some Neronian glamour to his regime by suggesting that Sporus appear on stage, taking a female part, but, rather contrary to his former lover's disposition, Sporus killed himself to avoid the shame (Dio, LXV 10.1). Vitellius wooed the plebs by staging lavish entertainments (Tac., *Hist* II 94–5).

Vitellius' major problem was, however, military. The death of Otho brought one round of the civil war to an end, but Vitellius' troops had not inflicted a militarily decisive defeat. Vitellius must have been aware that the legions of the East had been against him and had not been defeated. Like the legions in Germany in 68, they were potentially disaffected. Vitellius disbanded the praetorians who had shown such loyalty to Otho (Suet., *Vit.* 10), and also executed Othonian centurions in the Danubian legions (Tac., *Hist.* II 60), which may have removed some of his enemies but did not endear him to the legionaries and their surviving officers. Vitellius' military insecurity was such that he needed to maintain a very large garrison in Rome (20,000 troops), perhaps more to intimidate potential rivals among the governors than to control the city (Tac., *Hist* II 93). The concentration of these troops in Rome was at the expense of the garrison in Germany which lost many of its most experienced men. Vitellius' problems were increased by the revolt of the Batavians led by Julius Civilis (see pp. 159–63). The revolt involved the auxiliaries that Vitellius had recruited for his war effort. The forces led by Civilis and his German and Gallic allies caused havoc in Gaul and Germany and, although the chronology of these events is not altogether clear, Vitellius was unable to draw reinforcements from those areas.

The major threat was posed by the governors in the East. Initially, the Eastern armies (in Judaea, Syria and Egypt) accepted Vitellius, but it seems likely that this was only a temporary measure. On 1 July, Tiberius Julius Alexander, prefect of Egypt, administered the oath of loyalty to the legions in Egypt in the name of Vespasian. By 3 July, Judaea and Syria had followed. The declaration seems to have been somewhat untidy, with the initiative coming from a slightly unlikely quarter, but the speed with which the Flavians moved suggests that the declaration had been planned. Mucianus, governor of Syria, was sent West to lead the war effort while Vespasian himself went to Alexandria (Tac., *Hist.* II 79–82). Almost inevitably, the Danubian legions used the opportunity to move against Vitellius and, led by Antonius Primus, they marched on Italy without even waiting for Mucianus.

Although Vitellius had a significant force at his disposal in

Rome, and could call on limited support from the Western provinces, the Flavian forces were potentially overwhelming. Even as the legions crossed into Italy, it must have seemed likely that Vitellius would lose the war. This may explain the behaviour of Alienus Caecina, the leading general of the Vitellians who defected to the Flavians but was unable to bring his troops over with him (Tac., *Hist.* II 100–1).

The two armies met at Cremona and fought a night battle which culminated in the rout of the Vitellians. The Flavian forces captured their camp and drove on to Cremona itself. The city was sacked. The Vitellians were effectively beaten though resistance continued (Tac., *Hist.* III 16–35; Dio, LXV 11.3–15). Once Primus could tear his troops from the looting of Cremona, he marched towards Rome. There was a series of minor engagements, some of which produced successes for the Vitellians, but the overwhelming numbers of the Flavian forces led to further defections.

Vitellius entered negotiations with the Flavians in Rome led by Flavius Sabinus (Vespasian's brother) and, probably after receiving assurances for his personal safety, Vitellius abdicated, leaving the palace and entering the Forum as a private citizen. As Flavius Sabinus organised the takeover, the situation took a dramatic turn. Vitellius was returned to the palace forcibly and there were demonstrations in his favour. The Flavian party seized the Capitoline Hill where they were besieged by Vitellian forces. During the siege, the temple of Jupiter Capitolinus, the most venerable temple in Rome, was destroyed. The Vitellian soldiers defeated the senators holding the Capitol and Sabinus was executed. Domitian, Vespasian's younger son, escaped in disguise (Tac., *Hist.* III 67–74).

This extraordinary spirit of defiance continued despite the overwhelming odds. The Flavian legions arrived on the outskirts of Rome but did not receive the expected surrender. They forced their way into the city, but the Vitellians fought a hopeless yet valiant rearguard action across the city which culminated in the capture of the praetorian barracks. Vitellius himself fled the palace only to return later. He was captured and killed (Tac., *Hist.* III 79–85; Suet., *Vit.* 16–17; Dio, LXV 17–21).

As with Otho, Vitellius appears to have enjoyed notable political success. In the period from his appointment to the command in Germania Inferior until his death in AD 69, he managed to win the devoted loyalty of the German troops who fought two wars for him, many of whom must have been killed either at Cremona or in the last hopeless battle through the streets of Rome. He also seems to have won the loyalty of the people of Rome who backed him until the end, though the military skill of the Roman troops was such that civilians could not offer Vitellius effective aid. He had, however, failed to resolve the tensions in the Roman state and win the loyalty of the troops. Like Galba and Otho before him, he had failed to achieve political legitimacy.

Vespasian's position was far stronger than that of Vitellius. He had the backing of the legions of the East and had conclusively defeated the legions of the West. Also, the conflict in Germany and Gaul in 69–70 would lead to the defeat of the remaining forces in Germany. There was no substantial effective military force that could threaten Vespasian. At his side, he had Mucianus and Titus. Other generals, such as Petilius Cerealis, had distinguished themselves and some of Otho's generals were to be given positions of prominence. Antonius Primus, who had effectively delivered the empire into Vespasian's hands, may have been an effective general but his failure to preserve Cremona and his attack on the city of Rome had reduced his political standing. Vespasian could attempt reconciliation confident that he faced no immediate political threat.

'CRISIS' IN THE PROVINCES

The civil conflict in the Roman Empire was combined with provincial disturbances. There was a continuing rebellion in Judaea and fresh outbreaks in Britain, Germany and Gaul (the most notable rebellion), and along the Danube frontier. Such outbreaks seemed to threaten to overwhelm the Roman empire but, as we shall see, Rome easily re-established control and her authority was confirmed.

Judaea

The conflict in Judaea (see also pp. 127–8) had resulted in a series of hard-fought conflicts as Vespasian led his legions into the province. The course of the war was marked by long sieges in which the Romans were ultimately successful, though at great cost. The Jews had not the skill, the training or the technology to meet the Romans in open battle and so resistance took the form of siege warfare and sorties against the Roman forces. Vespasian's campaign was stopped when he became a contender for the throne and the campaign was resumed under Titus after Vespasian's victory in the West.

Vespasian needed a quick victory and Titus' task was to provide him with that victory. The pattern of the war was unchanged and victory could only come after the capture of Jerusalem. The Roman forces besieged the city. Josephus' account makes it clear that the siege was hard fought. Titus was unwilling to allow the war to drag on. He and Vespasian had other pressing business and it must have become obvious to all that the Romans did not intend simply to wait for the Jews' food and resolve to give out. The Flavians needed a triumph, a dramatic symbol of victory to enhance their prestige; this was especially important given the problems in the West. Storming Jerusalem was no easy task. The Romans had to bring siege equipment against the walls and force a breach in the defences. The Jews attempted to defend and repair the walls and launch attacks on the siege equipment. In this, they were notably successful, but they could not force Titus to break off the siege. There was a long period of attrition, but the Jews' forces were gradually weakened and the Roman siege became more intense. Eventually, Titus' troops breached the many defences of the city and exacted their revenge for such a bloody siege. The temple itself was sacked and destroyed.

The temple was the central monument of Judaism to which many Jews would travel at the various religious festivals. It was their holiest site, and it was also extremely rich since it received contributions from Jews in all provinces and those friendly towards the Jewish people also contributed to temple funds. In AD 71, the vast wealth of the temple was to be carried through the streets of Rome in a triumph (an elaborate parade with various associated religious ceremonies), which was depicted on Vespasian and Titus' triumphal arch (known as the arch of Titus). The temple was never to be rebuilt and its destruction encouraged fundamental changes in Judaism.

Further operations continued in the region with the siege of Masada and the suppression of 'bandit' activity, yet, although this campaign was hard, Vespasian and Titus were justified in seeing the fall of Jerusalem as marking the end of the major stage of the war.

The revolt was also contained. The Jewish populations of the neighbouring provinces may have wished to support their co-religionists, but their minority position was more likely to lead to their persecution by the pagan population than any mass outbreak.

The Danube

Little is known about the outbreaks in this period. Tacitus (*Hist.* I 79) tells us that the Rhoxolani, a tribe living north of the Danube, crossed the river during the reign of Otho and invaded Moesia, but were defeated. Similarly, in late 69, the Dacians crossed the Danube to raid. Although the garrison had been significantly weakened by the expedition to Italy under Primus, the Dacians unluckily ran into Mucianus and his legions heading west from Syria and were defeated (Tac., *Hist.* III 46). However, they may have continued to pose problems for the Romans throughout 69, and later, though the detail of these wars is lost. The Sarmatians also caused problems, though again little is known about these outbreaks (Tac., *Hist.* I 2, IV 54). Such outbreaks may signify growing problems in the lands north of the Danube and may be precursors of the much more serious threats to the Danubian provinces that were faced by Vespasian and Domitian (see pp. 174, 184–5). It seems more likely, however, that these were raids designed to take advantage of the temporary weakness of the Roman frontiers and did not pose a serious threat to Roman rule in the area.

Britain

We have no significant information about events in Britain from the departure of Suetonius Paulinus until AD 69, and one must presume that the latter years of Nero's reign were occupied by a policy of consolidation and pacification of areas disturbed by the Boudiccan revolt. In 69, there seems to have been conflict between the governor and the officers of the legion, conflict which reached such a pitch that the governor fled to join Vitellius. The fact that the legions also declared for Vitellius (though they were later to declare for Vespasian who had served in Britain, perhaps urged on by the Fourteenth Legion) suggests that the issue in question was not which candidate to support in the civil wars, but may have been corruption (Tac., *Hist.* I 59–60).

Vitellius returned the Fourteenth Legion to Britain in 69. The legion had been prominent among the defeated Othonian forces at Bedriacum and was mutinous (Tac., *Hist.* II 66) but, although convenient, the return of the legion may have been in response to a fresh outbreak of anti-Roman activity. Cartimandua, the queen of the Brigantes (a tribe of northern Britain) who had proved herself a friend of Rome since the conquest, was ousted in a coup staged by her former husband Venutius (Tac., *Hist.* III 45). Cartimandua was rescued by the Romans, but they were unable to secure the province and war continued into the Flavian period when Petilius Cerealis launched a major campaign into Brigantia (see pp. 174–5). It is very difficult to understand these events, especially as Tacitus' description reduces the politics of the revolt to a scandalous marriage within the royal household, but the fact that the Romans were not easily able to secure the region suggests that there may have been serious problems.

Germany and Gaul

We have already suggested that Gallic discontent fuelled the rebellions of Vindex and Vitellius. During Vitellius' reign, events took a different turn with the creation of the 'Empire of the Gauls', though this was an event subsidiary to the revolt of the Batavians.

The Batavians lived on a stretch of land along the Lower Rhine. They had long provided the Roman army with auxiliary units, which were particularly valued not just for their fighting prowess but also for their skill in fording rivers. There had been conflicts between the Batavians and other Roman troops before the outbreak of the civil wars, but Vitellius had attempted to patch together an agreement in order to secure the support of the Batavians in the forthcoming conflicts. Unfortunately for the Romans, the Vitellians' demand for troops led to heavy-handed and corrupt recruitment among the Batavians and to general discontent. Julius Civilis led the revolt. They were joined by their neighbouring tribe, the Cannenefates, and gained support from other Germanic tribes. The Cannenefates and Batavians attacked and massacred small local garrisons. A two-legionary army was sent against them, though the legions were depleted by troops levied by Vitellius. This force was defeated and forced to retreat to the legionary camp of Vetera (Tac., *Hist.* IV 12–18).

The next stage of the revolt was a mutiny staged by units of Batavians and Cannenefates with the Roman army, though their exact location at the time of their revolt is unclear (they were probably in Germania Superior heading towards Italy). Hordeonius Flaccus, governor in Germany, had to decide whether to oppose their march or allow them to join with Civilis. Flaccus was worried about the quality of troops at his disposal and the loyalty of the Gallic troops with his army. He allowed them to start on their march but instructed Legion I to intercept them. The legion was

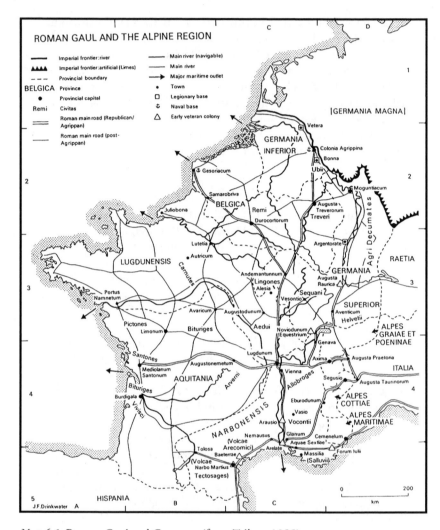

Map 6.1 Roman Gaul and Germany (from Talbert 1985)

heavily defeated and the Batavians made their way to join Civilis, adding substantially to his military strength (Tac., *Hist.* IV 19–20).

Civilis' forces had defeated three legions and established control over much of Germania Inferior. Already, two more tribes, the Bructeri and Tencteri, had joined the revolt and Civilis might hope for more support. The addition of the Batavian cohorts gave Civilis a core of well-trained and experienced soldiers around which to build his army. He became more confident and launched an attack on the legionary garrison in Germania Inferior in its camp at Vetera. The Batavians and their allies had not the equipment for storming the camp, though its fortifications may not have been strong, and were repulsed from the walls. The Romans did not have the strength to break out, however, and Civilis besieged the camp (Tac., *Hist.* IV 21–3).

The situation was perilous. Flaccus mobilised the resources of Germania Superior and sent his general Vocula north into Germania Inferior to face the Batavians and relieve Vetera. At this stage, news of the defeat of Vitellius seems to have reached Germany. The Roman troops stationed in Germany had shown great loyalty to Vitellius and the defeat of their comrades in Italy was likely to have affected morale. It may also have affected their view of their commanders. There was a suspicion that the Batavian revolt had been encouraged by the Flavians and that the legions were faced by enemies in both the Batavians and the new emperor. The smooth way in which the legions' commanders transferred their loyalty from Vitellius to Vespasian also caused the troops to doubt their former commitment to the Vitellian cause (Tac., *Hist.* IV 32). The troops may have felt betrayed.

Vocula marched on Vetera with a mutinous army. The relief column was attacked by Civilis but, with difficulty, Vocula drove off the Batavians. The legions managed to reach Vetera. They were, however, short of supplies. The situation was so serious that Vocula was forced to retreat, leaving a garrison in Vetera. Although the expedition to Vetera had not produced a decisive battle, the campaign had ended in Roman retreat, further increasing the prestige of Civilis and worsening the morale of the Roman troops (Tac., *Hist.* IV 33–7). On return to Germania Superior, the troops were openly mutinous: Vocula had to flee a lynch mob which claimed the life of Hordeonius Flaccus. Order was restored with difficulty, but the strategic situation had been made worse by the expedition. Civilis promptly besieged Vetera once more. German tribesmen now roamed across Germania Inferior and raided into neighbouring districts. There was little the Romans could do to stop them.

The anarchy which reigned among the legions, and their repeated defeat by Civilis, changed the political situation. The legions no longer seemed invincible and the Gauls looked for other means to secure their safety. Civilis had entered negotiations with Rome's Gallic allies and an alliance was formed involving the Treviri and the Lingones. The new allies appealed to all Gaul, seeking to form an Empire of the Gauls.

The alliance remained secret initially, though Vocula must have been aware that his position was serious. He decided to take the initiative by marching on Vetera once more. On the march, however, the Gallic auxiliaries defected and made overtures to the legions themselves. Vocula could not bring them to order and he was assassinated. The legions were enrolled into service with the new Gallic Empire. The troops besieged in Vetera were now without hope and surrendered. Both Germanies had fallen and at least parts of Gaul were now in rebellion (Tac., *Hist.* IV 54–60).

Almost as soon as the Gallic Empire was founded, it was under threat from both internal division and external intervention. The Flavians gathered a large army to invade Germany and Gaul under the command of Petilius Cerealis and Annius Gallus. The threat posed by eight legions was sufficient to force the Gauls into reconsidering their position. Gaul was not a nation state but a group of tribes politically independent of each other and often culturally diverse. Political divisions between the various tribes had been shown during the revolt of Vindex when tribes such as the Treviri and Lingones had not supported Vindex. Such recent bitter memories led to mutual antagonisms. Also, although the legionaries had come over to the Gallic Empire, they had suffered military defeat and were demoralised. They were not a realistic or reliable force with which to face the victorious Flavian legions and, although the Batavians and Gallic auxiliaries were more than capable, they were no match for the massed legions approaching them. The chances of the Gallic Empire surviving the coming assault were slim, and many of the Gallic tribes either failed to join the Empire or quickly returned to Rome (Tac., *Ann.* IV 68–9).

Cerealis led the advance with mixed success. The Treviri were decisively defeated but Cerealis himself suffered the embarrassment of losing his camp in a raid launched by Civilis, though he managed to regain the initiative (Tac., *Hist.* IV 71–7). The defected and defeated legions returned in disgrace. Eventually, Cerealis reached

Vetera where Civilis made his stand. The first battle resulted in a victory for Civilis, but the legions remained undaunted. Cerealis managed to out-manoeuvre Civilis and drive the Batavians back. Civilis launched a series of successful counter-attacks but was unable to halt the advance of the legions. The Batavians were forced to retreat to a territory known as the Island. The Romans were faced with a river crossing if they were to continue their pursuit, but were able to ravage Batavian land south of the Island. The result was stalemate. The Romans had failed to bring the Batavians to a decisive battle and looked unable to dislodge them from the Island. The Batavians had lost some territory but were in a position to continue the war. Petilius entered into negotiations which appear to have resulted in peace (Tac., *Hist.* V 14–26).

Conclusions

The revolts that swept the Roman world in this period can be related to problems that arose either during the latter years of Nero's reign or result from the military and political events of the civil wars. These revolts stretched Roman resources but, once the civil wars ended, there can have been little doubt that the Romans would restore the situation. The formation of the Gallic Empire may have seemed to threaten the dissolution of the Roman Empire, especially when considered in combination with the other revolts, but the Gallic Empire itself was illusory and in many ways shows the strength rather than the weakness of the Roman Empire. The Gallic communities did not attempt to establish independent tribal areas once more, but felt the need of a provincial structure. The Gallic Empire collapsed in the face of mutual hostilities and the failure to accept the authority of any individual. In spite of the trauma of the civil wars, Rome was able to restore her Empire without significant territorial losses. This was a major achievement and demonstrates the continued military prowess of the legions. The civil wars may have shown weaknesses in Rome's political and military organisation, but they also demonstrated the power and solidity of the Roman Empire.

CONCLUSIONS: AD 69 AND THE SECRETS OF EMPIRE

In AD 68–9, the military came to the forefront of political life. To a certain extent, the troops developed political attitudes independent of their commanders. Their disaffection was instrumental in the accessions of Otho and Vitellius and the troops fought long and hard for both men. The inability of men like Caecina to win over his troops when he defected to Vespasian, and the reluctance of troops in Germany to accept the accession of Vespasian when their officers seem to have accepted the political inevitability of Vespasian's success, shows that the troops were not simply manipulated by their officers into giving support to their chosen candidate.

Nevertheless, the problems candidates for the throne faced were as much to do with winning the loyalty of the political classes as with reconciling the soldiers. Galba offended the aristocracy and the soldiers. Otho and Vitellius had more success and were able to win over many of the aristocracy, but they both had to give rivals a reason to follow them rather than bid for the throne themselves. They needed to establish their legitimacy in the eyes of their social equals as well as with the soldiers. Vespasian was in a better position. He had the support of the legions of the East and had powerful allies in Mucianus, Tiberius Julius Alexander, Petilius Cerealis, and his own son Titus. Also, the important governorships were less of a threat. The Danubian legions had fought for Vespasian and could be relied on. The German forces had been weakened by supporting Vitellius and the war against Civilis. Vespasian had won, but to secure his regime he needed to build a powerful political alliance, and it is notable that Vespasian tended to concentrate political authority in the hands of his family and a few close friends to an even greater extent than the Julio–Claudians (see pp. 167–9). The events of AD 68–9 did not then uncover any great secret. The Roman emperor's most difficult task remained establishing his authority over the political elite.

Main events of AD 69–70

Date	Events
AD 69 January	Galba emperor and consul with Titus Vinius. Revolt of German legions in favour of Vitellius. Gaul and Britain join Vitellius. Adoption of Piso. Rising of Otho. Deaths of Galba, Vinius and Piso. Otho emperor. Preparations for civil war.
February to April	Invasion of Italy by legions from Germany. Danubian legions come over to Otho. False Nero in the East. Otho's forces win victories in Gallia Narbonensis, at siege of Placentia and outside Cremona. Battle of Bedriacum. Otho commits suicide.
April to July	Vitellius marches on Rome. Flavius Sabinus administers oath to the troops in Rome. Otho's supporters among the centurions of the Danubian legions killed. East accepts Vitellius. Vitellius wins support in Rome.
July to December	(1 July) Vespasian declared emperor in Egypt. (3 July) Syrian and Judaean legions support Vespasian. Danubian legions support Vespasian. Antonius Primus leads Danubian forces towards Italy. Mucianus leads Syrian legions to Italy. Primus invades Italy. Batavian Revolt. Revolt in Britain. Alienus Caecina defects to Vespasian. Ravenna fleet joins Vespasian. Battle of Cremona. Sack of Cremona. Collapse of Vitellian forces in North and Central Italy. Burning of the Capitol. Capture of Rome by Flavians. Death of Vitellius. Mucianus arrives in Rome. Civilis defeats Roman forces. Siege of Vetera. Defeat of Legion I. Vocula relieves Vetera, but forced to retreat. Siege of Vetera continues. Troops in Germany mutiny.
AD 70	Creation of the 'Gallic Empire'. Petilius Cerealis sent to Germany. Cerealis inflicts defeat on Civilis and invades Batavia. Cerealis and Civilis battle inconclusively. Peace negotiated. Siege and capture of Jerusalem.

7

VESPASIAN AND TITUS
(AD 70–81)

There is a change in the nature of our available source material from the reign of Vespasian onwards. For the narrative history of the period we have to rely on the fragments of Dio preserved in Byzantine epitomes (see p. 4) and it is frequently difficult to date events mentioned. Tacitus does write about the period but his observations are contained in the *Agricola* and the *Dialogus*, neither of which pretend to provide narrative histories of the period. Our other main guide is Suetonius, but the biographies of the Flavians are less detailed than those of earlier emperors. As a result, though we can perceive at least some of the more general developments, it is almost impossible to produce a detailed narrative of events during these years.

Vespasian associated his rule with his elder son, Titus. When the elderly Vespasian died, the succession was smooth. Titus took over as expected. Vespasian's reign has been generally well received by posterity. Titus' reign seems to have been regarded as almost a golden age. The reign, however, was short and he was replaced by his brother, the hated Domitian (see Figure 7.1).

POLITICS

Friends and Allies

On accession, Vespasian was the fifth emperor in a two-year period and, although he had no obvious rivals, he did not have such political authority that he could assume that the Roman aristocracy or the soldiers would offer him their loyalty. The Flavians were not a particularly distinguished family. Vespasian had failed to secure the aedileship (see p. 14 for the nature of this office) at his first attempt,

Figure 7.1 The Flavian family

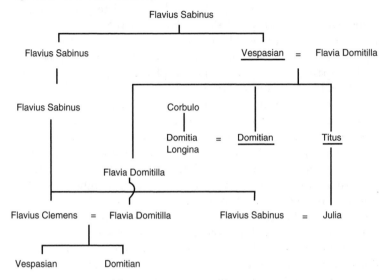

a sign that he did not have powerful political backing. When he eventually became aedile, he was famously dropped in mud by Gaius for not keeping the streets of Rome clean. His career may not have prospered until the reign of Claudius when he served with distinction in Britain and Germany. He was rewarded with a consulship in AD 51 and later governed Africa. He was in Nero's party that headed off to Greece, but supposedly slept through Nero's dramatic performances. In spite of this obvious breach of taste, Nero chose him to command the troops in Judaea (Suet., *Vesp.* 2–5). Vespasian achieved prominence with this command but he was certainly no more elevated socially than other provincial governors and was a less credible imperial candidate than Galba or Vitellius. Vespasian did, however, have powerful friends.

He was supported by Mucianus. Comparatively little is known about this man, though his authority and leadership were amply demonstrated by the way in which he took charge of Rome following Primus' rather anarchic seizure of the capital (see pp. 155–6). Mucianus appointed Vespasian's first praetorian prefects and probably appointed Petilius Cerealis to the Batavian campaign. Mucianus' role in Rome during the long period before Vespasian's arrival demonstrates Vespasian's trust in the man. He was rewarded with consulships in 70 and 72 after which time he remained in Rome, probably blending a political career with literary pursuits.

Titus was also prominent. He took charge of the war in Judaea and led the troops to a quick and bloody victory in capturing Jerusalem in 70 (see pp. 156–7). Although the war did not end until Flavius Silva (possibly a distant relative) stormed Masada in 73, Titus returned to Rome to share a lavish triumphal procession with Vespasian in 71. The triumph displayed Vespasian's power in a traditional style (triumphs had become the prerogative of the imperial family) and thus reinforced the legitimacy of his rule. By sharing the limelight with his son, Vespasian made it clear that he planned a dynasty. This was further marked by Vespasian and Titus holding a joint consulship in 70 (Vespasian's first as emperor). Titus was *consul ordinarius* in 72, 74, 75, 76, 77 and 79, a remarkable succession of consulships. As Vespasian also held eight consulships during his reign, the two virtually monopolised the ordinary consulships, though a large number of suffect consuls were appointed (see p. 253 for the differences between ordinary and suffect consulships). Titus was also appointed praetorian prefect (Suet., *Titus* 6), possibly as early as 71, and thus took charge of the largest military force in Italy and the emperor's personal security. Vespasian's reliance on him was clear.

Vespasian's other son, Domitian, was also honoured. He was granted suffect consulships in 71, 74, 76, 77 and 79, and ordinary consulships in 73 and 80. He wielded some authority in 70 as being the senior member of the Flavian family in Rome. His prominence in the consular lists shows that he was an important member of the regime.

Vespasian's brother, Sabinus, had been a prominent and seemingly popular senator (pp. 151–6) and although his death robbed Vespasian of his personal support, his son, also Flavius Sabinus, was granted a second consulship in 72 (he held his first in 69).

Petilius Cerealis, a relative by marriage, was also prominent (Tac., *Hist.* III 59). Cerealis had served in Britain in 61 when the legion he was commanding had been defeated by the Boudiccan rebels. He was in Rome when Vespasian made his bid for the throne, but managed to escape and led troops against the Vitellians. He was rewarded by being given the command against Civilis (see pp. 159–63) and a suffect consulship in 70. He was then sent to Britain to campaign against the Brigantes and probably returned in 74 when he was granted a second consulship.

Tiberius Julius Alexander received due reward. He had served the Flavian cause in Egypt and had presumably cemented his relationship with Vespasian during Vespasian's rather difficult stay in

Alexandria awaiting news from Italy. Alexander probably took part in the campaigns in Judaea under Titus and is recorded as being prefect of the Jews and procurator in Syria (*IGRR* III 1015). He may have journeyed to Italy soon after the conclusion of the Jewish war and there been Titus' colleague as praetorian prefect (*P. Hibeh*. 215). The exact chronology of his advancement is difficult to establish.

There were others of less prominence who were influential in the Flavian camp: men such as M. Ulpius Traianus, the father of the future emperor, who served in the Judaean war with Vespasian and Titus and who was subsequently rewarded with a consulship, provincial governorships and a priesthood (*ILS* 8970). We know less about the future emperor Nerva, who had risen to prominence by displaying loyalty to Nero during the Pisonian conspiracy and had been granted an ordinary consulship in 71 with Vespasian. The domination of the consulship by Titus and Vespasian was such that only Domitian and L. Valerius Catullus Messalinus (in 73), L. Ceionius Commodus and D. Junius Novius Priscus (in 78) and Nerva were allowed ordinary consulships during Vespasian's reign. The prominence of Nerva suggests that he was close to the centre of the Flavian group.

Reconstructing the friendships and alliances at the heart of the Flavian regime is complex and hazardous and the patterns of alliances will have changed as Vespasian promoted new men and gained the friendship and trust of others. One gains the impression that, although Vespasian was clearly in charge, his regime was based on more than the authority of a single man: Rome was ruled by a family and their friends.

Manners and the senate

It may seem inconsequential to discuss the manners of an emperor, but such matters were important. The senators formed a fairly small community and it mattered very much to them whether the emperor was friendly, whether he behaved as their superior or their equal, or whether he addressed them as a civilian or a general. They needed to know whether the emperor was one of them (a fellow senator) or their king.

Vespasian did not have the social status that would allow him to assert superiority over the senate: they knew he was of no better birth than them. It seems unlikely that anyone would take seriously a claim to divinity, and following the lead of Nero was problematic. Vespasian could rely on military power, but, as Claudius discovered, this would not lead to a peaceful life. Vespasian played the senator and stripped the imperial position of much of its ostentation. He did not live in the imperial palace but in a house in the Gardens of Sallust, a park in the centre of Rome. There, he received visitors from early in the morning. He made sure that the guard was not obvious and he gave up the practice of searching visitors. Personally, he was not above the banter of political life and rather liked to satirise his own pretensions (Suet., *Vesp.* 12–13, 21–2; Dio, LXVI 10–11). His most famous witticism is typical: as his last illness weakened him he is said to have remarked, 'Alas, I think I am becoming a god'. The recognition that his sons would deify him combined with a consciousness of his weakened state (Suet., *Vesp.* 23).

Vespasian represented himself in the mode of the traditional Italian aristocrat and there was a certain lack of refinement to his manner. He famously revoked a military command from a man who was over-perfumed (Suet., *Vesp.* 8) and he used obscenities in everyday speech. His desire for money rather than honours marked out his practicality. He may not have been what the senate wanted, but at least he was comprehensible. Vespasian had none of the terrifying unpredictability of the later Julio–Claudians.

Enemies and feuds

It would have been a mistake to underestimate Vespasian and to assume that his easy-going manner was a sign of personal weakness. Vespasian became emperor through civil war. He and his allies could be ruthless in maintaining their hold on power. Vespasian may not have purged the Roman aristocracy in quite the ruthless manner of the Julio–Claudians, but he was perfectly capable of removing his enemies.

His most famous political feud was with Helvidius Priscus. Priscus had been exiled by Nero and on his return to Rome became the leading member of the group that had grown up around Thrasea Paetus. The group continued its tradition of opposition (pp. 129–32). Vespasian's attitude towards them is unclear. Tacitus tells us that Vespasian had been friendly with Thrasea and Soranus (see pp. 129–32) during the reign of Nero (Tac., *Hist.* IV 6–7). Thrasea's status as martyr and leading senator may have encouraged those favourable to Vespasian to invent such a friendship, but the behaviour of the Flavians in the first months of the new regime suggests that they may have been well disposed to Priscus and his group. Such a relationship may explain why Musonius Rufus, another member of Thrasea's group, and Arulenus Rusticus (a close friend of Thrasea (see p. 131)) were chosen to lead a senatorial embassy to Antonius Primus to persuade him not to storm Rome in 69 (Tac., *Hist.* III 80–1). If this was the case, the accession of Vespasian would have raised the expectations of Priscus and his friends that they would be allowed to exact revenge on their enemies.

They did not wait long. Musonius Rufus launched a prosecution of Publius Celer (the prosecutor of Barea Soranus) immediately after the Flavian seizure of Rome (Tac., *Hist.* IV 10). Flavian support for Rufus suggests friendly relations with Priscus and his circle. Helvidius Priscus then launched his attack. Priscus and a certain Curtius Montanus attacked Eprius Marcellus and Aquilius Regulus, who had both been prominent prosecutors under Nero. Marcellus had brought the charges against Thrasea. The case was blocked by Domitian, presumably with the backing of Mucianus. The Flavians, like Otho and Vitellius, desired reconciliation and investigations into the events of Nero's reign could endanger too many powerful men. Priscus was not to be allowed his revenge (Tac., *Hist.* IV 40–4). The failure of the attack on Marcellus may have enraged Priscus and his supporters or they may have had other reasons to quarrel with Vespasian.

Priscus appears never to have fully recognised Vespasian's accession, but Vespasian seems to have ignored minor slights. More seriously, Priscus launched a direct attack on the Flavian dynasty. Dio (LXVI 12.1) preserves an account of Priscus attacking the Emperor in the senate-house with such vitriol that the tribunes stepped in and arrested Priscus, leading him from the house. Vespasian left proclaiming 'My son shall succeed me or no one shall'. If Dio has preserved the story correctly, then it would seem that the attack had focused not on Vespasian himself but on Titus. In so doing, Priscus struck at the heart of the regime.

Priscus continued to attack Vespasian, though we do not know the details of the conflict. Vespasian's response was to give a provincial governorship to Priscus' enemy, Eprius Marcellus (*IGRR* IV 524; *ILS* 992). By so doing, he removed Marcellus temporarily from the political scene and he may have hoped that tempers would calm. However, Marcellus was subjected to another prosecution on his return to Rome, probably to take up a consulship in 74. Tacitus tells us that Marcellus got the better of this conflict, perhaps suggesting that Priscus had lost the sympathy of the senate (*Dialogus* 5). Vespasian's response was to exile and then kill Priscus (Suet., *Vesp.* 15; Dio, LXVI 12.2).

Marcellus himself was to come to grief in 79. He was involved in a conspiracy with Alienus Caecina (see p. 155). Caecina was detected with a speech that he intended to deliver to the soldiers and was struck down by Titus at Titus' own dinner table, a deed reminiscent of the ruthless killings of the Julio–Claudians (Suet., *Titus* 6; Dio LXVI 16.3–4). The background to the conspiracy and the nature of Marcellus' involvement is unclear.

Some modern writers have seen in this conspiracy a violent resolution of tensions in the Flavian camp that had been simmering since 69, tensions which had disturbed the relationship between Mucianus and Titus. They have suggested that it was Mucianus who first extended his patronage to Marcellus, saving Marcellus from the wrath of the senate, to the displeasure of Titus, and that Mucianus prevented Titus from bringing his Jewish lover Berenice to Rome. There are suggestions that Titus forced Mucianus' devotion to literature late in life (Tac., *Dialogus* 37) and the arrival of Berenice in Rome has been seen as signifying his retirement some time before 75, a retirement which left Marcellus in a politically exposed position, resulting in his removal in 79. However attractive this is, there is no evidence for any breach between Mucianus and Titus and the reconstruction of the internal politics of the Flavian faction is fantasy.

The presumption that feuding between Titus and Domitian was the dominant political issue of the period is similarly fantastic, though this at least has some ancient support (Suet., *Titus* 9.3, 10; *Dom.* 2.3). Some of this is clearly later literary invention that serves to contrast the good (Titus) and the bad (Domitian). Yet, we need not see Domitian's comparatively minor role under Vespasian as an attempt to control an unruly young man. Domitian was not expected to succeed to the throne and was therefore not given the same kind of role as Titus. Titus was made his father's aide partly to secure the succession. When Titus came to the throne, the succession did not seem an immediate problem and Domitian's consulship in 80 with Titus demonstrates that there was no attempt to remove Domitian from positions of prominence, but it could not have been expected that, on the accession of Titus, Domitian would simply take over the duties that his brother had performed for their father.

Much else of the political history of the period is lost. Suetonius (*Vesp.* 25 cf. *Titus* 6) talks of many conspiracies against Vespasian, but provides no evidence, and the fact that both Suetonius and Dio note the relative paucity of senatorial and equestrian deaths rather suggests that these conspiracies, if they were not figments of

Suetonius' imagination, were not serious. Titus similarly killed no senators, though Suetonius tells us that he was threatened by a conspiracy (Suet., *Titus* 9).

Much of the opposition to the Flavians seems to have been very vocal and unafraid of the ability of the emperors to kill them. Whereas Thrasea Paetus attempted to avoid open conflict with Nero, Helvidius Priscus seems to have welcomed such public confrontations. Similar public confrontations were sought by two philosophers, Diogenes and Heras, who both spoke against Vespasian in the theatre. Diogenes was flogged. Heras, who came later, when patiences had been tried, was decapitated. One might guess that their philosophy taught them contempt for the world so that they had no fear of being deprived of life, and that advertising this contempt in the face of official pressure demonstrated the strength of their conviction and attracted attention and followers. Dictatorial regimes that rely on the character of those in charge to legitimate their control (as was the case with the Flavians) find those willing to expose their moral and political weaknesses immensely disturbing and those who do not fear death are almost impossible to control. Vespasian made a public example of Diogenes and Heras. Helvidius Priscus was more difficult, and Vespasian may have felt unwilling or unable to act until Priscus had lost senatorial support and his regime was relatively secure. Such discordant voices probably represent a much larger, silent element of the political classes. Yet Vespasian and Titus were not dethroned by their opponents and Vespasian had his wish in that he was succeeded (peacefully) by his sons. They may not have been universally popular, but Vespasian and Titus were remarkably successful.

MILITARY POLICY

Vespasian faced considerable problems when he came to the throne. There was war in Judaea, Germany and Britain and unrest along the Danube (pp. 156–63). In the East, Vespasian and Titus were mainly occupied with ending the war in Judaea. In the West, they were able to begin a process of renewed imperial expansion.

Judaea and the East

Titus' troops stormed Jerusalem in AD 70. The destruction of the temple brought the major part of the war to an end (pp. 156–7). Yet there remained pockets of resistance. From the very beginning of the conflict, some of the rebel groups had operated as bandits in the countryside. These were comparatively unaffected by the fall of Jerusalem and posed a significant problem for the Roman forces. Eventually, however, the main group were driven to the fortress of Masada where they were besieged by the Romans. In AD 73, the Roman siege machines were advanced to the walls. The besieged had no hope of survival and committed mass suicide. The war came to an end.

Vespasian annexed a number of client-kingdoms, Cilicia and Commagene being militarily significant. The annexation of Commagene involved a brief war (Jos., *BJ* VII 220–40; *ILS* 9198).

The rest of the East seems to have remained quite peaceful.

Britain and Germany

Vespasian and Titus followed an aggressive policy in Britain. Cerealis was sent from his campaigns in Germany to Britain where the Brigantes had been causing problems (see pp. 158–63). We know little about his campaigns but the archaeological evidence suggests that he pushed the Roman frontier to the north of Brigantian territory and established forts throughout what is modern Yorkshire. The Brigantes were defeated. He was followed by Julius Frontinus who campaigned in South Wales against the Silures. The campaign was probably successful. Julius Agricola, Tacitus' father-in-law, was sent to the province in 77/8 and campaigned throughout the next seven years. His campaigns took him from North Wales to the very north of Scotland. His victories seem to have brought much of Britain under Roman control, though Tacitus' claims for Agricola are undoubtedly exaggerated (Tac., *Agricola*).

We know less about the campaigns in Germany after peace was made with the Batavians. The frontier needed to be secured and the damage of the Batavian revolt repaired. In addition, relationships with the German tribes that had been disturbed by the revolt had to be restored. It is clear that the frontier was reorganised with a new camp built at Vetera and legionary forces stationed close to the Batavians. At some point, it seems to have been decided to go on the offensive. This can be traced in the Neckar valley between the Rhine and the Danube, where there seems to have been a Roman advance. New forts were built in this region. There may have been other military action further to the north but, in any case, the territory acquired cannot have been great.

Vespasian and Titus seem to have engaged in a period of consolidation, as one would expect at the end of a period of civil wars. They brought peace to areas where there were problems and secured their triumph in Judaea, a triumph they celebrated with some style if the huge arch of Titus is any guide. In contrast to the generally pacific policies followed by the Julio–Claudians, they seem to have developed a fairly aggressive policy in the West, campaigning in Britain and Germany, with significant territorial gains in Britain. In the East, the annexation of Commagene (and perhaps Cilicia) shows aggressive intent, though we know of no plans for expansion towards the East.

BUILDING AND FINANCE

The treasury was empty when the Flavians took over. The excesses of Nero, gifts to soldiers and the expenses of civil war led to a rapid depletion of funds. The damage to Rome and other cities needed repair and military expenses had to be met. Vespasian needed money. Taxes were raised (in some cases doubled) and new taxes invented, most notable being a tax on Jews, which was levied for the repair of the Capitoline temple and as a punishment for the rebellion, and a tax on urinals (about which he teased Titus). He was not above selling minor offices and even acquittals in legal cases. He may also have used his financial resources to corner the market in certain goods and then make a profit on their resale (Suet., *Vesp.* 16, 23.2–3).

This suggests financial desperation, but the measures seem to have worked. Vespasian met his obligations to be generous to his friends, to sponsor the arts, to entertain the plebs, and to provide emergency aid to communities in distress, and he also managed to embark on an ambitious building programme. On his death, the finances were sufficiently healthy that they could meet the very heavy expenditure of Titus' reign and the cost of the donatives paid to the troops on the accessions of Titus and Domitian.

Vespasian's major building project was to repair the damage caused by the civil war in Rome. The most notable casualty was the Temple of Jupiter on the Capitoline Hill. This was one of the oldest and most important sacred sites in the city. Its destruction was regarded as a national catastrophe and a symbol of the self-destructive nature of civil war. Vespasian himself supervised the clearance of the site, apparently carrying a load of rubble away on his head (Suet., *Vesp.* 8.5).

The focus of Vespasian's building marked a radical change from that of Nero's. Whereas Nero's most notable construction had been his palace (and in this he followed the pattern set by Gaius' additions to the Domus Tiberiana), Vespasian moved out of the palace and used the area of the Domus Aurea for public building projects. His most famous construction is the Colosseum, a huge amphitheatre in the centre of Rome. Although Vespasian claimed to be fulfilling a plan of Augustus in constructing such a huge building, the Colosseum was part of an attempt by the Flavians to win popular favour. For similar reasons, he rebuilt the stage building at the theatre of Marcellus (Suet., *Vesp.* 19). Vespasian rebuilt or completed a temple to the Divus Claudius. He built a large temple to Pax (peace) near the Forum. He also re-erected a huge statue (the statue of Nero from the Domus Aurea) either in or near the Forum which, Dio (LXVI 15) claims, had the features of Nero or Titus. The Arch of Titus was a monument to the Flavians' great military achievement in sacking Jerusalem.

Titus' reign was marked by massive expenditure. On accession, he needed to pay donatives to the troops. He completed the Colosseum, and added a set of baths to the amphitheatre. This was probably to demonstrate his personal involvement with the construction and ensure that not all the credit passed to his dead father. The Colosseum was opened with lavish shows, again partly to celebrate the new building, partly to demonstrate Titus' own generosity and care for the plebs (Suet., *Titus* 7.3, 8.2; Dio LXVI 25). The cost of these entertainments was probably dwarfed by the expenses of disaster relief and repair incurred during his reign. In AD 79, Vesuvius erupted. Pompeii and Herculaneum were destroyed. There was probably extensive earthquake damage in surrounding communities and the debris may have affected local agriculture. The following year, a fire swept through the centre of Rome, destroying many buildings on the Campus Martius. Again, those made homeless needed immediate help and the emperor was faced with the expensive task of repairing or rebuilding monuments. Titus himself is supposed to have responded to news of the fire merely by saying 'I am lost'. He used the statues from his own villas to decorate the public buildings (Suet., *Titus* 8.3–4; Dio, LXVI 21–4). Such generosity must have drained the public purse but will have won Titus many friends, especially among the lower classes. Titus, however, did not live long enough to enjoy his popularity. He died of a fever in September AD 81, aged 40.

TITUS' REPUTATION

History has been kind to Titus. Suetonius remarks on his personal skills and virtues, the generosity of his reign and the kindliness with which he dealt with friends and foes while he was emperor. This portrayal is in marked contrast with the treatment of his brother and it seems very likely that Titus' reputation has benefited from the comparison.

Titus' reign was sufficiently short that it avoided the gradual accumulation of animosities that marked every other reign and eventually led to conflict. There are, however, certain signs of tension between Titus and the Roman elite that give rise to the suspicion that such conflict would not have been avoided. Titus had been an active praetorian prefect and the cutting down of the conspirators of 79 showed a brutality that may have led some to fear his reign (see p. 172). His personal morality also may have led to doubts. His involvement with the Jewish princess, Berenice, was scandalous. Quintillian claims to have represented Berenice in a court case while Berenice herself sat with the judge (probably Titus), a clear abuse of power (Quintillian, *Inst.* IV 1.19). Such behaviour recalled the relationships of Caesar and Antony with Cleopatra, and some in Rome may have feared that Berenice would wield considerable authority when Titus became emperor. Berenice had come to Rome in 75 but left again before Vespasian's death. She returned when Titus became emperor but was sent back to the East, perhaps because of an adverse public reaction (Dio, LXVI 15.3, 18; Suet., *Titus* 7).

There were elements in Titus' life that would have allowed a creative biographer to have portrayed him as a second Nero. It is certainly possible that his interests in the Greek East and his concern to win favour with the plebs would have led to him evolving a rather different style of leadership from that of his father and that he would have come into conflict with more traditional elements of the Roman aristocracy. There were, however, no open conflicts. It seems clear though that the dismal years of Domitian's reign affected ancient perceptions of the reign of Titus and turned his two efficient and seemingly politically peaceful years into a time of tremendous hope and promise for the Roman people, which was ruined by their emperor's premature death.

8

DOMITIAN (AD 81–96)

With the sudden death of Titus, Domitian emerged from his brother's shadow to become emperor. He had played an important role in AD 69 when he had been the senior representative of the family in Rome, but had not enjoyed the same prominence as Titus during the reign of their father, nor had he come to the forefront of Roman political life with the accession of his brother. His reign is damned by the tradition. Tacitus, Pliny, Suetonius and Juvenal present extremely hostile portraits of the emperor. His personal behaviour, his handling of the senate and his conduct of military and administrative affairs are the main areas that drew ancient criticism. Any reconstruction of Domitian's reign is hampered by this almost universal hostility. It is also hampered by the absence of a full narrative account of the reign. We depend mainly on Byzantine epitomes of Dio and, as a result, the chronology of political and military events is somewhat confused (see p. 4). Almost of necessity, we must take a thematic rather than a chronological approach to the reign.

THE IMPERIAL COURT

Domitian seems to have been temperamentally unsuited to adopting the open and unassuming manner of his father and brother. He spent much of his time both before and after accession at Alba some distance from Rome where he is depicted in Juvenal, *Satire IV*, surrounded by a small group of intimates on whom he relied for advice. Good emperors were supposed to consult widely and take advice from the senate in public. Domitian enhanced the tendency for government to concentrate on the court.

Family

Domitian was emperor solely because of his birth. It was inevitable that he should attempt to elevate his family (see Figure 7.1, p. 167 for a family tree). Vespasian had been deified, Titus followed. Domitian's niece, Julia Augusta, was associated with Domitian's reign, appearing on coins from as early as *c.* 80–1 in association with Venus and being included in sacrifices for the safety of the emperor (BMC, *Imp* II p. 247). Julia and Domitian were rumoured to be lovers (Dio, LXVII 3.1–2), though the sexual habits of emperors were always a matter for (inventive) gossip.

Domitian was married to a daughter of Corbulo (see pp. 125–6), Domitia Longina. Domitia was initially prominent and Domitian was probably able to exploit this connection with the popular general. She fell from grace fairly early in the reign for alleged adultery with the actor Paris, who was killed on the street by Domitian. Although exiled, she returned to the emperor fairly quickly (Dio, LXVII 3).

Domitian's first consular colleague as emperor was a family member, T. Flavius Sabinus, a descendant of Vespasian's brother and husband of Julia. Sabinus apparently clad his servants in white, the same colour that Domitian used (Suet., *Dom.* 12). The close relationship of these two reflected the fact that the regime continued to be a family affair. In the event of Domitian's early death, Sabinus was to continue the Flavian line with a minimum of disruption. At some point (probably early in the reign), however, an attendant became confused between the two Flavians and announced Sabinus as imperator, not consul. Domitian regarded this as a usurpation of authority and Sabinus was killed (Suet., *Dom.* 10).

Flavius Clemens, the brother of Flavius Sabinus, became prominent when he held a consulship with Domitian in 95. Two of his sons were named as Domitian's heirs. As the father of the future emperors and a close adult male relative of the emperor, Clemens was in an important political position. He was killed, probably in late 95, and his wife was exiled on charges of atheism (Suet., *Dom.* 15; Dio, LXVII 14.1–2; see pp. 185–6).

A more distant relative, Arrecinus Clemens, may have been prominent in the early years of Domitian's reign, but was executed for reasons unknown (Suet., *Dom.* 11).

Friends

Julius Ursus was prefect of Egypt under Vespasian. He may have been Domitian's praetorian prefect. Dio (LXVII 3.1) credits him with sufficient influence to prevent Domitian from killing Domitia Longina after her alleged adultery with the actor Paris. Domitian quarrelled with Ursus in the mid-80s and Dio (LXVII 4.2) claims that Ursus' life was saved by Julia's intervention. He was honoured with the consulship in 84, suggesting that he was no longer praetorian prefect by that date and that the quarrel cannot have been serious. His later fate is unclear.

Juvenal's list of courtiers in Satire *IV* is an obviously distorted picture of Domitian's court. The courtiers summoned to consider the crucial issue of what to do with a very large fish were Pegasus (the urban prefect), Vibius Crispus, Acilius Glabrio and son, Rubrius Gallus (a military man later executed for an unknown crime), Montanus, Crispinus, Pompeius, Cornelius Fuscus (the praetorian prefect), Fabricius Veiento and Catullus Messalinus. We know very little about some of these men, but several were senior political figures. Vibius Crispus had been consul first under Nero and held a third consulship under Domitian. Acilius Glabrio's son was consul with Trajan in AD 91 but was killed in *c.* AD 95 (Dio, LXVII 14.3). Fabricius Veiento was expelled from Rome after publishing a scandalous mock will under Nero (see p. 111), but returned to become a close adviser of Domitian and was responsible for several prosecutions. His political skill was such that he retained prominence and power into the reign of Nerva and used that power to try and protect others who had collaborated with Domitian (see pp. 192–3). Catullus Messalinus was a notorious prosecutor of Domitian's enemies. His blindness seems to have added to the general fear he inspired. He had held an ordinary consulship with Domitian in 73 (see p. 253) – only Nerva had preceded Messalinus in this honour – and Messalinus was to hold a further consulship in 83.

Nerva's name is absent from most ancient accounts of Domitian's reign. He cannot, however, have been invisible in this period. He had been a prominent supporter of Vespasian and held an ordinary consulship as Domitian's colleague in 90. His rapid elevation to the imperial position in 96 and his protection of the former associates of Domitian suggest strongly that he, too, was a member of the inner circle of Domitian's friends, though there is some evidence to suggest that he may have somewhat distanced himself from the regime in 93 (see below).

There is no evidence to suggest a fundamental change in the composition of the imperial court between the reigns of Titus and Domitian. Domitian surrounded himself with experienced and politically astute men. The operation of the court is more difficult to establish. Juvenal portrays the *amici* (friends of the emperor) gathering suddenly and in terror. Pliny (*Pan.* 48) also describes how those who visited the emperor made every effort to leave quickly. *Amici* could be intimidated by the imperial presence and even the honoured may have been treated with suspicion. Hostile and frightened *amici* were hardly in a position to give good advice and a tyrannical emperor may only have heard what he wanted to hear. Domitian killed many of those closest to him (several in the last years of his reign) and was killed in a conspiracy of his freedmen which probably also involved both *amici* and family (Dio, LXVII 15). We should not dismiss altogether the ancient portrayal of Domitian as an emperor feared and hated by all. Nevertheless, it remains probable that Domitian's relationship with his friends and family changed during his reign. Increasing conflict between Domitian and the senate may have led to increasing paranoia. Those to whom he may have listened in the early years of his reign might have been rather more cautious in what they said during his later years.

POLITICS

Domitian's enemies are hardly better attested than his friends, and the picture we gain of them is equally distorted. Domitian's reign saw further conflict with the so-called philosophical opposition. This was certainly not the only group to suffer at the hands of Domitian and his supporters, but our sources are such that it is only the history of this group that can be traced with any confidence. The three most prominent victims were the younger Helvidius Priscus, Arulenus Rusticus and Herennius Senecio. The crimes of these men were literary. Helvidius published a farce which was interpreted as an allegorical attack on Domitian and his wife (Suet., *Dom.* 10.2). Rusticus published a work on Thrasea Paetus (see pp. 129–32) and Domitian took exception to lavish praise of a man who had been a thorn in the side of an emperor. Senecio's biography of Helvidius Priscus (the elder) (see pp. 170–1) was similarly impolitic. These men fell in late 93 (Suet., *Dom.* 10.2–4; Tac., *Agr.* 2; Dio, LXVII 13.2–3; Pliny, *Ep.* VII 33).[1]

Rusticus, Priscus and Senecio were not the only ones punished. Junius Mauricus, brother of Arulenus Rusticus, and Arria, Fannia and Gratilla, female members of the group, were also exiled (Pliny, *Ep.* I 5, III 11, VII 19). Other possible members include Maternus, a philosopher, who was killed for making a speech on tyranny (Dio, LXVII 12.5) and Hermogenes of Tarsus, a historian, who was killed for certain 'allusions' in his history (Suet., *Dom.* 10), and perhaps the Artemidoros whom Pliny visited in 93 was also exiled (Pliny, *Ep.* III 11). Pliny himself must have come very close to being prosecuted.

We know very little of the background to these cases, but it seems likely that relations between Priscus and his circle and Domitian had been tense for some years before 93. Domitian's connection with Corbulo (who had been on the edge of this circle) may have encouraged Domitian to seek a reconciliation with the circle of Thrasea and Helvidius. The accounts of the charges suggest that the opposition of these men had been clear long before their cases came to court: it is difficult to believe that these literary works were all recent publications. Nevertheless, Domitian had taken no obvious action to hamper the careers of these men and may even have aided their rise. Both Helvidius Priscus (date uncertain) and Rusticus (AD 90) held the consulship. Avidius Quietus, who had been a friend of Thrasea Paetus, received the consulship in 93, the same year in which Pliny was probably praetor, having been allowed by Domitian to stand for the praetorship a year early (Pliny, *Ep.* VII 16). Quietus was to be active in support of Pliny's attempt to gain revenge on those who had prosecuted Helvidius Priscus (Pliny, *Ep.* IX 13). Pliny claims that his career was subsequently blocked by Domitian (*Pan.* 95), but this is difficult to substantiate. Yet, by allowing these people to advance into prominent positions, he merely enhanced his later difficulties and the situation in 93, when a consul and a praetor were associated with the men who were tried for treasonable acts, may have been explosive.

Pliny gives an account of the events that led to the elimination of the 'philosophical opposition' and places these firmly in a senatorial context. Senecio and Pliny had been involved in the trial of a corrupt governor, Baebius Massa. They had effectively won the case, but Massa had not been punished. Senecio and Pliny pushed for harsh measures to be taken and Massa retaliated by prosecuting Senecio for *maiestas* (treason) (Pliny, *Ep.* VII 33). Subsequent events are unclear, but it seems that the fall of Senecio was taken as an excuse to remove many of Senecio's circle. Priscus and Rusticus seem to have fallen victim in this outburst of senatorial faction fighting. Massa was clearly threatened by ruin if the penalties for corruption were enforced and so his reaction was possibly not a surprise. Domitian's involvement is demonstrated by the involvement of men close to the emperor in the prosecutions and his failure to stop the prosecutions. As in the reign of Tiberius, the prosecutions were led by senators, but the emperor stood behind them.

Domitian's relationship with the senate was probably difficult before this point. The elimination of this group of prominent senators had, however, been avoided. It is probable that they were regarded by all as a symbol of senatorial liberty and their deaths marked the culmination of a process in which liberty was destroyed. After 93, there could be little pretence of cordiality between emperor and senate, and senators needed to behave as if he was their master to survive the *dominatio*. The breach in relations with the senate may have led to an increasingly paranoid atmosphere and, although we know virtually nothing about the subsequent purges of the aristocracy, it would seem that the emperor came to fear even his closest associates.

Suetonius (*Dom.* 10–11) and Dio's account of the later years of Domitian's reign (LXVII 11–14) list former consuls and others killed in this period and provide numerous examples of ludicrous charges. Aelius Lama was killed for a joke at Domitian's expense. Salvius Cocceianus was killed for commemorating the birthday of his uncle Otho. Sallustius Lucullus was killed for naming a new type of lance after himself. Mettius Pompusianus was killed after a prediction that he would become emperor. We cannot know whether these cases involved serious conspiracies or the destruction of political factions, and we cannot date the killings.

Some of the deaths of Domitian's reign cannot be connected to the 'philosophical opposition'. Antonius Saturninus, governor of Germania Superior launched a revolt in AD 89 but was not even able to gain the support of the legions of Germania Inferior and the revolt was quickly crushed. Domitian responded to the threat by taking measures to secure the loyalty of the army. The pay of the troops was raised from 225 to 300 sesterces per year and each legion was given a separate camp (Suet., *Dom.* 6.2; Dio, LXVII 11.1–3). It is not known whether Saturninus had any support in Rome for his revolt.

The atmosphere of the reign is attested by Pliny and Tacitus. In the *Agricola*, Tacitus talks of the years when speech was impossible and the senators grew old in silence, fearing that their words would be twisted by informants in order to bring them down. Pliny tells us of Corellius Rufus who, though suffering from a painful and incurable illness, put off his suicide to have the pleasure of outliving Domitian. Rufus sent all from the room when Pliny visited so that no one, not even his wife, could report his words (*Ep.* I 12). Pliny also tells us of a case in the centumviral court when he clashed with Regulus. The case turned on the legal opinion of a certain Modestus who had been exiled by Domitian. Regulus tried to discredit Modestus' opinion and asked Pliny what he thought of the man. To praise Modestus would have meant exile or worse and to attack him would have lost him the case. Pliny circumvented the issue by trying to bring debate back to the point of law and Pliny and Regulus became sworn enemies (Pliny, *Ep.* I 5).

WAR AND MILITARY POLICY

The best account of campaigns is limited to Roman expansion in Britain in the period 77/8–84/5. Agricola had campaigned for seven years before bringing the Britons to a decisive battle, though the literary form of the work more or less demanded a great set-piece scene in which Agricola's military and rhetorical virtues could be displayed and Tacitus may have considerably enhanced the importance of the battle. Yet the seizure of Northern Scotland was short-lived even if Agricola's success ever properly secured the territory. Domitian withdrew a legion to meet a crisis in Germany and Rome was forced to retreat from the newly conquered territory (Tac., *Agr.*).

The Rhine and Danube frontiers had been the scene of much activity during the reign of Vespasian and it seems probable that Domitian's wars should be seen as part of the same policy of gradual expansion in Germany. Domitian's German campaigns (conducted in person) were directed against the Chatti, and as early as 83 (the war probably started in the summer of 82) Domitian proclaimed victory. The literary tradition is more hostile and justifiably so. The Chatti were not subdued, although the defences of the frontier and communications may have been notably improved. They continued to pose a threat to neighbouring tribes and the frontier and even gave their support to Saturninus' attempted coup (Dio LXVII 3.5–4.2, 5.1; Suet., *Dom.* 6).

In 84 or 85, the Dacians crossed the Danube and invaded Moesia, killing the governor. Domitian and Cornelius Fuscus intervened and restored order (Dio, LXVII 6; Suet., *Dom.* 6). Fuscus took the initiative and launched an invasion of Dacian territory. His army was defeated and Fuscus himself was killed. In subsequent years, there were two or possibly three major campaigns in Dacia which brought a settlement of the frontier, though the Dacians had to be bought off. Domitian did not accept a triumph: he may have been aware that, although order was restored, the frontier was not properly secured (Dio, LXVII 7).

In the mid-80s, the Nasmones, an African tribe, revolted and, after initial success, were destroyed by the Roman governor. Changes in the frontier under Trajan perhaps suggest that there were other conflicts in North Africa (Dio LXVII 4.6).

Domitian seems to have followed a very similar policy to that of his father. He was interested in winning military glory and therefore pursued an active expansionist policy in Britain and Germany. He continued to make slow gains in Germany, but events on the Danube changed the military situation fundamentally forcing the relocation of units away from Britain and a limited retreat. It was these long Danubian wars which occupied much of Domitian's reign. Domitian's aggressive instincts are shown by Fuscus' unsuccessful attack on the Dacians and he may have intended to return to the offensive eventually. His reign was marked by defeat and consolidation rather than the acquisition of new territory, but the situation was such that we cannot regard him as militarily incompetent.

IMAGE AND PROPAGANDA

Domitian made some effort to win popular esteem. He maintained an image of personal conservatism and restraint in combination with exhibitions of largesse, especially directed towards the urban population and the military.

This conservatism was reflected in his religious policy. He collected the tax on the Jews with vigour (see p. 175). Suetonius tells that he was present at a public and humiliating examination of the genitalia of a ninety-year-old man to ascertain whether he was Jewish and should be paying the Jewish tax (Suet., *Dom.* 12.2). The use of informers probably increased abuses of the law since any who had flirted with Judaism might find themselves faced with a crippling tax bill and criminal charges.

Prosecutions for atheism in this period may also be connected with anti-Jewish feeling, but are perhaps more likely to be related to Domitian's use of the imperial cult as a way of displaying his authority. Dio's notice of Domitian's demand that the title *deus et dominus* (god and master) be used when addressing him is associated with the persecution of the 'philosophers' in 93 (Dio, LXVII 13.4; Suet., *Dom.* 13), prior to the prosecution of Flavius Clemens for atheism. Atheism could be understood as a political crime: an unwillingness to acknowledge the divinity of the emperor. *Deus et dominus* does not appear in official contexts, suggesting that its application was limited (perhaps it was only used to intimidate senators), and it is probable that it was never adopted as an official part of Domitian's nomenclature.

Domitian's religious conservatism came to the fore in the treatment of the vestals. The period saw two scandals, one involving the chief vestal. The traditional punishment for a vestal who broke her vows of chastity was to be buried alive. Cornelia, chief vestal, who had already been tried and acquitted once for failure to maintain chastity, was retried and found guilty. The traditional punishment was imposed. Three other vestals were allowed to choose their method of death. Most of those with whom they had supposedly offended were punished by death, though the former praetor who had confessed to the crime was merely exiled. The treatment of the vestals was so cruel (and the use of torture leads to considerable doubt about their guilt) that one senator supposedly expired in horror in the senate-house (Suet., *Dom.* 8; Dio, LXVII 3.3).

Domitian was generous to the plebs. He abolished the corn dole, but replaced it with civic banquets at which the emperor's largesse could be displayed. He also gave lavish games. He gave secular games and instituted a major new festival. He increased the number of circus teams and factions from four to six, presumably to add interest to the games. He also distributed money to the Roman plebs (Suet., *Dom.* 4, 7.1; Dio LXVII 8).

Domitian, like his father and brother, also had ambitious building plans. We do not know the full extent of Domitianic building in Rome, since after the *damnatio memoriae* (an official attempt to wipe out all trace of Domitian from the public records, including erasing his name from inscriptions and removing his statues from display) Domitian's name would have been removed from public buildings, and his successors associated themselves with projects started but incomplete at Domitian's death. He was engaged in major construction projects in the centre of the city. He started the Forum Transitorium, later known as the Forum of Nerva. This led from the Forum Romanum and Forum Iulium to the Forum Augusti and the temple of Pax, which is sometimes known as the Forum Pacis. This last was a Flavian construction and was probably finished by Domitian. There may have been Domitianic constructions in the huge area that later became the Forum Traiani. Alongside the Forum Romanum, Domitian completed the temple to his father and consecrated it to both Vespasian and Titus. He also remodelled the Domus Tiberiana and constructed a large three-storey structure (purpose uncertain) by the temple of Castor. He built himself a new palace near the Circus Maximus. He built a new temple to Jupiter Custos and renovated once more the temple of Jupiter Capitolinus. He constructed a new stadium and an odeion (Suet., *Dom.* 5). He built many arches, presumably to commemorate his military successes (Suet., *Dom.* 13.2). The list of buildings associated with Domitian is impressive (see Table 8.1) and the scale of activity can be assessed from Pliny's praise of Trajan (the oration was delivered before the building of the Forum Traiani) for his moderation in building (*Pan.* 51). Such a massive construction programme was clearly meant to inscribe his name and power on the city of Rome. Numerous statues were erected in gold and silver. Domitian's domination of the city was made concrete and visible.

Table 8.1 Domitian's new buildings and refurbishments to buildings

Altar incendii Neronis	Naumachia Domitiani
Arches of Domitian	Odeiom
Arch of Titus	Porticus of Minucius Vetus
Atria Septem	Porticus of Octavia and associated
Baths of Charinus, Claudius	temples
Etruscus, Lupus, Argentaria,	Stadium Domitiani
Agrippa	Temple of Castor
Camp of the fleet of Misenum	Temple of the Divus Augustus
Circus Maximus	Temple of Divus Vespasiani
Colosseum	Temple of the Flavian Family
Domus Augustiana	Temple of Fortuna Redux
Equus Domitiani	Temple of Isis Campensis
Forum Transitorium	Temple of Jupiter Custos
Four ludi	Temple of Jupiter Optimus
Granaries: Agrippiana, Piperataria.	Maximus
Horologium Augusti	Temple of Minerva Chalcidica
Horti Domitiani	Temple of Venus Genetrix
Janus Quadrifons	Theatre and Cryptum of Balbus
Julian senate-house	Theatre of Pompey
Mica Aurea	Tiberian Palace

FINANCE

Our understanding of Domitianic administration is closely connected to the interpretation of Domitianic politics. As far as the sources touch on the issue, it is (normally) to emphasise Domitian's cruelty. Attention has focused on his financial administration.

The case against Domitian argues that he bankrupted the state. It can be briefly summarised.

- Domitian is accused of killing senators and others in order to obtain their money.
- The administration of taxes seems to have been severe.
- Nerva established a commission to reduce public expenditure.
- The level of silver content in the coinage falls later in Domitian's reign.
- Domitian tried to compensate for the increase in the pay of soldiers by reducing the number of troops.
- Vespasian had left a full treasury.
- Taxes on inheritance were increased.

Domitian's expenditure was certainly heavy. Military pay was increased and this was probably the most significant part of the imperial budget. The building programme must have consumed large amounts of cash. He also had to pay off Decebalus, the Dacian king.

There is a counter-argument.

- 'Bad' emperors are frequently accused of financial mismanagement and greed.
- The disasters of the 70s considerably increased expenditure. Although Vespasian may have accumulated some reserves, these were depleted by the fire of Rome and the eruption of Vesuvius, as well as Titus' other expenditures and the gifts to the troops and Roman people on Domitian's accession.
- Domitian seems to have had a relaxed attitude towards debts.
- The collection of taxes was part of normal administration and Domitian's ferocious collection of the Jewish tax may be related to other aspects of Domitianic policy.
- Nerva and Trajan met the initial expenses of gifts to troops and people. It was in response to these outgoings that Nerva set up the commission on public expenditure, and although the commission saved virtually no money, Roman finances seem to have prospered.

• It is unclear whether the increase in inheritance taxes was a response to financial difficulties or simply a tightening of inheritance law.

A reduction in the silver content of coinage is evidence that the treasury was under some strain. We must not, however, exaggerate the scale of the problems and there is no evidence that Domitian seriously attempted to reduce expenditure (which he could have done comparatively easily by reducing the size of the building programme). It is also clear that although there may have been temporary problems at the start of Trajan's reign, Trajan was not short of money. This suggests that the fiscal fundamentals of the Roman state were comparatively good. The major increase in expenditure under Domitian, the army pay rise, could be met. Although the ancient sources emphasise Domitian's financial mismanagement, it seems unlikely that there was a financial crisis in 96.

ASSASSINATION

Domitian's unpopularity with certain elements of the senate increased the danger of assassination. The elimination of the so-called philosophical opposition showed that he was unable to build a consensus in the senate and conspiracies or supposed conspiracies after 93 added to paranoia. Even those closest to him were perceived as a threat and Domitian killed members of his family and court. Domitian may have been right to fear those close to him: after all, his assassination was carried out by members of his household. Yet, once Domitian became suspicious of his closest advisers, it was almost inevitable that those close to him would see his removal as their only chance of survival. The extent of the conspiracy is, however, difficult to assess. His assassins were all freedmen: Stephanus, Parthenius, Maximus and several others. Others were either involved or claimed later to have been involved, such as Domitia, the emperor's wife, and the future emperor Nerva. It seems somewhat odd that the conspiracy was led by imperial freedmen, who one would expect had most to lose from assassinating their emperor and also, being of lowly status, would be comparatively safe from Domitian's wrath. Yet the freedmen probably felt increasingly vulnerable after the death of Epaphroditus. This freedman had served Nero before working for the Flavians and had been one of the few who accompanied Nero's flight from Rome.

He had aided Nero's suicide (see p. 139), and it was this 'crime' that Domitian used to remove him, possibly feeling that having killed one emperor, he might kill another. Any illusion that the freedmen of Domitian were safe was dispelled. It is very likely that the conspirators had taken steps to ensure their continued security after the assassination and had received some undertakings from Nerva. The speed with which Nerva moved to claim the imperial throne suggests that he was the chosen candidate of the freedmen and was well aware of the conspiracy (Dio, LXVII 14.4–18; Suet., *Dom.* 14.4–17).

CONCLUSIONS

The history of Domitian's reign was written by his enemies. For them, Domitian was a tyrant. Although there have been attempts to react against the ancient interpretation of Domitian's reign, and we have seen areas in which the tradition has been grossly unfair to Domitian (such as in the treatment of his military activities and in his handling of the state finances), the authority of Tacitus, Pliny, Juvenal and Suetonius is not substantially undermined. We have, however, to beware of extreme interpretations. After Domitian's fall, the senate passed a *damnatio memoriae* but it was not prepared to see action taken against those who had collaborated with Domitian, with certain limited exceptions. One of the main themes of the *Agricola* is the defence of those who had worked with the tyrannous emperor. Tacitus' attitude to the 'philosophical opposition' was somewhat ambiguous (*Agr.* 40–2). They were martyrs to a cause, but their deaths were avoidable. One guesses that many in the senate may have felt similarly: they deplored the treatment of Helvidius, Rusticus and others, but felt that the confrontation could have been avoided. Many will have voted reluctantly for the condemnation of these men. Men such as the Helvidii, Rusticus and Senecio represented an extreme of senatorial behaviour and, although their elimination profoundly disturbed the political equilibrium, we cannot take them as representative of the majority of the senate in either attitude or behaviour. Most sought some accommodation with Domitian as they were to do with the new regime.

9

NERVA AND TRAJAN
(AD 96–117)

The reign of Nerva was so short and so closely related to the reign of his successor in the historical issues that arise that separate consideration would be futile. The tradition on Nerva is mostly shaped by Trajanic writers, especially Pliny, and since Nerva adopted Trajan, any criticism or praise of Nerva of necessity reflected on Trajan. The sources on Trajan tend to glorify his reign. Trajan was the conquering hero who personally led Roman armies to great victories against barbarian enemies. Politically, he shared Nerva's triumph of, in Tacitus' memorable phrase, 'integrating things previously opposed: principate and liberty' (*Agr.* 3). Pliny's *Panegyricus* presents us with an extended hymn to Trajan's political and military virtues. It is the eulogistic presentation of the emperor whom the senate chose to call '*optimus*' (best) that dominates the tradition.

THE LEGACY OF DOMITIAN

Domitian was killed on 18 September 96. On the very same day Nerva was declared emperor. It seems unlikely that Nerva's elevation was an accidental result of the conspiracy. The extent to which the freedmen responsible for killing Domitian had contacted other interested parties is unclear (see pp. 189–90). Being as closely connected with the regime as they were, they may also have sought to find someone who could be trusted not to embark on a witch hunt to remove those who were tainted by Domitian's tyranny. Nerva had enjoyed a glittering career under the Flavians, though his role in the last years of Domitian's reign is unclear. Pliny tells us that Nerva wrote to congratulate Pliny on his bold behaviour in 93 (*Ep.* VII 33), which would suggest that Nerva was not part of the group that engaged in the persecution of the 'philosophical opposition' in that year (see pp. 181–4). Indeed, it may have strained even the ingenuity of Pliny and Tacitus to present Nerva as the restorer of liberty had he been involved. Yet Nerva's close association with the Flavian family throughout his career probably meant that his closest political allies had also been prominent under Domitian. It was probably these connections that eased his path to the throne in 96.

The manner of his accession led to his condemnation of Domitian and an extension of protection to those who had been involved in the assassination. Domitian's treatment of the senate in the last three years of his reign led to inevitable calls for revenge. Senators who had suffered at the hands of their colleagues now looked to turn the tables. The returning exiles were to face those who had exiled them in the senate-house. Yet, those who had been close to Domitian had been exercising influence to aid their friends as well as harm their enemies. They had powerful support. Some had co-operated with Domitian to remove their personal enemies. Others had played less than honourable roles during the trials. It would be no easy task to bring down those who had been close to Domitian and, since some were probably still close to Nerva, such action ran considerable political risks. Nerva sought to paper over the cracks and institute an amnesty. Those who had suffered would not be allowed to continue the factional fighting into the next reign. Those who had served under Domitian were left in place. The replacement of Domitian did not lead to a purge and it was in the interests of the freedmen assassins to ensure the highest level of continuity possible between reigns.

There was no more obvious sign of continuity between the reigns of Domitian and Nerva than the career of Titinius Capito. After distinguished military service, he served in the household administrations of Domitian, Nerva and Trajan. He was a noted figure on the literary scene and is favourably discussed in Pliny's letters (*Ep.* I 17, V 8, VIII 12; McCrum, Woodhead 1966: No. 347). Despite being so close to Domitian, there was no obvious stain on his character and there is no evidence that he was a controversial figure.

Nevertheless, the political situation was tense and animosities could not be laid aside. Pliny himself led one attack in 97. He threatened to bring charges against the prosecutor of Helvidius. The debate in the senate seems to have been vitriolic. The majority of the senate may have had sympathy with Pliny, but there was a reluctance to open up fresh wounds and Veiento led a counter-attack. Pliny may have had the backing of other senior members of the senate such as Verginius Rufus, Julius Frontinus, Corellius Rufus and Avidius Quietus, though he claims he acted without seeking support in advance. Pliny carried the day in the senate in that his enemy was not allowed to hold further office, but he was unable to bring the case to court and had to be satisfied with publishing his speech in vindication of Helvidius. Before publication, his intended victim died (*Ep.* IX 13).

Another of Pliny's enemies from the reign of Domitian was Regulus (see p. 184). Again, Pliny may have made aggressive noises. Regulus sought some reconciliation but Pliny was unwilling to come to terms: he was waiting for the return of Junius Mauricus from exile. Mauricus was the brother of one of Regulus' victims, Arulenus Rusticus, and had the moral right to launch the prosecution in person (*Ep.* I 5). It seems likely that this episode can also to be dated to 97 and that on Mauricus' return they were either unable or thought it unwise to launch the prosecution, probably because Regulus had powerful protectors. Pliny had to be satisfied with literary attacks.

Nerva himself may have been trying to maintain a foot in both camps. The Domitianic court remained powerful, but Nerva attempted to maintain good relations with Pliny and his circle. His first choice as fellow consul was Verginius Rufus. Rufus' political activities during the Flavian period cannot be reconstructed, though his extraordinary prominence in 68–9 (see pp. 137–8) and his longevity established him as a leading senator. He had been a friend and protector of Pliny and one wonders whether he was excluded from the Flavian court. Nerva's decision to reward him with a third consulship and invitation to sit on a commission for the reduction of public expenditure suggests an attempt to associate his reign with Rufus, possibly a break with the Domitianic circle (Pliny, *Ep.* II 1).

The restoration of the exiled and Nerva's search for political support led to a change in the political balance. The tensions that arose were dramatised at a dinner party held by Nerva, probably in 97. Junius Mauricus and Veiento were at the table. Veiento was sitting in the place of honour, next to the emperor. Discussion turned to another notorious Domitianic courtier, Catullus Messalinus (see p. 180), who had died during Domitian's reign. Someone asked where he would be today and Mauricus asserted that he would be sitting at dinner with them (Pliny, *Ep.* IV 22). Veiento was meant to take offence. Nerva may have done so. The stresses of maintaining the peace between the two opposed groups were obvious and even at the emperor's own table tensions resurfaced.

These tensions led to a major crisis in 97 when the praetorians rose against Nerva. His political position became virtually untenable and he turned for political support to one of the leading generals, Trajan.

THE ADOPTION OF TRAJAN

In spite of eulogistic later treatments of Nerva, it is clear that the emperor failed to reconcile the disparate factions at the centre of Roman politics. His coinage issues proclaimed the restoration of liberty, the rebirth of Rome and the restoration of justice – themes close to the senators' hearts (*Libertas Augusta, Roma Renascens, Iustitia Augusta, Aequitas August*). Another major theme was the *Concordia Exercitum* (concord of the army). It is traditional to interpret this as a sign of Nerva's political uncertainty, a slogan reflecting more his hope than political reality, and understand the emphasis placed on the loyalty of the army to signify that the army was anything but loyal. This is perhaps the case, but we ought to see this coinage issue in the context of the other issues of the reign. Nerva's coinage celebrated the lifting of customs duty charged on the movement of goods in Italy (*Vehiculatione Italiae Remissa*), the end of the 'wickedness of the Jewish tax' (*Fisci Iudaici calumnia sublata*), the restoration of the corn supply (*Annona August*; *Plebei Urbanae Frumento Constituto*). Thus, the coinage proclaimed a fresh start with important groups: the senate, the people of Rome, the people of Italy (through the remission of taxation) and the army. We need not necessarily assume that Nerva thought the army was particularly likely to turn against him.

In 97, the simmering discontent started to unravel the fragile consensus that Nerva was trying to build. The first sign of this may have been a mysterious conspiracy launched by a certain Calpurnius Crassus, descendant of one of the great Republican families. The details of the conspiracy are not known and Dio recounts an anecdote in which Nerva, once the conspiracy had been betrayed, met the conspirators, gave them all swords and asked them to assess their sharpness. The conspirators did not use them and were not brought to trial (Dio, LXVIII 3.1–2). The whole anecdote is suspicious. Since the issue never came to trial, the evidence will not have been presented and the story may have first been circulated in public under Trajan who punished the same Crassus for conspiracy. The invention of an earlier conspiracy, or the recollection of a rumour which associated Crassus with a conspiracy against Nerva, would have aided Trajan's prosecution (Dio, LXVIII 16.2).

Casperius Aelianus was at the centre of a more credible threat to usurp Nerva's authority. Aelianus was praetorian prefect, a post he had held under Domitian. In such a role, it is inevitable that he would have been implicated in some of Domitian's misdeeds. It is likely, therefore, that he viewed the growing influence of anti-Domitianic groups with some fear. He harnessed the discontent of the praetorians to demand action. Nerva was besieged in his palace and forced to agree to execute Parthenius and others who had been involved in the conspiracy against Domitian (Pliny, *Pan.* 90; Dio, LXVIII 3.3).

Nerva's choices were now limited. His lack of power had been demonstrated. He needed to bring renewed legitimacy and authority to his regime in order to compete with or suppress Aelianus and his supporters. Like Galba, the aged emperor looked to establish a successor who would add lustre to the regime. He ascended the Capitoline Hill and, in the temple of Jupiter Optimus Maximus, adopted M. Ulpius Traianus (Dio, LXVIII 3.4; Pliny, *Pan.* 7–8).

Trajan was an interesting choice. Trajan's father had enjoyed a distinguished military career. He had served with Vespasian and Titus in Judaea and had become governor of Syria. His son's career needs to be reconstructed from Pliny's *Panegyricus* 14–15. He had started his military career with some distinction, serving with his father in Syria. Subsequently, he had been posted to Spain from where he journeyed with his legion to aid Domitian in the suppression of Saturninus' revolt. Pliny tells us that the revolt was already over when Trajan arrived in Germany. His show of loyalty led to a transfer to Germany where he served for an extended period, though his exact role is unclear. He was consul in 91 but returned to Germany and was governor of Germania Superior when Nerva chose him as emperor.

His long service in the provinces meant that he had been away from Rome during the crucial years of AD 93–6 and was untainted by association with the Domitianic terror. He and his father had also been prominent and powerful Flavian supporters and had been rewarded with key governorships. The friends of Domitian could look on him optimistically. The military power at his disposal ensured that he was a force to be reckoned with and would have made him a probable contender for the throne had the discontent with Nerva become civil war. In some ways, he was an ideal choice, a man who could enforce his authority and who offered some hope to both sides. He was in Germany, however, not in Rome, and was not in a position immediately to improve Nerva's political position. Nerva's struggle with Aelianus remained the struggle of unequals, though Aelianus was now threatened by the German legions.

Nerva wrote to Trajan to inform him of his adoption. Pliny makes allusion to various omens which had suggested that Trajan would become emperor (*Pan.* 5), but we cannot know whether Trajan was already making a bid for the throne. When the letter arrived, Trajan did not rush to his new father. The delay needs explanation. It is unlikely that order was restored in Rome merely by mentioning Trajan's name as Pliny claims. We can also dismiss moralistic interpretations: Trajan not wanting to be seen to be rushing to accept the power and authority granted to him or effectively usurp the power of his 'father'. The answer is probably more prosaic. Trajan seems to have spent the period visiting the troops, securing their loyalty. By the time he reached Italy, Nerva was dead. Aelianus recognised his authority and came to Trajan when summoned. Trajan executed him and purged the praetorian guard (Dio, LXVIII 5.4). One must wonder what the tradition hides and whether Aelianus might have expected to be treated very differently. After so intimidating Nerva and establishing his domination in Rome, one would assume that the next emperor would take action against this over-mighty prefect. Yet Aelianus went to Trajan. We could assume that he was politically bankrupt, threatened by overwhelming military force and in no position to oppose Trajan, but, in fact, Aelianus may have been hoping for some reward. He had, after all, precipitated the crisis that led to the adoption of Trajan.

We can arrive at two versions of Trajan's accession. In the first, as represented by our sources, the political crisis in Rome led to Trajan being chosen from all men in the empire as the best suited to bring peace. Order was restored. Eventually, Aelianus was killed for his undutiful behaviour towards Nerva. In the second, Nerva failed to secure general political support. Various individuals in the senate and elsewhere engaged in political manoeuvres designed to secure the dominance of their group or prepare for a bid for the throne. Aelianus moved first. Nerva, however, turned to Trajan who may or may not have been preparing to bid for the imperial position. Trajan secured the loyalty of the troops, as any usurper needed to do, and moved on Rome. There was an uneasy truce. Trajan asserted his authority by removing Aelianus and thereby disassociated himself from the former Domitianic circle. In other words, instead of an orderly succession through adoption, we have something approaching a *coup*.

A further break with the Domitianic past was signalled at games which were probably held very soon after Trajan's arrival in Rome. Informers were brought before the crowd, condemned and sent into exile (Pliny, *Pan.* 34). This was a theatrical display. The status of the various informers is not stated, but it seems likely that only minor characters suffered. Powerful senators such as Regulus remained untouched and Pliny never did bring about his downfall. Trajan's assertion of authority in 98 may have been dramatic and his break with the former courtiers of Domitian decisive, but he did not allow any revenge for the factional strife of the Domitianic period.

THE *OPTIMUS PRINCEPS*

There is very little information on which to base a political history of Trajan's reign. We do, however, have varied and quite full sources concerning Trajan's image. Much of this is related to his role as a conqueror (to be considered below). Apart from the mystery of the conspiracy of Crassus and attempts to divide Licinius Sura and Trajan by alleging conspiracy (Dio, LXVIII 15.3–16.2), there is no evidence of political opposition to Trajan, but it is reasonable to assume that the tensions he inherited from Nerva and Domitian continued to influence political life, and Pliny's somewhat confused depiction of the emperor suggests that Trajan was no more able to solve the various contradictions of the imperial position than any of his predecessors.

Pliny's *Panegyricus*

The *Panegyricus* is an extraordinary work. It is a speech in praise of the emperor. Pliny delivered the original version in AD 100 as a gesture of thanks to the emperor who had just made him consul. It was later reworked by Pliny for publication and even delivered again in a public reading that lasted three days (Pliny, *Ep.* III 13, 18). The composition of a panegyric posed certain fundamental problems of taste. Domitian and other emperors had received similar orations and it was felt that the whole rhetorical form had become debased: what more praise could be heaped on an emperor when so much that was insincere had been said on such occasions.

Pliny faced the issue explicitly at the start of his speech (*Pan* 2–3). His solution was to claim naivety: that his speech was different simply because it was sincere. As a rhetorical device this is clearly unsatisfactory, but represents a deeper tension in the work. Pliny praises Trajan the senator but, in so doing, the *Panegyricus* clearly shows that Trajan was more than a senator. If Trajan was 'one of us' (*Pan.* 3), then the *Panegyricus* was clearly unsuitable. The very act of presenting a panegyric associates Trajan with the more autocratic aspects of imperial rule even if the speech itself emphasises 'senatorial' or 'democratic' characteristics of the emperor. Throughout the *Panegyric*, Pliny is faced with this irresolvable problem and it is a problem that Trajan himself faced.

I take as an example the divinity of the emperor though there are others that could be chosen. 'Good' emperors did not become gods in their own lifetime. Trajan could not, therefore, be a god and did not claim to be a god. In *Panegyricus* 2 this is explicit:

> Nowhere must we flatter him as a god, nowhere as a divine power: for we speak not about a tyrant but a citizen, not of a master (*dominus*) but a parent. He himself is one of us – and in this he excels and shines most since he thinks he is one of us and remembers that he is no less a man than the men he commands.

Yet, even in the same section, Pliny talks of Trajan's *divinitas*, though it is Trajan's *humanitas* which encouraged the senators to celebrate him.

Later, Pliny declares that imperial power is equal to that of the gods, the unstated logic of the argument being that the wielders of those powers should be equal (*Pan.* 3). Trajan was adopted by the gods and then by Nerva (*Pan.* 5). Nerva, his father, becomes a god (*Pan.* 11). Trajan is compared to Hercules (*Pan.* 14). His achievements were worthy of divine honours, though Trajan moderately placed bronze statues of himself in the temple of Jupiter Optimus Maximus rather than the gold and silver statues installed by Domitian (*Pan.* 52).

The argument is ingenious: Trajan is not a god and does not present himself as a god, but has divine characteristics that lead to his association with gods. This is contrasted with Domitian's seemingly explicit claims to divinity. Yet, although Trajan's self-glorification had not by AD 100, or whenever this section of the *Panegyricus* reached its final form, extended to the placing of precious metal statues of himself in the most important temple in the city, he did place other statues of himself in that temple, thus inviting his association with the divine.

One could interpret the *Panegyricus* as Pliny's attempt to impose a senatorial ideal of the emperor on Trajan's principate and, if so, so much of what is said would become programmatic. It seems more likely that the confusion in the *Panegyricus* reflects Pliny's difficulties (and probably those of many of his contemporaries) in understanding and interpreting the role of the *princeps* in the first years of the second century AD. Pliny probably reflects a general view that, although the emperor should behave as if he is 'one of us', the vast power that he wields and the favours that the gods have bestowed on him mean that the emperor is superior to the rest of the aristocracy and is in a quasi-divine, quasi-parental role. This intellectual acceptance of the superiority of the emperor represents not just an acceptance of the necessity of monarchy (many may have seen this as a necessary evil from the reign of Claudius), but a willingness to work within an openly monarchic system. Pliny, a conservative, seems to be saying that as long as the emperor does not actually claim to be a god, we are willing to accept that his relationship to the senate and people may be like that of a god to mortals and thus divine imagery is appropriate for presenting the role of the emperor. This allows Pliny to publish a work filled with contradictions as a coherent speech in praise of the emperor. The same man who proclaimed that none should call the emperor *dominus*, wrote as governor to Trajan from Bithynia and each time addressed him as *dominus*. Pliny, and one suspects many others in the senate, had reconciled themselves to the loss of personal and political freedom that came with the monarchic system.

At about the same time as the *Panegyricus* was first delivered, Tacitus argued in the *Agricola* that even a bad emperor can be served without bringing dishonour. Agricola was a role model of the decent man serving his country and his sacrifices are explicitly contrasted with those of the senators who had opposed Domitian's tyranny publicly and paid with their lives. Agricola's life was of benefit to the state, while the sacrifice of others brought liberty no nearer (see p. 190). This would seem quite a radical agenda, but placed alongside the *Panegyricus* we perhaps see the end of a process of transformation in the attitudes of the Roman elite. The Roman elite adjusted its view of itself and of Rome to accept its subservience (though not exactly its enslavement) to the monarch. From the foundation of the Principate, Rome had been faced with

the problem of an independently minded powerful senatorial aristocracy that thought it should largely run the empire and a
monarchic system. This structural problem was being resolved.
Although our sources for the second century AD do not contain the
detail of our sources for the first, there does not seem to have been
the same level of strife between emperor and senate that so marred
the reigns of so many first-century emperors. The success of the 'five
good emperors' over the next eighty years may be more a reflection
of a change in attitude among the Roman political elite than the
greater political aptitude of these second-century emperors.

Trajanic images

Trajan made use of all traditional means for elevating his status and
winning the favour of his subjects. His arrival in Rome in AD 98
appears to have been marked by games and most significant events
in his reign were celebrated in a similar way. His victories in Dacia
led to major celebrations (Dio, LXVIII 10.2, 15.1). There were also
games in 109 to celebrate the opening of an aqueduct and Trajan's
baths. In 112, another set of games celebrated the opening of
Trajan's Forum and the Basilica Ulpia (*Fasti Ostienses*). On accession,
he curried favour with the plebs more directly by grants of money
and a similar gift was made in 107 (Pliny, *Pan.* 25; *Fasti Ostienses*).

Trajan also made use of divine imagery. Nerva was deified on
Trajan's return to Rome. More unusually, Trajan elevated the status
of his family. In his case, this involved making public reference to
his wife, sister and niece. These three all appear on coins of the
period and all received the title Augusta. He also deified Marciana,
his sister, when she died in 112. His elevation of the womenfolk
differs from Julio–Claudian and Domitianic emphasis on the imperial women. Trajan's position was certainly not reliant upon his
family's status. The special status of these women sprang from
Trajan's own authority and the divine honours granted to Marciana
signify that association with the emperor, rather than descent from a
particularly important family, was enough to elevate an individual
to the level of the divine. Deifying Marciana was a substitute for
deifying the emperor.

Perhaps the most obvious way in which Trajan elevated his status
was through his building programme. It was traditional for
emperors to leave their mark on the central area of Rome. Trajan
continued this tradition by constructing the largest of the imperial
fora. This Forum differed somewhat from earlier imperial *fora* in

that the architectural centres of the earlier fora were occupied by temples which dominated the spatial arrangements. In Trajan's Forum, the main court was dominated by a basilica which separated the main court from a subsidiary court. The basilica itself, unlike the temple of Venus Genetrix or the temple of Mars Ultor, was not a natural focus for the Forum. The rather cramped secondary court had a temple at one end, but this temple was not the focus of the area and was no more architecturally significant than the two flanking libraries. This area was dominated by its central monument, Trajan's column. The column celebrated Trajan's Dacian war and is an important source of information on the appearance of the soldiers of the period, though reconstructing a narrative of the war from the pictorial remains is somewhat problematic. The temple was dedicated to Divus Traianus, presumably by Hadrian. On the hill above the Forum stood Trajan's markets, presumably constructed to house those shopkeepers displaced from the area of the Forum.

The unusual design and evidence that other emperors had been involved in building projects in the area has led to disagreement among archaeologists and art historians as to how to interpret the Forum. No absolute answer seems possible since any answer must depend in part on individual artistic sensibilities. Those entering the Forum were probably not visibly aware of the column and temple standing behind the basilica. The outer court was also decorated with images from Trajan's Dacian triumph. Visitors who passed through the basilica would enter the inner court where Trajan's success was so grandly displayed with the column. The hiding of this court from those in the first courtyard may have increased the aesthetic impact on leaving the basilica. The confined space must have enhanced the impressiveness of the column. Yet visual clues do not lead the visitor directly through the basilica into an 'inner sanctum' of the second court. There is little sense of logical progression. The basilica effectively hides the inner monuments, suggesting that the spaces were to be interpreted differently and perhaps quite separately. The whole Forum reflects Trajan's Dacian victories and glorifies the emperor, but does so through different architectural and artistic media. Although one can still see this as part of one construction, conforming to a single plan, we perhaps see two distinct architectural elements combined. In any case, the Forum advertises Trajan and his conquests with a grandeur that certainly matches the achievements of those less popular emperors the tradition tends to see as megalomaniacs.

Trajan's military success was advertised in his Forum, his coinage and his name. It was an important part of Trajan's image. Most other emperors had made some attempt to associate themselves with the troops and military success. Trajan differed only in the scale of his involvement in military matters. His campaigns were largely aggressive and, although there may have been some strategic rationale for his campaigns in Dacia, the thirst for glory appears to have been the major motivating factor. His campaigns in Germany earned him the title Germanicus in the first days of his reign, Dacicus followed in 102 and Parthicus came in 116–17. There are two possible views of this desire for military glory. It could represent political insecurity. Trajan sought to secure his own position by military feats that rivalled those of Alexander the Great. One could, however, regard Trajan's aggressiveness as normal Roman behaviour. Previous emperors had not engaged in such campaigns because of political insecurity, pressing military problems or personal weakness. Nevertheless, such success was popular in Rome and it seems certain that diverting energies into foreign wars would have eased any difficulties in managing senatorial opinion.

WARS

When Trajan was adopted, he was an experienced general, though the exact nature of that experience is somewhat obscure. He immediately adopted an aggressive policy. The two areas of military activity were on the Danubian frontier and in the East.

Domitian had been beset with difficulties with the tribes beyond the Danube. His victories had brought some stability to the frontier zone, but attempts to assert Roman authority beyond the Danube ended in humiliating failure (see pp. 184–5). It is unclear whether the settlement was such that further military action would have been inevitable in order to retrieve Roman honour. The Romans had, after all, accepted disadvantageous settlements in Germany and the East at various times throughout the first century.

Trajan's first intervention in the region was before AD 100. Pliny noted that Trajan showed moderation in his recent campaign by not venturing beyond the Danube (*Pan.* 16). This suggests that Trajan had been involved in suppressing an incursion, probably by the Dacians, possibly as early as 97. This renewed outbreak provided a pretext for a more radical solution to this recurring problem. There is evidence to suggest a considerable build-up of forces along the

Danube as early as 100. The war was over by 102. Decebalus had sued for peace, his forces had been defeated at Tapae, and considerable territory had been lost. Trajan's willingness to accept the peace and failure to unseat Decebalus does, however, suggest that Roman successes had been mixed and the Dacians' formidable military force had not been decisively defeated (Dio, LXVIII 6, 8–9).

Trajan celebrated a triumph, but the very next year (103) the senate was persuaded once more to declare war on Decebalus. The war seems to have been extended. Decebalus explored the possibility of a diplomatic solution, but this was rejected. In the end, the king was captured and beheaded by a Roman cavalryman whose military career has been preserved on a comparatively recently discovered inscription (see p. 268). Dacia became a province and the Dacian capital was turned into a Roman colony. The decisive defeat of the Dacians must have increased the security of the Danubian provinces and probably acted as a check on the neighbouring tribes such as the Iazyges, yet it remains an open question as to what extent Dacia was pacified. C. Julius Quadratus Bassus, who was one of Trajan's leading generals and was involved in the conquest of Dacia, was later (at an uncertain date) appointed governor of the province. There he ended his long and distinguished career. We do not know how he died, but the inscription tells us that he was actively campaigning in Dacia. Hadrian laid down the procedures for his funeral (Smallwood 1966: No. 214). Dacia remained a trouble spot.

In *c.* 107, Trajan expanded the empire by annexing Arabia. Details of the campaign remain obscure. Indeed, it is possible that there was only limited resistance.

Trajan's next and final military adventure was a general assault on Parthia and the East. The exact chronology of the war is a matter of some dispute but, from 112 or soon after, Trajan was preparing his invasion. The Parthians seem to have been unsure as to Trajan's motives. The region had been reasonably peaceful since the campaigns of Corbulo. There were efforts to come to a diplomatic solution along similar lines to Corbulo's settlement. The Arsacid rulers of Armenia were prepared to surrender in public and provide Trajan with the kind of ceremonial victory that had satisfied both Augustus and Nero. Instead of simply restoring the Arsacids to the Armenian throne, however, Trajan decided to turn Armenia into a province.

War was inevitable and it seems very likely that Trajan was looking to inflict a decisive defeat on the Parthians and their allies and secure the Parthian empire for Rome. For generations, Roman leaders had looked for inspiration to the achievements of Alexander the Great, and the conquest of the Eastern Mediterranean put Roman forces in a position to emulate Alexander by defeating the successor state to the Persian empire.

Trajan made significant territorial gains. Armenia fell and he campaigned successfully in Mesopotamia. However, the problem with the region was not securing initial military success. Roman forces were consistently able to cross the frontier and take control of Armenia and Parthian territory. The problems the Romans faced were bringing the highly mobile Parthian forces to a decisive battle and maintaining control over the disparate peoples spread over this huge territory. The Parthian military and political system seems to have been extremely flexible and the Parthians showed an ability to raise troops in spite of what would appear to have been catastrophic military and political defeats.

Trajan's invasion of 116 culminated in the capture of the Parthian capital Ctesiphon. It is likely that Trajan thought the war was over. Instead of consolidating his control over this territory, he advanced towards the Persian Gulf, the effective limits of Alexander's empire. Yet the Parthians proved able to put an army in the field and, although Trajan had asserted Roman military power, he still did not have political control.

In 115, a major earthquake had destroyed the city of Antioch. It has been suggested that this event precipitated a significant revolt in the East. Between 115–17, Jewish communities in Cyrenaica, Cyprus, Egypt and probably Judaea revolted. There is no obvious explanation for this sudden outbreak of violence. The Jewish communities of the diaspora (those communities located outside the area of Israel–Palestine) had withstood periodic persecutions over the previous century without staging a revolt of this scale. There is no evidence to suggest that Trajan instituted any anti-Semitic policies. More likely, the Jewish communities were responding to a common cultural or political movement, perhaps of a messianic nature. Either the earthquake in the East or the war in Parthia, where there was a large Jewish community, were interpreted as religiously significant events which encouraged revolt. We do not have the Jewish side of the story. In any event, the revolt caused considerable disruption within the empire and forced the recall of units from Parthia.

In 116 or early 117, the recently conquered peoples revolted. Major campaigns were fought to hold the territory and the cities of

Nisbis, Seleucia and Edessa were sacked by Roman forces. Arabia revolted and Trajan himself was repulsed from the walls of Hatra. The Roman forces involved in the siege of Hatra were beset by illness caused by the insanitary conditions. Trajan himself became ill and died. Hadrian was unwilling to maintain control over the new provinces and came to a settlement with the Parthians by which he withdrew from much of the conquered territory (Dio, LXVIII 17–33).

Trajan's adventure to the East ended in ultimate failure. Trajan failed to secure political control of the area and perhaps failed to recognise the rather diffuse nature of power in the Parthian empire. The extent of the revolt and of Trajan's campaigns in 116–17 probably forced a recognition of the difficulties in governing the region. We know nothing of the causes of the revolt, but we may speculate that Rome attempted to establish provincial governmental systems. The tasks of pacification and turning the conquered territory into provinces were far from finished on Trajan's death, and further extended campaigning may have been distinctly unattractive to a new emperor unsure of his political position. Trajan's Eastern adventure ended, like so many other attempts to emulate the achievements of Alexander both before and after, in ultimate failure.

FINANCE

The evidence concerning the finances of Nerva and Trajan is somewhat confused. This is partly the result of a tradition that condemned Domitian for financial extravagance and saw in his treatment of the senate and other groups a rapacious desire for money (see pp. 188–9). It would seem that this interpretation was certainly encouraged by his successors and yet their own actions and generosity suggest that the finances of the state were not in too poor a situation in 96.

When Nerva became emperor Domitian suffered a *damnatio memoriae* (see p. 186). One of the beneficial effects of this was that Domitian's statues were destroyed and since at least some were of precious metal, they filled the coffers of Nerva (Dio LXVIII 1). Nerva also created a committee to produce advice on the reduction of public expenditure (Pliny, *Ep.* II 1). This suggests that he was under some financial pressure. He may also have raised some new taxes: Pliny refers to *plera vectigalia* (several taxes) being created. The only detail we have is a discussion of changes in the 5 per cent inheritance tax. The attestation in *Panegyricus* 37 is rather difficult to understand, but it seems that Nerva changed the grounds for exemption from inheritance tax which had the effect of increasing income. Pliny presents this as a measure which increased the equity with which the tax was administered.

The reduction in the number of prosecutions led to a fall in state income since at least part of the property of those convicted often passed to the state (Pliny, *Pan.* 36, 42). Property which had not been reclaimed by returning exiles (see below) was sold by Trajan (Pliny, *Pan.* 50). This would result in a loss of the income from the property and such selling of state assets may reflect cash-flow problems in Trajan's reign.

Nevertheless, the evidence for a certain prosperity in these years is compelling. Nerva presumably sought to secure the loyalty of the troops and plebs through the normal donations. He publicly proclaimed that the period of harsh imposition of the Jewish tax and a transport tax in Italy were over, though the Jewish tax was probably still collected. Nerva also had to meet the financial demands placed on the state by the returning exiles who claimed property confiscated by Domitian. Dio (LXVIII 2) claims that land worth 60,000,000 sesterces was returned, though the figure is certainly open to question. Nerva's building projects were not extensive, though he completed the Forum transitorum (or the Forum of Nerva).

Trajan was able to meet the normal donations to the plebs, though he only paid a half donative to the troops on accession (Pliny, *Pan.* 25). He gave lavish games (Pliny, *Pan.* 33). He also remitted taxation from Egypt and even sent emergency aid to the province, which appears to have had a disastrous harvest (Pliny, *Pan.* 30). Trajan's building programme was notable. Although Pliny praises Trajan for his moderation in building (in contrast to Domitian), he was already constructing a porticus, an arch and a temple in AD 100 (*Pan.* 51). He had also commenced major and expensive building projects in Ostia to improve the harbour and provide greater protection for the grain boats. In addition, he may have been engaged in major road construction in Italy (Pliny, *Pan.* 29). His greatest building works, the forum and related structures, the baths and the aqueduct were all completed much later, but it is likely that work on at least some of these projects started in the early part of his reign before his finances were boosted by the Dacian conquest.

The evidence of Pliny suggests that Trajan spent freely

throughout the early years of his reign. The *Panegyricus* does not give the impression that the Roman state was teetering on the brink of a financial crisis (though a panegyric could hardly be expected to be critical of an emperor's financial management), and Pliny's extended discussion of financial matters would perhaps have been impolitic if this were so. Unless Nerva and Trajan had worked some kind of financial miracle, it seems very likely that they had inherited a fairly healthy financial situation from Domitian and there were no great financial problems during the reign of Nerva or the early part of the reign of Trajan.

It is normally assumed that the success of the Dacian wars transformed Trajan's financial situation and allowed him to spend freely on monuments such as the Forum. As we have seen, his finances probably did not need transforming. It is also impossible to estimate the significance of the money that came from Dacia, and this looted wealth, as depicted on Trajan's column, must be set against the expenses of the war and the costs of establishing a new province.

Trajan's finances remained healthy. He was able to embark on ambitious expansionist plans, continue and complete wide-ranging building projects and also finance a new initiative in Italy. This was the *alimenta* scheme. This scheme was designed to provide a certain amount of poor relief for the children of Italy. The idea was that certain land-owners would mortgage land to the state. The interest on that mortgage would be paid into a fund to provide poor relief. The landowners were encouraged by a low interest rate on the loan, though it seems that in most cases only a small part of the estate was mortgaged in this fashion. Landowners were probably able to benefit from the injection of capital (which may have been in fairly short supply in the Italian economy) and this could be used either to improve or to extend their estates. The poor would benefit from the accumulated money and thus the population would be encouraged to grow. The financial burden of the system fell largely on the state. We do not know the extent of the *alimenta* system in Italy but it seems likely that it represented a massive financial outlay. This was a bold attempt to provide some financial security for the children of Italy. Although the demography of Italy had been a matter of some concern to the Roman state for centuries, this was a very direct and expensive intervention. Such an extension of imperial generosity (though of course the system created was nowhere near as extensive as modern welfare systems) symbolises the wealth, confidence and power of the Trajanic principate.

10

SOCIETY

SOCIAL ORDERS

The Romans divided the population into legal categories. The population of the empire was divided into Romans, Latins and non-Romans. Romans were divided into groups which we call 'orders', partly to differentiate these categories from social classes (a division broadly based on wealth). A slightly simplified version of these social orders is represented in Table 10.1. Latin status was an intermediate status between non-Romans and Romans. Latin communities in the empire had a constitution modelled on that of Rome, though it is unclear whether there was a significant number of Latin communities in the imperial period. Junian Latins were rather different and will be discussed below. The non-Roman communities were those cities and peoples of the empire who had not been given Roman or Latin status. These communities continued to be governed by their local traditions and showed considerably more variation in social organisation than is possible to represent here. Progressively, Rome came to influence the constitutions of many of these communities and they developed institutions more similar to those of Rome.

In these next sections, I will concentrate on Roman categories.

Table 10.1 Legal divisions in imperial society

Romans	Latins	Non-Romans (Peregrini)
Senators	Decurions	Decurions
Equestrians		
Ordinary citizens	Ordinary citizens	Ordinary citizens
Freed	Freed	Freed
Slave	Slave	Slave

Slaves

Slaves were owned. They had no control over their labour or bodies. They were property to be disposed of as their masters or mistresses pleased, subject to certain slight moral and legal constraints. Slaves were either born slaves or became slaves. They became slaves through capture in war or through the imposition of legal penalties. The free could also be kidnapped and thus enslaved. The exact legal process that transformed a free person into a slave is unclear. Slaves could be bought and sold and subjected to almost unlimited violence. That violence eventually must have ensured acceptance of unfree status. All societies in the ancient world maintained slaves. It was part of the common culture.

It is often said that slaves were treated as objects: that they were not regarded as men (or women) but as things devoid of souls: animals with voices. In legal and financial terms, this is largely true. The Romans were unsentimental about slavery. Slaves were economic units and were accounted for as such. Nevertheless, although at no time do we see any questioning of the institution of slavery, some Romans could show fellow-feeling for slaves. Vedius Pollio ordered a slave to be thrown to his collection of carnivorous fish for breaking a glass, but Augustus happened to be dining with him and the emperor intervened. The slave was pardoned. Augustus' intervention is inexplicable if he had regarded the slave as a 'thing' for Pollio to dispose of as he wished. Another example comes in the reign of Nero. Some slaves killed a particularly brutal *dominus* (master) who happened to be a high-ranking senator (see pp. 118–19). According to the law, all the slaves of the household had to be killed. The legal penalty was imposed after some disagreement in the senate and the urban plebs rioted against the sentence. Although not condoning the crime, the ancient reaction to the murder of the senator suggests that at least some free Roman citizens had some sympathy for the plight of the slaves.

The imperial period saw the institution of limited protection for slaves. Claudius ordered that slaves exposed to die near the temple of Aesculapius (the god of medicine), which was on an island in the Tiber, should receive their freedom and be exempted from the patronal authority of their previous *domini*. He also equated killing a sick or old slave with homicide. This gave some very slight protection, but it is probable that a master was still able to kill a slave if he could show 'good' cause and one must wonder at the chances of a successful prosecution (Suet., *Claud.* 25.2). The major reform of slave law seems to have been Hadrianic (HA, *Hadrian* 18) when slave prisons were banned, killing of slaves by their owners was made an offence, and owners were prevented from selling slaves into prostitution or to the gladiatorial school without reason. The extension of limited protection attests public attitudes. There was a perception that the *dominus* had a social responsibility towards his slaves and was expected to carry out that responsibility, as did the younger Pliny who took pains to look after his slaves when they were struck down with a mysterious illness (*Ep.* VIII 16). Taking some care of slaves made good economic sense and tempering the brutality and violence with certain privileges may have eased the problems of control, but we see in Roman attitudes towards slaves in this period more than managerial strategy. There were also some very faint glimmers of humanity.

The treatment of slaves probably varied greatly depending on their role within the household. The vast majority of slaves in Italy must have worked on the land. Those who worked with tenants may have been treated slightly better. The slave-run estates, however, may have been more abusive. The *ergastulae* (slave prisons) were notorious and it was common for slaves to work in chained gangs. The chances of freedom must have been slim. Slaves met even more brutal conditions in the mines where life expectancy must have been very short, though not as short as that for slaves condemned to the games. Being condemned to the mines or the games was recognised as a death sentence.

Slaves working as personal servants had an easier life. They would be subjected to the capricious cruelty of the *dominus* and *domina*, but freedom was a possibility and the work was probably not as hard. The running of an elite household also required skilled slaves. Such slaves would represent a considerable investment and many could expect eventually to receive their freedom. These trusted slaves were often paid, though their wages had no legal status: the owner could reclaim the money at any moment. Slaves or freedmen were involved in the financial management of the household. Some slaves were probably set up in semi-independent commercial enterprises to look after the master's business interests. Slaves would also cater for the cultural needs of the *dominus* by reading literary works to him (a skilled task) or running his library or helping him with his literary endeavours. Although not free, these slaves could become comparatively powerful. They controlled significant amounts of money and were relied on by their masters for advice.

Many non-elite households will have contained a small number of slaves. In these households, the tasks of the slaves must have been varied, but they probably represented a valuable source of labour and a considerable expense. No doubt some of these slaves were also harshly treated, but the welfare of an individual slave may have been far more important to smaller households.

The cases of brutality, abuse and murder of slaves must be balanced by the evidence of close co-operation between slave and *dominus*. There were examples of slaves showing outstanding courage in protecting their owner. The slave women of Octavia for instance supposedly withstood torture rather than falsely incriminate their mistress (see p. 111). Slaves were also taken as sexual partners. Claudius and Vespasian seem to have retained favoured concubines for extended periods and their behaviour was probably not very different from that of many other Roman men. (Roman women were not allowed to have sexual relations with their slaves.) Some of these relationships became marriages. Legally, slaves formed part of the *familia*, as did children. The Roman family was extremely hierarchical and paternalistic and the *pater* had great authority, though this does not mean that this power was exercised on a daily basis. It is certainly possible that some felt loyalty to their family.

We should be aware of gradations in treatment of slaves. All slaves were unfree and subject to the authority of the *dominus*. There is no doubt that there were good and bad *domini* and sometimes even the comparatively good could act with brutality. The literature of the elite characterised slaves as generally morally reprehensible, thieves and cheats, who could not be trusted. Their sexual morality was also dubious. They were regarded as inferiors. Yet, there was a recognition of the humanity of slaves, and even of gradations in the levels of their inferiority (some were less inferior than others) and it was possible for good relations to be established between slave and *dominus*. The evidence points to a slight improvement in the treatment of slaves in this period due to changes in attitudes and economic climate rather than any desire to reform the institution.

The importance of the institution of slavery for Roman social attitudes has often been stressed. The division between free and unfree has been seen as the fundamental division in Roman society. Those who were not slaves were free and the free would avoid any social situation that would lead to a threat to that freedom. The free man was independent, for a lack of independence brought him near to the status of the slave.

The freed

The law concerning freedmen was changed under Augustus by the *lex Aelia Sentia*. Before this law, all those freed by Roman citizens became Roman citizens. The *lex Aelia Sentia* introduced two further categories of freedmen. Slaves who had been tortured, branded or sent to fight in gladiatorial combat were to become *dediticii* (foreigners without a state) on being freed. They were not allowed to live within a hundred miles of Rome. A slave freed informally, that is not through the ceremony of manumission, by being included in the census or by will, became a Latin. Slaves under the age of thirty had to be manumitted and show just cause for the grant of freedom before a board of senators and equestrians or they would become Latins. Slaves over the age of thirty become Roman citizens on being freed.

The freedmen who became Latins joined a specific status group known as the Junian Latins. Freedmen with this status could not make a will or receive property through a will. A Junian Latin could obtain Roman citizenship by marrying a Roman and having a son who survived for one year or by serving for six years with the *vigiles* (the watch) at Rome, or (from an edict of Claudius) building a ship which could carry 10,000 *modii* (87,360 litres) of wheat and using it to transport the grain supply for six years, or (from an edict of Nero) investing 50 per cent of a census level of 200,000 sesterces or more in a house in Rome, or (from an edict of Trajan) operating a mill in Rome which ground 100 *modii* (873.6 litres) of grain each day for three years (Gaius, *Institutes* I 9–36).

Another Augustan law, the *lex Fufia Caninia* limited the rights of owners to bequeath freedom to slaves. A sliding scale operated (see Table 10.2) (Gaius, *Institutes* I 42–6).

The testamentary rights of freedmen were also limited. Freedmen who had no children were expected to leave half their estate to their

Table 10.2 Limitations of the *lex Fufia Caninia*

Number of slaves owned	Proportion of freed that can be created by will (percentage)
2–10	50
11–30	33
31–100	25
101–500	20
501 +	No more than 100 slaves

patron (former owner). In addition, an Augustan law, the *lex Papia Poppaea*, obliged a freedman with an estate of 100,000 sesterces or more to leave property to his patron. Again this was on a sliding scale. A freedman with one child left half his property to his patron, one with two children left one-third of his property to his patron and one with three children was under no obligation. Freedmen with less than 100,000 sesterces and one child were under no obligation (Gaius, *Institutes* III 39–44).

The freedom of the freed in relation to the patron was also limited. A freedman was bound by law to perform certain duties for his patron and presumably these could vary according to the form of manumission and the nature of the skills of the slave. Female slaves remained under the authority of the patron even when freed. The freedwoman was unable to enact any business without the authority of her patron, unless she happened to have four children after which, under Augustan legislation to encourage childbirth, she was permitted to control her own affairs. The freed were also not allowed to bring their patrons to court (a Claudian enactment) (Gaius, *Institutes* I 45–6, IV 183).

The tight regulation of freedmen in our legal sources contrasts somewhat with the representation of freedmen in literary sources. Literary sources consistently place emphasis on the wealth of the freed. The most obvious area of concern was the power wielded by imperial freedmen. Men like Pallas and Narcissus used their political power to amass huge fortunes and also to place relatives and probably supporters in high office. The pattern is reflected elsewhere. Petronius' satirical portrait of the freedmen Trimalchio is to be regarded with a certain caution, since it certainly exaggerates and the comic Trimalchio must be a distortion of the behaviour of real freedmen, yet the portrait would have had no satirical bite if there were no rich freedmen.

The ability of freedmen to rise up the social ladder is shown by Claudius' measures to punish freedmen who posed as equestrians (Suet., *Claud.* 25; see p. 215). Claudius' ruling could have been prompted by a single case, yet the perception that some freedmen could accumulate significant property does seem to have been general.

It can be argued that the freed were well placed to rise socially. Freedmen often remained within the household of their former master, performing the same services as before. Freedmen who were involved in the management of aristocratic households acquired certain skills that made them invaluable to the *dominus*. Financial rewards were likely to follow. Freedmen would be entrusted with aspects of the patrons' business interests and were probably encouraged by sharing (formally or informally) in the resultant profits. There were opportunities for enrichment and it is probable that some freedmen took advantage.

This was regarded as a problem by the Roman elite. At first sight, it is difficult to see why. Rich freedmen were creations of the elite and controlled by them. It was probably only those who could mix easily with the elite who achieved positions of prominence. The problem, however, lay not with the individuals but with the hierarchical dissonance that resulted: freedmen became more powerful than those to whom they should defer according to the theoretical structures of Roman society. The Romans were aware that the social, economic and political power of certain freedmen had allowed them to rise above free men and even above members of the upper orders. The discrepancy between socio-economic and legal status caused outrage among certain elements.

Ordinary citizens

These were the free-born Roman citizens who were not members of the higher orders. All Roman citizens had to have parents who were also Roman citizens, unless there was a special and particular grant of privilege. Technically, the Roman citizen body was further divided into status groups based on the census (property qualification) but, apart from equestrian and senatorial status, these can safely be ignored for our period.

A Roman citizen was governed and protected by Roman law. They were protected from magistrates by the *lex Iulia de vi publica* (the Julian law on public violence) and were able to appeal to tribunes to protect them from abuses of magisterial power. In the imperial period, this function of the tribunes was taken over by the emperor. Citizens were able to bequeath their property by will and receive bequests in return. Roman citizens in Italy were probably subject to only very limited taxation. They had to pay an inheritance tax and customs duties. In the provinces, they had to pay land taxes, but were normally exempted from capitation taxes. In Rome, some at least of the citizens received the corn dole.

Roman citizenship was not tied to residence or place of birth. Citizens could reside or be born in the provinces and provincials could reside in Rome. Provincial governors probably registered the

Roman citizens resident in their province either through a formal census or through registrations of births and deaths.

Citizenship was a legal status. It did not reflect economic or social status. Citizens could be poor or rich. In the provinces, citizenship may have been more closely related to high status. Some provincials of high social status were rewarded by special grants of Roman citizenship, though others of similar social status were not. The other groups resident in the provinces who gained Roman citizenship were the freed of members of the provincial elite who had Roman citizenship and army veterans. Neither of these groups enjoyed particularly high social status.

Equestrians

There were various formal ways of defining equestrian status. Originally, equestrians had been those who had the financial ability to equip themselves as cavalrymen. This was an archaic definition. In our period, equestrians were free-born citizens registered in the census as having property worth 400,000 sesterces or more. Equestrians were allowed to wear a toga with a thin purple stripe and also wore a gold ring. They were given a separate bank of seats in the theatre.

Augustus invented an equestrian career structure which was further developed by later emperors, as is discussed elsewhere (see p. 255).

It is sometimes argued that the equestrians were the business class of Rome. This is not supported by the available evidence. During the Republic, equestrians were allowed to bid for the lucrative state contracts for the collection of taxation, but these were phased out in favour of direct collection in the imperial period. There is no evidence to suggest that equestrian interests differed substantially from senatorial interests. Technically, sons of senators who avoided official posts remained equestrians. Equestrians appear to have been landowners, though, like senators, they often had interests in various economic activities.

Equestrians were the non-senatorial aristocracy of Italy and came also to incorporate the rich from across the empire as Roman citizenship spread. Equestrians ran their local communities and sat on local councils. Although wealth and Roman citizenship were the only formal criteria that seem to have operated, it is likely that equestrians regarded themselves as a hereditary elite with status passing from generation to generation.

Senators

Senators were those who sat in the senate. They were magistrates and former magistrates, or those who were granted magisterial honours without performing the functions. They wore a broad purple stripe on their togas.

Augustus introduced distinctions which transformed the senatorial group from merely those who held or had held office to a properly defined social order. He introduced a census requirement of 1,000,000 sesterces. In addition, he allowed the sons of senators to enter the senate as observers and to wear a toga with a broad stripe. The privilege was extended to members of equestrian families whom Augustus wished to encourage to enter the senate. Senators, their children and grandchildren were prevented by law from marrying freed people. Senators were given separate seats in the theatre. They were also given their own voting units (centuries) at the elections. By these measures, senatorial status was extended beyond the senators to their families.

The creation of a senatorial order may have reflected perceptions of senators as members of a stable, hereditary elite, some of whom could trace their ancestry back to the beginnings of Rome or even earlier. Status passed through the generations as the young males were regarded as future senators and the women as mothers and wives of senators. This was formalised by Augustus. The truth, however, was that the senate was a far more open elite than presented. Studies of consuls have shown that only about 26 per cent of consuls during the period 249–50 BC had no immediate consular or even praetorian ancestor. In the first century AD, 46–75 per cent of consuls had no consular ancestor. The senatorial order was not stable.

The system of orders suggests a fairly rigid social structure with an extreme consciousness of hierarchy. Attaching legal definitions to the different social status groups might be thought to have restricted social mobility. In reality, although the ideology of a largely unchanging social hierarchy in which social status was passed from generation to generation was maintained and, indeed, strengthened by various measures in our period, there was movement over generations between orders and changes in status within the social hierarchy within a single generation. These changes caused tensions within Roman society. To understand better the nature of these fluctuations, we need to look at society in a different way. Nevertheless, we should remember that the orders were probably the social categories that meant most to the Romans themselves.

WEALTH AND SOCIAL STRUCTURE

We have limited information at our disposal for relative levels of wealth. Table 10.3 is imperfect in that some of the figures are questionable and some social groups are not attested. What appears most clearly, however, is the relative inequality of Roman society. There are a number of incomes of about 1,000 sesterces per year. It seems a reasonable assumption that this income would provide a decent standard of living. An absolute subsistence income from which someone could buy enough food to live but have nothing else was approximately 25 per cent of that level. Pliny's income was about 1,000 times higher than this 'decent income'. His estates generated enough money to support about a fifth of a legion: he could maintain approximately 2,400 people at subsistence levels. Pliny was not one of the richest senators, but if we take his income as average for the senatorial elite, then the income of the senatorial elite could support about 1,200,000 people at subsistence levels or

Table 10.3 Relative wealth

Source	Income by period (in sesterces)	Annual income (in sesterces)
Subsistence (Grain price)	20/month	240
Subsistence (Digest)	40/month	480
Subsistence (Digest)	42/month	504
Veterans (Retirement bonus)	12,000 (capital)	720[1]
Subsistence (Digest)	83/month	996
Freedmen (Pliny's will)	18,666.66 (capital)	1,120
Soldiers (Pay)	1,200/year	1,200
Subsistence (Martial)	6/day	1,800[2]
Pliny (Estates)	20,000,000 (capital)	1,200,000[3]

[1] Assuming a return of 6 per cent.
[2] Calculated on the assumption of the client securing the gift on 300 days a year.
[3] Assuming a return of 6 per cent.

600,000 soldiers. This concentration of wealth in the hands of the elite gave great power to those at the top of the social pyramid.

The size of upper-class fortunes and the nature of the ancient economy suggests that great wealth was not generated by judicious investment, but was accumulated through inheritance. Pliny invested most of his money in land and it seems likely that this was typical of the Roman elite. The extent of the wealth of the elite would have encouraged a diversity of economic interests, but no source suggests that those other interests could supplant agricultural exploitation as the major source of income. Investment in land produced a long-term return, and economic stability appears to characterise our period (see pp. 231–2). Inheritance seems to have been the only way in which anyone could accumulate the vast amounts of property that were owned by the senatorial elite.

The Romans had a system of partible inheritance whereby property was divided equally at death between the surviving children. Since wealth was so closely related to status, the division of an estate between several children could bring considerable loss of status and some have seen this as a cause of downward social mobility. The Romans had certain mechanisms which would partially alleviate this difficulty. Property tended to be disposed of through wills. The bulk of the estate would go to heirs, but substantial legacies were frequently left to others. The normal demographic processes in a family would lead to the accumulation and dispersal of property as friends and family left bequests to an individual, and the individual then dispersed his property to children and friends at death. Thus, Pliny inherited property from his father and mother and from his uncle. He benefited under the wills of his friends and accumulated property by bequest and perhaps through some investment of profits from other estates throughout his lifetime. He had no children, nor any obvious close relatives. Some of his estate was left in trust to support his freedmen. His gifts to the town of Comum accounted for more of his estate, but his friends probably also benefited. As family lines died out or prospered, property moved through the upper classes, and presumably those who came from larger families would be somewhat compensated for the division of the estate on the death of their parents by receipt of legacies from family friends and perhaps from less fertile branches of the family. As long as the amount of land under the control of the elite and the numbers of the elite remained relatively stable, the partible inheritance system posed no real threat to the continuity of elite families.

The continual dispersal and concentration of estates did,

however, provide opportunities for social mobility. The elite gave property to their friends. They thanked the powerful for favours. They gave support and security to poorer friends. A person of low social status who happened to achieve a position of authority from where he could harm or help members of the elite could expect to be rewarded. The emperors accumulated and dispersed huge amounts of 'private' property. The imperial freedmen were probably also presented with legacies. Such legacies were a normal process of ensuring that friendship and support would be given to the next generation and was a form of repayment for services rendered. Lower down the political scale, a similar pattern was followed. Those who could form friendships with the elite were in a position to benefit. Those who established friendships with childless members of the elite could receive very substantial legacies. The freed, many of whom were educated and literate and many of whom will have been on friendly terms with their former masters, were in a better position to insert themselves into this pattern of dispersal and concentration of property than the free poor.

Worry about the rise of the freedmen was, therefore, in one sense real since freedmen could potentially accumulate wealth. In another sense, however, it was unreal since the reason these freedmen were selected for promotion was probably because they shared the same values as the traditional elite. The 'rise of the freedmen' (and we must remember that we have no idea how many freedmen rose) was thus part of this process of continual flux that does not obscure the essential social and cultural continuity. Since the freed became free and rose because they were socially and culturally indistinguishable from the elite, their rise did not entail the development of a new aristocracy and they were thus no threat to the social order.

GROUPS WITHIN SOCIETY: PATRONAGE AND SOCIAL COHESION

The landed elite also controlled other sources of social power. They were the political class who led communities locally and represented the community in Rome. They tended to represent the community to the gods, holding the important priesthoods and sacrificing on behalf of the community. They served as judges and ran the legal system. Many served as officers in the Roman army. They had political, economic, judicial, religious and, to a certain extent, military authority.

Their power was limited by the competitive nature of the elite. In the Republican period, the elite had competed for the votes that would secure them political power. The elite secured the support of the voters in various ways. Politicians could try to appeal to a mass audience by suggesting popular measures. They could also use their existing power to do favours on the understanding that the voters would turn out for them. Yet an individual could not hope to gather significant support through this process. The prospective candidate needed to turn to other members of the elite for support. These 'friends' would lend their support and that of their followers on the basis of being able to require that the favour was returned in some form. Friendships were central to the workings of the political system and continued to be so in the imperial period.

Such friendships extended beyond the political sphere. Marriages cemented alliances and friends would help friends of friends in the resolution of disputes, in obtaining military office or any other favour. The interrelationship of the Roman elite is complex, as we can see by studying the family of Thrasea Paetus and Helvidius Priscus and the friends of Pliny (see pp. 129–32). To take a single example, Pliny wrote a letter to Junius Mauricus in which he suggested a suitor for the sister of Mauricus' brother Arulenus Rusticus (a friend of Thrasea and Helvidius) (*Ep.* I 14). Pliny's chosen candidate was Minicius Acilianus, a slightly younger friend of Pliny. Pliny notes that he is a close friend who looks to Pliny for advice. Pliny then establishes his family history. Acilianus was a native of Brixia in Cisalpine Gaul and thus from the same region of Italy as Pliny. His father had remained an equestrian, though Vespasian had offered to raise him to among the former praetors in the senate (see also *Ep.* VIII 5). His maternal grandmother was also from the same region of Northern Italy. She was a native of Patavium, the home town of Thrasea Paetus. One can trace such connections throughout the Roman elite.

With Pliny, we can also observe the connections stretching to the lower orders. Romatius Firmus received 300,000 sesterces from Pliny to raise him to equestrian status (*Ep.* I 19). He tried to secure a military post (*Ep.* II 13) and then a senatorial position (*Ep.* X 4) for his friend and literary adviser Voconius Romanus (*Ep.* III 13, VI 15, 33). Voconius' father was an equestrian, but Voconius himself could not meet the census requirement for senatorial status. His mother, however, agreed to make over 4,000,000 sesterces for her son should Trajan decide to elevate him. Further down the social scale, Pliny's benefactions for Comum were expected to bring him popular favour as was his treatment of contractors and tenants (see pp. 233–4).

This system of alliances and mutual favours was social glue. The senior partner in the arrangement, the patron, spread his favours and those below spread their favours in an ever extending network of mutual obligations. The system of patronage linked social orders, but also formed links within orders. A young aristocrat seeking to make his way would rely on the support and advice of more senior figures and contract a series of obligations which, in turn, would be repaid to the benefit of other protégés of those who had aided his career.

Political and economic power established the patron. Since the emperor had in his gift the majority of senior and junior appointments, huge financial resources, and controlled the legal administration, he was able to establish himself as a universal patron, able to spread favours through the aristocracy and to the lower orders. Emperors delegated much of their authority, and senior figures within the administration would act as intermediaries, effectively distributing imperial patronage. Tacitus saw the emergence of the emperor as such a powerful patron as one of the keys to the establishing of the monarchy. The network of the patronage system spread through the social classes so that those whom Pliny helped in Comum would be loyal to Pliny, and since Pliny was loyal to the emperor, the loyalty of Comum to the emperor was assured.

The extensive use of patronage meant that ancient society operated in ways very different from those of modern societies. Instead of a horizontal stratification of society so that group loyalties were regulated by class or order, we have a vertical division of society. This transforms political and economic perspectives. What mattered was not whether a policy benefited a particular social category, shopkeepers for instance, but whether it benefited a particular social faction, the senator, his friends and his dependants. At the top of this social pyramid was the great aristocrat and, ultimately, the emperor.

In theory, these vertical groupings should have encompassed most members of society, and social competition should have been between these various groups. In practice, the patronage networks probably never involved all the population. Many of the urban and rural poor probably had little contact with patrons. In the imperial period, politicians became dependent for political success on their fellow senators and on the emperor. Since the elite no longer needed their votes, there was less pressure to extend patronage to the lower classes. It is, however, clear from our sources, both epigraphic and literary, that the behaviour of the elite did not change radically. The elite continued to be interested in securing the favour of their communities and went about securing that favour in a traditional manner. Throughout the first century, the elite continued to put money into projects designed to improve their standing with their local communities and the first century saw considerable and perhaps increasing expenditure by the elite on public buildings and festivals and this process.

Although elections seem to have become less important, popular opinion could be expressed through decrees of the local councils or through demonstrations in the theatre. These decrees often resulted in the erection of a honorific monument, often a statue, to the bene-factor. Indeed, there is some evidence to suggest that some cities became so crowded by such monuments that the councils simply changed the heads on existing statues to honour new civic benefac-tors. The theatre in Rome was a major medium of communication between the plebs and the emperor (see pp. 112–14) and it is likely that similar processes were at work in the theatres of the empire. We know of organised claques in Rome who supported Nero, and it is likely that there were similar groups elsewhere who could be encouraged to voice their approval of particular members of the community. The approval of one's local community seems to have been regarded as extremely important by the elite.

There were, however, signs of tensions within the social system. Martial complains bitterly about his treatment in the great aristo-cratic houses, which in itself would not be convincing evidence of a worsening of behaviour, but Pliny adds his voice to complaints. Pliny complains that at dinner parties the food was graded by the social status of the guest. This measure breached the illusion that at dinner all were equal: all were simply *amici* (friends). This was important since, although all may have been acutely aware of rela-tive social status, all were free and thus had at least to preserve the illusion of independence. To provide such *amici* with poorer food than that which the host ate was to demonstrate that they were inferior and probably dependent, and dependency carried with it the taint of servility.

Culture was also an important way of displaying status. Inevitably, those who were interested in literature dominate the surviving sources. Yet, the stress on culture seems to influence more than a small literary circle. The Roman elite was educated in classical literature and rhetoric. They were expected to be able to speak in public and present themselves before an audience. A gentleman was cultured. Pliny stresses the cultural achievements of those he recommended. Suetonius felt that the cultural interests of the emperors were sufficiently important that the rhetorical style and literary achievements of each needed some comment.

Roman patronage of Greek culture (and much of the Roman culture of the imperial period was heavily influenced by Greek precursors) encouraged the flourishing of arts in Italy and Greece. The end of our period saw the development of the so-called 'second sophistic', which was a cultural revival in the Greek East that looked back to the achievements of Greek culture in previous centuries, especially the fifth and fourth centuries BC. The language in which the ideas of the second sophistic were transmitted was often an old-fashioned form of Greek. In Italy, the Romans continued to look to the East for cultural inspiration, and never more so than in the reign of Nero. The literature and art of the period also seem to display a high degree of cultural sophistication. Most intellectual and literary production in this period seems to have been largely directed at a highly educated elite, and it seems unlikely that much of this would have been understood by the uneducated of Greece or Italy. Significantly, the cultural values of the Roman elite led to imitation of and participation in the cultural activities of the Greek elite. As a result, the Roman elite may well have had more in common with the Greek aristocracy than with their own poor.

Culture was not the only way in which distinctions could be made between the elite and other social groups. There may have been a change in relative incomes in the imperial period. When Augustus brought in the senatorial census level of 1,000,000 sesterces, several senators failed to reach this level. Augustus and Tiberius were forced to give grants of property to deserving senators and their children. Many senators will have had wealth far in excess of the census requirement, even in the Augustan period. Pliny's wealth was such that the census requirement was not a serious concern. Pliny's friend Voconius Romanus was to receive four times the census level from his mother should he be elevated to the senate by Trajan (see p. 220) and, since we must assume that Romanus was at the bottom of the senatorial financial scale, this suggests that a senator should have a minimum of 4,000,000–5,000,000 sesterces. It is probable that the average senator of the late first century was several times wealthier than his equivalent earlier in the century.

The increasing wealth of the elite can easily be explained. The expenses of political activity in the Late Republic had been great and the instability of the period threatened the fortunes of the elite, since the wealthy were targets for politicians often short of cash. Although the imperial period may also have seen some limited purges of the wealthiest members of the aristocracy to refill imperial coffers, the emperors also brought a level of security. The gradual influx of senators of provincial origin probably also affected the wealth of the elite and broadened economic horizons. It is likely that, overall, the Roman elite became richer and therefore more powerful as they became more integrated with provincial elites. Although our evidence is very limited, it suggests an increased differentiation between the rich and poor in Roman society.

Potentially, this social change could have increased social conflicts in Roman society but the continued expenditure of the elite for the wider benefit of their communities must have reduced social tensions and it seems likely that the elite came to exercise more control over the lower classes. This can be seen by examining those groups that might be thought to have posed a threat to elite power.

In the Republican period, popular discontent had been mobilised through *collegia*. These were 'clubs' of varying status and function. Little is known about the operation of these *collegia*. They appear to have performed social functions in providing some charitable support, religious functions (often based around a district of a city), or to have operated as trade associations. The involvement of such groups in urban violence led to various measures to ban *collegia*. Official opposition to *collegia* continued into the imperial period. When Pliny wrote to Trajan requesting permission to set up a fire brigade in Nicomedia, Trajan refused on the grounds that such groups often became involved in political activities (Pliny, *Ep.* X 33–4). Nevertheless, there is evidence that *collegia* remained prominent parts of the urban scene. These associations can be seen in the epigraphic evidence from the cities of the East and also from Ostia and Pompeii. In Pompeii, Eumachia had a large meeting house for the fullers built in a prominent position in the Forum. At Ostia, the activities of the *collegia* are represented in inscriptions and large meeting houses in various parts of the city. These buildings attest the wealth and prominence of the various trade groups.

Potentially, these groups could have been mobilised to challenge elite dominance of the city. It is, however, unclear whether this ever happened. The inscriptions from Ostia often attest aristocratic patrons for *collegia*. In Pompeii, Eumachia was probably not a fuller herself, rather a member of the local aristocracy. We cannot know how much influence the patron had over the activities of those in the *collegia* and, anyhow, such control varied from place to place and from time to time. On some issues, the elite may have been unable to prevent the *collegia* voicing their opposition, and on others the elite was probably able to smooth discontents. Control of trading activities by easily identifiable *collegia* allowed the elite to exercise greater control over traders since *collegia* had a leadership which could be pressured, cajoled and rewarded. The *collegia* could be seen as a method of social control.

Another rather surprising development in the imperial period is the rise of the *Augustales*. These were priests of the imperial cult who may have organised the activities of the imperial cult on a local basis within the city. There seems to be some variation in nomenclature of the cult officers and in their recruitment in different cities, but in at least some urban centres the posts were filled by freedmen. The prominence of freedmen in what one would have assumed was an important religious and political function for a community is unexpected and not yet properly explained. The epigraphic record suggests that *Augustales* formed an elite in parallel to the decurions (see p. 208). It seems unlikely that they were in any sense an alternative elite within the city. There was resistance among the upper classes to allowing freedmen to join the town council, and yet some of the freedmen had probably accumulated considerable wealth and some social prestige. The institution of the *Augustales* provided an opportunity for the urban community to obtain some of that money and to integrate the freedmen into the social and political life of the city. The origins and actual independence of the freedmen cannot easily be assessed from the inscriptions. It has been suggested that many of these freedmen in effect represented the aristocratic houses of a community and were sponsored by them and thus the prominence of the *Augustales* should not be seen as a major social development.

CONCLUSIONS

This period did see limited social change. The elite appears to have become richer. There is evidence that certain freedmen were able to accumulate significant amounts of wealth. The treatment of slaves may have improved very slightly. The treatment of the poor freeborn by the powerful in society may have deteriorated slightly. Yet there is no evidence that the power of the landed elite was seriously challenged. They were not threatened by the rise of a 'new elite', either of freedmen descent or those who owed their wealth from trade or even an elite drawn from the army. Those who managed to join the ranks of the elite from the lower orders probably did so simply because they were compatible and would not threaten the social system. Our evidence suggests that the elite controlled potential subversive organisations. Society may have been changing slightly, but the social order did not face any significant threat.

11

THE ECONOMY

In recent years much attention has been focused on the Roman economy. Historians have been asking fundamental questions about how the economy worked and what kind of economy it was. These questions have to be understood before we can look at the issue of economic change in the first century AD.

ECONOMIC STRUCTURES

Historians disagree as to the level of sophistication of the ancient economy. Some historians have seen broad analogies between the workings of the ancient economy and 'subsistence economies' of areas of the developing world. Other historians suggest that the ancient economy was complex and had more in common with modern economies. This debate has at times been vitriolic and part of the reason for this difference of opinion lies in the nature of the source material.

Sources and approaches

Our major ancient literary sources make virtually no mention of macro-economic issues (issues affecting the whole economy). They do not discuss the economic fortunes of regions or the productivity of the Roman empire, levels or distribution of employment, demographics, or any of the other issues that have become central to modern political and economic debate. If the emperors had anything approaching an economic policy, this is not discussed by our sources. There are a number of figures in our sources which historians have treated as statistically valid, such as population figures for certain communities, prices for certain goods and certain rates of pay. Some of these figures are trustworthy, though some are invented. These statistics (both trustworthy and untrustworthy) are so few and often so difficult to interpret that everyone agrees we have nothing approaching an adequate statistical base from which to write economic history.

Two approaches are open to the historian. The first is to patch together the inadequate material available to attempt to reconstruct the ancient economy from literary attestations, archaeological excavations and documentary studies. The second is to develop theoretical models to explain how the economy might have worked and then examine whether the evidence we have fits those models. Both approaches have serious methodological weaknesses. The first approach may mean that too much weight is placed on anomalous evidence and that the general picture of the economy cannot be perceived because of the many and various pieces of evidence: no clear picture of the wood emerges because of a concentration on individual trees. The second approach runs the risk of over-simplifying the economy and, perhaps more seriously, of distorting the evidence to fit the model. The success of the second approach has been that it has allowed historians to think about the economy generally and has generated much modern debate that has led to a better understanding of this issue. It has also allowed historians to make use of evidence which previously had not seemed to be of much relevance to economic history. Used sensitively, this second approach can offer valuable insights into the ancient economy.

All such theoretical models should be treated with caution. They are 'ideal types', designed to provide a simple theoretical explanation for the workings of the economy rather than describing any real situation. This can be best illustrated by considering the 'ideal type' of a family. One could draw up a list of characteristics of the average family, as various market research organisations do. It is understood that families may differ radically from that 'ideal type' and even that the 'average family' probably does not exist in reality. The non-existence of the 'average family' does not mean that the concept of the 'average family' is not useful since, although all families differ, many will differ only insignificantly from the ideal type. It is to theoretical models we turn first.

Theories and models

The city

One of the best known economic models is that of the consumer city (see Figure 11.1). In this model, members of the elite own farms in the countryside and reside in the city, which is the centre of political activity. All cities need an influx of goods from the countryside to feed their populations, and in this model those goods are mainly brought in through taxes, rents or the produce of the farms of the elite.

The model of the consumer city (Figure 11.2) can be compared to the medieval producer city. In this model the city supports itself by trading in goods, either goods manufactured in the city or goods marketed in the city. The elite reside mainly in the countryside and the city is not the centre of political power.

Figure 11.1 The consumer city

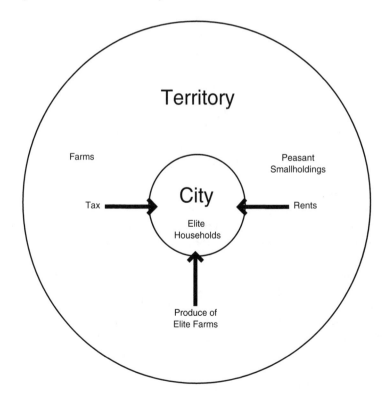

Figure 11.2 The medieval producer city

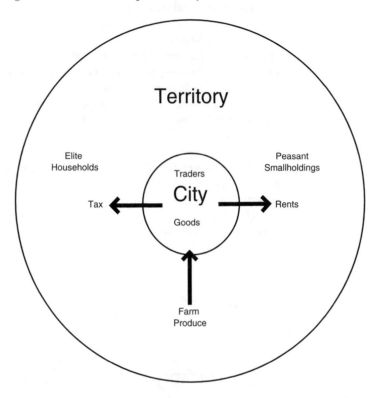

Everyone agrees that these models (even in more complex presentations) are over-simplified, but they focus our attention on perceived differences between cities of various periods. The 'consumer city' model suggests that cities were a focus of political life and were likely to be beautified by members of the elite competing for political status. Trade was unimportant since the city survived from taxes and rents. There is unlikely to have been a large manufacturing centre, therefore, and few will have made significant amounts of money from trade or manufacture. In the 'medieval producer city', trade is important since the city survives on the income produced from exchange of goods. Thus, we see powerful trade guilds in the medieval city. However, the elite tended to live away from the city and the cities were not centres of political power and were unlikely to receive large benefactions from members of the elite seeking to secure political popularity.

The attitudes of the elite towards trade can be used to support the theory of 'the consumer city'. Evidently, the majority of the elite, both equestrian and senatorial, invested the majority of their wealth in land. Farming was the only honourable profession for a gentleman and elite writers tend to be rather rude about those involved in trade.

The agricultural economy

Various trading activities are attested by our literary sources and are attested in abundance by archaeology. The problem is the significance of these activities. Here we need to make a series of hypotheses and observations.

- All pre-modern economies were agricultural, i.e. the majority of the population were involved in agricultural work. The Roman economy was also agricultural.
- Much pre-modern agricultural production was for subsistence and not for the market. The Roman economy had a large subsistence base.
- Transporting heavy goods was extremely expensive and would prevent the development of large-scale trade. Economies, therefore, of necessity tended to remain local.
- The concentration of the wealth of the elite in land prevented capital being invested in trade and manufacture, so that these sectors were starved of investment preventing economies of scale and technological development.
- The legal structures of the Roman state tended to emphasise individual responsibility and were reluctant to allow liabilities to be shared or limited and were very cautious concerning the use of agents of individuals in business. These laws effectively limited the ability of the Romans to pool resources and risk in companies.
- The elite tended to manage property conservatively, being more concerned with passing their estates to their heirs than expanding on those estates. The elite tended to be involved in political life and so surpluses were invested in social events or constructions rather than in economically productive areas.

The resulting picture of the Roman economy is one which emphasises stability and local activity. Without technological change or a change in attitudes, this was an economy in which there was very little scope for economic change. If smallholders were not involved in the market, they would not be affected by changes in the nature of that market. Local movement of goods reduced the opportunities for businessmen to make huge profits. The economy was not integrated and so events even close to a certain community, such as warfare in the territory of a neighbour, may have had very little effect on the economy. The economy of the empire could survive shocks to any one part without the other parts being damaged.

Much of this is undeniable. Most argument concerns the variations from the model. It makes a difference whether the city derived 2 per cent or 20 per cent or 40 per cent of its income from trade and manufactured goods. Similarly, the extent to which goods were produced for the market is important. Also, the percentage of land that was in the hands of smallholders and what those smallholders did with their land shapes the economic history of the period. This information cannot be derived from theory. We need to look at the evidence.

Evidence

The absence of any discussion of macro-economic matters in our literary sources is in itself evidence. Two obvious explanations suggest themselves. First, the literature of the period was written for the elite, people who had considerable personal wealth. It may be that this wealth insulated the elite from the realities of economic life so that they were either unaware of, or did not care about, the fluctuations of the economy which affected their social inferiors. Perhaps a more likely explanation lies in the nature of the economy. If the economy did not fluctuate, then discussion of the state of the economy and the collection of information from which to study the economy would be unnecessary.

Literary sources contain snippets of information and do discuss micro-economic matters. Writers such as Columella provided advice to landowners on how to run their estates. Pliny the Younger provides us with a great deal of incidental information on how he ran his estates. Other literary sources tend to provide anecdotal information which is difficult to evaluate. Domitian passed a decree which outlawed the planting of vines and ordered that the acreage of vines in the provinces be halved (Suet., *Dom.* 7; see p. 244). Anecdotal information about, for instance, the size of individual fortunes or the time in which a journey was completed must be treated with caution since so often we know it is the exception (which is why it is reported) rather than the rule.

Pliny's *Letters* attest his generosity to friends and fellow towns-folk. They also show something of Pliny's management of his estate. He had several farms around the town of Comum, some of which he inherited from his parents. His parental estate was regarded as special and when a friend expressed interest in purchasing property near Lake Como, he offered her the pick of his estates except those he had inherited from his parents (*Ep.* VII 11). He took a close interest in the management of his estate, though he tends to joke about his ability to lose money. One of the more interesting letters concerns the failure of a grape harvest. Pliny had sold the harvest while it was still on the vine. However, the crop failed and threat-ened to ruin those who had purchased it. Pliny stepped in to remit some of the money owed to him and it is likely that he thereby prevented many of these purchasers going out of business. The purchasers were intending to pick and sell the harvest. Since harvesting and marketing were major and specialised tasks, Pliny's use of contractors made good economic sense. His support of them in this crisis was also rational since, if they were ruined, Pliny may have had difficulty in finding people prepared to contract for these tasks in subsequent years and his subsidy would probably encourage the contractors to take further risks on his grape crop (*Ep.* VIII 2). The letter hints at Pliny's economic power. He was dealing with a large number of contractors and was probably able to exercise a great deal of control over their activities. Since Pliny was probably the major landowner in the district, some may have been financially dependent on the work he provided.

Not all Pliny's crop was sold to such people. He tell us that he spent time supervising the grape harvest and checking the wine-making. The grapes may have come from land leased to tenants or farmed directly through members of Pliny's household. The harvest was brought in with the help of a gang brought by Pliny from the city (*Ep.* IX 20).

Pliny seems to have had problems with his tenants. He was forced to reduce rents, but arrears continued to build up and indeed rose to such a level that the tenants lost hope of payment. Pliny could have dispossessed the tenants and looked for new people to take up the tenancy, but this would have brought him a certain unpopularity with the tenants and their associates, many of whom were probably living close to his estates. Instead, Pliny chose to institute a share-cropping scheme whereby he received a proportion of the produce in rent. His rent would thus be adjusted according to the productivity of the land, but there would still be an incentive for the tenants to increase production (*Ep.* IX 37).

The texts we have show Pliny playing the kindly landlord and fulfilling social responsibilities by not extracting maximum profit from his tenants and contractors. Pliny's generosity was tempered with self-interest. If he had bankrupted his contractors, he may have caused considerable damage to the local economy and, although he offset some of the losses of the contractors, he clearly made money on the whole transaction. If he had dispossessed his tenants, he would have been faced with trying to find new tenants for his farms, and finding farmers experienced in the local conditions was probably not easy. There was no guarantee that the new tenants would be more efficient. Retaining his tenants would be popular, but also probably in Pliny's long-term financial interests. He was interested in generating money from his estates, and although he did not squeeze every penny from his dependants each year, this may have been sensible management.

The literary record can be supplemented by archaeology, which has improved knowledge of the economy through two main areas of research: distribution of artefacts and distribution of sites. Surveys of large areas have tended to uncover large numbers of small or very small ancient sites. These surveys have shown that the old idea that much of Italy was dominated by *latifundia*, huge estates worked by slaves, is insupportable. The countryside remained thickly populated and excavated estates seem to have been, as far as one can judge, quite small establishments. The archaeological evidence cannot currently tell us very much about the crops grown on these small farms. Detailed excavations can produce this information, but too few rural sites have been excavated to allow us to get a clear picture. Ownership of estates cannot be established. A small farm could be owned and run by a farmer, or the farmer might lease the land from a great landowner, or the land might be exploited directly through slaves and a bailiff. Nothing would appear in the archaeological record which would allow us to distinguish between these possibilities.

The great landowners appear to have had a number of topographically distinct farms, rather than a single large farm. In economic terms this made sense. Whereas concentration of landholding in modern farming offers considerable economies of scale, ancient farming was not so mechanised and dispersal of plots (as long as the parcels were not very small) would only have a limited effect.

Dispersal also spread risk. Climatic conditions and disease were a major threat and dispersal of farms provided some insurance against crop failure. The pattern of acquisition and disposal of estates discouraged concentration of landholding. The division of estates on the death of the owner probably led to the acquisition of small parcels of land. Purchase and sale would allow some rationalisation, but there is no evidence to suggest that the Romans regarded holding neighbouring farms as necessarily advantageous. Although separate farms would have made assessing the profitability of estates and parts of estates more complex, this does not seem to have been beyond Roman estate management and Pliny certainly could assess the profitability of individual parcels of his estate (*Ep.* II 15).

Archaeological survey in Italy gives the impression of a thickly populated countryside. It also gives the impression of a comparatively wealthy countryside. In many areas, in fact, there is little evidence of the poor. It is possible that this is because the poor were too poor to be archaeologically detectable. Many ancient sites are identified because of the presence of pottery, especially the higher quality pottery. This means that poor farmers who could not buy the latest high-quality pottery cannot always be identified in the archaeological record: the peasant-agriculturists who farmed barely enough land to live off, and were so beloved of traditional Roman moralists, are difficult to find. Many of the poor may have become dependent labourers – people such as Pliny's tenants or those even lower down the social scale. Peasant farmers almost certainly existed, but their economic importance was probably not great. Medium-sized farms seem to have been more important and these are not just attested in the archaeological record, but also by inscriptions, especially those related to the *alimenta* scheme (see p. 207). These farms were not subsistence farms: the farmers were clearly producing for a market, almost certainly an urban centre.

Archaeological exploration of urban centres offers some further insights. Although absolute population figures cannot be discovered through archaeological excavation, some idea of the size of the urban community can be gained. Large numbers of shops have been found in urban centres, and other retail sites such as *macella* (a kind of market hall) and *fora* provide evidence for trading activities. Investigations at Pompeii have suggested that at least some of the shops were owned by members of the elite, and that they were probably run by servile members of elite households. Such evidence shows some elite involvement with trade. Excavations at Ostia also demonstrate the importance of trade. Ostia was at the mouth of the

Tiber and much of the naval trade for Rome must have passed through the port; this probably distorted the economy of the city, but trading *collegia* (see pp. 224–5) appear to have been a prominent and economically important part of the city.

Distribution of artefacts also provides clues to the workings of the economy. Artefacts have to get to where they are found and thus often attest to trade. The monetarisation of the ancient economy is attested by the thousands of ancient coins that were in circulation and by the appearance of coins at most sites in the empire. Although the appearance of coins does not in itself show that many transactions occurred, or even whether monetary transactions were the norm, they do show some trade. Historians dispute the means by which coins entered particular areas and were circulated within those areas. The army is normally seen as an important source of coinage, especially in the West. In the East, coins had been in more extensive use for longer. It has been argued that coins did not circulate freely even in the East and that what are called 'coin populations' remained fairly stationary. This means that once a particular group of coins entered a particular region, they tended to circulate locally.

Pottery is another easily detectable artefact. Some agricultural produce was moved round the Mediterranean in large pottery jars known as *amphorae*. Millions of these have found all over the Empire. Various centres of production appear to have operated simultaneously, though the styles of *amphorae* appear to have been fairly uniform. Massive numbers of broken *amphorae* have been excavated in southern Gaul, where the Mediterranean trade would have entered the Gallic river system. Great mounds of pottery have been found at many other sites. The volume of such finds is impressive, but ultimately difficult to comprehend, especially since they represent deposits over hundreds of years. Yet, the *amphorae* provide clear evidence for long-distance trade.

The situation with good-quality pottery (fine wares) is more complex. Various locally produced Italian wares do seem to be very widely distributed in the first century, though Eastern wares continued to be produced and circulated throughout the East. The pottery does not show the same kind of uniformity of style as *amphorae* and there were regional distribution networks, yet the wide distribution of certain wares again provides evidence for long-distance trade.

The cheapest pottery tended only to circulate locally within a region of a province or throughout a province. Although some of these wares did cross provincial boundaries, this was probably related to military demands that could not be satisfied locally rather than a developed trade network.

Conclusions and regional variations

Although the information at our disposal is far from perfect, we do seem to be able to construct a reasonable picture of the Italian economy. This economy appears to have been dominated by medium-sized farms, most of which probably produced for both domestic and market consumption. The Italians exported their agricultural produce. The monetarisation of the economy of Italy and the gradual monetarisation of the economy of the rest of the empire is notable. Money is useful for trade (and paying taxes) and this suggests that trade was an important element of the economy. There is evidence of economically significant trade both between town and country and between regions of the Empire.

If we return to the theories outlined in the first sections of this chapter, we can now add modifications. The economy of Italy and the Roman Empire was an agricultural economy. It does, however, appear to have been rather more developed than a 'subsistence economy': much agricultural production was destined for urban markets. Similarly, the 'consumer city' model can be seen to apply. Much of the wealth of the city was derived from taxes and rents. Nevertheless, trade was important for some cities and a certain proportion of the urban population must have relied on income derived from trading with the rural population and their landlords. We must also build long-distance trade into our model. Economies were not purely local.

Much of this relates to the Italian economy. The economies of other areas are less well understood. It is clear, however, that there was considerable variation in economic systems. Britain, for instance, had few urban centres at the time of the conquest, whereas the East was heavily urbanised. The dominance of the medium-sized farm in some areas of Italy is not a feature of the Eastern economies of Egypt, Palestine and Syria, where the exploitation of extremely small parcels of land by villagers appears to have been a normal pattern of land use. The economy of Greece seems to have been more mixed with villas and villages, while that of the Danubian regions is something of a mystery. Northern Gaul may have had a village economy, while parts of Spain appear to have had medium-sized farms. Yet all these areas contained a multiplicity of different types of settlements and different ways of exploiting the countryside. The pattern of exploitation of the land varied from area to area and the level of integration with the 'Mediterranean economy' must also have varied. The economy of all areas may have been agricultural, but there were considerable variations within this broad descriptive category.

ECONOMIC CHANGE

The Empire

The first century AD saw the urbanisation of many areas. Roman-style cities appear across the empire, sometimes in provinces which previously had few urban centres. This change has been interpreted as a sign of economic growth.

It seems unlikely that there was a simple relationship between urbanisation and economic growth. Urbanisation is a complex phenomenon and is not necessarily related to fundamental changes in the economy. In the pre-Roman West, the elite may have displayed its wealth through personal ornamentation: jewellery and weapons, or through ownership or use of high-status goods such as foreign slaves, Roman wine, etc., or through maintaining a large band of followers. It is also possible (even probable in some places) that this elite did not congregate in urban centres. Surpluses were extracted from the local farmers, but these surpluses were not used to develop urban centres. Roman urbanisation may have changed the way in which the elite displayed their status, and the concentration of the elite in urban centres may have made the surpluses generated more archaeologically visible. Nevertheless, the extent of urbanisation, the distribution of trade goods, including money, the evidence for the development of new areas of agricultural exploitation, and an improvement in the quality of some buildings in the countryside in many regions lead most historians to take a fairly optimistic line about the first century. The developments across the empire suggest that the changes were more than cosmetic. There does appear to have been economic growth in the first century AD.

It has been suggested, rather against modern preconceptions, that the imposition of taxation was partly responsible for economic growth. The argument is outlined below.

- The Romans imposed taxation across the empire.

- The locals needed to find money to pay this tax.
- To obtain money, the locals needed to trade with money-rich markets and the most obvious markets were provided by the soldiers.
- The locals needed to grow goods for sale and needed to generate a sufficient surplus to trade with the soldiers.
- The economic specialisation that resulted led to improvements in efficiency and the growth of a market economy.
- Since most expenditure was on the army which was stationed on the fringes of the empire, taxation and government expenditure would mean that the under-developed provinces on the fringes of the empire would tend to receive more money, which should have caused economic growth in the least developed regions.

Such a model works best in the 'barbarian provinces' of the West and North. The monetarised and sophisticated economies of the East were probably less affected by the stationing of a Roman garrison and there was not the same shortage of coin in provinces which had been monetarised for centuries. Still, it is to be assumed that stationing several thousand well-paid troops in a province would have an effect, though we can hardly know whether this would compensate for the taxation of the province. Also, the theory tends to assume that farmers in the provinces were subsistence farmers and sent little of their crop to market before the Roman invasion. This is certainly questionable for many of the more developed regions, and even in Britain local elites may have extracted surpluses from the farmers. In many areas, the imposition of Roman taxation probably did not have a great deal of effect on local farmers. Also, in some highly urbanised areas the stationing of legions may not have brought sufficient change to affect the economy of the province as a whole.

In the West and North, we see a close relationship between urban development and the location of Roman garrisons. The stationing of troops on the Rhine especially may have encouraged the development of long-distance trade. The river valleys of southern Gaul allowed the fairly cheap movement of goods across the province and the Rhine itself allowed easy transportation. Much of the trade entering Gaul from the Mediterranean may have been destined for the legions stationed near the Rhine, but the wealth generated by this trade probably encouraged the development of southern Gallic production designed to meet the needs of the troops.

Another possible explanation for economic growth in this period is the 'Roman peace'. The process of Roman conquest was often brutal and disturbed the economic infrastructure. Wars were fought across territories. Populations were shifted. Cities were destroyed. People were enslaved or killed. The economies of Italy and the provinces suffered dislocation as a result of warfare.

The propaganda of the Augustan Peace was of a restoration of prosperity and a renewal of the fertility of Italy. The propaganda expressed this in religious terms, rather than the economic terminology which would be natural to modern politicians, though Augustan claims were no more or less credible. Yet, the general increase in political stability should have had an economic effect. The gradual stabilisation of the provinces probably encouraged investment. Although the provinces had to meet the demands of Roman taxation, deal with corrupt Roman officials, face the occasional war – and it is probable that many local problems were not noted by our sources – it seems very likely that the provinces were more peaceful in the first century AD than in any previous period.

Rome provided the Mediterranean with a huge market. As a city of probably about one million people, goods were brought to Rome from across the Mediterranean. The soldiers also provided traders with a market. There were probably about 300,000 troops in the Roman army. The political conditions of the Roman empire allowed provincials to seek to exploit these markets.

Rome itself organised some trade. The grain supply was heavily administered. The grain from Egypt was collected in taxes and transported to the port at Alexandria. From there, it was loaded on to the grain boats. Soldiers supervised the transportation of grain down the Nile, though it is unclear whether they simply handed over the grain to the shippers in Alexandria or supervised procedures more closely. Shippers, like those bringing the grain to Alexandria, were responsible for the safe delivery of their cargo and had to provide a bond in case they failed in their duties. The ships themselves were privately owned and, since the grain was not sold, there must have been a fixed payment for transportation. Supplies for the Roman troops must have been secured in a similar fashion. This trans-Mediterranean trade must have led to the construction of merchant fleets and it is probable that these fleets were also used to move other goods.

The resulting expansion of long-distance trade brought more

markets within the reach of farmers and must have encouraged farmers to grow produce for these markets. Relative peace further encouraged trade and the profits of trade must have encouraged further investment in the land, either by buying more land or investing in the land to bring more of it into production or to produce higher value crops. Vines and olives (the major cash crops in antiquity) are capital intensive. They are expensive to grow and take a long time to produce a return. Most farmers probably continued a mixed agricultural regime, growing fruit crops, cereals, vines and olives. Yet changes in the balance of crops grown could have considerable economic effects.

The most obvious areas to benefit from the prosperity of the first century were those on the major trade routes or with easy access to the Mediterranean. Spanish oil jars and Gallic wine *amphorae* become more common. Major potteries have also been found near Alexandria and on some Mediterranean islands. Prosperity was not confined to these regions. We see the emergence of 'villa estates' in many areas. Many of these villas, especially in Britain, were comparatively humble affairs and often differed little from Celtic farms (apart from the fact that the main buildings were not circular and they were at least partially constructed from stone). Such developments represent an investment in agricultural buildings and the gradual growth of many villas suggests an increasing prosperity in the countryside.

We should not, however, be too optimistic. There were regional variations. Archaeological studies have shown that some villages seem to have remained largely untouched by this Mediterranean market, and the first century of Roman domination seems to have brought considerable economic problems to parts of the East. The adjustment of local communities to new economic and political structures took time and there was probably considerable exploitation of the rural population. The damage caused by the wars of conquest in the East and by exploitative Roman officials may have reduced economic activity to a fairly low base from which it began to rise in the first century AD. It is also evident that local markets remained crucial to the success of a region. Although long-distance trade increased, it probably only accounts for a small fraction of the production of the empire as a whole. Most agricultural production must have been for local consumption and numismatic studies suggesting the coins tended to move from region to region only very slowly seem to confirm this.

There does appear to have been limited economic growth in this period, though we are not looking at an economic revolution. Change was comparatively slow and differed in pace from region to region. These processes worked over centuries of Roman rule and in some regions may have produced little observable change during the century that we are studying. The causes of this transformation are also complex, but it can partly be explained by the imposition of Roman administration which led to a certain integration of the economy of the Roman empire. It is even less clear whether these developments led to an improvement in the standard of living of the average inhabitant of the Roman empire. It seems very likely that the period saw an increase in the resources controlled by the elites of the empire. The lot of the poor was probably little improved by these developments.

Italy

Historians have seen crises in the Italian economy in most epochs and the first century AD is no exception, though the 'crisis' has been limited to the last years of the century. This crisis has been related to an alteration in the relationship of Italy to the Roman empire. The great conquests of the Republic had driven the Italian economy. Rome's armies plundered the Mediterranean basin and extracted great wealth in money, material goods and slaves. They were followed in their depredations by tax collectors and corrupt governors who maintained the flow of revenue to Rome. The money enriched the Roman elite and some of this money must have been invested in land. In addition, wars brought slaves. The development of a large slave workforce probably significantly reduced labour costs in Italy and allowed the further development of commercial farming. The development of a slave labour force also probably displaced large numbers of rural poor from the countryside. The most visible element of the problem was the rapid growth in Rome and the increased visibility of the urban poor. Various methods were tried to solve this problem: repatriation of non-Romans and, most importantly, colonisation. By the middle of the first century BC, however, the problem does not appear to have been serious. The corn dole gave a certain security to the urban poor and the only attempt at establishing a colonisation programme for the urban poor appears to have failed for lack of senatorial or popular support. Colonies set up in the first century BC were intended to provide some support for veteran soldiers and not to move the poor from Rome.

The civil wars must have disrupted economic life. There was

considerable fighting in Italy in the first decades of the first century BC and some fighting in the period 49–36 BC. Confiscations of property from political enemies or to create veteran colonies were also disruptive. The activities of leaders such as Sextus Pompeius, who raided Italian ports, probably had a deleterious effect on trade. The Augustan peace brought this to an end.

It is very difficult to assess the health of the Italian economy in the early first century AD. The period did see substantial urban development, i.e. the erection of new civic structures. Some of this can be related to the increasing concern to be seen to be honouring the imperial family. Some have suggested that the granting of civic benefactions by the aristocracies of the Italian towns slowed in the late first century AD. This judgement depends on the number of surviving inscriptions attesting such grants. However, the patterns of preservation and discovery of inscriptions distort the evidence and also patterns of civic benefactions may have changed: elite expenditure on a festival is less easy to detect than expenditure on a large public building. In any case, even if the elite started spending less on their various communities, this does not necessarily mean that they were less wealthy.

The Principate brought changes to the relationship between Italy and the provinces. It is arguable that provincial administration improved since more taxes were collected directly and the emperor took an interest in supervising his governors. The slowing of conquests must also have reduced the flow of money into Italy. The flow of slaves was also reduced. Landowners were probably faced with increased labour costs and had to rely more on tenants. The benefits of empire were thus reduced. Equally important was the change in the stationing of the army. Legionaries now lived, worked and spent their cash in the provinces. Money, therefore, flowed out to the provinces, though the contribution of Italy to the imperial budget may have been comparatively slight since there were few direct taxes levied on the Italian population. Any immediate decline that this may have caused was probably compensated for by the development of markets and secure trade routes in the empire. By the middle of the first century, however, competition for the commercial markets was becoming more fierce and Spanish, Gallic and later African production was to supplant Italian dominance.

We can certainly identify factors that might have led to a partial decline in the Italian economy. There is some evidence that has been used to support a theory of decline at the end of the first century:

Domitian's edict on vines, the introduction of the *alimenta* scheme and Pliny's problems with his estate.

It has been argued that Domitian's edict, which forbade the planting of new vineyards in Italy and ordered the destruction of 50 per cent of provincial vineyards, was designed to reduce provincial competition with Italian vineyards (Suet., *Dom.* 7). This is not what Suetonius tells us. Suetonius explains the development by suggesting that it was a response to a grain shortage and a bumper grape harvest. There seems to be no reason to dispute that interpretation.

Trajan's *alimenta* scheme (see p. 207) also does not suggest economic hardship. There was a long tradition of Roman leaders being concerned with the well-being of the poor and the young. The military traditions of Rome (dear to Trajan's heart) depended for their continuation on the supply of young men strong enough to fight, and the furtherance of the Roman people depended on the next generation of mothers. Augustus had introduced measures which, at least in part, had been designed to increase the Italian population and Trajan acted with similar motives. The provision of poor relief to support the next generation is better seen as a continuation of a general concern than a response to a specific crisis. In fact, the success of Trajan's scheme in at least some areas demonstrates prosperity. The government had significant sums of money to invest in the next generation. The influx of capital into the agricultural sector may even have been economically beneficial since it might have encouraged further investment.

Pliny's problems on his estates appear to have lasted for more than a single year. His move to a share-cropping system was induced by falling income from his estates. There could be local reasons for this: soil exhaustion, a run of poor seasons, crop disease, or Pliny's previous management of the estate may have been at fault. After all, his letters continually lay emphasis on how busy he was. Purchase of new estates may also have discouraged Pliny from investing in his current estates and it is possible that he had set rents too high in the first place. We may also note that although Pliny complains, his complaints do not suggest much suffering on his part. Nevertheless, it does seem that Pliny was grappling with real problems.

Archaeological evidence is inconclusive. Studies of the distribution of settlements and the excavations of specific sites appear to show that there were economic changes in some areas at the end of the first century AD, but there were significant regional variations and the evidence does not point to a widespread decline in Italian agriculture.

The accumulated evidence is inconclusive and it is safest to conclude that there was limited change in the Italian economy in this period. In the early first century, the economy appears to have been relatively prosperous. It is probable that commercial farming continued to develop and more produce was destined for non-Italian markets. The elite continued to accumulate land and wealth. The cities may have enjoyed greater prosperity supported by the generosity of local elites. Towards the end of the first century, there may have been some readjustment. The Italian economy may have lost some ground to Spain and Gaul and this may have affected the returns of some farmers. The great advantages that the Italian economy had enjoyed in the first century BC and earlier became less significant towards the end of this period. Yet, it would seem extravagant to elevate the grumbles of Pliny into a general economic crisis, and perhaps we should see the changes in the first century as part of the ebb and flow of the ancient economy with areas rising and then declining in relative prosperity, combined with a certain adjustment to the new economic conditions and competition brought by the very partial integration of the imperial economy.

12

ADMINISTRATION

INTRODUCTION AND PROBLEMS

This chapter considers the working of the various political institutions of the Roman Empire. We shall examine not just the administrative structures that were in place, as far as they can be discerned, but also how this administrative structure was used by political leaders. The administrative system was a mechanism by which power was exercised and transmitted. The authority at the centre of the system was, inevitably, the emperor and it is with the emperor that this study starts. Before looking at administrative structures, we shall examine the problems the Roman administration faced, the resources available, and the nature of Roman imperial administration.

It is important to consider the size of the Roman empire. Telecommunications and modern methods of transport have reduced the importance of distance in the modern world, but for Roman administrators, distance was a major limitation on their ability to act. We can illustrate some of the problems by considering the revolt in Judaea. The revolt broke out in Jerusalem in the early summer of AD 66 and a message was sent from the city to the Roman authorities in Syria. The governor of Syria (Cestius Gallus) then needed to discuss his course of action with his friends, mobilise his troops, and march on Jerusalem. Mobilisation probably presented few problems and those troops posted to parts distant from the legionary camp could be quickly recalled or expected to meet the army on the march. Defeat followed in October 66 and Cestius retreated in some disarray. A report then had to be composed and sent to the emperor. Nero, who was in Greece, then had to decide what to do, recruit the senior officers for the army, send instructions to the various other governors who were to provide Vespasian with troops, and the army had to reach the rebellious lands. It was only in the summer of AD 67, a year after the outbreak of the rebellion, that Vespasian was able to make serious inroads into rebel territory. The distances involved and the technology of transport and communications meant that the Roman empire was something of a giant dinosaur: large, powerful and slow-moving.

Most modern states have extensive bureaucratic structures and the buildings which house the bureaucrats are often rather visible parts of the topography of the capital city. There was, however, no Whitehall in Rome. There was central administration, as we shall see, and there must have been extensive archives, but the administration based in the city of Rome appears to have been small.

Some have argued that Roman government was largely non-interventionist. Rome did not have the administrative resources to control the day-to-day activities of the peoples of the Empire. Governors exercised a personal and, in law, an almost unlimited authority in the provinces. Yet, this power was limited by practical considerations. The governor could not be everywhere at once and, although he had aides, the communities of the provinces were only subjected to occasional visitations. Most of the time, the governor was unable to exercise much practical authority. What he could do was deal with crises either by visiting the affected region or by deploying Roman military might.

The style of Roman government seems to have been rather personal. The emperor and the governors communicated directly to their people and much of the language of this communication was set in terms of personal relations: friendships rather than administrative hierarchies. Decisions were granted as personal favours by the authorities and seem to have been treated as such by the favoured. This was a traditional aristocratic method of government. Yet, as we shall see, there is considerable evidence of a bureaucratisation of government, a development which was in some tension with traditional informality. Laws, edicts and imperial pronouncements represent an increased regulation of the way government was conducted. These developments created a tension between the personal and the bureaucratic which is a recurring theme of this chapter.

THE EMPEROR

The emperor was the supreme authority in the Roman state. His main legal powers consisted of consular *imperium* (power) which gave him authority in Italy and Rome, *imperium maius* which gave him power greater than that of all the other governors, *tribunicia potestas* which gave him authority to intervene in legal cases and technically gave him a veto over all other magistrates, and proconsular *imperium* which gave him authority over a large number of those provinces which had significant military garrisons. Since he also enjoyed exemption from the laws, the emperor's authority was absolute. He had the legal authority to do what he wished.

The emperor delegated his authority to senators, equestrians and members of his family and personal staff. His power depended on the extent to which he could control those to whom he delegated. All to whom authority was given could be seen as part of the administration, whether they held formal office or not. At the centre of this administrative system was the imperial household, and it is with the household that we start.

The women of the imperial family did not hold political office, but they helped manage imperial relations with groups in the elite. Emperors also relied on male family members and close friends, people such as L. Vitellius who was close to Gaius and Claudius. The emperor had a *consilium* (a body of advisers) with whom he would consult. Augustus established an official *consilium principis* with family members, friends, senators and the consuls, but it is likely that most emperors also had a less formally constituted group of friends who provided advice. It is probably this group that is portrayed advising Domitian on the giant fish (see pp. 178–81).

In addition to his friends and family, the emperor also relied on his freedmen, who have sometimes been described in terms analogous to ministers of state. The major freedmen offices were the *ab epistulis* (who dealt with correspondence), *a rationibus* (keeper of the accounts), *a libellis* (who dealt with petitions) and the *a studiis* (whose role is not entirely clear). These officials rose to prominence under Claudius (see pp. 79–80), but were influential from the very beginnings of the Principate. They ran the 'imperial office'. Naturally, when the succession was dynastic, the new emperor inherited his predecessor's freedmen and tended to leave them in positions of authority. This continuity seems also to have been a feature of non-dynastic succession. The Flavians inherited some Neronian freedmen. The freedmen could thus serve a series of

emperors and would provide a certain continuity in Roman administration.

The management of the imperial household seems to have been
based on the methods adopted by other members of the elite to run
their households though, obviously, the number of those involved,
the division of duties, and the amount of work undertaken were
rather different. Most members of the elite will have had a small
group of family members (including freedmen) and friends who
provided advice and help. Prior to the imperial period, Roman
magistrates had only limited official administrative support and so
turned to their households to run government business. Since part
of the rhetoric of the imperial position under emperors such as
Augustus, Tiberius, Claudius and Vespasian was that the emperor
was a senator and thus like all other senators, the extension of
household administration to deal with the administration of the
empire was a natural progression. The use of freedmen in important
posts is a reflection of the domestic nature of the management of
the imperial household. Initially, therefore, no member of the elite
would have served in the household of another since this was tanta-
mount to accepting servile status and so the administration of the
imperial office came to rely on freedmen.

Many emperors, true to the household ethos of the administration, continued to operate as if they were ordinary senators. Early
each morning, at the *salutatio*, every important Roman received his
clients (followers) at his house. They would crowd into the *atrium*
(hall) to greet him and his family and put themselves at his service.
It was a time when they could also present him with requests. The
emperor, too, greeted his friends and clients at the morning
salutatio. Much of the political business was conducted through a
network of 'friendships' and thus accessibility and affability were
highly desirable attributes. The informality of such contacts allowed
transgression of normal social and political structures: imperial
wives and freedmen would also be present on occasions such as the
salutatio.

This personal and somewhat informal governmental style
extended beyond the management of the Roman aristocracy.
Provincial communities were often in contact with emperors and
frequently stressed pre-existing ties of friendship between the
emperor or members of his family and the particular community.
Cities also emphasised the importance of individual citizens who
had been particularly favoured by the emperor. Such communities
sent petitions and embassies to ask for specific favours, but also sent

greetings on the imperial birthday and congratulations on special occasions.

It was not just communities which could reach the emperor, but individuals could also deliver petitions. It is likely that this was considerably more difficult for provincials than Romans since they had to travel from the province and may have required permission to do so. The *Digest*, a sixth-century collection of legal rulings, contains many summary responses to legal problems that had been presented to the emperor. These rescripts appear to have been in response to petitions presented by members of most social groups.

The emperor was bombarded with written and oral requests and government seems to have consisted largely in responding to these problems. The emperor often responded by granting favours, and these established a personal relationship of mutual friendship between the emperor and the beneficiary. The emperor had powers to intervene in legal cases and also financial authority which would enable him to respond to specific requests. In addition, the emperor had in his direct gift most of the important appointments in the empire. His legates (representatives) governed the military provinces, and he also influenced appointments to other provinces and to the magistracies in Rome. Patronage brought the emperor power. The face-to-face nature of much of this exercise of patronage minimised bureaucracy.

This household administration, however, was based on an illusion. Everyone recognised the fact that the emperor's power was far greater than that of a senator. Everyone wished to be a friend of the emperor and the withdrawal of imperial friendship meant the end of an official career. At the morning *salutatio*, it seems that all available senators (possibly as many as 600) would gather to greet the emperor. The senate would thus assemble in the emperor's house, though this would not normally constitute a formal session. Since the emperor was a friend to all senators (almost by definition) favours had to be granted to all groups. Monopolisation of favours by a particular group in the senate was likely to lead to senatorial discontent. It is likely that various gradings were introduced in the *salutatio* by Claudius so that the important would join him first and the lesser grades be admitted later. Vespasian operated a similar system (though perhaps less formal) whereby his close friends would meet him in his bedchamber and he would meet the rest presumably in the *atrium*. Yet, this was still probably a ceremonial occasion. To avoid causing offence, Claudius probably decided who was going to be in the first wave of visitors by rank and not by political loyalty. Since it was quite evident under most emperors that not everyone was really a friend of the emperor, the *salutatio* ceased to have real political meaning. The emperor could not be seen to show bias to a particular group. In the event, in order to avoid open conflict or a breach with a section of the senate, favours needed to be distributed to a wide range of people, which explains why seemingly hostile senators received magisterial posts under Domitian (see pp. 181–2). The ceremonial nature of much of this activity must have transmitted itself to all concerned and thus senators will have been aware that even if they received favours they may have been regarded with suspicion or hostility by the emperor. To be declared to be no longer a friend of the emperor or a member of the imperial family was to be excluded from these ceremonial events and was a first step towards becoming an enemy of the state (see pp. 33–4, 131–2 for exclusions from imperial friendship). Tacitus stresses the hypocrisy of all involved and the difficulties this posed for successful administration. The personal nature of administration, which was the very essence of the system, was eroded.

This process can be seen elsewhere. Imperial communications with provincial communities became increasingly formalised, as can be seen in the development of the imperial cult (see pp. 309–12). The worship of deified emperors provided an opportunity for gestures of loyalty on the part of local elites and these gestures were communicated to the reigning emperor through embassies. Many speeches were made in praise of the emperor or Rome or both. It mattered little who was on the throne: the gesture was important and the words themselves were devoid of meaning (see pp. 197–8).

One of the incidental benefits of the imperial position was that the emperor accumulated vast wealth. Formally, this money was held separately from the state finances and the emperor probably did not benefit directly from the seizure of property by the treasury or from taxation. It is evident from the vast amounts of money that Augustus donated to the state from his private resources that the emperor was extremely wealthy and, although there were considerable drains on the private finances of the emperor, gifts and testamentary bequests as well as the wealth that flowed in from judicious land investments boosted the private finances. It was these that were presumably supervised by the *a rationibus* (freedman in charge of accounts). State finances were supervised by senators and, theoretically, were separate from those of the emperor. The financial boundaries, however, quickly became blurred with the emperor taking control over land confiscated because of legal penalties, land which had no legal owner, and mines and quarries. The mechanism behind this process is unclear, but it may have taken place more rapidly in the provinces than in Italy. Imperial freedmen were employed to supervise imperial assets in the provinces, but these procurators are also found dealing with non-imperial finances and the use of equestrian procurators, presumably initially to manage state assets, further confuses the situation. The result, however, is clear: the finances of government (both state and imperial) were effectively controlled by the emperor.

The process of 'formalisation' and transformation of a household administration into a state bureaucracy was slow and was certainly not completed by the end of the first century. One sign of the transformation was the appointment of equestrians to the major household offices. These offices had come to be considered offices of state, not offices of the emperor's household. The very conception of the imperial administration as domestic administration and separate from state administration was under threat. The administration surrounding the emperor and the emperor's own role was evolving and becoming more bureaucratic.

THE SENATE AND SENATORS

Major reforms of the senate were introduced by Augustus. The number of senators was reduced, the required property level for enrolment was increased (see p. 216) and a series of minor administrative posts were created in a reform of the senatorial career structure. Most senators appear to have had a fairly regular career. They served first in a series of very minor posts (collectively called the *vigintivirate*) which involved supervision of the mint, supervision of public executions and some minor judicial duties. From there, they progressed to a military tribunate. There were normally six tribunes to a legion, one of whom was of potential senatorial status. Election to one of the twenty quaestorships followed and this brought membership of the senate. The next stage was either to become one of the ten tribunes or one of the six aediles. Members of patrician families (a higher status group within the senate) were excused this stage on the career ladder. The next stage of a career was a praetorship. Under Tiberius, there were twelve praetors and so there would be competition for office, but the number edged upwards until eighteen praetors were often appointed in the Flavian period. The consulships underwent similar inflation. Under

Tiberius, there were four consuls per year, two *ordinarii* who held office from 1 January and after whom the year was named, and two *suffecti* who took over for the second half of the year. The *ordinarii* (ordinary) consulships were the most prestigious. This number was again increased by the Flavians so that there were between six and ten consuls per year (two of whom were ordinary). It should, however, be remembered that the Flavians tended to restrict ordinary consulships to family members and very close associates.

Once a man entered the senate by becoming quaestor, progression was almost automatic until the elections for the praetorships. At this stage, presuming none had died in the interim, eight men would fail to progress under the Julio–Claudian system, though there would only be two disappointed under the Flavians. The consulship seems to have been the only post for which competition would have been particularly fierce. In addition to the Republican offices, there was a series of new administrative posts (see Table 12.1).

The role of the senate was changed by the advent of imperial power. The emperor's powers were so great that senators could not question his authority and, throughout our period, the senate gave way when faced with a dictatorial emperor. Some have concluded

Table 12.1 The new administrative posts

Title	Function
Praefecti frumenti dandi	Distribution of the corn supply
Curatores viarum	Care of roads
Curatores aquarum	Care of the water supply
Curatores riparum et alvei Tiberis	Care of the banks and bed of the Tiber
Curatores locorum publicorum iudicandorum	Care of court buildings
Curatores tabularum publicarum	Care of public registers
Curatores aedium sacrarum et operum locorumque publicorum	Care of sacred temples and public works
Praefecti aerarii Saturni	Prefects of the state treasury
Legatus legionis	Commander of a legion (normally a former praetor)
Praefectus urbi	Prefect in charge of urban administration (a post held by a senior senator)

that the senate was powerless and a shadow of its Republican precursor, but the senate was sufficiently useful or powerful that no emperor seems to have seriously contemplated closing it. The senate's power had always rested on its personnel. This did not change in the imperial period. Most of the senior figures in the state sat in the senate. Most of the governors of the provinces, and hence the commanders of the army, were also senators. The senate contained some of the most powerful men in the empire. The emperor needed to conciliate the senate or face down those who might support its rights.

In law, the senate's status was actually improved in the imperial period since the decrees it passed, which had before been merely advisory, were given the force of law by Tiberius. In addition, the senate started to exercise more control over its membership. Popular election in some form or other continued into the late Augustan period. After this, the popular assemblies still met, but it seems probable that the senate only allowed the nomination of as many candidates as there were posts so that there was no competition and no decision for the assemblies to make.

In spite of these changes, the Principate did lead to the senate losing political power and to a gradual change in the role of the senate. From the Augustan period onwards, there is evidence that some men refused to embark on or withdrew from senatorial careers. People could exercise political authority without being senators and some senators probably felt that they had no political power. Augustus failed in his attempt to create a self-perpetuating oligarchic group in which father would follow son into the senate. In the period up to AD 54, only just over half of all consuls (54 per cent) had a consular father, grandfather or great-grandfather. In the Flavian period, this figure fell to just under a quarter (24 per cent). This compares with a Republican figure of 62 per cent. The period also sees the gradual incorporation of men of provincial origin into the senate. Claudius supported the introduction of men from Gallia Comata into the senate and may have been encouraging men from other areas as well. Trajan himself was of Spanish origin and Flavian interest in Spain may have enabled significant numbers of Spaniards to rise in the senate. Men from the East and Africa also achieved senatorial status. By Trajan's reign, about a third of the senators were of provincial origin.[1]

The effect of these changes is difficult to establish. Tacitus noted a change in membership in the Flavian period, and it seems possible that this brought a change in attitude towards the role of the senate and its relationship to the emperor. There is no straightforward correlation, however, between origins and political attitude and all we can safely say is that the Flavian senate was rather different from that of the Republic. Senators were less of an aristocracy of birth (owing their power in the senate to their ancestors) and more of an aristocracy of office (owing their power to the posts they had held).

EQUESTRIANS

Another of the great innovations of the imperial period was the development of an equestrian career structure. This, like so much else, appears to have been Augustus' creation, though most of our information concerning the equestrian career pattern dates to later periods. In the pre-Claudian period, there was a certain irregularity in the career patterns, and assessing them is made more complex by the fact that careers are sometimes listed in reverse chronological order, but a standard pattern is given in Table 12.2. Claudius reformed the equestrian career structure (Suet., *Claud.* 25), shown in Table 12.3.

Table 12.2 Pre-Claudian equestrian career structure

Centurion
Military Tribune
Praefectus Equitum
Praefectus Fabrum
Procuratorships
Great Prefectures

Table 12.3 Post-Claudian equestrian career structure

Centurion
Praefectus Cohortis
Praefectus Equitum/Alae
Military Tribune
Procuratorships
Great Prefectures

Such schema conceal variations. In the early period, there were other offices, such as prefectures of cohorts and veterans. The post of *praefectus fabrum* (probably a staff-officer) could be held at various points in a career. In the post-Claudian period, equestrians sometimes served a fourth military prefecture as prefect of a double strength cavalry unit. In both periods, many did not enter the career structure through the centurionate and most combined a Roman equestrian career with holding several magistracies in their own communities. There appears to have been a hierarchy in the procuratorships in the second century, but it is unclear when this developed. Clearly some procuratorial tasks were more important than others. Procurators collected taxes, supervised state assets, supported provincial governors, and some governed the smaller provinces. No clear distinction can be seen between equestrian and freedmen procurators. The great prefectures were those of the praetorian guard, the *vigiles* (watch), the urban cohorts, the corn supply and of Egypt. Two praetorian prefects normally held office jointly. Since these men were responsible for the security of the emperor and of Rome, the post was given to the most trusted.

Equestrian careers show a certain irregularity. People could jump posts. The mechanism for promotion is uncertain but, if we take the evidence of Pliny's letters, recommendation appears to have played an important part. The fact that some managed to combine their equestrian careers with an active role in their local communities suggests that there were periods, probably quite long ones, when these men were without an equestrian posting; thus it would appear that people did not move smoothly from posting to posting.

The equestrians were clearly an important arm of the administration, though the irregularity of the procuratorial office means that any estimate of the number of equestrians employed at any one time would be little more than a guess.

PROVINCES

The provinces can be divided into two basic types: those ruled directly by the emperor and those whose governors were appointed (in theory) by the senate. Apart from the titles of the governors, it is unclear whether this made any difference to the governing of the province. Imperial provinces were mostly governed by legates, either of consular or praetorian status. Some provinces were governed by equestrians, but most of these (with the exception of

Egypt) were comparatively unimportant and had only small military garrisons. There was a vague hierarchy of provinces, normally based on the size of the garrison. The two Germanies and Syria appear to have been the most important provinces. The senatorial provinces were governed by proconsuls or propraetors. After the reign of Gaius, none of these provinces had any significant military garrison. The most prestigious postings were Africa and Asia.

The governor exercised supreme authority within the province. He was at once the senior financial, judicial and military officer and would probably be active in all these areas. The governors seem to have had a limited staff of advisers who were either appointed separately or chosen by them. Some provinces had a legal officer. There would also be officers dealing with financial matters and military officers, depending on the nature of the garrison of the province. There may also have been a number of other equestrian officials. In Egypt, for instance, where the administration is very well attested, various regions were supervised by equestrian officers known as *epistrategoi*. Prefects were appointed to supervise regions in other provinces. A senior centurion (almost the equivalent in status to an equestrian procurator) sparked a revolt among a German tribe through too harsh an interpretation of a tax burden (Tac., *Ann*. IV 72), and Pliny heaps praise on a prefect of the Pontic shore for the efficiency with which he administered his district (Pliny, *Ep*. X 86). There appears to have been a certain flexibility in the way in which procurators were used. There would also be an indeterminate number of imperial freedmen dealing with taxation and the management of imperial property, and the governor may have brought with him a number of *amici* to whom he could turn for help, though the evidence for such groups is much better for the Republican period. In a province in which there was a large garrison, the governor could turn to his senior military officers for administrative support, and even in comparatively lightly garrisoned provinces there was probably normally a small number of troops at the governor's disposal who could be used for administrative tasks. In provinces in which the governor was unable to make extensive use of military labour, the number of Romans he could call upon was surprisingly small.

The governor could, however, turn to local resources. The evidence from Pliny's letters from Bithynia (the most extensive archive concerning the activities of a governor) suggests that Pliny had some records at his disposal in the province, but not a complete archive of imperial documentation (Pliny, *Ep*. X 56, 57, 58, 79,

108, 112, 114). Some of his material may have been found in local archives and petitioners presented copies of edicts which affected them, but it seems likely that there was a central archive. We know there was such an archive in Alexandria concerning the administration of Egypt.

More important to the successful administration of the province were the local authorities. In all the provinces of the empire, the Romans appear to have encouraged cities to take an active administrative role. In some places, of course, cities simply continued to operate in ways similar to those which they had been using for centuries. In others, the development of a city-based administrative system was innovative. The cities tended to be governed by councils of varying size composed of decurions, normally members of the landed elite, and the magistrates of the cities were drawn from this council. There seem to have been variations in the way that these urban centres related to surrounding communities. In some cases, the surrounding communities may have been largely independent of the urban authorities and were administered by a combination of officials imposed by the Roman authorities and members of the local communities conscripted into performing public offices. In other cases, the administration of the surrounding territory may have been the responsibility of the urban community and tax collectors and other officials were sent out from the city.

The constitutions of these cities also varied. We know that some cities were 'free', meaning that the governor had little or no legal authority over the communities, though it is likely that these communities were often forced to accept the *de facto* authority of the emperor's representative. Other cities may have had very little freedom of action. Several inscriptions have been discovered in Spain which contain fragments of the constitutions of various communities. The Flavians appear to have extended municipal status to several Spanish towns. As part of this grant, the towns were given new constitutions which were probably all adapted from a single source, possibly an Augustan law which established the framework for such constitutions. This law not only established the procedures for the internal administration of the city and the formation of the council, but also limited the powers of local magistrates. Serious legal cases were referred to the governor. It was an option, in any case, for those who fell within the remit of the council's authority to appeal to the governor, though he could refuse to hear the case or pass it down to a minor official.

Governors took an active role in the administration of the

province. They exercised their authority by touring the province and during their visits to the various cities they would receive petitions and hear legal cases. They would thus be closely involved in the administration of a particular community. The governor's representatives could also visit a community and would be expected to report back to the governor on any disturbing activity. The numbers of officials stationed in local communities cannot be established, but we have ample evidence for the use of centurions in this kind of supervisory role. The stationing of Roman representatives in local communities provided the governor with a valuable source of information and these men could also act as representatives of Roman authority in times of disturbance.

In addition to formal contacts with local communities, the governor probably received many less formal contacts. The visit of a governor was an important occasion and the elite of a community probably set out to impress. The council and people would meet the governor before he entered the city and escort him within. His visit may often have coincided with festivities. He would be welcomed and entertained by the elite and it is reasonable to expect that those who set out to befriend would, on occasion, succeed. The hospitality offered by a community created a mutual obligation and it is likely that some would seek to exploit that connection. Not only could individual members of local elites make representations, but also the masses could probably make their voice heard at the theatre or other gatherings. The crowd could present grievances to an official at games through chants and acclamations. If a community was divided or otherwise troubled, it is very difficult to see how such information could be kept from a visiting governor.

The governor could, therefore, have been kept informed about the various communities in his charge. Was he, in addition, able to do anything? It is probable that the ability of the governor to act varied from province to province. The virtual absence of the governor from the events depicted in Apuleius' novel, *The Golden Ass*, have been taken as reflecting a situation in which local authorities were largely left alone and Rome had very little administrative control. This fictional representation can, however, be compared with other evidence which shows the imperial administration at work. We shall examine the workings of the administration in two areas: population registration and the suppression of banditry.

Population registration

The Romans introduced poll taxes into several provinces of the empire. They therefore needed a list of the taxable population. This list was drawn up by holding a census of the population. Our information on the workings of the system comes mainly from the Egyptian census, though, of course, the most famous census is described in Luke 2.1–5. All members of and property belonging to each household in Roman Egypt were registered. The names, relationships and ages of the household members were listed. This list was probably used to either draw up or amend the poll tax register. In addition, the register needed to take account of those who died or left the area, of change in residence (so that the tax collector could find the individuals involved), and of the status of the individuals, since rates of tax varied according to legal status. The tax collector would be armed with a list of those eligible to pay and would then look for those men. In the event of the men having moved away, the tax collector had to discover their location and this involved circulating lists of the disappeared. From time to time, the authorities would crack down on those avoiding the poll tax, seemingly by staging a sweep through the countryside and arresting all who did not have appropriate documentation. The success of the Roman administration is difficult to establish, though the tax continued to be collected into the third century AD, but the ambitious nature of the project is notable. The registration and subsequent monitoring of the entire population was a major task which the Romans thought they could accomplish. The administration of the census may not have been so elaborate in provinces other than Egypt and, indeed, some provinces may not have held a census regularly, but their administrative ambition should tell us something about Roman capabilities.

Banditry

Banditry was a problem throughout the Roman period, though it was a problem that often escaped the notice of our literary sources. We know that there were certain areas that were associated with bandit activity. Judaea, Galilee and the Syrian mountains suffered from such activity. Bandits were active in Sardinia and Corsica, and banditry seems to have been almost endemic in Cilicia. It seems likely that frontier areas were also subjected to bandit threats from Arabic tribes or the Mauretanians or the tribes beyond the Danube.

Banditry was a problem that the Romans could not easily solve and in some areas was part of the political culture. Local aristocrats maintained armed gangs to further their interests and since it was these aristocrats that the Romans would expect to act against bandits, official action was unlikely to have much effect. Accepting that banditry could not be completely eliminated, how did the Romans control it? The Romans seem to have devoted considerable time and expense to limiting bandit activities. Watchtowers (*purgoi* or *stationes*) were built to monitor movement. Locals were recruited to guard important points. Soldiers were sent on guard duties to supervise local communities. Larger-scale expeditions were launched against bandits. As with the census, it is less the success that is important than the ambition the activity attests. The Romans thought that their power was such that they could influence the behaviour of provincials at a local level and prevent them becoming bandits. The Romans seem to have believed that their power could be felt by small communities.

We should not assume that Roman administration worked in the same way in all the diverse provinces of the Empire. Political, social, cultural and military factors will have influenced the administration of each province. Some provinces may have been like the province in which *The Golden Ass* is set, virtually devoid of Roman administration, though even here soldiers play an important role in at least one episode. In other provinces, it seems likely that the governor could influence events in quite small communities and would have had considerable information at his disposal in order to make decisions. We should not, of course, compare the level of administration to that of a modern state: ancient states had far more limited aims. Nevertheless, the provinces appear to have been quite closely administered by Roman officials.

COMMUNICATION AND CONTROL

The political imperative for most emperors was retaining control of power and thereby maintaining their personal security. The major threats to the position of the emperor stemmed from the powerful within the political system: the senators and the governors. The emperor controlled most of the major offices of state and could ensure that his enemies did not reach powerful positions, though there were limits on the effectiveness of this policy (see above). He could avoid giving control of the major legionary garrisons to his enemies. The emperor could also manage the senate. The emperor could take soundings of senatorial opinion through his council and also through more informal contacts. He could also prime certain senators before debates. Senators who were thought to be aware of the emperor's view were more closely regarded and their stated opinions would inevitably gain some support. Since the emperor could chair senatorial debates, he could shape opinion by calling members in a particular order or by showing partiality for a particular view. The emperor could make use of intermediaries (such as the praetorian prefect) for at least some of these tasks.

Another way of controlling the activities of senators was through the use of *delatores* (informers). The extent to which informers were used to spy on the activities of the aristocracy is arguable. '*Delator*' was used as a term of abuse, especially in the post-Domitianic period. Those who spied on the aristocracy and those who conducted the prosecutions were tarred by the same label. Both Tacitus and Pliny (see pp. 183–4) depict the impact of *delatores* on the activities of the elite in dramatic terms. If these descriptions were remotely correct, certain members of the elite were constrained by fear of being denounced. Almost by definition, the activities of spies are not fully documented. We only hear about the prosecution of the elite and cannot know whether the lower classes were subject to similar attentions. The emperor had several possible groups available for espionage. He could use the military forces stationed in Rome to report what they saw when they wandered the streets. But, in a society which still conducted its business personally, it would seem unlikely that a praetorian could infiltrate the household of a dissident without being recognised or having his background checked. The imperial intelligence service probably relied more on the activities of amateurs, lured on by the rewards of a successful prosecution, to report on the private activities of the Roman population. It was such amateur espionage which led to the uncovering of the Pisonian conspiracy (see p. 133). The threat to the senator stemmed from his own household, his friends and his neighbours, and from malicious prosecution.

Controlling the activities of senators in the provinces was a little more difficult. We have already seen that authority was concentrated in the hands of the governors. To control these men, the emperors needed independent information. This could be provided from two main sources: the Romans with the governor in the province and the provincials themselves. It has often been suggested that procurators were used to check the authority of the provincial governor and could be used effectively since they were directly answerable to the emperor. There is, in fact, very little evidence for this. There were clashes between procurators and governors, as can be seen in Suetonius Paulinus' difficulties after the Boudiccan revolt (see p. 123), but these problems concerned the specific issue of Paulinus' treatment of the defeated rebels and are not evidence of a general hostility between procurators and governors. The few senior Romans in a province probably needed to work quite closely together. Also, after service, the procurator would not want to have a powerful or potentially powerful senatorial enemy. We should remember that the Roman aristocracy, both senatorial and equestrian, would have shared similar values and may have been friends or had friends in common. There was not necessarily a great divide between the two groups.

The provincial elites represented a different source of information. Emperors seem to have encouraged a flow of communication between provincial communities and the emperor, some types of which have been outlined above. The ceremonial contacts between emperor and provincials were useful since they provided the emperor with some opportunity to establish friendships with provincials and these provincials could then monitor the activities of the provincial governor. Such informing on the behaviour of the governor could in itself become formalised, as in the decrees passed by provincial councils concerning a governor's term in office (see pp. 123–4).

The workings of the system can be seen in the fall of Flaccus, the prefect of Egypt (Philo, *In Flaccum*; see p. 71). Philo represents Flaccus responding to his insecure political position by seeking the support of the Alexandrian Greeks and sacrificing the Jewish community to win that support. The thought was, presumably, that the Alexandrian Greeks would send back glowing reports on Flaccus. Flaccus was, however, brought down. The Jewish community had sent a loyal address to the emperor on his accession and this had, apparently, been suppressed by Flaccus. News of this, and probably other aspects of the mistreatment of the Jews, was passed to Gaius by Herod Agrippa. The attack on Flaccus was pressed, however, on rather different grounds by two Alexandrian Greeks whom he had previously expelled. The hostility of provincials combined with a suspicious emperor to bring down a governor.

The governor was also subject to possible prosecution on return to Rome, though prosecutions were complex and difficult. Governors had to be particularly careful when dealing with Roman citizens who could expect some protection under the *lex Iulia de vi publica* (see p. 214). On the whole, governors seem to have been reluctant to take action against Romans in their province and to have preferred the safe course of passing Roman citizens to the emperor for trial and punishment.

In a similar way, governors may have wished to pass difficult or potentially controversial administrative problems to the emperor. The majority of the tenth book of Pliny's letters is devoted to the correspondence between Pliny and Trajan concerning various problems that arose during Pliny's governorship. These give a fascinating insight into provincial administration and must have meant that the emperor was comparatively well informed about developments in the province (especially if we assume that he was also in receipt of considerably more information in the form of official reports). It is possible that the correspondence between Pliny and Trajan was atypical. Trajan had taken a special interest in the appointment because of financial problems in the province resulting from the corruption of previous governors. Pliny himself, though an experienced administrator, was not an experienced governor. Yet, the peculiarities of the appointment and of Pliny's previous experience did not necessarily influence the nature of the correspondence. Pliny felt it necessary to refer for guidance to the emperor on even quite minor matters.

It is unlikely that all governors behaved in exactly the same way. Some, like Piso (see pp. 35–8), may have taken an independent stance. Yet, the political uncertainties of the period probably discouraged governors from taking dramatic initiatives. The emperors watched their governors and had some control over them.

The size of the empire forced emperors to devolve much of their authority to representatives, both in Rome and in the provinces. Imperial power depended on how closely the emperor could control his representative and how closely his representatives could control those they administered. The key to successful administration was flow of information, and it seems that the diversity of material which flowed through the administrative system would have ensured that governors knew something of what the provincials were doing and that emperors had some independent information concerning the activities of their governors. Acting on that information may have been rather more difficult, but the knowledge that information would filter through the administrative machinery to the emperor was probably sufficient to keep governors and provincials in check.

13

THE ROMAN ARMY AND MILITARY POLICY

THE REPUBLICAN AND AUGUSTAN BACKGROUND

It is a matter of some disagreement exactly when the 'professional' Roman army came into being. It is generally agreed that the army of the third and second century BC was an amateur citizen militia with troops raised on an annual basis from the whole body of Roman citizen men. These troops served for the duration of the campaign (ideally a single year) before returning to their pre-enlistment professions. It is also accepted that the army of the mid-first century AD, about which we know a great deal from literary and documentary sources, was much closer to what we would now characterise as a professional army with troops serving for twenty or twenty-five years. Historians have traditionally placed this fundamental change in the nature of Rome's armed forces at the end of the second century BC and have associated this development with the great Republican general Marius. More recently, the extent to which Marius changed the army has been questioned and historians have pointed to continuities between the army of the mid-second century BC and that of Caesar. It is becoming increasingly clear that, although the army can be seen to play a more direct role in politics in the first century BC, the institutional structures which transformed the army were only gradually put in place and that far-reaching changes were instituted during the reign of Augustus. Many of the Augustan reforms were not yet properly operational by AD 14 and there were important changes in the army's organisational structure after this date. Nevertheless, Augustus developed the framework for the later army. He established terms and conditions of service, the legal framework which governed the soldiers while in service, the benefits which the soldiers received on discharge, the standing units into which the soldiers were recruited, the fiscal system which was to pay for the troops, the political framework in which the army was to operate, and he developed (though it is unclear quite what is Augustan) the auxiliary system (see below).

Nevertheless, Augustus was not a radical military thinker: the political situation forced him to institute fundamental changes. After the defeat of Antony and Cleopatra, Augustus had a massive army at his disposal. The question arose as to how that military force was to be organised in the now peaceful empire and how Augustus' military supremacy might be institutionalised. It was decided as part of the political settlement of 28–27 BC that Augustus would be given authority over a huge area of the Empire. This provincial command brought with it the vast majority of the army. Augustus justified this command (which seemed to bring excessive personal power) on the grounds of the military sensitivity of these areas. As the Principate achieved political stability, so military organisation ossified. Legions which might in theory have been recruited for a single campaign were now stationed in provinces for extended periods on the (spurious) grounds that the military situation remained insecure. The result was the birth of the standing army.

Troops had served abroad for extended periods during the Republic. Previously, such extended service could be treated as an anomaly, but Augustus was forced to face the reality of a professional army and develop the regulatory and administrative infrastructure to deal with this creation. This was a slow process and the imperial system emerged from *ad hoc* developments. The first major series of institutional reforms is dated by Dio to 13 BC (Dio, LIV 25). This was seventeen years after the victory over Antony when many of the troops recruited for the Actium campaign would have retired or have been looking to retire. There was a second series of reforms in AD 5 (Dio, LV 23). It was only in this year that Augustus, against much opposition, set up the *aerarium militare*, a treasury designed to meet the pay (900 sesterces per year) and retirement bonuses (12,000 sesterces) of the soldier. This treasury was initially funded by direct grant from Augustus, though a new tax was developed for its long-term funding. This system was clearly not working as late as AD 14 when the soldiers of the Rhine and Danube legions revolted over their conditions. Their complaints included the prolongation of service beyond the legal maximum and improper payment of bonuses (see pp. 31–3).

Although the standing army had come into being with the political settlements of 28–27 BC, the administration to cope with this new army was not fully functioning more than forty years later.

MILITARY ORGANISATION

The legions

The legions remained the backbone of the Roman army during the first century AD. Historians, however, disagree about even such fundamental questions as to how many troops there were supposed to be in a legion. A legion consisted of ten cohorts. Each cohort was composed of six centuries of about 80 men. The first cohort could be of double strength. Sometimes a small body of cavalry was attached to the legion. There is some disagreement as to the number of junior officers and whether they were 'supernumerary' to the strength of a century. The theoretical strength of the legion can be estimated at c. 4,800–6,000 men. There is evidence, however, that the size of the legion would vary according to military circumstances. When the legion was preparing for war, more men would be recruited. In peacetime, the legion would be allowed to fall beneath its 'paper' strength.

The legionaries were recruited for twenty-five years. There was probably a physical examination to ascertain whether the recruit was fit and above a certain height, though the stringency with which the rules were applied is difficult to assess. It seems that most troops were recruited between the ages of 18 and 24 (as one would expect), though there are examples of younger and older recruits. Although the Roman authorities retained the legal power to conscript, it seems that most of the troops were volunteers.

Legionaries were supposed to be Roman citizens. This rule seems to have been maintained during the imperial period, but gradually the recruiting officers of the legions ceased to look to Italy for fresh supplies of troops. Legionaries began to be recruited from the provinces. Some of these provincial recruits would have been Roman citizens before recruitment. They were either descended from a previous generation of Roman soldiers who had settled in the province or from Roman settlers who had come to the province for some other reason. Some, however, were probably given citizenship on enlistment and thus the 'Romanity' of the legions was preserved. Slaves and freedmen were not allowed to join the legions.

The senior officers in a legion were drawn from the Roman aristocracy. Legions were commanded by a *legatus*. This man was appointed by the emperor and would normally be of fairly senior senatorial rank. Six tribunes served under the legate. These were recruited from junior senators and from more experienced equestrians. Below this group was the senior centurion, the *primus pilus*. This man was either an equestrian officer starting on his career, or a man who had risen through the ranks. The next rank was the centurion. These officers would be a mixture of equestrians who had joined at centurion level, and those promoted from more junior posts.

The officering of the legion reflected the structure of Roman society. The majority of senior officers were of elite birth. Their social status gave them authority. Their ability to assume senior commands, often at a young age, does not seem to have been questioned. A minority of officers rose through the ranks. We cannot, however, know whether the original social status of those who reached the rank of centurion or above was somehow superior to those others who failed to make the grade. Reaching the rank of centurion or above, or even just becoming a junior officer, may have improved the social status of individuals. The army was, however, only a limited avenue of social mobility and dramatic progress must have been unusual. The limitations on careers can be illustrated by the career of Tiberius Claudius Maximus. This man achieved fame and the notice of the emperor when he killed Decebalus, the Dacian leader (see p. 203). He fought in Parthia and received further decorations for bravery. This was a major military achievement and one might have expected that his rise would be meteoric. He was promoted, but only reached the rank of decurion (see below; Campbell 1994: 32–3). The anomalies of the third century AD, by which men could rise through the ranks to become emperor (if often only briefly), were not a feature of first-century military life.

Auxiliaries and other units

There were various types of auxiliary units. The main two were the *ala* (a cavalry unit of about 500 men) and the cohort (an infantry unit of about 500 men). In addition there was a mixed cavalry and infantry unit of about 400 infantry and 120 cavalry. There were some double strength units. Various other types of units existed, but *alae* and cohorts comprised the vast majority of auxiliary units in the first century AD.

Auxiliary units were distinguished by number and name, like the legions. In many cases, the names of the auxiliary units referred to an ethnic origin. It seems likely that this referred to the place where the unit was originally recruited, though it is possible that in some cases it referred to its first station.

There were Republican precursors to the imperial auxiliary units. Rome had for centuries recruited her *socii* (allies) to fight alongside the legions. These *socii* were a valuable part of Rome's military effort. Their organisation is unclear, but they were probably raised and largely officered by their native aristocracy. Caesar made extensive use of troops provided by his Gallic allies during the conquest of Gaul, and rival generals accepted help from all quarters during the civil wars. It is only after the reign of Augustus that we can identify auxiliary units of the imperial type, though Augustan units appear to have had a slightly different pattern of nomenclature from the units of the mid-first century and later: units were frequently named after a commanding officer, often a Roman.

It is unclear how many auxiliary units existed under Augustus, but under Tiberius the auxiliary forces were roughly equivalent to the legions in strength. It is likely that their organisation was somewhat irregular in this early period. Some units were probably recruited for specific campaigns and may have been discharged after those campaigns. Allied states were expected to contribute troops to Roman expeditions. Other peoples, such as the Batavians, may have effectively paid their taxes in men (see pp. 159–60) and special units of such troops retained an ethnic identity and solidarity. One may question the extent to which the organisation of such units would have been romanised. Gradually, a more regular system of nomenclature, pay and rewards, and officering emerged and much was probably in place when Claudius reformed the equestrian career structure (see pp. 255–6).

Much of our information concerning auxiliary units comes from a series of bronze diplomas. These documents attest the grant of citizenship to those leaving auxiliary units after their term of service. We have a few diplomas from the period before AD 69, but it is only after AD 69 that these documents appear to be issued regularly. It seems likely that there was a change in the privileges granted to auxiliaries at about that date, and this is one aspect of the steady evolution of auxiliary units during the early first century AD.

Originally, auxiliary units were mostly recruited from non-Romans, though some people with Roman citizenship did join auxiliary units. It is probable that the troops were originally recruited from one province and served in another. The link with the original province was quickly lost and the auxiliary recruiting officers turned to more convenient sources of manpower.

Auxiliaries served for twenty-five years. After AD 69 they were rewarded with a grant of citizenship on completion of their service. Their children would also be given citizenship. This would considerably boost the legal status of the men and their families.

The units were commanded by equestrian prefects. The second grade of officer in the *alae* were the decurion. These commanded *turmae* of about thirty men. The cohorts were divided into centuries commanded by a centurion.

SOLDIER AND CIVILIAN

Hostility

There is abundant evidence which attests hostility between civilians and soldiers during this period. Bullying, violent soldiers appear in Petronius' *Satyricon* (82), Juvenal, *Satire* XVI, the New Testament (especially Matthew 27.26–35, Mark 15.15–19, John 19.23–4, Luke 3.14), and Epictetus, *Discourses* IV 1.79. The historians are often critical of soldiers, especially in times of civil war. The corruption of the soldiers in Britain was a major contributory factor in the outbreak of the Boudiccan revolt (p. 123), and the behaviour of soldiers in Judaea brought the country on occasions to the verge of rebellion. A yet more extreme manifestation of hostility comes in the *Satyricon* (62) when a soldier turns out to be a werewolf.

The tradition of criticism of soldiers can be traced in certain texts of the first century BC and into the later imperial period. The violence of soldiers is depicted as a feature not only of their technical ability, but also of their political power. Soldiers were able to make or break an emperor and it is argued that this resulted in not only the granting of privileges to soldiers, but also a reluctance to enforce military discipline.

Although there is no doubt that soldiers abused their authority, we may question the extreme presentation of Juvenal and others. Roman society was conservative and hierarchical. Status was important and was established by birth. Members of the Roman aristocracy regarded political authority as their birthright and the essential stability of Italian society meant that this ideology could be maintained. The elite was hostile to those who threatened its position. Foreigners and freedmen were to be suspected since they might just oust the traditional aristocracy (see pp. 213–14). Soldiers also posed a threat.

Our information about social origins is negligble, but it seems that soldiers tended to be of the lower social classes and anyone of elite status would join the Roman military as an officer. As soldiers came increasingly to be recruited from the provinces, the Italian elite may have had difficulty in seeing these men as Romans rather than barbarians. These lower-class barbarians were, however, in a position to threaten the elite. The accession of Claudius was, to a large extent, a result of a recognition by the political elite that they could not control the soldiers (see p. 78). Roman aristocrats did not have significant armed force at their disposal and were collectively and individually unable to defend themselves against military force. Soldiers sent by the emperor, or even soldiers acting illegitimately, could threaten or kill members of the elite. By so doing, soldiers inverted the social system and exercised authority over their social superiors.

The criminal activities of soldiers cannot be quantified and we cannot use the criticisms in the literary sources as a guide. It would be the equivalent of using tabloid newspapers to assess crime or sexual mores in modern British society. The everyday does not necessarily get coverage and a soldier going peaceably about his duty would not be commented on. A better indicator might be the willingness of the elite to exercise authority over corrupt soldiers. Although we are hampered by a shortage of direct evidence, certain governors acted with an exemplary brutality in order to enforce discipline. Soldiers could be punished with death, with prolonged duties or with hard labour. The behaviour of martinets such as Cn. Piso, Corbulo or Galba may reflect the indiscipline of the troops, but also shows that some Romans were able to enforce extreme disciplinary measures. Although the soldiers of the Rhine and Danube armies mutinied in AD 14 (see pp. 31–3), the description of their working conditions does not suggest a military force able to cow its generals and achieve excessive rewards. The Roman authorities were usually willing to promulgate edicts which attacked abuses by those in power, officials or soldiers, and although we may doubt the effectiveness of such measures, it certainly seems possible that they would be willing to act. Soldiers were punished in Judaea and people still thought it worth complaining about soldiers. Apart from in certain extreme circumstances, such as the civil wars of

AD 68–9 and especially the sack of Cremona, we do not get the impression that the soldiers were out of control.

There was corruption, but we should beware exaggerating the social power and political influence of the soldiers.

A military society?

Roman troops served for twenty-five years. We can find their camps across the empire, often located in frontier regions. In the West, long-term occupancy of a camp often led to the development of an urban centre nearby. In the case of legionary camps, this centre was often given the status of a Roman colony (e.g. Colchester). Land would be given to the colonists and a Roman community would be established. Although nominally civilian, such settlements had a military function in that they replaced the legion as effective garrison of the area and acted as a centre of political authority. It is normally assumed that the communities which grew up in the environs of camps, often called *canabae*, were settled by former soldiers and camp followers: 'wives' and families and purveyors of those goods and services demanded by the several hundred or several thousand men stationed in the fort.

When colonies were not established, it is difficult to assess where veterans settled. Some returned to the area from where they were recruited. Others might have been attracted to particular areas in which they had served or where they had friends and connections. Others remained near the camp. Many soldiers spent most of their careers operating out of a single camp. In such circumstances, staying in a familiar environment may have been attractive, especially if the soldier had settled his family in the vicinity. During the second century AD, there were increasing numbers of soldiers in the army who claimed not a town or province as their *origo* (place of origin), but *castris* (camp). The army was recruiting more from the sons of soldiers. The trend developed in the first century AD alongside the increased enlistment of locals into the army.

In spite of this trend, most recruits were probably drawn from areas other than the immediate environs of the camp. Even recruits who remained in their native province may have served at some distance from their homes. Legions tended to recruit from their own and nearby provinces, but a few recruits served at the opposite end of the empire from which they were born. The pattern for the auxiliary units has not been the subject of detailed study, but it seems likely that it was similar to that of the legions. There are examples of non-legionary units recruiting from distant places. A unit stationed in Egypt received 126 men (about 25 per cent of their manpower) on a single day from the province of Asia (*PSI* IV 1063). The fleet stationed at Misenum in Italy recruited heavily, though not exclusively, from Egypt. Although trends can be observed in patterns of recruitment, they show irregularity not regularity.

The army appears to have recruited through two main procedures. First, men would volunteer. Service in the army was probably financially attractive to many provincials and offered other benefits (status and power) which would outweigh its manifest disadvantages. However, joining the army was probably not straightforward. It is likely that there was some competition in normal times. The papyrological evidence suggests that potential soldiers had to secure an introduction. Their entry into the army had to be eased by influential friends and possibly by bribes. Thus, those already with military connections would stand the best chance of being recruited.

The second procedure was through the *dilectus*. The recruiting officer would visit a community and either enrol volunteers or conscript recruits. When war broke out, the army needed to recruit large numbers of troops quickly and war may also have discouraged volunteers. The first place a recruiting officer could look would be in the communities near the camp, but they could also look elsewhere, or to other provinces, or 'borrow' recruits from other armies. All these procedures would lead to irregularities in recruitment patterns. Also, once recruits had been drawn from a particular community, that community had a connection with the unit and those wishing to join the army might have better luck when attempting to enlist in a unit in which their former neighbours were serving. A recruiting officer might be tempted to look to those areas from where he had drawn recruits in the past. Many of the soldiers (those who did not stay in the vicinity of the camp) probably returned to the village or city from which they originated. Although recruitment was conservative in that recruits tended to be drawn from the same areas, the irregularity of recruitment patterns encouraged a diversity of origins in the Roman army. This diversity of origins probably encouraged a diversity in settlement pattern. It seems unlikely, except in very recently conquered provinces, that all veterans remained close to their colleagues in camp: veteran settlements should not be seen as military islands surrounded by hostile civilian communities.

Soldiers had a rather peculiar legal status: they were not allowed to contract legal marriages; they were not allowed to own land in the province in which they were serving, except under special circumstances; they could not be summoned away from the standards to perform civilian legal business, and civil cases against soldiers were suspended for the duration of their service unless it could be shown that the soldiers had entered service to avoid their legal responsibilities; the property of soldiers was not treated as part of the property of their family under the control of the *paterfamilias* in the normal Roman fashion; and soldiers had the right to be tried on criminal charges in the camp, not in the civilian community where the offence may have taken place. This package of measures effectively isolated soldiers from many aspects of normal society.

It is apparent, however, that whatever the intention behind the regulation of soldiers' lives, soldiers interacted in many areas with civilian communities. They formed long-term relationships with women which they treated as marriages. The Roman authorities even came to acknowledge the existence of these relationships and, although they were not recognised as marriages during the military careers of the soldiers, the diplomas issued on the retirement of auxiliary soldiers retrospectively recognised the legitimacy of the relationship and of any children that resulted. In addition, the Roman authorities developed extraordinary legal procedures so that the children of these soldiers could be instituted as the legitimate heirs of their natural fathers.

The work of the soldier also brought the troops into contact with civilians. Troops did not just prepare for and fight in major conflicts. They were involved in building projects (military and non-military), in supervising the state's economic assets (guarding quarries and mines, etc.), in gathering supplies and in the supervision of tax collection; they were occasionally used as a convenient labour force, and in duties which we would describe as policing. On many of these duties, soldiers must have worked closely with the civilians and, in so doing, many soldiers spent much of their time away from the camp. The stories in our literary sources which depict soldiers appearing suddenly on street corners should not be dismissed as fabrications or evidence that soldiers were allowed to roam free. At least some of the soldiers were probably at their station, ensuring the security of the province.

It should come as no surprise that we see soldiers integrating with the local population. They contracted relationships with local women; some of them may even have been born locally; and they worked with the provincials throughout their careers. At Cremona, the battle was turned decisively when the Flavian forces turned to greet the rising sun (see p. 155): the German legions thought they were greeting reinforcements and fled. The greeting was non-Roman, a manifestation of the easternisation of the legions. The Roman army developed local characteristics, and such cultural assimilation suggests interaction with and not segregation from local communities.

The extent of this interaction varied from province to province. The legions in Britain under Nero were probably faced with a fairly hostile environment. The province was in the process of being conquered. Native cultural activities may have been scorned as barbaric by non-Britons. Integration was probably slower than elsewhere, and further slowed by major revolts which increased the mutual suspicion of the communities. In other provinces, cultures of troops and natives were probably more similar, and more peaceful circumstances allowed more rapid integration. Yet, even in a province in which one would have thought there were almost insuperable boundaries to integration, there is limited evidence of this process. In the New Testament, *Acts* 10 tells of a centurion from Caesarea named Cornelius who was perhaps the first non-Jewish convert to Christianity. Even in Judaea, a measure of integration was possible (cf. Matthew 8.5–13).

Soldiers and veterans as an elite

It is reasonable to suggest that soldiers and veterans did not form a separate society, but the nature of their relationship to the civilian community is more difficult to establish. In the provinces, most of the population did not have the privilege of Roman citizenship and were thus subjected to the full authority of Roman magistrates and their own local officials. Soldiers either had citizenship at the point of enlistment or were given citizenship when discharged. Romans in the provinces could claim protection under Roman law and limited exemptions from local jurisdiction. They enjoyed a legally privileged status. As Romans among the provincials, they could claim elite status.

Whether they were treated as an elite probably depended somewhat on political circumstances. In Britain, for instance, the province was insecure and the governors needed the support of all Romans in the province, especially those with military training. In provinces such as this, the governors were probably more inclined to take any claims of the soldiers to elite status seriously. In more settled provinces, the governors had less need of the troops. Also, in many provinces there was an easily recognisable pre-existing native elite. This elite, often familiar with classical culture, was entrusted with much of the day-to-day administrative business of their communities and could be relied upon politically. The Roman aristocracy probably had more in common with this group than the generally lower-class soldiers and veterans. In such areas, the military's claim to elite status was more difficult to sustain.

The annual income of soldiers and veterans was probably quite substantial. Before Domitian's pay increase (see p. 183), ordinary legionaries received 900 sesterces per year. This was raised by Domitian to 1,200 sesterces. If veterans lived off their discharge bonus, they would probably have had an income somewhat above 640 sesterces per year. In addition to this, pay records make clear that soldiers built up substantial savings which could have been invested on retirement. This probably provided a moderate income, though the real aristocracy of the empire had a far higher income (see pp. 217–18).

STRATEGY

It might seem self-evident that a state as militarily powerful as Rome would have a strategy. Historians have disagreed, however, as to whether one should talk about Roman military policy in terms of strategy.

Defining terms: strategy and tactics

Discussions of military affairs normally distinguish between two levels of military thinking: the strategic and the tactical. Here, we shall use a third. Tactics are, in effect, what happens on the battlefield. The way a general places his troops and what he gets them to do are tactics. The placing of camps in defensible locations is also tactical. The Romans thought about and discussed tactics. Although some battles lacked obvious tactics, literary accounts make clear that the better generals employed tactics.

Strategy involves the deployment of several armies and the organisation of troops over extended territories. There are obvious difficulties of definition. The placing of a single camp may be tactical. The placing of several camps may be a result of several similar tactical decisions. At some point, those camps may become connected by a road. Is the placement of the camps now strategic? When does a frontier cease to become a tactical arrangement and become a strategic boundary?

The issue is complicated by a further level of thinking: the grand strategy. This is used by ancient historians to refer to a set of principles that govern military policy across the whole empire or nearly the whole empire over an extended period. For a strategy to be a grand strategy, it must survive changes of emperors.

Grand strategy

There is very little discussion in our literary sources of anything that can be described as 'strategy' after the Augustan period. This is surprising. Although the focus of Tacitus, Dio and Suetonius was on affairs in Rome, there is much in these accounts which relates to military activity. Those emperors who either did not engage in conquests or limited the extent of conquests tend to be criticised, but the decision to stop expansion is nearly always represented as a political decision.

The predominance of political decision-making lies at the heart of the debate. Historians who do not see the empire as pursuing a conscious strategy tend to argue that military decisions were taken for purely political reasons. They argue that if there had been any strategic discussion in Rome, it would surely have been reported by our sources. It has also been suggested that in all areas of Roman administrative and political activity the emperor tended to respond to problems. If government was solely responsive, there could be little debate or ideological discussion.

A third area of discussion has concentrated on the concepts that lie behind modern strategic thinking. Historians have questioned the level of knowledge available to the Romans about the frontiers. Romans tended to discuss peoples rather than land forms (ethnography rather than geography). In a world in which political organisation was based on connections to a city, and in which Greek or Roman communities could be planted in territories that had been populated by Gauls or Syrians, the link between nation and land, so prevalent in modern thought, was much less developed. In such circumstances, an ethnographic rather than a geographic understanding of the world was far more practical. It is also argued that the Romans did not even have the basic concept of a frontier. The word used in the fourth century AD and later for frontier, *limes*, seems to mean a military road, and such roads in the first century

tended to lead into enemy territory rather than delineate boundaries. It is argued that the Romans did not have sufficient grasp of
geographical techniques or understanding of the physical geography
of their empire to create anything that approximates to a strategy.

It seems clear that whatever the Roman thought about military
policy, their thinking is likely to have been in terms different from
those in which modern strategic thinkers consider the world. We
must return to essential issues to understand this problem.

Concepts of empire

The modern word 'empire' derives from the Latin word *'imperium'*.
The primary meaning of *imperium* is power. It is used to describe
the power held by Roman magistrates. From this meaning a
secondary usage developed, closer to our concept of empire.
Imperium came to have implications of territoriality, so that a
magistrate would have *imperium* over a particular area, an area
normally referred to as the *provincia*. The Romans could understand
the territorial limitations of a particular grant of *imperium* and that
there was a border across which *imperium* had no legal force. Much
of provincial law depends on this concept. From the sacred
pomerium (boundary) of the city of Rome to the River Rubicon
which Caesar crossed to start the civil war, Roman history is
littered with clearly defined boundaries. Yet the concept of
imperium allowed a certain flexibility. The *imperium Romanum* did
not merely constitute those areas under the direct control of a
Roman magistrate or his representatives. Roman power extended
beyond this region. Thus, the so-called client kingdoms were
within the Roman Empire. 'Client kingdom' is the modern term
used to describe states over which the Romans exercised influence.
Client states could vary from states with which the Romans had
treaty relations, but very little influence over, to states which the
Romans controlled by appointing the monarch and closely supervising his or her activities. Roman power was exercised over the
territory of the client state.

There was a certain elasticity of the concept of *imperium*. A state
might come into contact with Rome and acknowledge Roman
power through a treaty. They would become a friend of Rome, but
through that treaty Rome's power would be felt in that region:
Roman *imperium* was extended. Obviously the Romans would have
been aware of degrees of dependence from the province to the client
king to the kingdom with which there was a treaty relationship,

but *imperium* allowed a blurring of frontiers so that the limits of Roman power could not be clearly established and there was room for dispute over the degree of integration.

This can be illustrated by the story of the Boudiccan revolt. The area of the Iceni tribe seems to have been territorially within what we think of as the boundary of the province. Yet under Prasutagus, the kingdom retained a certain independence. It was a client state and therefore within the *imperium* of Rome. When the king died, the Romans changed the administrative arrangements of the area, but did not thereby alter its status as part of the empire. The Iceni thought otherwise. By the same logic, the Romans could establish client kingdoms from provinces without causing an outcry in Rome over loss of territory. They could impose tribute on client states. They could impose provincial government on kingdoms that had previously enjoyed a fragile independence. Roman *imperium* was not thereby extended or diminished. The flexibility of *imperium* meant that the boundaries of the Roman empire (defined as the area over which the Romans exercised political authority) were in fact negotiable and uncertain.

The Romans exercised power over people. In such a conception, an exact territorial division between those barbarian lands within the empire and those outside was of little use to the Romans. Many of the borders of the Roman world were surrounded by tribal groupings whose precise zones of influence were probably not understood by the Romans and were probably shifting and uncertain anyway. The ethnographic view of the world made sense within this framework. The geographical precision with which modern states draw their frontiers was inappropriate to the political circumstances of much of the Roman empire.

We should not, however, over-estimate Roman geographical vagueness. The Romans imposed administrative and tax-levying structures on the provinces. Since they taxed goods, heads or land, and to tax all three they needed to establish a boundary across which the taxable unit might cross or within which they might fall, a precise definition of a frontier was administratively desirable. Even if the collection of this taxation was devolved to local communities, they had to decide who was subjected to that Roman taxation and who was beyond the administrative boundary. Roman surveying techniques were comparatively sophisticated and, even if they devolved responsibility for some of these decisions to local communities, they were able to divide territories and construct boundaries.

The use of geographical skills at the level of the individual city or the village or the field is a rather different activity from the use of geographical skills to plan military campaigns and manage frontier zones. Nevertheless, the Romans did collect material which might have allowed them to construct usable maps. We see some interest in distances between communities in Strabo and Pliny the Elder. We also know that Augustus' colleague Agrippa was involved in geographical survey, though the nature of the map produced cannot be deduced. A senator under Domitian was charged with *maiestas* partly because he had a depiction of the Roman empire on his bedroom wall (Dio, LXVII 12.2–4). This was presumably taken as evidence that the senator was planning some kind of *coup*. For our purposes, it is significant that a map might be thought to have useful information for a prospective emperor.

Territory beyond the Roman provinces must have been much less well known, but again we should not underestimate the knowledge available to the Romans. Large and small military expeditions penetrated these regions. Information was gathered from natives and traders, and anyway much of the zone beyond the Roman provinces was controlled by friendly powers. The Romans were almost certainly not as well informed about their neighbours and enemies as modern states, yet the emperors probably had sufficient information at their disposal to be able to make informed judgements on strategic grounds.

It remains to be considered whether this potential for informed policy making was ever realised.

Roman policy

Statements of Rome's broad strategic policy are very few and very simple. During the Republic, Rome's empire expanded to incorporate most of the lands surrounding the Mediterranean and much of western Europe with little obvious discussion of policy. Strategic decisions were taken at various times. Decisions must have been taken not to extend direct Roman rule into Greece during the early second century BC. Pompey's settlement of the East in 62 BC must have been based on a series of political and strategic decisions which he needed to justify on his return to Rome. Yet, even if we understand the senate to have been a policy-making forum, it was composed of individuals and groups who probably had many different policies. With the pressures on leading politicians to achieve military glory, foreign policy was subject to rapid change.

More important than any supposed senatorial policy were the social, economic and political pressures that led Rome to adopt an extremely aggressive foreign policy from at least the third century BC onwards. The politicians wanted to lead armies in wars and the beneficial effects of successful warfare on the Roman economy, and for the individuals who fought with the armies, encouraged the lower classes to support aggressive military policies. The impetus for the accumulation of territory was not strategic thinking, but an aggressive disposition.

The stability in political leadership that came with the domination of Augustus was an essential precondition for the development of a strategy. From 28–27 BC, a consistent policy could be followed over an extended period, but the statements of policy we get in the Augustan period are notably inconsistent. Early in the reign, the poets proclaim the domination of Augustus and claim that world conquest will follow. Augustus' own military imagery presents that conquest as being imminent. No boundaries were set to Roman power. Augustus was also responsible for the acquisition of a great deal of territory and, by including those lands which had been subjected to Antony and Cleopatra and to Sextus Pompeius in the list of conquered territory in his *Res Gestae*, Augustus laid claim to having conquered much of the known world. Yet, explicit statements of strategy reported in Dio (LIV 9, LVI 33, LVI 41) and Tacitus (*Ann.* I 11), the first of which is dated to 20 BC, claim that Augustus followed a non-expansionist policy.

The discrepancy is almost beyond explanation and has led to anachronistic claims that Augustus sought to expand the empire to its 'natural frontiers' (wherever or whatever they might be). The concept of natural frontiers is, however, modern. Even as a modern concept, defining the natural frontiers of a state is problematic and the drive to expand to a natural frontier has been used by various imperialists as an excuse to invade their neighbours. The concept would probably have been foreign to Augustus.

The elastic conception of *imperium* may help resolve the difficulty, since it allows us to see most (though certainly not all) of Augustus' campaigns as attempts to alter the status of areas in which Rome already had influence and were therefore already 'within the *imperium*'. Yet, Augustan expansion in Germany, the Alpine region and along the Danube would require a very flexible conception of Roman influence to be regarded as a facet of a policy of non-expansionism.

Tiberius adopted Augustus' stated policy and largely kept to it.

Our sources do not represent the expansionism of later emperors as being a breach with Augustan or Tiberian policy, or as being a result of a reconsideration of strategic policy. Gaius threatened Britain and Germany and expanded into Mauretania. Claudius invaded Britain. Nero considered expansion to the East. Vespasian and Titus were involved in campaigns in Germany, as was Domitian. Domitian attempted to expand across the Danube after temporarily stabilising the provinces of the area. Trajan launched invasions of Dacia and Parthia. There may have been a political or strategic rationale behind all these campaigns, but our sources consistently fail to place any weight on such discussions. There was no need to justify invasions of enemy territory. Glory was enough of an excuse. Agricola's campaigns in northern Britain were not justified by Tacitus in strategic terms. The conquest of Britain was an aim in itself. As far as the elite was concerned, the empire had no boundaries. Expansion was natural.

In spite of this, Roman expansionism slowed notably in the imperial period, which has encouraged historians to take Augustus' precept seriously. How can we account for this historical development?

One could look to the nature of Rome's enemies. In Africa, expansion to the south was distinctly unpromising. Much of the East faced on to desert regions populated by nomadic or semi-nomadic tribes: not a promising area for conquest. Parthia was a powerful state, the conquest of which would be rather difficult, as various Roman leaders discovered. In the North and West, the various border tribes were formidable, and it could be argued that these regions were underdeveloped and politically unstable. It would be too difficult to establish direct political control and diplomatic measures would produce better results. Such arguments are, however, specious. The Romans could have made the same arguments about Britain or Gaul, or various states and peoples conquered during the Republican expansion. The problems presented by these peoples were different from those the Romans had faced before, but not sufficiently different to prevent conquest. The explanation must lie in the internal politics of Rome.

Although the development of monarchy altered the political landscape, military success continued to bring popularity and acclaim and was an important way in which an emperor could establish his credentials. Yet, as Nero showed, it was possible to be an emperor without being a military figure. More important than the emperor's own military success was that no challenger should emerge as a military leader to threaten the emperor. The great campaigns of the period tended to be conducted by members of the imperial family: Germanicus in Germany, Claudius in Britain, Titus in Judaea, Domitian in Germany and on the Danube, and Trajan's campaigns. There were exceptions, such as Corbulo's campaigns in Germany and Armenia. Yet, Corbulo was closely monitored and forced to recall his troops from an expedition deep into Germany. In the East, he was notably cautious and steadfastly refused to go beyond his remit without consulting Rome. Nero still had him killed (see p. 136). Augustus could turn to his family to lead the troops. Tiberius had Germanicus, but his death robbed Tiberius of his leading general. His own son, Drusus, had been given early military experience, but was not entrusted with major campaigns, perhaps because of uncertainty at Rome. After Drusus' death, Tiberius had no male relative to whom he could entrust such campaigns. Gaius was in a similar position. Britannicus and Nero were too young to be given such responsibility by Claudius. Nero was similarly without obvious trusted relatives. Vespasian used Titus in Judaea, but then felt that he needed him in Rome to control the praetorians. Domitian and Trajan fought their own wars. After Augustus, the emperors were notably short of trusted agents to conduct great campaigns.

The political pressures of the period meant that most emperors feared the senate. They wished to remain in close contact with Rome and trips to the frontiers took time. Emperors were generally reluctant to make those trips. Since the impetus for large-scale expansion came to depend on the availability of the emperor or his deputy, and since emperors had many other constraints on their time, the rate of expansion inevitably slowed. This was a feature of political structures, not of grand strategy.

Local and regional policies

There were general changes in Roman military organisation across the Empire during this period. These included the development of fixed camps where units were stationed for extended periods and the development of what used to be thought of as fixed frontiers, but is perhaps better characterised as lines of defence stretching over very long distances. Hadrian's Wall is, of course, the most famous of these, though it is outside our period. There were also defensive lines in Germany, along the Rhine and between the Rhine and the

Danube, and probably in Africa. In other places, roads may have marked the division between different districts of the empire.

These developments were certainly not directly contemporary and cannot result from an imperial directive. The similarities between the constructions in Germany, Hadrian's Wall and the later Antonine Wall in Britain, and a fortified line in Africa are notable. The situation was rather different in the East. The Romans established control over the very long frontiers by controlling the limited routes of communication in these areas. In many cases, a single fort could accomplish tasks for which a defensive line was needed in the West. Although there was not a fortified barrier, the forts of the East probably controlled access to a defined region. The marking of a boundary must represent a similar perceived need (probably to control access to the provinces). The development of these defensive fortifications shows shared perceptions and military thinking. It is certainly possible that there was transmission of ideas from one region to another, possibly through senior officers or imperial involvement. It is through developments at this local or regional level that we can see military thought and the development of military policy.

Political factors will have been important in the development of military policy in the various regions, yet we can also see a geographical and strategic rationale behind many of the decisions. Some of the best examples fall outside our period, but since the processes of thought attested are likely to have been current in our period, they can be cited as evidence. Hadrian's Wall was positioned along a geographically sensible line of defence, though it may have made little sense in relation to tribal groupings (some tribes may have been divided by the Wall). The Augustan conquest of the Alpine region and campaigns into Pannonia followed what seems to have been a predetermined plan of conquest with troops invading from north and south to secure this extremely difficult terrain. Again, this showed a sophisticated deployment of military resources over a vast region. In the Flavian period, Domitian and possibly his father and brother engaged in bitter wars over an area known as the Agri Decumates, a stretch of territory between the Rhine and Danube. It is very difficult to escape the conclusion that a major aim in the campaign was to shorten the existing defensive line between the two rivers. This may have been as a preliminary to further expansion and it is clear that Roman power was felt across the Rhine, but this does not obscure the original strategic rationale.

There were military events which appear, at first sight, strategically irrational: the conquests of Britain and Dacia and the invasion of Parthia. All these were clearly influenced by political factors. Yet, if we accept that the strategic aim of Rome was world conquest, then neither the invasion of Britain nor the invasion of Parthia seem particularly irrational. Dacia is a different issue, but the Dacians had been causing problems on the frontiers for some time and, although the conquest may look ridiculous on a map of Europe, the exertion of direct military force beyond the Danube did allow the Romans to place increased pressure on other tribes north of the Danube, especially those now threatened by Roman incursions from Dacia to the east, Pannonia to the south and Germany to the west.

The Romans do appear to have developed military policies to deal with local problems. These policies were clearly influenced by political factors, but can be understood in geographical and strategic terms.

Conclusions

The Romans did not have a grand strategy. Roman policy aims remained static and simple. They aimed to conquer the world. This aim often conflicted with the political aims of emperors. They wanted to stay in power. To do so, they had to restrain their ambitious generals and monopolise military prestige. This resulted in a slowing of the process of expansion. The Romans did, however, think strategically. Much of the military activity of this period made strategic sense in terms of the region in which they were operating. The Romans do not appear to have launched their armies at random, but planned military installations and campaigns with some geographical sophistication. There was certainly no Department of Strategic Studies in Rome, but the Romans did develop military policies and apply them over large areas. By our definition, this seems to be strategy.

THE ARMY AND POLITICS

In Western democracies, the army is supposed to be an apolitical force concerned with the defence of the state against foreign enemies. The Roman army was also concerned with the security of the Empire and with foreign wars. This was, however, only one of the army's roles.

The Augustan settlements established a constitutional frame-work for the monarchy. As part of that settlement, the standing army was created and most of the troops were stationed in the provinces. Since the emperors took control over the appointment of generals, much of the political feuding that had marked appointments to important commands in the Republic seems to have disappeared, or at least was contained within the doors of the palace. We should not, however, be lulled by this silence into believing that the army was depoliticised. The army continued to play an important political role, both in the provinces and in Rome.

Military units in the provinces were often dispersed. Soldiers were sent on duties which varied from supervising grain supply to building bridges to acting as the political police. Certain provinces have produced more evidence for Roman military involvement in policing than others. The involvement of soldiers in policing activities in Jewish regions of the Near East and in Egypt is comparatively well attested. Here, the soldiers dealt with bandits and other local problems. They ensured the smooth working of the local administrative and security system. They represented Roman military force and, since a soldier was potentially supported by several thousand of his fellows, he wielded considerable authority. In these regions, the soldiers were there to ensure internal security. Their stations probably related as much if not more to political geography than strategic geography. Traces of this dispersal can be found in other regions. Some soldiers are depicted on tombstones carrying writing tablets and staffs as well as swords. The staff could be used to beat the locals. The writing tablets probably represented the role of the soldiers in policing the province. Varus, the Roman general whose legions were massacred in AD 9, was criticised by Dio for sending his soldiers in small numbers to the various settlements in Germany to act as police. Dio did not criticise the dispersal itself, rather the incorrect perception on the part of Varus that the province was peaceful. Dispersal was the norm.

The troops were in sufficient numbers that they could bring Roman power to the smallest of communities in military provinces. They could also provide the governor with detailed information about the state of the province. They were a powerful instrument of political control.

It was not just in the provinces that the army could be deployed in this way. The praetorian guard and the urban cohorts provided the emperor with a powerful instrument of political control in Rome. There were probably around 4,000 praetorians in Rome under Tiberius. These were supplemented by the urban cohorts, about 1,300 men. Although comparatively small in an urban population of about one million, the guard was a significant military force and could certainly enforce discipline in the theatre and other areas. The fleets stationed in Italy at Misenum and Ravenna provided another nearby military resource, and it is probable that considerable numbers of troops were in transit through Italy on various tasks at any one point.

The troops in Italy were an important resource for an emperor. The praetorians were a major factor in the accessions of Claudius and Otho. Claudius openly acknowledged his debt to the praetorians through his coinage. It was to the praetorians he fled when news of Messalina's conspiracy broke. The praetorians obviously provided military protection for the emperor and could intimidate the senate and the urban mob. They could be used symbolically. The presence of a few soldiers with the emperor gave him status and was an implied threat. The clatter of the armour and the gleam of the weapons were obvious symbols of power. Sejanus, Macro, Burrus, Tigellinus, Titus and Casperius Aelianus used their control of the praetorians to build a power base in Rome.

The extent to which the praetorians were used as a political police force is unclear. Soldiers were sent to encourage the recalcitrant to suicide and to arrest the 'criminal'. Praetorians may have been involved in the torture of supposed conspirators. There is little evidence to suggest that they were regularly employed as *delatores* (informers), though it is possible that some emperors employed praetorians in this role.

The frontier armies only rarely became involved in the political struggle. Some opposed the accessions of Tiberius and Claudius. They were crucial in the events of AD 68–9 and 97–8. The emperors made every attempt to secure their loyalty. The most concrete measure was the payment of the troops. Troops were paid in coin (all with the head of the emperor on it) three times a year and would also receive regular donatives (presents of money) which would encourage their loyalty. The troops also had ceremonials and symbols which would reinforce loyalty. They carried images of the emperor on their standards. It was probably to these images that they swore oaths of loyalty on 1 January each year. The imperial birthday was celebrated, as were the birthdays of other important members of the imperial family. Such ceremonials bound the troops together and cemented their loyalty. Potential usurpers had to subvert these expressions of collective loyalty to win over the troops.

The army retained a political role in the imperial period and there was no attempt to depoliticise it. Every measure was taken to ensure that the army remained a political force, but a force solidly in support of the emperor.

14

WOMEN

Study of the status of women in Roman society is made difficult by the nature of our sources. We are comparatively well informed about the legal status of women. The social status of women and the way in which women interacted with men are rather more difficult to understand. Our substantial problem is that the literary and epigraphic sources tend to represent extreme views of women. These depictions of women conform to stereotypes. They are either chaste, supportive and loyal or deceiving, promiscuous and avaricious. Neither Juvenal's misogynistic *Satire VI* nor the funerary inscriptions noting the manifest virtues of the departed may bear any relationship to the behaviour of contemporary women. Legal sources tell us about law and not behaviour. Legislation against adultery for instance tells us that adultery was a criminal offence, but not how widespread or socially acceptable adultery was. These sources do, however, attest ideologies. Funerary inscriptions suggest the virtues that represented an ideal of womanhood and we may assume that women were under some pressure to aspire to those virtues. Pliny's idealised women again show us an ideological representation of women, and the ideology – whether or not it was shared by women – may be assumed to have had some social effect. Similarly, Juvenal's *Satire VI* suggests that an ugly misogynism (however seriously we regard the depiction) was not completely foreign to Roman manhood. In some rare sources, however, depictions of women do not seem to conform to stereotypes and these, together with the attested ideologies, allow some progress to be made.

THE LAW

Nearly all Roman children were born into a family dominated by a *pater* (father or head of family). The *pater* exercised *potestas* (power) over his family. He controlled all the family property and could punish all members of the family as he thought fit. The authority of the *pater* extended to his children, and any grandchildren born to his sons. On the death of the *pater* all his children became independent. It was possible for children to be manumitted, and thereby given their independence, before the death of the *pater*, though it is unclear how common this was. In certain circumstances, a woman could also pass from the *potestas* of her father to that of her husband on marriage, though it seems that this was extremely rare. A woman would, therefore, normally remain under the authority of her father or grandfather even after her marriage. Her husband and his family had very little legal authority over her. On the death of her *pater*, the woman would become legally independent. The law, however, judged that women were not normally legally capable. This meant that to perform any legal action, such as marrying or divorcing or selling or buying property, a woman would need the authority of her *tutor* (legal guardian). This duty would probably normally be carried out by a close male relative or friend. A woman, therefore, needed male authority to conduct any public business. This control was somewhat lessened since a woman could always apply to a magistrate to have an inefficient or otherwise difficult *tutor* removed. In addition, a freeborn woman who had three children or a freedwoman who had four children was judged legally capable and given control over her own affairs.

A woman normally had property in two forms. Her dowry was passed to her husband at marriage. This property was supposed to be used to maintain the woman though it seems probable that husbands could make a substantial profit from dowries. Dowries were managed as part of the husband's estate. The only difference was that such property could not be mortgaged or sold (though the woman's holdings could be adjusted), since the woman always had first legal claim on the property. At the dissolution of the marriage, the property would be returned to the wife. It seems that in most senses the dowry was the property of the wife though the usufruct of the property (the right to exploit and manage the property) belonged to the husband.

A woman could also hold property separate from her dowry in the same manner as property was held by a man. This could be property inherited or purchased and was in no way subject to the control of her husband.

Marriage and divorce were comparatively informal legal procedures. A man and woman were judged to be married if they cohabited with that intention. Divorce was simply the ending of that intent. Practically, a man and woman could move into the same house and announce their marriage in some way and it would be taken to be a marriage, if there was no legal impediment. Normally, a dowry would be given as a symbol of that union. Divorce normally entailed notification of the end of the marriage and the restoration of the dowry. In theory, both partners were equally able to divorce, though a woman without legal independence would need the authority of her *pater* or *tutor* and the restoration of the dowry could be made difficult. A woman did not normally form part of the *familia* of her husband. She was often legally a stranger within his household. She could be removed or remove herself comparatively easily. She did not, however, have any rights over children or over her husband's property. Unless a woman maintained a separate household of her own (and the very wealthy probably did), divorce could render a woman homeless.

The sexual behaviour of women was controlled by law. Adultery by women was punishable by partial confiscation of her dowry and exile. Adultery was defined as sexual relations with any man not her husband. A man committed adultery through sexual relations with married, respectable women and an adulterous man could also be exiled. Sex with slaves, prostitutes or unmarried women was not regarded as adultery whatever his marital status. Husbands and fathers could exercise a certain amount of violence against those caught in adultery, provided that the couple were caught in the act, and the level of allowable violence increased if the male party was of low status. Husbands who killed allegedly adulterous wives could be prosecuted for homicide. In law, the husband was bound to divorce an adulterous wife. She could then be prosecuted for adultery. If he failed to prosecute a wife divorced on the grounds of adultery, after a suitable delay, any other citizen could prosecute. If he failed to divorce a wife convicted of adultery (and anyone could bring a charge of adultery, though they should allow a husband a certain amount of time after the alleged act to bring a prosecution), he could be prosecuted as a pimp.

The effect of the law on the lives of women probably depended on the manner in which it was applied. A *tutor*, for instance, may have simply acted as the woman wished, provided that nothing illegal or clearly against her interests was proposed, or he could have effectively blocked all her transactions. The independence of a woman from her husband's family could diminish her authority within her husband's household or provide her with financial and legal independence. Although the system was clearly patriarchal, recent studies have stressed how the regulations protected women's interests. The legal separation of a woman's property from that of her husband and the institution of guardianship prevented a husband from pressurising his wife into giving over management of all her property and provided some insurance against the loss of her dowry. Men who married for money could not normally take control of that money if the marriage was dissolved. Roman law provided the wife with some protection from her husband.

SOCIAL STATUS

Legal regulations assume that one of the major threats to the interests of a woman stemmed from her husband. This reflects an assumption that the woman would be the weaker party in any relationship, an assumption which seems generally to have been true. Roman society appears to have been patrilocal – a woman entered her husband's household. In general, women tended to marry at an earlier age than men. Establishing age at marriage is rather difficult, but it seems there was a general assumption that women would be married by the age of twenty, though women could marry as early as twelve. Men tended to marry later in life and Augustan legislation encouraged male marriage by the age of twenty-five, though it seems likely that many married much later. There was normally a notable discrepancy between the ages of spouses. Such differences in age, experience and authority placed the woman in a subordinate position to her spouse.

This subordination was a fundamental part of Rome's patriarchy. It can be seen in some of the depictions of 'ideal women'. Pliny gives us several. Arria, for instance, was married to Caecina Paetus who was implicated in a revolt against Claudius. Among her many other acts of personal bravery, she supported her husband to the end and encouraged him to suicide by first stabbing herself (Pliny, *Ep.* III 16). Another unnamed woman threw herself from a balcony into Lake Como where she presumably drowned. She had tied herself to her husband who had a seemingly fatal and painful disease (Pliny, *Ep.* VI 24). Pliny describes his wife affectionately and notes that she spent her time managing the household, memorising Pliny's literary masterpieces and even setting some of them to music (Pliny, *Ep.* IV 19). Discounting for a moment the possibility that her behaviour displayed a highly developed sense of irony, such devotion seems to reflect the balance of power in the relationship. There are other examples of this kind of devotion. Some of these women were clearly personally impressive, but instead of being in any sense independent agents, their roles were so closely bound up with those of their husbands that life without their husbands became impossible. They were not independent figures.

This ideology can be seen in other areas. Although women were encouraged by Augustan legislation to remarry after divorce or the death of a husband, women who were *univira*, married only once, were particularly honoured. When two girls were put forward for a single vacancy among the vestal virgins, the selection was made on the basis that one had a mother who was a divorcée and the other's mother was *univira* (Tac., *Ann.* II 86). In the Augustan period, Propertius (IV 11) sang the virtues of Cornelia, one of which was to be *univira*. These sources present an ideal of a woman who subordinated herself to a single man and who was devoted to him to the point of death.

INDEPENDENT WOMEN

There are depictions of women which contrast with this ideal. One thinks automatically of the women of the imperial household: Livia, the Agrippinas, Messalina, Poppaea, Domitia Longina and others. The depictions of these women in the literary sources stressed their powerful and independent role in Roman political life and it was an independence which, in some cases, allegedly affected their sexual behaviour.

There are grounds for treating the portrayals with a great deal of caution, but our sources are fairly uniform in their judgement and, in general terms, credible. It is fair to wonder whether Tacitus could have accepted a version of the elder Agrippina's role that was a complete fabrication and ran contrary to the normal expectations of female behaviour. The younger Agrippina appeared in official depictions, such as coins, which shows that her political prominence was not just a feature of an inventive literary tradition. This does not mean that we should accept all the stories which circulated about the imperial women. The Roman elite was prone to gossip. The sexual relationships of members of the imperial family were of obvious interest and could provide scope for scurrilous invention (see pp. 22, 91–4 for discussions of this issue).

One must ask whether the behaviour of the women of the imperial family can be taken to reflect the behaviour of women of other social groups. Here, the evidence becomes rather thin. Under Tiberius, a Vistilia attempted to avoid prosecution for adultery by registering as a prostitute. The emperor took a rather dim view of this evasion of the law (Tac., *Ann.* II 85). There were various prosecutions of women for adultery or for other crimes, sometimes of a political nature, though it is difficult to ascertain whether these crimes were real or just a result of malicious gossip. Similarly, the depiction of women in poetry so thoroughly mixes fact and fiction that reality cannot be discerned.

We are on safer ground with the portrayal of someone such as Ummidia Quadratilla. This lady kept a troupe of mime artists, a form of art noted for its erotic content, and had private performances. The troupe was renowned. She built a theatre in which they could perform and they appeared at the games in Rome (*ILS* 5628). It was not something she wished to hide, though Pliny claims that she rigorously excluded her grandson from all performances (Pliny, *Ep.* VII 24). Pliny's embarrassment is almost palpable and the letter seems designed to dissociate Pliny's protégé, her grandson, from the 'immoralities' of the grandmother. One can imagine the fun that Juvenal could have had with such a character.

Women are quite frequently attested as civic benefactors in both Italy and the provinces, especially Asia. In the East, women were given magistracies, though it seems likely that these were often merely financial duties and did not bring political or legal power. The duties performed show that women were both wealthy and prominent members of the local aristocracies. The prominence of these women can, in some ways, be seen to duplicate the prominence of imperial women.

The influence of these women should not obscure the social constraints which operated. Women of the imperial family were still technically subordinate to the male members of the family. In the various political struggles, the imperial women were not able openly to oppose the male emperors. Their power was a function of their relationship to the men of their family and in some senses they were representatives of their menfolk. In the same way, the women who acted as benefactors in the East and in Italy represented their families. Often their families had been prominent for generations and often (though not always) the inscriptions that celebrate their achievements noted their male relations. Sometimes the monuments which they paid for were family monuments. It may be argued that this was often the case with men also. Men were seen as representatives of a family tradition. Thus, when Pliny cites the suitability of Minicius Acilianus, he discusses the qualities of his family (*Ep.* I 14; see p. 220), and Pliny's letter concerning Ummidia Quadratilla was a reaction to the stigma that might have attached to his friend because of the grandmother's rather dubious hobby.

We see powerful women in this period, but these women do not appear to have been independent in any modern sense: they were still part of a family and individual interests tended to be subordinated to the interests of the family.

LOWER-CLASS WOMEN

The lives of less wealthy women are almost unattested. The epigraphic evidence suggests that the ideology of those who could afford tombstones differed little from that of the aristocracy. Women were praised for the piety and fidelity and affection shown to their husbands and children. Some women kept shops and performed various forms of paid labour. Further down the social and economic scale, prostitution was a generally accepted part of urban life, though it is possible that most prostitutes were of servile origin. The brutality of the life of a prostitute was recognised when it was made an offence to sell a slave into prostitution without 'good cause'. This level of society is generally not discussed by our sources, though hints can be found in the graffiti on the walls in the bars of Pompeii, and in the stories of imperial sorties to the taverns of Rome and Petronius' *Satyricon*. The lives of rural women are even less well attested. It is not known, for instance, whether significant numbers of women were engaged in agricultural labour or whether women, as is sometimes suggested, were expected to remain at home. In the study of women of antiquity, as in the study of so many aspects of ancient society, we can only guess at the lives of lower classes.

CONCLUSIONS: CHANGES IN IDEOLOGY

The Late Republic saw an increased concern about the moral fabric of society, perhaps partly in response to the civil wars. The literature of the period is filled with women who did not conform to traditional moral stereotypes. Augustus introduced a series of reforms intended to regulate sexual behaviour. These laws were directed at two perceived social evils: adulterous women and unmarried men. Augustus' extension of state interference was radical though his intentions were conservative. He was introducing a new moral foundation for the Roman state, the first major victim of which was his own daughter.

The success of Augustus cannot easily be assessed. Tacitus tells us that there was no appreciable change in Roman behaviour, though this can only be an impressionistic judgement (Tac., *Ann.* III 25–8). The anecdotal evidence suggests that 'high society' continued under the Julio–Claudians very much as it had done before the reforms. Indeed, the examples provided by emperors such as Gaius, Claudius and Nero were not calculated to encourage a new moral conservatism. Tacitus does, however, point to a general change in attitudes towards *luxuria*. The end of Nero's reign saw an end to extravagant meals, great palaces and huge private entertainments (Tac., *Ann.* III 55). The new emperors brought a change in moral tone and there was a change in the aristocracy. New Italian senators restored a 'small town conservatism' to Roman society, and in this they were led briefly by Galba and then by Vespasian. Although not explicit in Tacitus, *luxuria* was often also related to sexual behaviour.

In place of the excesses of the Neronian period, *moderatio* became an important symbol of worthiness. The new moral tone was, of course, not really new and had its roots in developments in Greek philosophy long before this period. It has been argued that Augustus encouraged this development by, contrary to normal Roman practice, associating his family very firmly with his rule. His authority was shared and his family formed a partnership which dominated Roman society and politics. Similarly, there appears to have been an emerging perception of man and wife forming a partnership, part of which involved an increasing domestication of men. Men spent more time with their families and status was asserted more in the environment of the family than in the public arena. The process was very gradual and we do not see its completion even by the fourth century AD, but the change seems discernible by the end of the first century. Writers such as Plutarch (admittedly in a Greek context) laid stress on the joint venture of married life. Plutarch's ideal couple both lived sexually restrained lives and sex was strictly for procreation. In such circumstances, men were also forbidden extra-marital relationships. The man remained the dominant partner. This was similar to the pattern that can be observed in the partnerships of the Arriae and Fannia. These women supported their husbands in their dangerous political courses and also in death.

An increased stress on the conjugal relationship had its advantages. The status of women within the relationship probably improved. The aristocratic man and his wife both had a public role to fulfil. A hardening of public opinion probably effectively circumscribed the activities of men. Such a change would, however, also limit the activities of women. Changes in expectations of behaviour may have made divorce, for instance, more difficult. Status may have improved, but a woman remained subordinate and did not enjoy increased freedom. Fundamentally, little changed.

15

PROVINCES AND CULTURE
Romanisation and Hellenisation

This chapter concentrates on the issue of cultural change and no attempt will be made to provide a comprehensive survey of developments in each province. The cultural changes of this period are normally described by the terms 'Romanisation' or 'Hellenisation', by which is meant the process by which local cultures became more Roman or more Greek. This process of fusion of local traditions has been seen as crucial to the pacification of the Roman empire due to a resulting possible modification of local identities and the emergence of a new Roman imperial identity.

ROMANISATION AND HELLENISATION

The development of urban centres on a Roman model is one of the most obvious facets of Romanisation. Such settlements can be seen in all the conquered lands of the West. Typically, the centre would have a regular street plan where the intersections of the streets formed regular rectangular blocks. The two main streets (the *cardo* and *decumanus*) ran through the geometric centre of the city and, near where these streets crossed, the Forum would be situated. The Forum would have a basilica, temples and other Roman-style buildings. The city would normally also be provided with baths.

In the countryside, the development of villas also attests the importation of Roman culture. There is some disagreement about the classification of villas. Archaeologists have tended to define as villas rural structures which have both a rectangular ground plan and stone footings. Such a definition may work for Britain, but clearly cannot apply to many other areas of the Empire where the native architectural style was for stone, rectangular farmhouses. Some early British villas show little sign of Roman influence other than the ground plan and building materials, though these were notable developments. In other provinces, rural properties began to develop more 'Roman' features, such as bathhouses or mosaics. In southern Gaul and Spain, structures similar in style to Italian farms developed. In Germany, northern Gaul and Britain, the style of development was rather different: corridor villas (a series of rooms connected by a passage running alongside the rooms) were common. In Gaul, the first century AD saw the development of some elaborate villas with suites of rooms arranged on three sides of a courtyard. Although problems of categorisation remain, and many buildings which have been classified as villas were built on or near the site of pre-existing native farms, few doubt that the emergence of these new architectural styles was in some way related to Roman conquest.

Other developments also attest Roman influence. The Romans tended to honour religiously significant sites and, indeed, on occasions sponsor their development. One of the best examples of this is at Roman Bath (*Aquae Sulis*), where a site which was of some religious significance prior to the Roman conquest was heavily developed in the Roman period with the construction of bathing establishments and a large classical temple, seemingly dedicated to a fusion of a Celtic deity (Sulis), and a Roman one (Minerva). This tendency towards syncretism (fusing of deities) is commonly attested. It was not just a Roman phenomenon, but was also a feature of Greek and Egyptian reactions to the many and multifaceted gods they came across.

We find similar types of high-quality pottery across the empire and the distribution of *amphorae* (jars used for the transportation of trade goods) suggests that wine and oils were shipped all across the empire and would have been available in every province (see pp. 236–7). Trade led to some integration of the imperial economy and goods of non-local origins found their way to local markets, so that farmers in Britain could have dinner parties at which they used Gallic pottery, drank Italian wine and cooked their food in Spanish oil.

Inscriptions also appear in many provinces of the Empire. Some provinces did not use inscriptions before Roman conquest, and the development of a tradition of Latin 'private' inscriptions across the West shows not only a growing familiarity with Latin, but also a willingness to invest money in inscriptions. Even in the East, where inscriptions had often been used for centuries, there were developments in epigraphic style which often suggest a growing Romanisation of practice.

In town and country, in language and religion, in art, in food and drink, we see evidence of an assimilation of Roman culture in the West.

In the East, Roman culture tended to be transmitted through the medium of Greek culture, and since Roman culture was heavily influenced by Greek culture anyway, Romanisation and Hellenisation appear as equivalent processes. In addition, many of the Eastern Mediterranean lands had been influenced by Greek culture since at least the fourth century BC, and interaction of the various cultures of the region led to significant cultural developments long before the arrival of the Romans. In these areas, it is far more difficult to establish what was a Roman cultural development and what was due to pre-Roman Hellenisation. Yet, as we shall see, similar processes were at work in the East as in the West.

THE NATURE OF CULTURAL CHANGE

Few would disagree that local cultures changed in the first century AD. Assessing the nature and significance of those changes is, however, rather more difficult.

Many of the cultural changes outlined above were longterm and took place over centuries rather than decades. The construction of significant numbers of large, elaborate villas in Britain, such as Chedworth or Lullingstone, was a phenomenon of the third or fourth century rather than the first. Simpler architectural forms tend to dominate the architectural record from the first century. Similarly with urbanisation, the first century saw gradual developments which often only came to fruition in later periods. Urban developments in Britain, for instance, seem to culminate in the early second century and, although patterns vary from province to province and city to city, a similar pattern can be discerned for both Africa and Egypt. We should not exaggerate the pace of change.

The evidence for cultural change is mainly archaeological. This presents certain problems in assessing the extent of change. The development of cities leaves extensive archaeological remains. Urban public buildings were built either by the Romans or by local political authorities, and it seems reasonable to believe that Romans and the local elites would wish to give the impression of thriving Roman communities. The reality of urban life may have been rather different. It is almost impossible to estimate the population of most towns of the Roman Empire, but it seems likely that some at least of the towns of Roman Britain and other frontier provinces had very small populations. Some urban housing was comparatively lavish and filled much of the available space in cities. Other cities seem to have had areas within the walls which were never occupied. The public buildings of these communities suggest that they were a success, but the private buildings tell a slightly different story.

Assessing the cultural importance of changes on previously existing urban centres presents similar problems. Changes in the public buildings of the cities and the development of more Roman-style buildings were again a direct result of imperial patronage and local endeavour, but there is no obvious way to ascertain what effect these buildings had on the cultural values of individuals within the city.

Evidence from inscriptions would seem to be more easily assessed. The preservation of large numbers of privately erected Latin inscriptions (mainly funerary inscriptions) from the Roman West and Greek inscriptions from the East would seem to attest widespread knowledge of Latin or Greek. Yet, we have to deal with the issue of absence. Although we have thousands of such inscriptions, we have only a tiny number of inscriptions in proportion to the population of the Roman Empire. We may assume that most of the inscriptions that there were in antiquity have been lost, but it is probable that many and probably the majority of the imperial population did not commemorate their deaths in stone. How then are we to judge the culture of the absent when we have no evidence for them? It is also possible that the majority of our privately erected inscriptions emanate from a relatively small sector of society. Very large numbers of the inscriptions from Roman Britain involve soldiers and their families. Many African inscriptions again come from a similarly military context. It is certainly arguable that these provide us with virtually no evidence for the culture of the majority of the population.

Other sources do provide evidence for linguistic usage. It is clear from later developments and Eastern sources that pre-conquest languages continued in common use in Africa, Egypt and Syria and we may assume similar linguistic continuities in Celtic areas. Recent studies on the Latin in use at the Roman fort at Vindolanda on Hadrian's Wall and in the fort at Bu Njem in Tripolitania show influence of non-Latin languages. Even in these military contexts and in contexts in which some trained scribes operated, we can detect native influences on Latin (though it seems likely that Latin was spoken at both forts). Latin or Greek was used for all official purposes in the Roman Empire, but it is unclear to what extent these languages were spoken or understood on the streets and in the villages of the empire.

Small finds, pottery, jewellery, etc., also present problems. Roman goods spread beyond the frontiers of the Empire. Roman wine circulated in Britain before the conquest and Roman trade routes extended into Scandinavia and to India. It seems unlikely that those places which received Roman goods were thereby Romanised to any significant extent. Yet, if these goods do not represent Romanisation outside the empire, can they represent Romanisation when discovered within the Empire?

It is also apparent that many of these trade goods were not of Italian origin. Goods from Spain and Gaul appear in Roman Britain and goods circulated in the East without ever going near Rome or Greece. Trade shows contacts between communities in the Mediterranean, but this does not necessarily mean that cultural change resulted or that any cultural change should be described as Hellenisation or Romanisation. To take a rather different example, inscriptions in Britain of the Roman period attest the worship of gods such as Mithras, Serapis and the *Tres Matres*. None of these gods was particularly Roman. Can we interpret their presence (with its obvious inference of cultural change) as evidence of Romanisation? Further, Rome itself had always been open to external cultural influences. Greek and Etruscan cultures exercised considerable influence, but also we find traces of Egyptian and Jewish culture. These influences are most easily seen in religious matters, but the fact that Romans might worship Isis did not thereby make them Egyptian.

Questions of cultural identity are very sensitive. We need to be able to understand what people thought they were doing when they drank wine from the Mediterranean region in the northern provinces, or when they worshipped a native god in a classical temple, and also what other people thought they were doing. They may have thought they were behaving like Romans when the local governor thought they were behaving like natives. The cultural interchanges that took place in the imperial period seem undeniable, but there is little evidence to decide whether the elements of cultural continuity or cultural change were more important in defining cultural identity.

Another approach to the issue of cultural change is to examine social and political structures to discover the extent to which these were modified by Roman imperial influence. Fundamental changes in political and social structures are likely to reflect and be reflected in cultural change.

Many civic buildings may be interpreted as political representations. These architectural developments were paralleled by the development of new ceremonials. Such processes can be seen throughout the empire, but can perhaps best be illustrated by festivals related to the imperial cult. Civic ceremonials celebrated imperial birthdays and dates of accession. Also, more traditional festivals were modified so that some part of the ceremony came to be devoted to the imperial house, even if only so that a prayer could be offered for the safety of the emperor. Temples to specific emperors, general temples, such as *Sebasteia* or *Caesarea*, and small shrines or statues of members of the imperial house adorned cities and may have often received some recognition in ceremonials. The elites of the provinces used all available opportunities to display their loyalty to Rome and to win the favour of the Roman authorities. The Romans would respond by granting favours to the elites. A typical pattern is perhaps attested in Claudius' 'letter to the Alexandrians' (Smallwood 1967: 370). Claudius responded to an embassy by first praising the ambassadors, then discussing and accepting most of the various honours granted to him before considering the various requests made by the delegation. One guesses that this represents the normal procedure of embassies – introduction, honours, requests. Rome's response to elite support was to support their allies.

The effect of this policy was probably to maintain the political *status quo* in many communities. The Roman elite identified with the urban elites of the various provinces and lent them their support. Such groups came to identify with Roman power and their own power was thereby increased. In Gaul, this policy seems to have increased the authority of the local 'tribal' leaders, many of whom seem to have quickly made the transition from Gallic warlords to Roman aristocrats, perhaps aided by service in the army in command of an auxiliary unit. In Britain, the situation may have been made more complex by a difficulty in defining the elite, though there is certainly evidence to suggest that certain members of the old tribal aristocracy were rewarded for their support of Rome (Tac., *Agr.* 14; *RIB* 91). In such circumstances, it would seem that local social and political (and cultural?) structures were likely to be maintained since the local tribal leader would continue to be in control. We cannot assume, however, that the old native elite maintained control in all areas. We simply do not have enough evidence to trace continuities over the period of conquest. It would, however, be a natural assumption that the elite of the Iceni and Trinovantes came under great pressure in the period immediately after the conquest of Britain. The Boudiccan revolt can in part be seen as a response to the threat to native aristocratic control (see p. 123). In Gaul also, the evidence that certain families maintained political control must be set against our ignorance of the origins of many members of the Gallic elite. There was continuity, but the extent of that continuity cannot be assessed.

Regions such as Egypt and Judaea-Palestine that had social structures which meant that elites were not necessarily drawn from the landowners, saw the emergence of new elite groups. In Egypt, this new elite was drawn from the more Hellenised elements of Egyptian society and, although it is probable that there were no large privately owned estates in Egypt at the time of the conquest, such estates emerged with remarkable rapidity in the first decades of the first century AD. It seems that a completely new elite replaced the old priestly leadership, but no significant political problems are attested as a result of this political transformation. It seems likely that this had a marked effect on the public culture of the cities, though the cultural values of the lower classes are almost impossible to disentangle even in this best attested of provinces.

In Judaea-Palestine, the evidence suggests that there was some overlap between the new elite of the Roman province and the old Jewish religious leadership, but discontinuities were as marked as continuities. The new elite probably had different cultural values, but the oddity of the population in having a monotheistic religion seems to have led to significant problems. It was to be expected that the population would be hostile towards religious innovation, but aspects of Graeco–Roman culture which did not, in fact, involve religion were also rejected, probably partly because all things Greek came to be associated with pagan religion. These cultural tensions probably undermined the power of the elite, and the failure of the elite to carry sufficient popular support was one of the major causes of the revolt of AD 66.

The pattern of change in political leadership probably varied from region to region and by social class. There was cultural change in the first century AD and the interaction of the cultures of the empire was leading to a gradual erosion of differences, but the pace of cultural change was not even and cultural continuities were as marked as discontinuities. It would seem likely that cultural change would initially affect those classes for whom Rome's support was most important. Further down the social scale, the attitudes of the elite may have been very important in spreading Roman or Greek culture, but the ability of the elite to persuade the rest of the population to follow their lead must have varied.

Finally, we should question some basic assumptions. Most interpretations of cultural change have seen a direct relationship between cultural identity and political loyalty. In so doing, the rhetoric of modern nationalism has been carried over into the study of ancient society. There is perhaps some support for this in Tacitus (*Agricola* 21), who presented cultural change as a means by which the Empire was pacified. The mechanisms of this pacification are not, however, obvious. It is possible that Tacitus viewed the increasing Romanity of Britain as an erosion of local identity: since the British increasingly behaved as Romans, they would identify with the Roman state. It is also possible that encouragement of cultural change was aimed at disrupting the traditional elite and the means by which traditional elites competed. If, as is often assumed, the British elite was a warrior aristocracy in which status was asserted on the battlefield, changing the social circumstances so that the elite asserted their status through building Roman houses and through competition in the rhetoric of the law courts had obvious political implications.

There is very little evidence to judge between these views. It is clear, however, that local loyalties were always important in the ancient world. People were loyal to their communities within the larger state and, when the Roman Empire suffered difficulties, as in the third and fourth centuries AD, these local identities re-emerged. Nationalism, with its ideal of self-government by those who shared the same cultural identity (a nation) does not appear to play a major part in ancient thought. Yet, it is also the case that after our period a recognisable 'Roman' identity is attested among the aristocracy of the provinces. The fact that local loyalties were never completely subsumed under Roman identity does not mean that people felt no loyalty to the Roman state. Conversely, the existence of this Roman loyalty did not prevent men defending their communities when threatened by the Roman state: there were revolts throughout imperial history. We see in the first century the development of overlapping loyalties and identities. Romanisation meant that one could be both a Roman and a citizen of London. The relationship between cultural identity and political affiliation was uncertain.

Cultural change in the Roman Empire is a very complex issue and although one can see cultural changes throughout the empire, these processes worked in different ways in different regions and affected different social groups within those regions at different rates. The pattern of cultural change was incoherent. Nevertheless, we may safely conclude that local cultures remained distinctive throughout our period and, although the Romans may have been striving towards cultural unity within the Empire, they still had a considerable way to go in AD 117.

16

RELIGION

This chapter will concentrate on issues of religious change in the imperial period. We shall look at Judaism, Christianity, the worship of Isis and the development of the imperial cult. Understanding these changes in religious practice in the Roman Empire in this period requires an examination of the nature of religion, and it will be argued here that the close relationship between religious, political and social structures was central to the ancient religious mentality and that the modern distinction between sacred and secular was much less clearly drawn in the ancient world.

POLYTHEISM AND RELIGIOUS DIVERSITY

The religions of the Roman Empire, with the exception of Judaism and Christianity, were polytheistic. Polytheism often poses significant problems for those educated in a Judaeo–Christian tradition. There is a tendency to view polytheism as primitive and regard monotheism as a more logical system of religious belief. This is to misunderstand fundamentally the nature of religion in this period. Jewish, Christian and Islamic traditions tend to view religion as a coherent system. Paganism was incoherent. There were very many gods. There were gods of particular places and particular functions, and even gods such as Apollo had many separate aspects and his powers were divided between his many temples. This multiplicity of different gods and different divine names and the multiple divisions of gods between different functions and locations posed no significant problems for ancient writers until the Christian period. This incoherence was an important feature of religious practice. It meant that Romans could respect gods that did not conform to Roman norms. Even the coherence implied by the phrase 'Roman religion' may be misleading: the Romans worshipped gods as it suited them and a Roman could worship Juno one day and Isis another without any conflict. There was a pantheon (group of gods) which was sanctified by tradition, but new gods could be added to that tradition. The Romans were open to new religious influences throughout their history and Roman religious practice was notably diverse. Such acceptance of diversity and of new cults implies an acceptance that current religious practice was incomplete and that, therefore, the universe could not be explained through the gods that were currently worshipped. There was no universal system of religious authority (such as exists in Islam, Christianity and Judaism with all things stemming from a single creator) and there is little evidence that the Romans saw a need for such a system.

The unsystematic nature of religion allowed assimilation and syncretism (the identification of different cults as one). Since there were many gods of particular places, the Romans accepted the existence of local provincial gods and, since gods had many different aspects and names, the Romans accepted that foreigners could worship familiar gods under a different name. Such openness to local custom was an important precondition for the Romanisation of religion. It also meant that a concept such as a 'national religion' made very little sense to the Romans. It was recognised that different ethnic groups had different traditions of worship, and religious practice was an important way of distinguishing between ethnic groups, yet the Romans were frequently prepared to accept the validity of foreign gods and often to worship those gods themselves.

RELIGIOUS AND POLITICAL AUTHORITY

Religious authority was closely related to political authority. The highest religious offices in Rome were held by senators who, as they represented and led the community in political and military affairs, also led in religious matters. State-run religious practice was governed by various groups of priests organised into colleges. These colleges, often in association with magistrates, were responsible for public sacrifices and festivals. The emperor was a member of all the important colleges and also took overall authority over religious matters through his office of *Pontifex Maximus*, which came to be recognised as a supreme priesthood.

The close connection between political and religious authority was a feature of most Graeco–Roman urban centres. Religion was integral to the operation of a state. Religious practice secured the *pax deorum* (the goodwill of the gods) and prevented divine retribution striking the city. In circumstances in which natural disaster, plague or the failure of a harvest could threaten even the most seemingly prosperous of communities, divine retribution may have seemed a very real threat. Since priests represented the community to the gods and led the community in important public ceremonials, priests acquired considerable prestige and it should come as no surprise that the political elite tended to monopolise religious authority. Religion could be used to legitimise the political order, but it would be a mistake to see religion cynically, as a means of asserting political legitimacy. The interrelationship between religion and politics was too close for this. Political authority also brought legitimacy to religious authority: the political leaders were those one wanted to represent the community before the gods, as one wanted them to lead the people in peace and war. It was expected that politicians would secure the prosperity of the state through the performance of rituals as they would look after the finances and military affairs. Religion and politics were not separate matters.

This integration of politics and religion can be seen very clearly in the development of the imperial cult.

IMPERIAL CULT

The first two emperors were particularly important in the development and spread of the cult. After Tiberius, the cult continued to flourish, though it became less a cult particular to an emperor and more of a generalised cult in which the emperor would be worshipped alongside his predecessors. Shrines and temples were built throughout the Empire. In some cities, temples to the imperial cult were placed centrally, in the *agora* or the *forum*, and a temple to the emperor was often placed at the centre of fora when they were remodelled. It was not just new buildings that were dedicated to the imperial cult. Existing temples were often extended to include a room dedicated to the emperors or received statues of the emperors. Statues could receive religious worship and fugitives could even take sanctuary by seizing the emperor's statue. The penetration of the imperial cult into public space was paralleled by the development of domestic cult and, although such practices are less well attested than public cult (for obvious reasons), the imperial cult came to be associated with the *lares* (domestic gods) in at least some households.

The cult spread throughout the East and West and throughout Italy. A centralised structure developed in some provinces and provincial gatherings (for festivals, etc.) incorporated some kind of ceremonial connected to the imperial cult. An imperial cult centre at Lyon was to serve all three of the Gallic provinces. The temple at Ephesus was for the use of all Asia, though Miletus seems to have rivalled Ephesus under Gaius. The temple at Nicomedia may have performed the same function for Bithynia. Galatia was served by the temple at Ancyra (on which the *Res Gestae* of Augustus was inscribed). It is probable that the Claudian temple at Colchester was intended as a provincial centre as well. There was probably similar centralisation in Germany. At local level, there appears to have been a certain heterogeneity in organisation which suggests that these cults were not imposed from Rome. Indeed, the rich epigraphic evidence from the East suggests that the initiative for establishing the imperial cult nearly always came from the cities and not from the emperors. The standard procedure appears to have been that a city would vote to ask permission to build a temple or set up cult worship and that the decree would be sent to the emperor who would either accept, reject or modify the honours proposed.

The imperial cult was built on a tradition of cult offerings to Hellenistic kings and to some provincial governors, and the earliest cults to Augustus date from immediately after the victory over Antony which, of course, was the first opportunity for the Eastern cities to propose these honours. Cities throughout the East very quickly began to adopt the cult and the Romans sought to impose some order on this developing religious phenomenon.

There is a greater possibility that the cult was imposed on the West, since there was a greater level of uniformity in cult organisation, yet, in most cases, we do not know where the initiative to develop the cult came from and it is possible that the visible uniformity arose from the development of a standard procedure for approving requests and from the transferral of organisational frameworks from one community to the next. By the Flavian period, the imperial cult was a very visible part of religious life in the East and West.

The meaning of the imperial cult is a matter of some dispute. It was a political symbol: destroying imperial images or stopping sacrifices for the emperor was an act of rebellion and this appears to have been recognised by all. To sacrifice before the imperial image was to assert political loyalty. Similarly, we could interpret the imperial cult as merely a metaphor by which to represent the elevated status of the emperor for whom normal honours were insufficient and who had to be honoured *as if* he was divine. These are, however, insufficient explanations for the cult. There is some evidence that contemporaries found the imperial cult problematic as a religious concept. There was cynicism concerning the elevations of Drusilla (see p. 59) and Claudius (see pp. 103–4) and Vespasian's premonition of his own forthcoming divinity was interpreted as evidence of humour (Suet., *Vesp.* 23.4). Nevertheless, this same Vespasian was able to heal the lame by touch (Suet., *Vesp.* 7.2–3). The lauding of emperors as divine figures in so many of our sources has to be taken seriously.

The divinity of the emperors was somewhat fudged. Only Gaius appears to have made explicit his divine pretensions. Augustus became a *divus* after his death. This made him a god, though the use of *divus* rather than *deus* demonstrated his mortal origins. This manufactured divinity applied to those emperors who received the posthumous honour, but could not be translated into Greek. In the East, emperors and Olympians were *theoi*, and it seems that not only was the distinction between *divus* and *deus* blurred, but the distinction between the deified and ruling emperors was also fudged: the ruling emperor could receive worship. Emperors also allowed the worship of their *genius* (divine spirit) or their *numen* (divine power). Sacrifices were offered for the safety of the emperor and all his house.

In fact, this was not particularly problematic. The Romans believed in a spirit world of ghosts and made offerings to the spirits of the dead. Worshipping the spirit of the living was a natural extension of perceptions of the divine. The Romans of the first century AD did not view the gods as inhabiting a mythological past. The omens that fill the pages of Tacitus, Suetonius and Dio are examples of manifestations of the divine. Romans of our period believed themselves as likely as Romans of earlier times to meet a god walking the street. The divine surrounded the Romans and there was nothing particularly incongruous in having one who was destined to be a god among them.

If we consider the power of the emperor, then his association with divinity becomes clearer. Imperial control over the military, wealth, political structures and the law brought unprecedented power to a single man. This power was wielded by a man frequently remote and known only from his images. The emperor communicated to the people through symbols and they granted him honours in kind – statues, shrines, rituals and temples. The imperial cult was an organised system of symbols by which the provincials demonstrated their loyalty and through which the emperors could show their favour, and should be interpreted in parallel to all the other forms of communication between an emperor and his subjects. It was of political and religious significance. The imperial cult was one way of making sense of the emperor's power.

RELIGIOUS DECLINE

Roman religion was always changing. Some rituals fell into disuse and others were developed as new religious influences were felt and society changed and yet Roman society, like most other societies, presented its religious beliefs as archaic. Change threatened the *pax deorum* (goodwill of the gods), though sometimes the *pax deorum* needed to be secured by the invention of new rituals.

It suited Augustus to 'restore' religion by repairing and rebuilding temples to leave his mark on the city. The 'restoration' of religion was, however, propaganda. The Romans were often worried by a perceived decline in religious rituals. Shrines which were no longer used became an obvious symbol of religious decline, while new shrines were ignored by the anxious in the last years of the Republic. Nevertheless, there is no substantial evidence for a decline in religious practice in the Republican or the imperial periods.

CHANGE: CHRISTIANITY, JUDAISM AND ISIS WORSHIP

Although there was no obvious decline in religious practice, there were changes. We have already seen one major change in the development of the imperial cult and, in Rome itself, the institutional dominance of the emperor brought about a change in the administration of Roman religion. The period also sees an increasing prominence for cults and religions foreign to Rome. Christianity was a development of the Imperial period. Judaism was far older and there was an established Jewish community in Rome at the start of our period. The other cults we shall look at are those from

Egypt. The worship of Isis and Osiris or Serapis had reached Italy centuries earlier, though seems to have grown in popularity during the first century BC. Both Judaism and the worship of Isis appear to have become more popular in the first century AD and parallel the growing importance of Christianity. There were many long-established foreign cults in Rome besides these. The cult of Dionysius had caused something of a panic in the early second century BC when cult members were suspected of various nefarious deeds. Since worship was covert, the fears of the elite were increased. The cult of Magna Mater, an officially organised introduction from Asia Minor, was deemed more acceptable in spite of the perceived oddity of her castrated priests: the Galli. There was a vast range of cultic activity in Rome and Italy by the late first century BC and this reflects the increasing cosmopolitanism of the city of Rome as people and ideas from across the Mediterranean reached the city.

Isis worship

There had been some resistance to the worship of Isis in Rome. It probably required specialist priests and it seems unlikely that members of the Roman elite could either have acquired the necessary religious knowledge or ritual purity to become priests. Hence, the cult could not be so easily controlled by the senate and may have been served by mainly by non-Roman priests. In spite of official suspicion, worship of Isis in Rome was established by Antony in 43 BC. Thereafter, it developed quickly. Tiberius took action against Egyptian rites in Rome (Suet., *Tib.* 36), but Caligula rebuilt the Iseum Campense and Nero introduced Isiac festivals into the Roman calendar. Domitian once more rebuilt the Iseum Campense while the Iseum at Beneventum, where his portrait as pharaoh was exhibited, may have been constructed during his reign. Rome had three large Isea: the Campense, one in Regio III and one on the Capitol; there were also smaller temples on the Caelian, Esquiline and Aventine Hills.

Judaism

The fortunes of the Jewish community were more varied. The Romans were officially tolerant of established Jewish communities and extended protection to the Jews in the various cities. There were exceptions and the effectiveness of Roman protection may be doubted, especially in periods of tension such as years of the Jewish war. Gaius' plan to place a statue of himself in the temple at Jerusalem (p. 72) and his emphasis on his own divinity placed great stress on the Jewish community. Tiberius also acted against the Jews, for reasons which are unclear, probably at the same time as he acted against those following Egyptian rites (see above). The community had been restored by the reign of Claudius, who again expelled the Jews from Rome, probably because of problems within the community concerning the emergence of Christianity and perhaps resulting violence (Suet., *Claud.* 25). The Jewish revolt must have increased tension and Vespasian imposed a punitive tax on the Jewish community in the aftermath of the revolt. Domitian levied the tax with a certain barbarity (see pp. 185–6) and, although Nerva may have relaxed the methods of collection (see p. 194), the tax continued to be levied.

Modern Judaism is non-proselytising (i.e. it does not actively seek converts) and this has often meant that there has been little communication on religious matters between Jewish and non-Jewish groups. By contrast, although some in antiquity saw Jewishness as being transmitted through descent from the patriarchs and thus not open to converts, others seem to have been more open and there is considerable evidence of communication between pagans and Jews in religious matters. Some Jews were more willing to accept those who followed the teachings of Judaism as Jewish and there even appears to have been an intermediate status between a Jew and a Gentile. These 'god-fearers' were allowed some status within the community and their presence may have blurred distinctions between Jews and non-Jews.

Many Jews lived as ethnic minorities throughout the Empire. In the Eastern cities, these communities adopted aspects of Greek culture, and Greek seems to have been widely used alongside Aramaic (the language Jesus would have used) and Hebrew in Jewish communities. There was a certain assimilation of Jewish communities and Hellenisation affected Jewish culture as it affected other Mediterranean cultures. Members of the Jewish elite appear to have been able to mix easily with the Roman aristocracy. Members of the Herodian royal family were frequently in Rome and appear to have been close to Claudius and (rather strangely) Gaius. The prominence of the Jewish princess Berenice and other Jews at the courts of Vespasian and Titus may also have encouraged interest in Jewish matters in the Flavian period (see pp. 172, 177). Flavius Josephus, the Jewish historian, was in the city and there may have been others whose behaviour during the Jewish war made their homeland 'uncomfortable'. Tiberius Julius Alexander, the former prefect of Egypt, was also prominent under Vespasian. Although not a Jew himself, he was descended from Jews and may have retained connections with the Jewish community.

The situation may, however, have been changing in the aftermath of the Jewish war. The punitive taxes introduced following the Jewish revolt probably led to the creation of a register of Jews to enable the collection of the tax. People were therefore forced to declare their Jewish identity. Those who avoided paying risked punishment. Domitian's severe enforcing of religious and fiscal regulations seems to have meant that denial of Jewish identity would not be accepted as sufficient grounds for exemption from the Jewish tax. Once registered as Jews, people had to remain Jews. Also, it probably made conversion or adopting the intermediate status more difficult, since it would appear that such behaviour would lay people open to the charge of atheism and, as the emperor was a god (or almost so), atheism was almost equivalent to treason. Domitian used atheism as a political charge, and the persecution of those who showed an interest in Judaism offers some parallels to the persecution of Christians to whom we now turn.

Christianity

Considerable attention has been paid to the development of Christianity in this crucial formative period. Christianity seems to have spread quickly to the Jewish communities of the Empire. Non-Jews were also converted and Christianity established itself as a separate religion. We have no figures for the rate of conversion or the size of Christian communities, but it is normally assumed that conversion was fairly gradual and steady, with ever-increasing numbers. The Christians in Rome, however, were already notable by the reign of Claudius, and Nero instituted the first persecution. They were clearly sufficiently numerous to be the subject of such official attention.

Pliny also tells us that there had been a considerable number of Christians in Bithynia. He had started persecuting the Christian community but, in the process, uncovered more information which led him to contact the emperor. He tells us that large numbers of people were potentially implicated, but that many had ceased to be Christians at some point before the persecution started. Tellingly, he notes that meat from sacrifices was now selling on the market (*Ep.* X 96). This suggests that the Christian community must have been sufficiently large to have had a noticeable effect on the market. Evidence from later centuries suggests that there were still large numbers of pagans in the fourth century AD and it may be that numbers of Christians fluctuated rather than steadily increased.

It is unclear how Nero's persecution was organised. He may have made Christianity illegal by decree or acted against the Christians under other legislation, perhaps in connection with the fire or with 'impiety'. Pliny's letter to Trajan concerned the exact charge against the Christians. Pliny was uncertain as to the legal basis of his proceedings: was he prosecuting these people because they were Christians or because of what Christians did? If the latter, then his investigations had uncovered little criminal behaviour. Trajan wrote back to Pliny to clarify procedures. Pliny was told that he was not to hunt out Christians. He was not to respond to anonymous pamphlets. Former Christians were to be released provided that they offered prayers to pagan deities. Current Christians were given the opportunity to deny the charge. If they refused, they were to be killed. No mention is made of other crimes and it is to be presumed that Christians were to be punished because they were Christians (Pliny, *Ep.* X 97).

Pliny was active in the law courts at Rome and his ignorance of procedure in relation to the Christians suggests that persecution of Christians was comparatively rare. In spite of Pliny's ignorance, he had been executing Christians who refused to sacrifice because of their failure to obey a Roman magistrate.

Official hostility seems to concentrate on the Christians' monotheism. The Jews were also monotheistic but, in spite of occasional official hostility, there is no suggestion that being a Jew was ever a crime. Christian monotheism was treated differently. There are two probable reasons for this. Christianity was relatively new and did not have the authority of centuries of tradition. Christianity was also actively proselytising.

Roman religious practice tended to be conservative. The *pax deorum* was secured by following ancestral custom. Judaism was part of an established world of religious cults. The continuation of Judaism did not affect the *status quo*. Christianity, however, did alter religious practice in that those who had previously worshipped at the city altars were drawn away. This threatened the *pax deorum* and could lead to popular fears about Christianity. Conversion also caused problems. Religion was not just a matter of public cult, but there was also worship in the home and gods were asked to bless significant acts. Withdrawal from these domestic ceremonies had implications for participation in family ceremonies. Unless the whole family converted, Christianity could cause domestic rifts.

Withdrawal from public cultic activity had other implications. The public cults were closely bound to the political structures of the city and the Empire. Avoidance of participation in sacrifices would have meant that men would probably have been unable to be magistrates. Sessions of the senate, for instance, commenced with a libation (an offering of wine) and this custom may have been followed by many local councils. Christianity also ruled out participation in the imperial cult. It was the failure of the Christians to make offerings to various gods and to a statue of Trajan which so annoyed Pliny that he felt it right to put them to death without further enquiry. Withdrawal from the imperial cult was seen as a denial of the political and religious order. In Pliny's view, such disloyalty had to be punished.

CONCLUSIONS

The increased popularity of Isis and interest in Judaism and the development of Christianity attest to a certain religious energy in this period and a willingness to innovate (seen also in the development of the imperial cult). These developments cannot be seen as manifestations of a decline in religious activity or of a sudden desire on the part of the Romans for 'a more fulfilling religion'. They do, however, require explanation. Although historians have tended to emphasise continuities in religious practice, the rejection of traditional religion by a portion of the population in favour of Christianity is of major historical importance and has no obvious rationale (unless one is a committed Christian).

Part of the appeal of these cults and religions may have been their slightly subversive nature. The traditional cults of the Graeco–Roman cities were so much a part of the traditional power structures of those cities that to reject the cults was implicitly a political act as well as being of religious significance. Cities and citizens tended to define themselves through participation in religious events. So, the citizens of Ephesus gathered for sacrifices and for processions at the great temple of Artemis and the great processions displayed the city to visitors and to the citizens themselves. Like many ceremonials, ancient and modern, ancient religious rituals were often demonstrations of community identity.

This religious community was coming under pressure in the

Roman period. The political independence of urban communities was eroded by the Roman empire and new political structures were reflected in the provincial and inter-provincial organisation of the imperial cult. Inevitably, community identity came under threat from the increased political and cultural dominance of Rome (see pp. 298–306). Christianity was not particularly related to issues of local identity, unlike pagan cults. It mattered little whether a Christian was from Ephesus or Rome. Christianity escaped from local identity. In so doing, it responded to the broader perspectives offered by the political unity of the empire. It is no coincidence that several of the apostles are said to have left Judaea after the death of Jesus and taken the message to other provinces. John's travels throughout the Eastern empire symbolise an important development in religious thought that is reflected in Christianity. In a world in which the centrality of the local community and of the city state was being undermined by the world empire, Christianity also escaped local limitations. Part of the success of Christianity lay in its ability to adapt to the new conditions and become an imperial religion.

Similar processes can account for other religious changes. The changes in political structures in the imperial period in Italy and the provinces led to people questioning their religious identity. The development of the imperial cult was a way of trying to understand and make room for imperial power in the traditional local urban panthea of the Greek cities. The increased interest in Eastern cults and mystery religions is part of the same phenomenon in which the religious community of the city became less important as the new community of the empire became more influential. These are gradual developments, but in a world in which religion and politics were so closely linked, such a fundamental political change as the development of the Roman empire was bound to affect the religious outlook of all the inhabitants of the empire and lead to attempts to define their place within this new world. The religious developments of this period are intimately connected with the changes in political and social life that came about with the creation of the Roman empire.

GLOSSARY

Ala   Cavalry unit of about 500 men.

Amphora   Large pottery vessel used for trade goods, often wine or olive oil.

Auctoritas   Personal authority.

Century (military)   A unit made up of approximately 80 infantrymen.

Century (voting)   An electoral unit into which men of similar wealth were grouped.

Client king   A monarch under the protection of or appointed by Rome.

Cohort   Infantry unit of about 500 men.

Colony   Settlement established as a self-governing community of Roman citizens often including former soldiers.

Consilium   Council of advisers.

Consul (*ordinarius*)   One of the first pair of consuls of the year.

Consul (*suffectus*)   One of the replacement consuls.

Curule chair   The chair on which a magistrate would sit, especially the consul.

Damnatio memoriae   A measure by which the name of an individual would be erased from all public records.

Decurion   Town councillor.

Decurion   Military officer in charge of about 30 cavalry.

Delator   Informer.

Donative   Gift of money.

Epitome   Byzantine summary account of a literary work.

Equestrian   See p. 215.

Faction   Political group of friends and family.

Genius   Divine spirit.

Hymn of the Salii   An archaic hymn sung by a group of priests and performed with a dance.

Imperium   Magisterial power.

Legate   Representative. Normally used of the legates of the emperor who were governors of the imperial province or, in the case of a *legatus legionis*, commander of a legion.

Lex   Law.

Maiestas   Treason.

Modius   A Roman unit of volume of about 8.736 litres.

Mores   Social customs.

Numen   Divine power.

Pax deorum   Goodwill of the gods.

Pomerium   Sacred boundary of the city of Rome.

Potestas   Power.

Procurator   An equestrian or freedman official appointed by the emperor to perform various tasks often of a financial nature, but they also could govern provinces.

Salutatio   The morning ceremony in which clients visited the houses of their patrons (see p. 249).

Senator   See pp. 216–17.

Toga virilis   Toga of manhood given to a boy when he reached adulthood.

Tribunicia Potestas   Power of a tribune (see p. 15–16).

Triumph   A religious victory procession through the streets of Rome.

Turma   Unit of about 30 cavalry.

Villa   Roman-style rural house or farm.

FURTHER READING

GENERAL

Boatwright, M. T. (1987) *Hadrian and the City of Rome*, Princeton.

Bowman, A. K., Camplin and E., Lintott, A. (eds) (1996) *The Cambridge Ancient History, second edition, Volume X: The Augustan Empire, 43 BC–AD 69*, Cambridge.

Brunt, P. A. (1977) 'Lex de imperio Vespasiani', *JRS* 67: 95–116.

—— (1990) *Roman Imperial Themes*, Oxford.

Dudley, D. R. (1967) *Urbs Romana*, London.

Edwards, C. (1993) *The Politics of Immorality in Ancient Rome*, Cambridge.

Ehrenberg, V. and Jones, A. H. M. (1976) *Documents Illustrating the Reigns of Augustus and Tiberius,* Oxford.

Finley, M. I. (1974) *Studies in Ancient Society*, London, Boston.

Garnsey, P. and Saller, R. (1987) *The Roman Empire*, Gloucester.

—— (1982) *The Early Principate: Augustus to Trajan. (Greece and Rome, New Surveys in the Classics* 15), Oxford.

Jones, A. H. M. (1960) *Studies in Roman Government and Law*, Oxford.

Lewis, N. and Reinhold, M. (1990) *Roman Civilization*, New York, Oxford.

Millar, F. G. B. (1977) *The Emperor in the Roman World*, London.

MacCrum, M. and Woodhead, A. G. (1966) *Select Documents of the Principates of the Flavian Emperors including the Year of Revolution, AD 68–96*, Cambridge.

MacDonald, W.L. (1982)*The Architecture of the Roman Empire: an Introductory Study*, New Haven, London.

Mattingly, H. (1932–62) *Coins of the Roman Empire in the British Museum*, London.

Meiggs, R. (1973) *Roman Ostia*, Oxford.

Patterson, J. R. (1992) 'The city of Rome: from republic to empire', *JRS* 82: 157–64.

Richardson, L. (1992) *A Topographical Dictionary of Ancient Rome*, Baltimore.

Smallwood, E. M. (1966) *Documents Illustrating the Principates of Nerva, Trajan and Hadrian*, Cambridge.

—— (1967) *Documents Illustrating the Principates of Gaius, Claudius and Nero*, Cambridge.

Syme, R. (1979–91) *Roman Papers*, vols I–VI, Oxford.

—— (1986) *The Augustan Aristocracy*, Oxford.

Talbert. R. J. A. (1985) *Atlas of Classical History*, Beckenham, Sydney.

Wallace-Hadrill, A. (1981) 'The emperor and his virtues', *Historia* 30: 298–323.

—— (1982) '*Civilis princeps*: between citizen and king', *JRS* 72: 32–48.

Ward-Perkins, J. B. (1971) *Roman Imperial Architecture*, Harmondsworth.

Wells, C. (1984) *The Roman Empire*, London.

Wiedemann, T. E. J. (1989)*The Julio–Claudian Emperors: AD 14–70 (Classical World Series)*, Bristol.

Wiseman, T. P. (1985) *Roman Political Life 90 BC–AD 69*, Exeter.

Yavetz, Z. (1969) *Plebs and Princeps*, Oxford.

INTRODUCTION

Brunt, P. A. and Moore, J. M. (eds) (1967) *Res Gestae Divi Augusti*, Oxford.

Jones, A. H. M. (1970) *Augustus*, London.

Jones, C. P. (1971) *Plutarch and Rome*, Oxford.

Martin, R. (1981) *Tacitus*, London.

Mellor, R. (1983) *Tacitus*, London.

Millar, F. (1964) *A Study of Cassius Dio*, Oxford.

Millar, F. and Segal, E. (1984) *Caesar Augustus: Seven Aspects*, Oxford.

Raaflaub, K. and Toher, M. (1990) *Between Republic and Empire: Interpretations of Augustus and his Principate*, Berkeley.

Shotter, D. A. (1991) *Augustus Caesar*, London, New York.

Syme, R. (1939) *The Roman Revolution*, Oxford.

—— (1958) *Tacitus*, Oxford.

—— (1986) *The Augustan Aristocracy*, Oxford.

Wallace-Hadrill, A. (1983) *Suetonius: the Scholar and his Caesars*, London.

—— (1986) 'Image and authority in the coinage of Augustus', *JRS* 76: 57–66.

—— (1989) 'Rome's cultural revolution', *JRS* 79: 157–64.

—— (1993) *Augustan Rome*, London.

Woodman, A. J. (1977) *Velleius Paterculus: the Tiberian Narrative*, Cambridge.

—— (1983) *Velleius Paterculus: the Caesarian and Augustan Narrative*, Cambridge.

Woolf, G. (1996) 'Monumental activity and the expansion of empire', *JRS* 86: 22–39.

Zanker, P. (1988)*The Power of Images in the Age of Augustus*, Ann Arbor.

EMPERORS

Tiberius

Levick, B. (1976) *Tiberius the Politician*, London.

—— (1983) 'The senatus consultum from Larinum', *JRS* 73: 97–115.

Rogers, R. S. (1935) *Criminal Trials and Criminal Legislation under Tiberius*, Philadelphia.

Seager, R. (1972) *Tiberius*, London.

Shotter, D.A. (1992) *Tiberius Caesar*, London, New York.

Gaius Caligula

Barrett, A. A. (1989) *Caligula and the Corruption of Power*, London.

Ferrill, A. (1991) *The Emperor Caligula*, London.

Claudius

Levick, B (1990) *Claudius*, London.

Momigliano, A. (1961) *Claudius, the Emperor and his Achievement*, Oxford.

Nero

Boethius, A. (1960) *The Golden House of Nero: Some Aspects of Roman Architecture*, Ann Arbor.

Elsner J. and Masters, J. (eds) (1994) *Reflections of Nero: Culture, History and Representation*, London.

Griffin, M. (1984) *Nero: The End of a Dynasty*, London.

Griffin, M. T. (1976) *Seneca: A Philosopher in Politics*, Oxford.

Rudich, V. (1993) *Political Dissidence under Nero: The Price of Dissimulation*, London, New York.

—— (1997) *Dissidence and Literature under Nero*, London, New York.

AD 69–70

Greenhalgh, A. L. (1975) *The Year of the Four Emperors*, London.

Wellesley, K. (1989) *The Long Year, AD 69*, Bristol.

Vespasian and Titus

Braund, D. C. (1984) 'Berenice in Rome', *Historia* 33: 120–3.

Crook, J. (1951) 'Titus and Berenice', *AJPh* 72: 162–73.

Jones, B. W. (1984) *The Emperor Titus*, London.

Rogers, P. M. (1980) 'Titus, Berenice and Mucianus', *Historia* 29: 86–95.

Domitian

Jones, B. W. (1992) *The Emperor Domitian*, London.

—— (1979) *Domitian and the Senatorial Order: a Prospographic Study of Domitian's Relationship with the Senate*, Philadelphia.

Rogers, P. M. (1984) 'Domitian and the finances of state', *Historia* 33: 440–56.

Southern, P. (1997) *Domitian: Tragic Tyrant*, London, New York.

Sutherland, C. H. V. (1935) 'The state of the imperial treasury at the death of Domitian', *JRS* 25: 150–62.

Syme, R. (1930) 'The imperial finances under Domitian, Nerva and Trajan', *JRS* 20: 55–70.

Nerva and Trajan

Bennett, J. (1997) *Trajan: Optimus Princeps: A Life and Times*, London, New York.

Claridge, A. (1993) 'Hadrian's column of Trajan', *JRA* 6: 5–22.

Lancaster, L. (1995) 'The date of Trajan's markets', *PBSR* 63: 25–44.

Lepper, F. (1948) *Trajan's Parthian War*, Oxford.

Packer, J. E. (1994) 'Trajan's column again: the column and the temple of Trajan in the master plan attributed to Apollodorus(?)', *JRA* 7: 163–82.

SOCIETY

Bradley, K. (1987) *Slaves and Masters in the Early Roman Empire*, Oxford.

Garnsey, P. (1970) *Social Status and Legal Privilege in the Roman Empire*, Oxford.

Giardina, A. (ed.) (1993) *The Romans*, Chicago.

Hopkins, K. (1978) *Conquerors and Slaves*, Cambridge.

—— (1983) *Death and Renewal* , Cambridge.

MacMullen, R. (1967) *Enemies of the Roman Order*, Cambridge MA, London.

—— (1974) *Roman Social Relations*, New Haven.

Rawson, E. (1987) 'Discrimina ordinum: the *lex Iulia Theatralis*', *PBSR* 55: 83–114.

Saller, R. P. (1982) *Personal Patronage in the Early Empire*, Cambridge.

Sherwin-White, A. N. (1973) *The Roman Citizenship*, Oxford.

Wallace-Hadrill, A. (ed.) (1989) *Patronage in Ancient Society*, London, New York.

Wiedemann, T. E. J. (1987) *Slavery (Greece and Rome: New Surveys in the Classics)*, Oxford.

THE ECONOMY

Barker, G. and Lloyd, J. A. (eds) (1991), *Roman Landscapes: Archaeological Survey in the Mediterranean Region,* Rome.

D'Arms, J. H. (1970) *Commerce and Social Standing in Ancient Rome,* Cambridge MA.

Duncan-Jones, R. P. (1983) *The Economy of the Roman Empire,* Cambridge.

—— (1990) *Structure and Scale in the Roman Economy,* Cambridge.

—— (1994) *Money and Government in the Roman Empire,* Cambridge.

Engels, D. W. (1990) *Roman Corinth: An Alternative Model for the Classical City,* Chicago.

Finley, M. I. (1973) *The Ancient Economy,* London.

Garnsey, P. (1988) *Famine in Food Supply in the Ancient World,* Cambridge.

Garnsey, P., Hopkins, K. and Whittaker, C. R. (eds) (1983) *Trade in the Ancient Economy,* Cambridge.

Greene, K. (1986) *The Archaeology of the Roman Economy,* London.

Harris, W. V. (1971) *Rome in Etruria and Umbria,* Oxford.

Hopkins, K. (1980) 'Taxes and trade in the Roman empire (200 BC–AD 400)', *JRS* 70: 100–25.

Howgego, C. (1992) 'The supply and use of money in the Roman world, 200 BC–AD 300', *JRS* 82: 1–31.

—— (1994) 'Coin circulation and the integration of the Roman economy', *JRA* 7: 5–21.

Jongman, W. (1988) *The Economy and Society of Pompeii,* Amsterdam.

Morley, N. (1996) *Metropolis and Hinterland: The City of Rome and the Italian Economy 200 BC–AD 200,* Cambridge.

Potter, T. (1986) *Roman Italy,* London.

Rickman, G. (1980) *The Corn Supply of Ancient Rome,* Oxford.

ADMINISTRATION

Brunt, P. A. (1990) *Roman Imperial Themes,* Oxford.

Crook, J. (1955) *Consilium Principis: Imperial Councils and Counsellors from Augustus to Diocletian,* Cambridge.

Gonzalez, J. (1986) 'The Lex Irnitana: a new copy of a Flavian municipal law', *JRS* 76: 147–243.

Hopkins, K. (1983) *Death and Renewal,* Cambridge.

Levick, B. M. (ed.) (1985) *The Government of the Roman Empire,* London.

Lintott, A. (1993) *Imperium Romanum: Politics and Administration,* London, New York.

Millar, F. (1981) 'The world of the Golden Ass', *JRS* 71: 63–75.

—— (1983) 'Empire and city: Augustus to Julian: obligations, excuses and status', *JRS* 73: 76–96.

Nippel, W. (1995) *Public Order in Ancient Rome,* Cambridge.

Reynolds, J. (1982) *Aphrodisias and Rome: Documents from the Excavation of the Theatre at Aphrodisias* (*JRS* Monographs 1), London.

Robinson, O. (1992) *Ancient Rome: City Planning and Administration*, London, New York.

Rogers, G. M. (1991) *The Sacred Identity of Ephesos*, London.

Shaw, B. D. (1984) 'Bandits in the Roman Empire', *P & P* 105: 3–52.

Talbert, R. (1984) *The Senate of Imperial Rome*, Princeton.

THE ROMAN ARMY AND MILITARY POLICY

Alston, R. (1994) 'Roman military pay from Caesar to Diocletian', *JRS* 84: 113–23.

—— (1995) *Soldier and Society in Roman Egypt: a Social History*, London.

Braund, D. C. (1984) *Rome and the Friendly King*, London.

Breeze, D. J. and Dobson, B. (1976) *Hadrian's Wall*, London.

Brunt, P. A. (1974) 'Conscription and volunteering in the Roman army', *Scripta Classica Israelica* 1: 90–115.

Campbell, J. B. (1984) *The Emperor and the Roman Army 31 BC–AD 235*, Oxford.

—— (1994) *The Roman Army: 31 BC–AD 337: a Sourcebook*, London, New York.

Davies, R. W. (1989) *Service in the Roman Army*, Edinburgh.

Elton, H. (1996) *Frontiers of the Roman Empire*, London.

Ferrill, A. (1992) *Roman Imperial Grand Strategy*, Lanham MD.

Holder, P. A. (1980) *Studies in the Auxilia of the Roman Army*, Oxford.

Isaac, B. (1990) *The Limits of Empire: the Roman Army in the East*, Oxford.

Keppie, L. (1984) *The Making of the Roman Army*, London.

Luttwak, E. (1979) *The Grand Strategy of the Roman Empire*, Baltimore, London.

Mann, J. C. (1983) *Legionary Recruitment and Veteran Settlement during the Principate*, London.

Millar, F. (1981) *The Roman Empire and its Neighbours*, London.

Nicolet, C. (1991) *Space, Geography and Politics in the Early Roman Empire*, Ann Arbor.

Nippel, W. (1995) *Public Order in Ancient Rome*, Cambridge.

Rich, J. and Shipley, G. (eds) (1993) *War and Society in the Roman World*, London, New York.

Richmond, I. A. (1982) *Trajan's Army on Trajan's Column*, London.

Roth, J. (1994) 'The size and organisation of the Roman imperial legion', *Historia* 43: 346–62.

Saddington, D. B. (1982) *The Development of the Roman Auxiliary Forces from Caesar to Vespasian 49 BC–AD 79*, Harare.

Sasel Kos, M. (1978) 'A Latin epitaph of a Roman legionary from Corinth', *JRS* 68: 22–6.

Wells, C. M. (1972) *The German Policy of Augustus*, Oxford.

Whittaker, C. R. (1994) *Frontiers of the Roman Empire: a Social and Economic Study*, Baltimore.

WOMEN

Bauman, R. A. (1992) *Women and Politics in Ancient Rome*, London, New York.

Bradley, K. R. (1991) *Discovering the Roman Family*, Oxford.

Bremen, R. van (1996) *The Limits of Participation*, Amsterdam.

Cameron, A. (1980) 'Neither Male nor Female', *Greece and Rome* 27: 60–80.

Cameron, A. and Kuhrt, A. (1983) *Images of Women in Antiquity*, London.

Clark, G. (1989) *Women in the Ancient World (Greece and Rome: New Surveys in the Classics 21)*, Oxford.

Dixon, S. (1988) *The Roman Mother*, London.

Gardner, J. (1986) *Women in Roman Law and Society*, London, New York.

Hopkins, K. (1965) 'The age of Roman girls at marriage', *Population Studies* 18: 309–27.

Lefkowitz, M. R. and Fant, M. B. (1992) *Women's Life in Greece and Rome: a Source Book in Translation*, London.

Rawson, B. (1986) *The Family in Ancient Rome*, London.

Saller, R. (1994) *Patriarchy, Property and Death in the Roman Family*, Cambridge.

Saller, R. P. and Shaw, B. D. (1984) 'Tombstones and Roman family relations in the principate: civilians, soldiers and slaves', *JRS* 74: 124–56.

Shaw, B. D. (1987) 'The age of Roman girls at marriage: some reconsiderations', *JRS* 77: 30–46.

Treggiari, S. (1991) *Roman Marriage. Iusti Coniuges from the Time of Cicero to the Time of Ulpian*, Oxford.

Wallace-Hadrill, A. (1981) 'Family and inheritance in the Augustan marriage laws', *PCPhS* 27: 58–80.

PROVINCES AND CULTURE

Adams, J. N. (1994) 'Latin and Punic in contact: the case of the Bu Njem ostraka', *JRS* 84: 87–112.

Alcock, S. (1993) *Graecia Capta: the Landscape of Roman Greece*, Cambridge.

Blagg, T. and Millet, M. (eds) (1990) *The Early Roman Empire in the West*, Oxford.

Bowersock, G. W. (1969) *Greek Sophists in the Roman Empire*, Oxford.

Bowman, A. K. (1986) *Egypt after the Pharoahs*, London.

Drinkwater, J. F. (1983) *Roman Gaul: the Three Provinces 58 BC–AD 260*, London, Canberra.

Fear, A. T. (1996) *Rome and Baetica*, Oxford.

Frere, S. S. (1978) *Britannia*, London.

Goodman, M. (1987) *The Ruling Class of Judaea: the Origins of the Jewish Revolt Against Rome*, Cambridge.

Henig, M. (1995) *The Art of Roman Britain*, London.

Hopkins, K. (1980) 'Taxes and trade in the Roman empire (200 BC–AD 400)', *JRS* 70: 100–25.

Keay, S. (1988) *Roman Spain*, London.

MacDonald, W. (1986) *The Architecture of the Roman Empire II. An Urban Appraisal*, New Haven.

Mattingly, D. (1995) *Tripolitania*, London.

Millar, F. (1968) 'Local cultures in the Roman Empire: Libyan, Punic and Latin in Roman Africa', *JRS* 58: 126–34.

—— (1983) 'The Phoenician cities: a case study in hellenisation', *PCPhS* 29: 55–71.

—— (1993) *The Roman Near East 31 BC–AD 337*, Cambridge MA.

Millett, M. (1990) *The Romanization of Britain: an Essay in Archaeological Interpretation*, Cambridge.

Momigliano, A. (1979) *Alien Wisdom*, Cambridge.

Rajak, T. (1983) *Josephus: the Historian and his Society*, London.

Reynolds, J. (1982) *Aphrodisias and Rome: Documents from the Excavation of the Theatre at Aphrodisias* (*JRS* Monographs 1), London.

Rogers, G. M. (1991) *The Sacred Identity of Ephesos*, London.

Smallwood, E. M. (1967) *The Jews under Roman Rule from Pompey to Diocletian*, Leiden.

Wacher, J. (1974) *The Towns of Roman Britain*, London.

Woolf, G. (1994) 'Becoming Roman, staying Greek: culture, identity and the civilizing process in the Roman East', *PCPhS* 40: 116–43.

RELIGION

Beard, M. and North, J. (1990) *Pagan Priests*, London.

Fishwick, D. (1987) *The Imperial Cult in the Latin West*, London, New York, Leiden, Köln.

Frend, W. H. C. (1984) *The Rise of Christianity*, London.

Liebeschuetz, J. H. W. G. (1979) *Continuity and Change in Roman Religion*, Oxford.

Meeks, W. A. (1983) *The First Urban Christains: the Social World of the Apostle Paul*, New Haven, London.

North, J. (1986) 'Religion and politics from republic to principate', *JRS* 76: 251–8.

Price, S. R. F. (1984) *Rituals and Power: the Roman Imperial Cult in Asia Minor*, Cambridge.

Reynolds, J. (1982) *Aphrodisias and Rome: Documents from the Excavation of the Theatre at Aphrodisias* (*JRS* Monographs 1), London.

Rogers, G. M. (1991) *The Sacred Identity of Ephesos*, London.

Roullet, A. (1972) *The Egyptian and Egyptianizing Monuments of Imperial Rome*, Leiden.

Sordi, M. (1983) *The Christians and the Roman Empire*, London, Sydney.

Witt, G. (1971) *Isis in the Graeco–Roman World*, London.

NOTES

2 TIBERIUS

1 Tacitus uses the phrase in connection with AD 23 (see p. 40), though it seems more appropriate in this context.
2 Seager, R. (1972) *Tiberius*, London, p. 173.

3 GAIUS CALIGULA

1 The honouring of Germanicus by naming centuries within the electoral assembly after him would make little sense if the assembly never met (see p. 36).
2 Placing information in the public domain had not been a feature of Tiberius' later government.

4 CLAUDIUS

1 The *pomerium* could only be enlarged if the territory of the Roman empire had been increased.
2 Equestrian governors must have exercised legal authority before this ruling. This regulation therefore probably relates to the normally financial posts held by procurators in other provinces.
3 Those who celebrated triumphs were permanently allowed certain symbols of their victory, including clothing. From 19 BC, it had been common to reject triumphs, but to accept the marks of increased status that went with them.
4 Levick (1990) *Claudius*, London, pp. 64–7.

5 NERO

1 Even Tacitus regards it as unlikely that Nero was responsible.
2 Griffin (1984) *Nero: the End of a Dynasty*, London, p. 102.
3 There must be some doubt as to Tacitus' accuracy here since it is hardly likely that he had demographic information on which to base this assertion.
4 Griffin (1984) *op. cit.*, assesses Nero's building programme.

5 Rudich (1993) *Political Dissidence under Nero: the Price of Dissimulation*, London, New York.

8 DOMITIAN

1 Tacitus *Agr.* 45 tells us that Agricola died (August AD 93) just before the prosecution of Senecio and Pliny, *Ep.* III 11 that Pliny (who was praetor in 93) was still praetor after the trials.

12 ADMINISTRATION

1 See the detailed presentation of this material in Hopkins (1983) *Death and Renewal*, Cambridge, pp. 120–200.

INDEX